North Sea Crossings

North Sea Crossings

The Literary Heritage of Anglo-Dutch Relations 1066–1688

Sjoerd Levelt and Ad Putter

with contributions by

Robyn Adams, Moreed Arbabzadah, Anne Louise Avery, Jack Avery, Edward Holberton,
Elisabeth van Houts and Kathleen E. Kennedy

BODLEIAN
LIBRARY
PUBLISHING

Contents

This book and the exhibition it accompanies arise from two projects: the outreach project *North Sea Crossings*, funded by the National Lottery Heritage Fund and the University of Bristol; and the research project *The Literary Heritage of Anglo-Dutch Relations, c.1050–c.1600*, funded by the Leverhulme Trust. We gratefully acknowledge the support of our funders. We have been fortunate to be able to work on *North Sea Crossings* with the creative arts charity Flash of Splendour, the Bodleian Libraries and Aardman Studios, and we thank them for their collaboration. We are also grateful for the financial support provided by the Master and Fellows of Emmanuel College, Cambridge, by the Fellows' Research Fund of Pembroke College, Cambridge, and by the T.S. Eliot Foundation.

We would like to thank the librarians and support staff at the libraries where we carried out our research: first and foremost the Bodleian Library, where we received much help and expert advice from Alan Coates, Sallyanne Gilchrist, Matthew Holford, Martin Kauffmann, Madeline Slaven and Mike Webb; the Brotherton Library of the University of Leeds; Cambridge University Library; the University of Bristol Library; the Koninklijke Bibliotheek in The Hague; the Library of the University of Utrecht; the British Library; and the many libraries that have made manuscripts and printed books available digitally.

Many colleagues and friends have answered queries and offered suggestions. We are thankful for the help received from Chloe

Acknowledgements

Biddle, Liesbeth Corens, John Gallagher, Tracey Hill, Steven Van Impe, Emma Josephine Levelt, Eylem Levelt, Bex Lidster-Lyons, Nicholas Rogers, David Rundle and Elsa Strietman. We received valuable comments from the readers of early drafts of parts of this book: Rik Van Daele, Lynda Dennison and Paul Wackers. Similarly helpful were the suggestions from Samuel Fanous, Janet Phillips and Leanda Shrimpton of Bodleian Library Publishing, and from the anonymous readers for the press. We were saved from many errors and inconsistencies by our copy-editor Jacqueline Harvey and our proofreader Alison Effeny. The book was brought to fruition under the watchful eyes of Susie Foster and Deborah Susman, and beautifully designed and typeset by Dot Little. Hatsuko Matsuda provided valuable assistance with the preparation of the bibliography and the index. We are especially grateful to Anne Louise Avery and Steve Pratley, who enriched our research both by contributing their own expertise and by showing us directions towards new audiences.

This book would not have been possible without the generous con-tributions of authors who have written parts of individual chapters: Robyn Adams, Anne Louise Avery, Jack Avery, Edward Holberton and Kathleen E. Kennedy. Moreed Arbabzadah and Elisabeth van Houts are acknowledged as co-authors of three chapters, but have, as our collaborators in the Leverhulme-funded research project, been instrumental at all stages of the planning, research and execution of this book.

Sjoerd Levelt
Ad Putter

When Queen Elizabeth pledged her support for the people of the Low Countries in 1585 she referred to her own people as their 'ancient allies and familiar neighbours'. The close relations she alluded to, which still exist today, have a long history. The Norman Conquest of 1066 brought a Flemish-born queen, Matilda, to the throne, and accelerated a process of migration that included people not only from present-day France but also from Flanders. By the twelfth century, over fifty colonies of Flemish speakers could be found across England, Scotland, Wales and Ireland. Some six centuries after the Conquest, in 1689, the 'ancient alliance' culminated in the coronation of William III, stadtholder in the Dutch Republic, as king of England, Scotland and Ireland, who had been invited over to 'save English liberties'.

This book, together with the exhibition at the Bodleian's Weston Library which it accompanies, documents the remarkable cultural heritage of Anglo-Dutch relations between the Norman Conquest and the 'Glorious Revolution', shown through a selection of manuscript and printed books, as well as through archival records from the Bodleian Library. The selection shows not only the wide range of the library's collections but also the profound consequences of Anglo-Dutch relations on texts, manuscripts and book production on both sides of the North Sea. It includes beautifully illuminated manuscripts made in the Low Countries for English audiences and those made in England by migrant artists and scribes; early printed books in Dutch produced in England and volumes printed in English by early Dutch printers; and chronicles that document intense rivalries and alliances. There are maps made by Dutch and English map-makers working in

Foreword

close collaboration, and early translations from Dutch into English such as Caxton's *Reynard* and *Everyman*. But there are also documents that reveal ugly responses to multiculturalism, such as the 'Foreigners Out!' diatribe that was stuck on the Dutch Church in London in 1593.

The heritage of medieval and early modern Anglo-Dutch relations is rich, complex and illuminating of many aspects of our historic interactions, and in many ways the Bodleian Library and its collection are themselves part of this heritage. The oldest part of the Bodleian, 'Duke Humfrey's Library', is named after Humfrey, duke of Gloucester, who claimed the title of count of Holland, Zeeland and Hainault through his marriage to Jacqueline of Hainault (1423). The library was re-founded by Thomas Bodley, formerly English ambassador to the Netherlands. Many of its medieval Dutch treasures were collected and bequeathed to the library by Thomas Marshall, chaplain to the Merchant Adventurers in the Dutch Republic. *North Sea Crossings* tells the story of these and many other contacts between English and Dutch speakers, and celebrates the lasting legacy of Anglo-Dutch relations in the books and written records that survive to this day. I would like to express my huge admiration and thanks to the editors of this volume and the curators of the exhibition which it accompanies, for producing such a compelling account of the cultural, historical and intellectual exchange between Britain and the Low Countries, and for helping us to appreciate the value of maintaining those connections in our current world.

Richard Ovenden OBE
Bodley's Librarian

1037 Queen Emma of Normandy, mother of Edward the Confessor, takes refuge in Flanders

1051 Judith of Flanders, daughter of Count Baldwin IV of Flanders, marries Tostig Godwinson, brother of Harold, future king of England

1052/3 William, duke of Normandy, marries Matilda, daughter of Count Baldwin V of Flanders

c.1058–1107 Goscelin of Saint-Bertin, writer of Latin saints' lives from Flanders, moves to England, where he remains for the rest of his life

c.1069–85 Folcard, Latin hagiographer originally from Saint-Bertin, is acting abbot of Thorney Abbey in the Fens of Cambridgeshire

1066 Norman Conquest: William of Normandy invades England, with many Flemish knights in his entourage, and becomes King William I

11th century First wave of Flemish weavers migrate to England

c.1100 Earliest snippets of Dutch secular verse, written by a Flemish migrant at Rochester Abbey

1108–10 Henry I orders the settlement of a colony of Flemish people in Pembrokeshire, Wales

1120s Flemish noblemen, some coming from Pembrokeshire, enter the service of King David I of Scotland

1121 Henry I marries Adeliza, daughter of Count Godfrey of Louvain and Brabant

c.1136 Geoffrey of Monmouth writes his *History of the Kings of Britain*, which is soon taken up by writers in the Low Countries

c.1143 Alfred of Beverley, the Yorkshire chronicler, is the earliest of many

historians to include the Flemish as one of the 'nations' of England

c.1148 Latin poem about Reynard the Fox, *Ysengrimus*, composed in Flanders

1157 Henry II signs England up to the Hanseatic League

1164 Thomas Becket, archbishop of Canterbury, travels through Flanders on his way to Burgundy

c.1180 Nigel of Whiteacre, a monk at Canterbury, writes the satire *Speculum stultorum* (*Mirror of Fools*), perhaps under the influence of *Ysengrimus*

c.1190 The Anglo-Norman chivalric romance *Boeve de Haumtone* is written, and soon inspires versions in Middle English and Middle Dutch

1215 Magna Carta; mercenaries from Flanders and Brabant are banned from England

1253 Linen manufacture introduced into England from the Low Countries

1270 Henry III attempts to establish a cloth-making industry in England and invites Flemish cloth-makers to settle in England

1290 Edward I's daughter Margaret is married to John, duke of Brabant

c.1290 The Dutch chronicler Jan van Heelu dedicates his verse chronicle account of the Battle of Woeringen to Margaret of England, duchess of Brabant

1293/4–1381 Jan van Ruusbroec, Dutch mystic whose works are influential in England in Latin translation

1294–1303 Anglo-French war: Edward I allies himself with Flanders and Holland against France

1296 Flemish merchants die defending the 'Red Hall', their factory in

Berwick-upon-Tweed, against the English forces of Edward I

1297 John, count of Holland, marries Elizabeth, Edward I's daughter

1318 John Crabbe, a Flemish pirate, makes Berwick-upon-Tweed his base and helps defend it against the English

1328 Edward III marries Philippa of Hainault, daughter of Count William III of Holland

1339–40 Jan van Boendale, secretary of the city of Antwerp, is paid for his services by Edward III during Edward's stay in Brabant

1340–96 Walter Hilton, English mystic whose *Scale of Perfection* is influential in the Low Countries in Latin translation

1343 An English staple is established in Bruges, moving to Calais in 1363

1381 The Peasants' Revolt; riots in London target the Dutch-speaking community

1387–1400 Chaucer writes his *Canterbury Tales*; 'Flaundres' features prominently as a setting

1413 The Dutch poet Dirc Potter visits England

1423 Humfrey, duke of Gloucester, marries Jacqueline, countess of Hainault and Holland

1447 Henry VI revokes privileges of the Hanseatic League, leading to war between England and the Hanseatic League

1449 Mary of Guelders marries King James II of Scotland

1468 Marriage of Margaret of York and Charles, duke of Burgundy; the lavish celebrations in Bruges are witnessed by John Paston

1473 William Caxton prints his first English book in Flanders

Timeline

1474 Treaty of Utrecht ends the Anglo-Hanseatic War

1480 Johan Veldener prints his Middle Dutch *Fasciculus temporum*, including a Dutch chronicle of England

1481 Caxton publishes the first printed edition of *Reynard the Fox* in English, his own translation from the Dutch

1484 Richard III exempts producers of books from commercial restrictions affecting foreign merchants and artisans

1488 Duke Humfrey's Library, based on gifts of books from Humfrey of Gloucester, opens in Oxford

1492 The English poet John Skelton crowned poet laureate in Louvain (Leuven)

1499 Desiderius Erasmus visits England, leading to lifelong friendships with fellow humanists John Colet and Thomas More

*c.*1499 First illustrated edition of *Reynard the Fox* is printed by Caxton's disciple Wynkyn de Worde

1508–9 Alexander and James Stewart, sons of King James IV of Scotland, are tutored by Erasmus in Italy

*c.*1510–25 *Everyman*, translated from the Dutch, is printed by Robert Pynson

1517 Evil May Day: riots in London against 'alien' merchants and bankers; many immigrants, including Dutch speakers, are murdered

*c.*1518 The Dutch publisher Jan van Doesborch prints *Mary of Nemmegen* (translated from Dutch) for the English market

1521 Edict of Worms, outlawing Martin Luther, leads to an influx of Protestant immigrants into England

1535 First complete printed English Bible, the Coverdale Bible, is produced in Antwerp

1550 The Dutch Church in London is formally established by Royal Charter to cater for the large number of Dutch-speaking immigrants

1569 Edmund Spenser's earliest work, *A Theatre for Worldlings*, based on Jan van der Noot's *Het theatre oft toon-neel*, is printed in London by John Day

1570 The map-maker Ortelius (from Antwerp) publishes the first geographical atlas, *Theatrum orbis terrarum*; Humphrey Llwyd prepares maps of England and Wales for the 1573 edition

1579 Union of Utrecht: the Netherlands (the Dutch Republic) declare independence from Spanish rule

1585 Elizabeth I supports the Dutch Republic against Philip II of Spain; in retaliation, Philip sends the Armada to invade England

1588–97 Sir Thomas Bodley, founder of the Bodleian Library, is ambassador to the Netherlands

1599 Emanuel van Meteren, friend of Sir Robert Cotton, nephew of Abraham Ortelius and consul for the Dutch traders in London, publishes the first complete history of the Dutch Revolt

1602 Foundation of the Dutch East India Company

The Bodleian Library opens

1613 Richard Verstegan publishes his *Nederlantsche antiquiteyten*, a history of the Netherlands largely adapted from his English history, *Restitution of Decayed Intelligence* (1605)

1635 John Selden publishes *Mare clausum*, a response to the Dutch legal scholar Hugo Grotius's *Mare liberum* (1609)

1641 Mary Henrietta Stuart, eldest daughter of Charles I, marries William II of Orange; she arrives in Holland in 1642

1648 The first English–Dutch/Dutch–English dictionary is published by Henry Hexham

1648–60 Charles II moves to Holland not long before the execution of his father, Charles I, and spends much of his time in the Low Countries until the Restoration (1660)

1650–72 Thomas Marshall, who donates his vast collection of printed books and manuscripts to the Bodleian Library, is stationed in the Dutch Republic as chaplain to the Merchant Adventurers

1652–4 The first of the Anglo-Dutch Wars, fought by the navy of the Dutch Republic and England's Royal Navy

1655 Franciscus Junius (from Leiden), scholar of Old English poetry, publishes his 'Cædmon' edition

1659 *The Learned Maid, or, Whether a Maid May be a Scholar?*, English translation of a work by Anna Maria van Schurman, is published

1665–7 Second Anglo-Dutch War

1667 The Raid on the Medway. The Dutch navy sails up the Thames Estuary to inflict one of the Royal Navy's worst defeats

1672–4 Third Anglo-Dutch War

1677 Franciscus Junius gives his manuscript collection to the Bodleian Library, and his printing materials to the press of the University of Oxford

1688 'Glorious Revolution': King James II is overthrown by English Parliamentarians and Prince William of Orange

1689 William of Orange is crowned king of England, Scotland and Ireland

die hi wt romē ōdreuē hadde geiiage eñ wert te rome geblocht daer vp wt grot ē ſtark indē indē kerker eñ wert begrauen in ſinte peters kerck. ¶ Int iaer ōs he ijc. wort dz eerſte guldē iaer igeſet vā deſe bonifati? die allē kerſkē mēſcē ōleende mē oflaet vā allē zōdē die te romē quamē eñ ōſochtē mz deuotiē die heilige plaet ſtedē ō heiligē apoſtelē eñ martelarē goods eñ hi ōleēde dz oflaet tot allen c. iaer de daer gingē binen i ōt iaer eñ wt der ſtat vā romē alled age ijc. m. mēſcen behal binn der ſtat woenden Anno m. ijc. rcviij. kepſeren

ert? hertoghe vā oeſtēryc dpe i. des voer noēde coninc rodolphus zoendoen zijn
Jan van hollant die rvij. graue.

tē hi regeerde r. iaer.   ¶ Van ioncheer iā vā hollāt eñ van
rchden eñ was die rvij. graue vā hollāt zeelāt eñ heer vā vrieſlant. Dat ij. capitel.

The dokes cryden as men wolde hem quelle;   [ducks; kill]

The gees for feere flowen over the trees;   [fear; flew]

Out of the hyve cam the swarm of bees.

So hydous was the noyse – a, benedicitee! –

Certes, he Jakke Straw and his meynee   [followers]

Ne made nevere shoutes half so shrille,

Whan that they wolden any Flemyng kille,

As thilke day was maad upon the fox.   [that; made]

GEOFFREY CHAUCER, *The Nun's Priest's Tale* [1]

This is a book about the relations between the Low Countries and Britain (especially England) in the Middle Ages and the early modern period, and about the impact these relations had on literature and book production in both regions. It was written to accompany an exhibition at the Weston Library of the University of Oxford. This explains why the written and printed artefacts we discuss are selective: our focus is on items displayed in the exhibition, most of which come from the vast collections of Oxford's Bodleian Libraries. Our subtitle, *The Literary Heritage of Anglo-Dutch Relations 1066–1688*, may be open to misunderstanding, and so some historical background and clarifications are necessary.

Our period is bookended by the Norman Conquest of 1066 and the so-called Glorious Revolution of 1688. Both events were watersheds in British history and both involved North Sea crossings. The Norman Conquest brought to the throne not only a king from Normandy but also a Flemish-born queen, Matilda, daughter of the count of Flanders, while the 'Glorious Revolution' ushered in the reign of a Dutch king, William III.

'Anglo-Dutch relations' is a convenient shorthand for the contacts and exchanges between speakers of Dutch and speakers of English. In this book 'Dutch', 'English' and 'Anglo-Dutch' refer to languages and

Woodcut illustrating the *Divisiekroniek* (*Division Chronicle*), a history of Holland printed in 1517 (detail of fig. 1.4)

not to our modern nations, which were yet to be born. What did exist was a lowland region, known today as the Low Countries on account of the flatness of the coastal plains. The area covers the Netherlands and Belgium; geographers also include the Pas-de-Calais, the area of Germany bordering on the Netherlands, and the northern tip of Luxembourg. The flatness of this geographical region has not changed, but the political landscape has, for none of these countries existed in their current form before the nineteenth century. In the Middle Ages, the Dutch-speaking countries known today as the Netherlands and Belgium were a patchwork of dominions: Friesland (where Frisian was also spoken), Holland, Zeeland, Utrecht, Flanders, Limburg, Guelders and Brabant. Medieval Flanders at times stretched much further south than it does today, as far as Boulogne-sur-Mer, covering what nowadays is called French Flanders, the north-western corner of France. Gradually the southern border of Flanders fragmented into smaller units such as the counties of Boulogne, Ardres and Guines, and Saint-Pol.[2]

The Low Countries were thus not one political entity, but rather a conglomeration of mostly self-governing principalities ruled by counts (e.g. Flanders, Limburg, Holland), dukes (e.g. Brabant) or bishops (e.g. the bishopric of Utrecht, which covered most of the northern Low Countries, including Groningen). Formally, however, these local rulers had two main overlords: the part of Flanders that lay west of the River Scheldt belonged to the kingdom of France, while all the other territories fell under the authority of the German king, whose official title was Holy Roman Emperor.

Towards the end of the Middle Ages a third feudal power appeared alongside these two: the House of Burgundy.[3] In 1369 Philip the Bold, the youngest son of King John II of France and duke of Burgundy, married Margaret III, daughter of Count Louis II of Flanders. When the count died, Flanders fell to the duke and duchess of Burgundy. Under Philip's grandson, Philip the Good (1396–1467), the Burgundian domain grew larger still, absorbing various other territories, including the Dutch-speaking principalities of Holland, Zeeland and Brabant. After the death of Mary of Burgundy in 1482, the Burgundian Netherlands passed to the Austrian Habsburg dynasty and then to the Spanish branch of that dynasty. During the 'Dutch Revolt', also known as the Eighty Years War (1568–1648), the Low Countries rebelled against Spanish rule. The northern Netherlands, predominantly Protestant at this point, won independence from Catholic Spain and became the United Provinces. These provinces, which went back to the medieval principalities, were now part of an independent state, the predecessor of the modern Netherlands. The Protestant Queen Elizabeth I of England was invited to become the sovereign. When she declined, the country became a republic, officially headed by members of the House of Orange-Nassau. A United Kingdom of the Netherlands, which included Belgium and Luxembourg, was established in 1815. Only when Belgium and Luxembourg seceded in 1830 and 1839 respectively was the present status of these countries as separate nation-states finally reached. It would thus be misleading to talk of Dutch or Belgian nationals in the context of pre-modern history. 'People from the Low Countries' may sound vaguer but is less misleading.

While our use of 'Dutch' to refer to speakers of Dutch rather than to 'Dutch citizens' avoids anachronistic assumptions based on notions of the modern nation-state, it should be recognized that assumptions about languages have also changed. What it meant to be 'Dutch speaking' and 'English speaking' was not the same in the past as it is now. In linguistic terms, Dutch is a West Germanic language. Other members of that language family include German, English and Frisian, which is still spoken in the northern tip of the Netherlands. The variety of Dutch spoken in Belgium, while not regarded as a different language, is nevertheless often referred to by a different name, Flemish ('Vlaams'), just as the Dutch-speaking part of Belgium is now known as Flanders ('Vlaanderen'), despite the fact that historically Flanders and Flemish refer to the County of Flanders.[4] In the Middle Ages and the sixteenth century, the terms for the Dutch language were even less precise, because 'standard' languages and 'national' languages did not exist. Speakers of other languages often used 'Flemish' to refer to Dutch speech and Dutch speakers generally. The term 'Dutch' – Latin *Teutonicus*, Middle Dutch *Diets*, Middle English *Douche* – was even more general: it was used to refer to Germans and their language as well as to the language and people we now call 'Dutch'.[5] ('Middle' in Middle English and Middle Dutch refers to the form of the language used from around the twelfth to the fifteenth centuries; their predecessors were Old Dutch and Old English.)

Secondly, it should be remembered that in the medieval and early modern periods many Dutch speakers, especially if they were educated, nobly born or merchants, spoke more than one language. French was widely spoken by the aristocracy, particularly in the County of Flanders.[6]

This was true in England too.[7] The Norman Conquest of 1066 put a French-speaking king and a French-speaking elite in charge, and even two and a half centuries later French remained a living vernacular of medieval England. Latin too had an important role: it was the language of the church, at least until the rise of Protestantism, and the principal language of scholarship for long after that. This pervasive multilingualism meant that both English speakers and Dutch speakers often communicated in other languages. It also explains why some of the books and texts we discuss are in Latin and French: Anglo-Dutch relations were not exclusively carried out in Dutch or English.

The third point that needs to be emphasized is that the areas where Dutch and English were spoken in the past only roughly map onto the areas where they are spoken today. The English-speaking area was smaller. Welsh was spoken both in Wales and along its borders, while Cornish was a living language in parts of Devon and Cornwall. Gaelic was spoken in Scotland. Around the time of the Norman Conquest, the English–Gaelic language border was north of the Forth, and it moved steadily northwards during the later Middle Ages. By the early sixteenth century, when the language that Scottish speakers once termed 'Inglis' had become what they now began to call 'Scottis', the language border coincided roughly with the 'Highland line', running from Glasgow to Inverness and beyond.[8] The Dutch-speaking area, by contrast, was larger then than it is now. In present-day Belgium the language border between French-speaking Wallonia and Dutch-speaking 'Flanders' runs roughly in a horizontal line from Visé (between Liège and Maastricht) in the east to Mouscron (north of Lille). It is clear from historic place names, however, that this border has shifted north over the centuries. For instance, Tournai, south of Mouscron, was once Doornik, and French Flanders, which historically belonged to the County of Flanders, was also Dutch-speaking. In the fourteenth century, the French–Dutch language border ran roughly in a line from Wissant (Witsant) to Saint-Omer (Sint-Omaars), and from there down to Merville (Mergem).[9] Five centuries earlier it was even further south. Bilingualism must have been the norm along the language border. Dutch was also spoken in parts of Germany bordering on what is now the Netherlands, notably in cities such as Cleves and Emden.[10]

English, now an international language, had no status abroad during our period, although it was spoken in Calais. The town had been captured by the English in 1347, during the Hundred Years War against France. The legendary story of how six burghers from the town of Calais offered themselves up to King Edward III for execution, so that Calais and its people might be saved, is told by the fourteenth-century chronicler Jean Froissart. Through the intercession of King Edward III's wife, Philippa of Hainault, the burghers were spared, but Calais was then colonized by the English, and it remained an English colony until it was retaken by the French in 1558. For over two centuries, then, Calais was an English town in Dutch-speaking lands (for it lay north of the historic French–Dutch language border).[11] This remarkable situation explains why Lord Hastings, Lieutenant of Calais, seeking a new clerk of the kitchen in 1476, was advised by Sir John Paston to appoint one Richard Stratton: 'He is well spokyn in Inglyshe, metly [fairly] well in Frenshe, and verry parfite in Flemyshe.'[12] It also explains why we find Dutch in the fifteenth-century letters and papers of the Cely family,[13] who traded in wool from their base in Calais, and why a native of Calais, Laurence Andrewe, found it easy to translate Dutch into English. Born and bred in Calais, Andrewe acquired both languages, and profited from his language skills by working as a Dutch–English translator, first for other printers in Antwerp, and then for himself when he started printing in London in 1529.[14] The willingness shown by English speakers of that time to learn languages other than their own, including Dutch, is worth noting, and is explained by the simple fact that no one else could be expected to speak English. Rather like Dutch speakers today (who know they will not be understood abroad if they speak their mother tongue), the English found it necessary and therefore psychologically easier to learn other languages.

The first phrase of our title, 'literary heritage', also needs some clarification. By 'literary' and 'literature' we do not mean 'high art', as distinct from more mundane kinds of writing. Our concern is with texts and books, plain and deluxe. Our 'literature' certainly includes writings of recognized artistic and intellectual quality such as *Everyman* (*c.*1500, translated from the masterpiece of Middle Dutch drama *Elckerlijc*) and the works of Thomas More and Erasmus. Special mention should be made of the wonderful stories of Reynard the Fox and of William Caxton's *History of Reynard the Fox*, which Caxton himself translated from Dutch into English. But our coverage also includes scraps that have no great 'literary' merit, but owe their existence and human interest

to the historical circumstances that brought them into being. So we also discuss, for instance, an early twelfth-century pen trial by a Flemish monk living in Kent and a 'Foreigners Out!' diatribe that was attached to the wall of the Dutch Church in London in 1593. All these and many other types of writing, such as chronicles and saints' lives, are included in the 'literary heritage of Anglo-Dutch relations'.

Our book has two related themes: first, the encounters between Dutch-speaking and English-speaking people in medieval and early modern times; second, the legacy of these encounters in the surviving literature of the Middle Ages and the early modern period. We thus bring together the domains of social history and literary history. Relations between the literatures from the Low Countries and England can usefully be examined in terms of textual sources and influences, but in a period without wired or wireless communications ideas, texts and books naturally could not travel without humans. Every instance of 'literary influence' or 'borrowing' therefore presupposes a chain of human contact. By combining insights from the fields of history and literature, we can obtain a more rounded picture.

This book also differs from conventional histories and literary histories in that it explores and illustrates the literary heritage of Anglo-Dutch relations with specific reference to the unique collection of manuscripts, early prints, maps and other writings from the Bodleian Library in Oxford. If it is the case, as we believe, that the crossing of Dutch and English lives had important consequences for literature, then we must let works of literature do the talking. We have therefore chosen to unfold the story of Anglo-Dutch relations through a selection of treasures and curiosities from the Bodleian Library, occasionally supplemented with items from other collections. This focus on material texts – the physical objects, such as manuscripts and early printed books, through which the literary heritage is preserved and transmitted to us – adds a third dimension to the perspectives of history and literary history: that of the history of the book, from the handwritten codex to the early printed edition, and from manuscript illuminations to woodcuts and engravings.

Why focus on the Bodleian? As will become clear, any English cultural institution with a history that stretches back far into the past has felt the impact of Anglo-Dutch relations, and we do hope that others will take up the challenge of telling those stories. The Bodleian Library, however, was shaped by these relations to such an extent that the institution and its collections are themselves part of Anglo-Dutch heritage. The oldest part of the Bodleian, Duke Humfrey's Library, is named after Humfrey, duke of Gloucester, who claimed the title of count of Holland, Zeeland and Hainault through his marriage to Jacqueline of Hainault in 1423; the library was re-founded by Thomas Bodley, formerly English ambassador to the Netherlands; and many medieval Dutch treasures in the collection were collected and bequeathed to the library by a former chaplain to the Merchant Adventurers in the Dutch Republic, Thomas Marshall.

In fact, the Dutch connection can be taken further back still. The earliest records of learning and study in Oxford date from the late eleventh century – before the university was officially established in 1231.[15] Only a handful of names of students and scholars in Oxford in this period are preserved. The first recorded international student came from the northern Low Countries: Emo of Huizinge (in the province of Groningen).[16] Whether his mother tongue was Dutch or Frisian we do not know, but it is likely that Emo could speak both languages. Around 1195, at the age of about twenty, he went to England, as he tells us in the chronicle he later wrote of his monastery in Groningen, 'causa studii litterarum quod fuit Oxonie' ('for study of the liberal arts then available at Oxford').[17] His biographer, Menko, later added that he was accompanied by his brother Addo, who encouraged him to study law. In Oxford both brothers made copies of Gratian's *Decretum*, the standard canon law text. After Oxford, Emo, like so many of his contemporary 'wandering scholars', continued his studies at Orléans and Paris before returning home. He brought back the learning he had acquired in England and France, and put it to use for the benefit of his monastery, Bloemhof, in Wittewierum in Groningen. The only record of Emo's time in Oxford is the chance survival of the chronicle of his monastery.

The six chapters that follow explore the cultural consequences of Anglo-Dutch contact. The first is devoted to the writing of history, real and imaginary. The second, third and fourth chapters, on manuscripts, early printed books and maps, show how North Sea crossings affected book production and map-making. The fifth chapter examines aspects of the social history of migration, including the networks of Anglo-Dutch intellectuals and the institutional legacy of these networks, with special

reference to the Bodleian Library itself. The final chapter provides a case study of literary and artistic diffusion by examining the evolution of stories and visual representations of Reynard the Fox, who was born in Flanders but soon made his way across to England and who became part of a literary and iconographical tradition that was cherished and shared on both sides of the North Sea.

While the richness and breadth of the literary heritage of Anglo-Dutch relations will become clear in these chapters, the writings of Geoffrey Chaucer (1340–1400), the 'Father of English Poetry' (as John Dryden called him), can provide us with a useful indication of the diversity of cultural impacts. Chaucer was well acquainted with Dutch speakers for a number of reasons. As a customs official, he knew all about the wool trade, and he had also travelled through the Low Countries, first as a soldier and later in royal service. Just as important, however, was his life in London, a city with a notable presence of Dutch speakers.[18] Repeated references to the Dutch Low Countries and to Dutch speakers in Chaucer's work emphasize these connections. The Merchant of the *Canterbury Tales* trades between Middelburg and Suffolk and wears 'a Flaudryssh bever hat'.[19] Flanders is again prominent in the geography of the Shipman's Tale, where Bruges features as the centre of international finance that it was indeed becoming at the time.[20] Chaucer's Miller's Tale seems to have been influenced by the Middle Dutch comic tale *Heile van Berseele*, though some think the influence was the other way around.[21] The Pardoner's Tale is situated 'in Flaundres',[22] but when the father of Sir Thopas is described as having been born 'in fer [distant] contree, / In Flaundres, al biyonde the see / At Poperyng',[23] the description is pointedly parodic. At a time when travel by sea was often easier than travel by land, Flanders was London's nearest neighbour abroad, while Poperinge was decidedly in the lower division of cloth-producing towns, behind more glamorous cities such as Ghent and Bruges. The hero of the tale, 'Sir Thopas', Chaucer implies, is not really properly chivalric but bourgeois. Chaucer, the merchant's son turned gentleman, here taps into a common species of class prejudice, that of knights looking down on artisans. As we shall see, the prejudice had a long history and afterlife in descriptions of the Flemish. For his part, Chaucer's Cook, whose world does not extend much beyond London, has nevertheless managed to pick up some Dutch himself, citing a Flemish proverb: '"sooth pley, quaad pley", as the Flemyng seith.'[24] Chaucer did not think that the Dutch 'quaad' in this proverb ('a true jest is a bad jest') required translating, and remarkably some scribes were able to cite the proverb in an even more fully fledged Dutch form, writing Dutch 'spel' (play) instead of 'pley'.[25] The host of the Tabard Inn, Harry Bailey, has a troublesome wife who is named after the patiently submissive Flemish saint Godelieve, but she is an innkeeper who is nothing but trouble, living up to the reputation that Dutch speakers in London had for their role in both beer production and prostitution.[26]

The Dutch connection is also central to the Nun's Priest's Tale, which can in fact be characterized as the most Flemish of Chaucer's *Canterbury Tales*. It is a retelling of an episode from the Reynard the Fox cycle, the collection of fables about the trickster fox. Chaucer's immediate source was in French, but the story originated in Flanders and remained closely associated with the region as it developed. Symptomatic of this association is that the housewives that set off in pursuit of the fox invariably go armed with distaffs. This tool of the weaver's craft was so strongly associated with Flanders that two Dutch words for it, *rok* and *spinrok*, were taken over into English. The latter first occurs in a book printed by William Caxton, and the former crops up in various texts, the most interesting one being another Middle English Reynard poem, the fifteenth-century *The False Fox*:

> The good-wyf came out in her smoke
> And at the fox she threw hir rok.[27]

The Reynard tradition itself was repeatedly marked by North Sea crossings, and Chaucer associated the story with Flemings, as becomes clear in his description of the chasing of the fox by the villagers, whom he describes as shouting at least twice as loud as Jack Straw, the leader of the Peasants' Revolt of 1381, and his followers, 'whan that they wolden any Flemyng kille'.[28] Such targeted killings of Flemings indeed took place during the Peasants' Revolt, and Chaucer was not the only one to mention them. It is, however, striking that he reserves his only explicit reference to the Peasants' Revolt – the events of which horrified contemporaries – for this one comment. In his retelling, the chased fox takes the place of London's Flemings.

We shall return to various elements of this brief episode in Chaucer's *Canterbury Tales* in the subsequent chapters of this book: Chaucer's stories were initially transmitted in handwritten books, and we find the scene of the fox being chased by women with distaffs in decorated manuscripts. The *Canterbury Tales* were first printed by William Caxton, England's earliest printer, who had started printing in the Dutch Low Countries, where he had no doubt picked up the word *spynroke* ('distaff'), which he introduced into the English language. He also personally translated from Dutch his bestselling *History of Reynard the Fox*. The English geographical imagination, which is limited to London and its immediate surroundings in Chaucer's Cook's Tale but broadens out to include the Low Countries in many of his other tales, was further expanded by Dutch map-makers. Dutch speakers in England and English people who spent time in the Netherlands helped shape English cities as well as English institutions, including the Bodleian Library. Finally, we shall return to Reynard the Fox, the role that Anglo-Dutch relations played in the development of his stories and the impact of Dutch Reynard stories in England: a heritage of Anglo-Dutch relations that endures to this day.

Detail of a map of Britain and Ireland showing the North Sea, from Joan Blaeu's *Atlas*, c.1645–54. © Bodleian Library, Oxford, Gough Maps 91.

**Sjoerd Levelt, Elisabeth van Houts,
Moreed Arbabzadah and Ad Putter**

> This our realme of England and those countries
> have bene by common language of long time
> resembled and termed as man and wife.

Queen Elizabeth I, 1585

The medieval and early modern chronicles and histories from England
and the Low Countries are important sources for the history of relations
between Dutch and English speakers in the period. They not only provide
us with accounts of events, but also tell us how and why these events
mattered to contemporaries. Chroniclers recorded happenings from
the distant or recent past that struck them as memorable and relevant:
migration, exile, marriage, diplomacy, trade, wars, plagues and so on.
That so many chroniclers took the trouble to record contact situations
between Dutch and English speakers, some even commenting on personal
experiences, makes their writings significant to us. Events that happened
in different countries were often overlooked. If English historians
recorded things that happened in the Low Countries, and vice versa, these
must have mattered, so reciprocal reporting is of considerable interest.

Another reason for our interest in historical writings may be less
obvious to readers who expect historians from the past to be like
historians today. Historians writing in the Middle Ages and the early
modern period tended to be less concerned with historical accuracy,
'truth' in the modern sense, than with 'truth' in the dominant older sense
of the word, that is, how things should be, knowing right from wrong.
This cultural difference explains the generous scope afforded to 'myth'
(as we would now call it) in the histories we are about to survey. For if
historians concern themselves with life as they think it should be, morally
or politically, then the past must be reconfigured to form a suitable back
story to this moral/political agenda. That some of the encounters between
Dutch and English speakers described in chronicles are imagined rather

King William III's entry into The Hague, from a 1692
engraving by Govard Bidloo (detail of fig. 1.17)

than real does not make them less important. On the contrary, the ways in which writers in the Low Countries and England imagined each other's cultures and histories provide telling evidence of mutual perceptions. Their writings show the roles that English and Dutch speakers attributed to each other in the formation of their own histories and collective identities.

Our purpose in this chapter is therefore to examine what chronicles and histories of the period tell us about Anglo-Dutch relations, real *and* imagined. Our story moves between different languages and different rulers; it takes us to different parts of England and Wales and to the different principalities of the Low Countries (mainly Flanders, Brabant and Holland); but, as we cross back and forth between England and the Low Countries to see how historians on both sides of the North Sea recorded and responded to Anglo-Dutch exchanges, we will keep a roughly chronological course. We begin with the Norman Conquest, which brought a Flemish-born queen to the English throne, and we end with the so-called Glorious Revolution, culminating in the coronation of a Dutchman as king of England, Scotland and Ireland.

FLEMINGS AND ANGLO-NORMAN ENGLAND

The invasion by Duke William of Normandy (1027–1087) in 1066 was recorded with equal measures of horror at the bloodbath of Hastings, condemnation of William's coup and admiration for his military audacity.[1] The contemporary perception in Flanders was generally positive, not least because William's wife, Matilda, was Flemish and had financed his flagship, according to the so-called Ship List of William. This text, uniquely preserved in Oxford, Bodleian Library, MS. e Musaeo 93, fol. 8v (fig. 1.1),[2] describes Matilda of Flanders' contribution to the Conquest, and her subsequent reward:

> Matildis, postea regina, eiusdem ducis uxor, ad honorem ducis fecit effici nauem que uocabatur Mora, in qua ipse dux uectus est. In prora eiusdem nauis fecit fieri eadem Matildes infantulum de auro, dextro indice monstrantem Angliam et sinistra manu inprimentem cornu eburneum ori. Pro quo facto dux concessit eidem Matildi comitatum Cantie.

> *The duke's wife, Matilda, who later became queen, in honour of her husband had a ship made called 'Mora', on which the duke crossed. On*

1.1 The Ship List of William the Conqueror, describing the commitment of his nobles to supply vessels for the conquest of England. The page shown has a description of the ship financed by Matilda of Flanders. Manuscript from c.1130–60. Oxford, Bodleian Library, MS. e Mus. 93, fol. 8v.

Willelm' dux normannoꝛ uemens
in anglia ob adq'rendu regnu iu
re sibi debitu habuit a Willelmo
dapifero filio Osb'ni. sexaginta
naues. Ab hugone p'ea comite de
cestra: totide. Ab hugone de mu
fort': quinquaginta naues. & sexagin
ta milites. A romo elemosinario tel
canni. p'ea epo lincoliensi. una
naue cu xx. militib3. A nicholao
abbe de S'co dudoeno. xv. naue
cu c. militib3. A rob'to comite
augi. sexaginta naues. A fulco
ne daurno. xl. naues. A geroldo
dapifero: totade. A will' comite
deuroul. octoginta naues. A ro
gero de mungumeri. sexaginta
naues. A ruſo de baumunt. lx.
naues. Ab idone epo de baios:
c. naues. A rob'to de moroten.
c. xxx. A waltio gisfardo. xxx.
cu c. militib3. Ext hal naues que
coputate simul. oꝫ efficiunt.
habuit dux adq'buſda suiſ hoibʒ
ſedꝛ poſſibilitate ſuiꝰ cuiuſ
multaſ aliaſ naueſ. Mathild'
poſtea regina eidem ducis uxoꝛ.
ad honoꝛe ducis ſibi effecit naue
que uocabat moꝛa. iꝗ ipe dux
uect' eſt. Inſupra eidem naueſ. fec
fieri eadem matildeſ infantulu
de auro dext' indice monſtran
te angliam. & ſiniſt' manu iꝓ
inꝛe coꝛnu eburnu oꝛi. Proꝗ
hacto dux ꝯceſſit eidem matilth.

solamini. Nec eni celestis eius spe
aliter opatus est: quam si interim re
dituro corpe suo cotidie veniret.

Ve originarii sui diuersarumqz habitatum ciuitatum
eorum aut qui ipe eorum archiepos iste fuit.
et qua occasione eum in hiis locis se derelinq...

De ciuitate franc̃os qua referunt sc̃m
ynouem et fr̃em eius beatum athana
rium ē natum. in eadem regnauit p̃
cor rex nomine yomos. et regina ysca
lua mr eorxdem. Athanathus aut fr sc̃i
ynouis: in nemore quodam heremiticam
dux̃t uitam. quo dñs p̃ merita hactru
miranda facit miracla. Sanctus uero y
no patronus nr inqua ciuitate natus.
estituit et epc. Postea quoqz p̃ ea̅ e̅ q̃ua
tione electus: in ciuitate astania ad ar
chiepm. in qua puigil sup gregem sui
sibi comissum dvo devote obseruelans
p̃uauebat. donec p̃ter peccata p̃pli ta̅
ta fames et tam ualida ibi incruit: ut
mater filiam. et filium pr. mutuoqz plan
subditu s̃ p̃plm comedent. Quod si
eius ozone et fr̃is sui inpellatione ad dñi
p̃pls ñ ect quodam fructu cio donate
sustentatus. tota terra illa et totus p̃
pls famis imanitate devastata. et c̃et. Pro
inde p̃r. uiri religiosi et mentes in
inuicem elegerunt eadem in pata et con
stiuct tota p̃pria se uelle et regna p̃ter
amorem dñi omnino derelinqueire. et
totas tras p̃gnando rñ̃sincare. Qui eu
ad romam p̃uenissent: et silio pape qui
tunc tempc fuit: et ipor electione sepa
rati ab inuicem: ui quisqz eor pse uiam
suam tetendit. Alius p̃uiam lauicana̅.

alius p̃uiam nuñitanam. Ali p̃uia̅ scla
ram. steqz omñ p̃uiam p̃ierunt electam.
Tandem ad dispositione patronus nos
tes yno archiepe cu sithio nepote et iuxta
cognato suo. aliusqz cu decem sociis itala
p̃ p̃stra: allobrogu gentes et galliarum
regione rñ̃sincata. ad illum locum s̃ adeo
destinatu p̃uenit: quo huc usqz nomo e
omnipo de p̃ ei merita murtice p̃muulgat.
Fr̃ uero eius beato athanatho ruente
ad p̃priam heremiteam sedem deo duce
te euenit. qui siut ex duodecim suis patri
bus qui ita ut supra dixi se se in peregnati
ne dederunt. Locus aut ille ubi corpus e̅
excelso monte ad huc incorruptum p̃ma
net monachor collegio honoratur: ut uno
quoqz siue monachi ad p̃destinati. unguet
manuu e̅ incidunt. et capillos rondent.
omniqz ab gente illius regionus in grecia
ut sc̃s demetrius in prima regione ho
noratur et colitur.

Verba certo caro
sius heubro. iteru̅ naminius. sacal
hic fr Corelinus. Incipit plog̃ de uita
discotum ab diiu... nr archiepus ut offt...

ye de uita beati y
nonis referuntur
a uenerabili abbate
andira celebrata nos
cuntur: qui de angl
ad diuica̅ urbem ierl'm
peregrinat̃ ta̅ archiua

uitam exercuit. ut ei credere nullus
fidelis dubitauerit. Testabatur ingra
cia ei nom̃ et uitam. et gestis multis mi
raculis haberi clarissima: et uno odue

xpi gīarum longe lateq; notissima ipsius preconia.
Ab inuentione ū & reuelatione & pdigia que hic
precessor scribit tā oclis uisa qm fidelium testimonio
cōpbata: adhuc pene omniū frm ramesiensiū
nonnulloruq; forensiū cordibz memorabilius qm
in libro sunt scripta: & scriptis luculentius memo-
rant aliqua premissa. Hec q gra huj patris
sčissimi: totusq; huj conuentus carissimi peti-
cione uenerabili paulo breuius collegi: quatinus
in paruo facilius qm in uita multa qd querit in-
ueniat: citiusq; breuiori uia qm longo ambi-
tu ad tmnū pueniat: & de confecta mensula
qm de horreo paratus edat: & de fonticulo g-
tius qm de fluuio bibat. Nec adeo de copia te-
nui inopiā: nec intellectus uel condimentū te-
nui decett qd opinio supstuit. is m modulus
mediet. qn nec auidior nec fastidiosior offendat.

Hec amabili & eterne memorie tue honorificen-
tissime alba in sacratissimo patre yuone condi-
dim: qn cum suscepisti uenerandū tue salutis
pnapem cū pnapatu ramesiensi: quatinus sicut
hic ipm honorificauerit & colueris: ita te insine
assumat in gaudia sue lucis. Expliciut plogus.
Incipiunt miracla beati yuonis archiepisopi
ac confessoris.

Doctor Apticus. &
ueri solis nuntius.
yuo presul inclitus:
in psida ut oriene-
tale sidus & ortus:
finibz occiduis bri-
tannie a dīo desti-
natus. Relicta dulce patam ut exilium: conti-
nuit supnarum immū: & pegnus xpi in toto
mundo ad eternū tendebat regnū. Quocūq;
deuenit suis radiis refulsit: omnia etingulis

xpi semiuerbiis repleuit. gentes & nationes
documentis ac exemplis: atq; innumeris mi-
raclis ad saluatore traxit. Post magnā asiā.
p illiricū. p romā. p innumeras urbes & po-
plos trisacros gallias penetrauit: ibiq; in
chilomiis tantis signis chorusceauit: ut eius
celestem uitā & anglicam doctrinam mirifice
titures loquerent. Cūq; cum rex francor &
optimates regni ac popli tanqm anglin dei
dignu honoribz retinere temptarent: ille qui
parentalem mundi gsām exulando fugerat:
& p multas tbulationes intrare in regnū di
decernabat. nulla gra terrena retineri potat.
Omnibz q confirmatis in fide: tnstterauit cū
dignis comitibz ac sociis in candidā albionem
britannie. gentē candidā patria miseratus
pietate tā signis qm pdicatione put dīo ido-
late absoluit errore: & uerius candificauit
baptismate. Sequebat q; amaīnissimū prem
adolescens pātie dignitatis. uocatus patruus.
cuidam senatoris filius: qn amore x p ipm scm
yuone uocantis ū solū dulces natales & pa-
trios honores postposuit: uersieuā desponsatā
s uginem cū tota spe seli intactam deseruit:
dulcq; magistro tā caritate qm imitacione
inseparabilis adhesit. Beatus. qui illius im-
ui pectoralis xpi iosus exemplū assecutus est.
Deinde salutifer aduena yuo in puinciā
meruor pgrediū ad oppidū qd hun-
tedun appellat: & in pxima uilla queslepe
uo cat. iam se intelligens a dīo ad certū locū
deduci: multis annis pseuerauit ad uitte
extium. Hic ū tanta flagitia celestem con-
uersacione induit: qm tue denū cepisset:
& qm p longam sitim fontem petrum re-
pisset. Hic inqm tā sue qm omniū salim

its prow Matilda had [a statue of] a golden child fitted, who with his right index finger pointed to England and with his left hand held an ivory horn to his mouth. In return for this the duke granted Matilda the earldom of Kent.

Matilda's father, Count Baldwin V of Flanders (r.1035–67), had also supported his son-in-law by allowing many Flemish soldiers to join in William's venture.[3] They were richly rewarded with lands, especially in Lincolnshire and East Anglia. Their new-found wealth made them a target for Continental fundraisers, such as the monks of Laon in northern France, who travelled through England *c.*1100 showing off their own relics as part of the fashionable *circumlationes*, or 'funding tours' (more literally 'trips carrying things round'), to solicit donations for the repair of the cathedral of Laon.[4]

The North Sea crossing was also made by a number of Flemish monks, who travelled to England as professional biographers of saints and royalty. Goscelin (born *c.*1035) was especially prolific, producing *Vitae* (saints' lives), for numerous English abbeys, including Wilton, Sherborne, Barking, Ely and Ramsey. Having started his career at Saint-Bertin's monastery in Dutch-speaking Sint-Omaars (modern Saint-Omer), he travelled to England to join Bishop Herman in Wiltshire. After Herman's death, Goscelin was (in his own words) 'forced to wander the land',[5] but in the 1090s he ended up at St Augustine's Abbey, Canterbury. He was still writing as late as 1099 and probably died *c.*1107 at the age of about seventy. His contemporary Reginald of Canterbury called him 'Musarum dulcis amicus' ('a sweet friend of the Muses').[6] The chronicler William of Malmesbury (died *c.*1142) described him as 'insignis litterarum et cantuum peritia' ('famous for his expertise in literature and singing') and rated him second only to Bede as a hagiographer of English saints ('nulli post Bedam secundus').[7] Much of what we know about pre-Conquest English saints comes from Flemish writers, and Goscelin in particular. Manuscripts with lives of these saints were repeatedly copied in the centuries following the Norman Conquest, thus conveying the religious heritage of pre-Conquest England to new generations of monastics, often themselves immigrants from the Continent. Oxford, Bodleian Library, MS. Bodl. 285 (fig. 1.2) is one such manuscript. It was produced in the thirteenth century, quite possibly at Ramsey Abbey, with which both St Ivo and Goscelin had been associated.

I.2   *previous pages*   Opening of the life of the Cornish bishop and hermit St Ivo, by the Flemish monk Goscelin of Saint-Bertin, from a thirteenth-century manuscript from Ramsey Abbey, where the saint's relics were kept (until *c.*1100) and Goscelin wrote his life (*c.*1090). Oxford, Bodleian Library, MS. Bodl. 285, fols 99v–100r.

A Flemish monk like Goscelin probably had a linguistic advantage when it came to working in England.[8] Goscelin remarked on some of the similarities between English and Flemish in his *Liber confortatorius* (*Book of Consolation*), and his good knowledge of English allowed him to make use of English sources for his works.[9] His facility in Latin would also have been prized, because not every monk in the medieval world was capable of writing Latin hagiographies. Though it is easy to assume that every monk spoke Latin, it has been argued that comparatively few monks really did.[10] The standard of reading and writing Latin was also perhaps not necessarily as high as might be imagined. About a century after Goscelin, Gerald of Wales has an anecdote about an abbot of Malmesbury whose Latin was so poor that he utterly misunderstood the word *repente* ('suddenly').[11] In comparison with English monks, Goscelin had an advantage when it came to learning Latin because in Flanders he would have been exposed to French,[12] a language much closer to Latin than English was.[13] Being a Flemish monk at a wealthy monastery was therefore in many ways the ideal grounding for a life as a Latin hagiographer of English saints. His early life in Flanders provided knowledge of both a Romance language and a Germanic language, which facilitated the later learning of Latin and English respectively. The wealth of Saint-Bertin then provided the books and environment necessary to develop a great deal of expertise in Latin and hagiography. The literary output of Flemish authors like Goscelin thus made a lasting contribution to the heritage of the English church.

FLEMISH SETTLERS IN TWELFTH-CENTURY ENGLAND, WALES AND SCOTLAND

The majority of the Flemish elite that gave military support to Duke William came from the southern province of Artois.[14] By 1086, the Flemings and Picards formed approximately 5.7 per cent of the newly established foreign landed elite in England.[15] In their wake followed Flemish men and women of humbler backgrounds. The chroniclers William of Malmesbury and John of Worcester (died *c.*1140) recorded this in texts that are preserved in Bodleian Library manuscripts. They described how in 1108–10 King Henry I of England, son of the Conqueror, ordered the forced resettlement of one Flemish colony.[16] Flemish peasant farmers and artisans had originally made a home in Cumbria. John of Worcester tells us that they were then ordered to go to Pembrokeshire in south Wales: 'Rex Anglorum Heinricus Flandrenses qui Norðymbriam incolebant, cum tota suppellictili sua, in

Waloniam transtulit, et terram, que Ros nominatur, incolere precepit' ('Henry, king of the English, removed to Wales some Flemings, who were living in Northumbria, together with all their chattels, and made them settle in the district which is called Rhos').[17] The strategic settlement of these foreigners met with fierce local resistance, according to the same chronicler:

> Walenses in defensione sue natiue terre, non solum a Normannicis diuitibus, sed etiam a Flandrensibus multa perpessi pluribus utrinque peremptis, deuictis tamen ad ultimum Flandrensibus, non cessant in circuitu omnia uastare, uillas ac castella uastando comburere, omnes resistentes sibi simul cum innocentibus et nocentibus neci tradere.

> *In the defence of their native land, the Welsh were hard pressed not only by the powerful Normans, but also by the Flemings. Many were killed on both sides, but in the end the Flemings were beaten, and the Welsh laid waste all around them, setting fire to townships and castles, killing all who resisted, whether innocent or not.*[18]

Nevertheless, Flemings long remained a recognizable settler community in south-west Wales. They were vividly recorded by the historian Gerald of Wales, whose brother Philip had married into a Flemish family. Passing through the area on his *Itinerarium Kambriae* (*Journey through Wales*, 1191), Gerald describes them as follows:

> Gens fortis et robusta, continuoque belli conflictu gens Kambrensibus inimicissima; gens, inquam, lanificiis, gens mercimoniis usitatissima; quocunque labore sive periculo terra marique lucrum quaerere gens pervalida; vicissim loco et tempore nunc ad aratrum, nunc ad arma, gens promptissima.[19]

> *They are a brave and robust people, but very hostile to the Welsh and in a perpetual state of conflict with them. They are highly skilled in the wool trade, ready to work hard and to face danger by land or sea in the pursuit of gain, and, as time and opportunity offer, prompt to turn their hand to the sword or the ploughshare.*[20]

He tells in particular of their custom of scapulimancy: foretelling the future using the shoulder bones of rams stripped of their meat. He gives various examples of the uses to which these Flemings applied the custom, but these become increasingly ridiculous, finishing with an example from their country of origin:

> Contigit etiam in Flandriae finibus, unde gens ista descenderat, viro quodam vicino suo os hujusmodi ad inspiciendum transmittente, quod portitor obiter fossam transiliendo fissa nate crepitum dedit, quem statim viri naribus, cujus causa vexabatur, verbis et votis adoptavit. Ille vero cui portabatur, armo inspecto, illico subjecit; 'Sed tu, frater, quod mihi optaveras in naribus habeas.'[21]

> *The story is told in Flanders, the land from which these people come, that a certain person sent one of these bones to his neighbour for inspection. As he jumped over a ditch, the man who was carrying it let out a fart through his exertions, and wished the stench on the nostrils of him to whom he was taking it. The man who received the bone turned it over and said without more ado: 'Well, brother, what you have wished on my nose you can stuff up your own!'*[22]

It was not just their customs that were imported from the Continent: later, writing in 1207–13, Gerald recalled that they continued to speak their own language, not just among themselves, but also to his brother.[23]

Gerald's personal views of the Flemish were negative. In England, too, the influx of Flemish speakers troubled the natives. The 'journalists' of their day were increasingly worried about Flemish immigrants and soldiers. In his chronicle about the war between Scotland and England in 1173–74, Jordan Fantosme heaped scorn on the many Flemish mercenaries who had flocked to the service of Henry II's rebellious sons and King William the Lion of Scotland, parodying their chivalric pretensions by presenting them as being interested mainly in stealing the wool of England and being nothing more than weavers:

> Seignurs, ço est la verité: li plus furent telier,
> Ne sevent porter armes a lei de chevalier.

Lords, the truth is that most of them were weavers,
they do not know how to bear arms like knights.[24]

Chaucer's parody of the Flemish bourgeois knight Sir Thopas in *The Canterbury Tales* continues where Fantosme leaves off. Adapting a passage from Bede's *Ecclesiastical History*, in which the five languages spoken in Britain (English, British, Scottish, Pictish and Latin) were listed,[25] Henry of Huntingdon's *Historia Anglorum* (*History of the English People*, the first version of which was finished by 1131)[26] explained how five 'plagues' (*plagas*) had been inflicted on Britain by God: the Romans, Picts and Scots, English, Danes and Normans, all of whom had successively harried or conquered the land.[27] Alfred of Beverley, a historian who wrote *c.*1150, imitated Henry's list, but instead counted six peoples, adding the Flemish as the sixth.[28] It should be stressed that Alfred, a canon at Beverley, lived in one of the areas near the Humber populated by William the Conqueror's Flemish followers in the post-Conquest period. These followers were numerous enough for the town of Beverley to have a ward known as 'Flammengaria', later 'Flemingate'.[29] The presence of Dutch speakers in Britain was recorded not only in histories, but also in the island's place names.

Flemish immigrants also came to Scotland, but mostly indirectly as a result of the Norman Conquest of England. As with the Cumbrian Flemings who were resettled in Wales, there is evidence for the early twelfth-century migration of people with Flemish names from England to Scotland. We should see this move as part of the invitation by King David of Scotland (r.1124–53) and his grandson King Malcolm IV (r.1153–65) to Continental settlers to move north to help settle the borderlands. Robert de Quinchy, for example, belonged to a family that had come to England from French Flanders near Béthune, and as a member of a younger branch he moved to Scotland; Baldwin the Fleming was Malcolm's sheriff in Lanark, where the Olifard family settled.[30]

A FLEMING IN HOLLAND: JACOB VAN MAERLANT

We have so far looked at authors who were active in England and Wales, and who were writing in Latin. From the thirteenth century onwards, however, writers increasingly worked in the vernacular, and writers of Middle Dutch engaged in highly imaginative ways with the history and culture of their neighbours across the North Sea. The composite manuscript bearing the shelf-mark MS. Canon. Misc. 278 (fig. 1.3) provides an interesting example of the international context in which the texts we describe here circulated. The manuscript was acquired by the Bodleian Library in 1817 as part of an Italian collection of over 2,000 manuscripts. The fifteenth-century compilation is witness to a vibrant multilingual culture, containing Middle Dutch, French and Latin texts.[31] How it came to Italy in the later fifteenth century has been reconstructed with reasonable precision. The first recorded owner, in 1467, was the Bruges merchant Jan van Hersvelt, who was particularly active in the Venetian trade and had a franchise in Venice, while also trading in Rome. The manuscript also contains an itinerary of a journey from Bruges to Venice, and back and forth between Venice and Rome. This context of international commerce also had an English dimension, as the trade between the Dutch Low Countries and Italy was, in practice, part of a triangular one that also included England.[32] Another Middle Dutch manuscript that was once part of the same Italian collection, now London, British Library, Add. MS. 10802, contains a Dutch–Italian phrase book and concludes with a letter in Italian urging its readers to seek contacts in Antwerp for trade with England.[33]

Among the various texts in the Bodleian manuscript is a series of three didactic poems, known as the *Martijns*, by the thirteenth-century author Jacob van Maerlant. For successive generations of authors he was 'de vader der dietse dichtren algader' ('the father of all Dutch poets'). The Dutch text of the poems is given in the Bodleian manuscript together with a Latin translation. Presented as a dialogue between the author, Jacob, and his friend, Martijn, the first of these poems is a discourse on divine and worldly love. The two speakers discuss a range of subjects, which all address the causes of the poor state of the world, such as (bad) counsel, social inequality and infidelity:

1.3 Fifteenth-century manuscript of Jacob van Maerlant's late thirteenth-century Middle Dutch poem *Wapene Martijn*. The manuscript was brought to Italy by a Flemish merchant shortly after it had been written, and was acquired by the Bodleian Library in the nineteenth century. Oxford, Bodleian Library, MS. Canon. Misc. 278, fol. 23r.

Wat zal zeghel ende was
Ende brieven die ghewaghen das
Van dat deese heeren gheven?
En es al niet dan een ghedwas
Also lief hadt my een Zas[34]
Oft een Vriese bescreven.
Trauwe es broocher dan een glas.[35]

*Why use seal, wax and letters to record the
commitments of these lords? It's all for nought, a
chimera; it's worth as much to me as if it had been
written by a Saxon or a Frisian. Fidelity is more
fragile than glass.*

This poem is not the only place where the prolific Maerlant wrote
disparagingly about Frisians and Saxons. To explain why he singled
out these particular peoples and lumped them together to serve as
a textbook example of treachery, we need to look at his historical
writing. Historical works from the later medieval period often reflect
the interests and affiliations of the noble dynasties who normally
commissioned such works and whose patronage chroniclers sought to
attract.[36] In the thirteenth- and fourteenth-century Low Countries,
notable patrons were the counts of Holland, the dukes of Brabant
and the more prominent among their vassals. When Maerlant made
a Middle Dutch verse translation of the Latin historical compendium
Speculum historiale (*Mirror of History*), written by the French Cistercian
monk Vincent of Beauvais, he was inspired by his patron's diplomatic
entanglements to make certain interventions, touching particularly
on Holland's and on England's history.[37] Maerlant originated from
Flanders, but his patron was Count Floris V of Holland (1254–1296),
who was pursuing an alliance with England. Floris's daughter Margaret
had been engaged to Alphonso, earl of Chester, son of King Edward I.
When the engagement was cut short by Alphonso's early death in 1284,
Floris's one-year-old son (who later became Count John I of Holland)
was betrothed to Elizabeth, Edward's daughter (fig. 1.4). From that
very early age John was raised at the English royal court.[38] The alliance
between Holland and England had a direct impact on Maerlant's
treatment of his sources.

Throughout his reign King Edward strove to appropriate the figure of King Arthur in British history to his own ends: he visited Arthur's supposed grave at Glastonbury and commissioned a reproduction of the Round Table at Winchester, in part to legitimize his territorial claim to Wales.[39] Maerlant, noticing that his principal source, the *Speculum historiale*, included scant reference to Arthurian history, decided to consult the most appropriate and opportune source: Geoffrey of Monmouth's *Historia regum Britanniae* (*History of the Kings of Britain*). Geoffrey's *Historia* survives in over 220 medieval manuscripts, which shows just how popular and readily available it was at the time;[40] and the largest concentration of manuscripts outside Britain is found in the Low Countries.[41] Maerlant added to Vincent of Beauvais's account by translating from Geoffrey's elaborate Latin history of Britain, from the first arrival of Brutus and Corineus and their followers on the island of Albion (which they renamed Britain after Brutus), to the reign of King Arthur, the invasions by Saxons and Angles, the resulting downfall of the British kingdom and the establishment of the English as rulers of the island.[42]

Certain touches in Maerlant's account also betray his local outlook, reflecting the interests of the counts of Holland. He emphasizes that the Saxons who arrived in Britain, home to the previously Christianized Britons, were 'heidinen honden' ('heathen dogs')[43] – this is an addition to Geoffrey of Monmouth, who, although he identifies them as pagans (i.e. heathens), does not use explicitly derogatory terms. An added emphasis on the Saxons as being from the Continental North Sea coast may at first sight seem inspired by a desire to connect the English to Holland, but turns out to be just the opposite: the Saxons, Maerlant asserts, 'were Frisians' – not Hollanders.[44] Jacob van Maerlant's interventions in the narrative serve to identify King Arthur, the Christian king fighting pagan Frisians, not only with Edward, but also with Count Floris V himself, who was engaged in repeated expeditions against rebellious Frisians in the lands over which he claimed jurisdiction.[45] In his work

1.4 Woodcut depicting Elizabeth, daughter of King Edward I, and her husband, Count John I of Holland. From the *Divisiekroniek* (*Division Chronicle*), a chronicle of Holland printed in Leiden in 1517. The woodcut was originally made in Gouda to illustrate a different text. Oxford, Bodleian Library, Vet. B1 d.9, fol. 184v.

we see a Dutch author's genuine interest in English history paired with a drive to shape that interest according to local political considerations. This duality was to continue to exert an influence over later authors: even after the Frisians had been definitively incorporated into the domains of the counts of Holland, Maerlant's identification of the Saxons as Frisians appealed to the minds of historical writers.

BRABANT: JAN VAN HEELU AND JAN VAN BOENDALE

While Holland was governed by the counts of Holland during this period, Brabant was ruled by the dukes of Brabant. Like the counts of Holland, they actively pursued intimate relations with the English monarchy:[46] Duke John II of Brabant married Margaret of England, another daughter of Edward I (and thus sister of Elizabeth, the betrothed of the young John of Holland) (fig. 1.5). To celebrate the union, the Middle Dutch poet Jan van Heelu dedicated a verse chronicle about the history of Brabant to Margaret:

> Vrouwe Margriete van Inghelant,
> Die seker hevet van Brabant
> Tshertoghen Jans sone Jan,
> Want si dietsche tale niet en can
> Daer bi willic haer ene gichte
> Sinden van dietschen gedichte,
> Daer si dietsch in leeren moghe.[47]

> *Lady Margaret of England, who is*
> *engaged to John, son of Duke John of*
> *Brabant, because she does not know Dutch,*
> *I am sending her a gift of Dutch poetry,*
> *through which she can learn Dutch.*

Heelu's work is part chivalric romance, part chronicle account of the Battle of Woeringen (5 June 1288), in which Brabant won a decisive victory over the archbishop of Cologne, extending the power of Brabant's dukes over the duchy of Limburg. It is not known whether the chronicle helped Margaret to learn Dutch, but the language did play an important role at the duke's court at this time: Margaret's father-in-law, Duke John I, had himself written courtly love poetry in Dutch. Margaret continued to live in Brabant even following her husband's death, and eventually died in Brussels in 1333.[48]

Margaret and John's only son, John III (1300–1355), became duke in 1312. His reign was marked by shifts of alliance back and forth between France and England. Anglo-Dutch relations had a particularly significant impact on the work of the author Jan van Boendale (*c*.1280–*c*.1351),[49] who, as secretary of the city of Antwerp, had close connections with the court of Duke John III of Brabant. Records of payments made to him in King Edward III's wardrobe accounts show that he was also known at the English court.[50] Edward had established an alliance with Holland by his marriage in 1328 to Philippa of Hainault, whose father was the count of Holland, Zeeland, Hainault and Avesnes. Further expanding his power base in the Low Countries, he resided in Brabant, in Antwerp, in the years of these payments (1339 and 1340), where he sought support for his war against France. Boendale wrote a series of didactic and historical works, all of which were shaped by contacts between the duchy of Brabant and the kingdom of England.

The Bodleian Library holds a manuscript that is of particular importance for the transmission of Boendale's works, MS. Marshall 29 (*c*.1375). The manuscript is named after Thomas Marshall (1621–1685), scholar of older Germanic languages and before that chaplain to the Merchant Adventurers in Holland, who bequeathed his fine collection of books and manuscripts (including Dutch ones) to the Bodleian Library. MS. Marshall 29, alongside works by other authors, contains three of the major works ascribed to Boendale. One of these is his *Boec vander wraken* (*Book of Vengeance*), which tells of the working of God's justice through historical examples. In it we find a vivid account of the spread of the Black Death in the late 1340s, with this fascinating anecdote about how the disease made the North Sea crossing to England:

> Mi vertrac een goet man,
> Daer trouwe ende ere lach an,
> Dat een scep quam uut Inghelant,
> Dat over woude in Zelant,
> Want het was vanden Briele.
> Oec nam hijt op sijn ziele,

1.5 Portrait (centre) of Margaret, daughter of King Edward I, and wife of Duke John II of Brabant, as depicted in a late thirteenth-century Anglo-Norman chronicle roll of the kings of England. Oxford, Bodleian Library, MS. Broxbourne 112. 3, section 7.

Dat waer was al
Dat ic u hier segghen sal.
In dat scep waren danne
Meer dan .XX. vromer manne.
Doen si dus in die zee quamen,
Saghen si ende vernamen
Dat een groet pert te hen waert quam,
Ende een man daer op ocht hi was gram,
Die opt water quam te hen wert.
Si worden alle zeer vervard
Om dat pert opt water liep,
Dat soe wijt was ende soe diep.
Doe hi hen bi quam sprac hi:
'En vervaert u niet van mi,
U en sal gheen arch ghescien.'
Doen sprac een van dien
Die daer in scep waren:
'Wij sien u over twater varen,
Des soe heeft ons wonder groet.'
Die ghene sprac: 'ic ben die doot
Die nieman en can verdraghen
Dien God wilt hebben verslaghen,
Ende ic come uut Vranckeryke,
Ende van anderen lande des ghelike,
Daer ic hebbe ghedaen sulc ghebot
Als mi gheboot Onse Here God.
God en heeft vergheten niet
Die grote scande ende tverdriet
Ende die sunderlinghe scade,
Die de Sarrasine daden.
Des es nu .LX. jare
Datsi met bloetstortinghen zware
Akers wonnen, die goede stat,
Daer Kerstenheit doen in sat,
Daer si in versloeghen dan
Meneghen goeden kersten man.
Die crucifixe ten selven stonden
Die si in die kerken vonden

Sleypten si onwaerdelike
Achter straten inden slike,
Ihesum Cristum te blamen.
Des hem Kerstenheit mach scamen.
Ende om dat God ghene vriende en vint,
Die hem der wraken onderwint,
Ende dien es Gods scande,
Soe wrect inden lande
Ende sonderlinghe in Vrankerijke,
Welx coninc mechtich es ende rike
Ende wel ghereet daer toe,
Ende der Kerken goet daer toe alsoe
Heeft over al in sinen lande,
Daer hi mede wreken soude Gods ande.
Daer om datten Onse Here
Gheplaecht heeft herde zere,
Ende noch meer sal in corter tijt,
En si dat hi hem wel castijt.
Nu soe vaer ic tInghelant wert
Om te doene dat God beghert.'
Mettien verloren sijn doe
Ende dat visioen, si en wisten hoe.[51]

*A virtuous, reliable and honourable man told me that a ship came
from England, intending to cross over to Zeeland, for it was
originally from Brielle. He swore on his soul that what I will tell
you here was all true. There were more than twenty brave men
on that ship. When they came to sea, they saw a large horse coming
towards them over the water, ridden by a man who appeared angry.
They were all astonished because the horse trod over the water,
which was so vast and so deep. When the man approached them, he
said: 'Do not be afraid of me, you will not be harmed.' One of the
people on the ship said: 'We see you riding over the water, which is a
marvel to us.' The rider said: 'I am Death, who cannot be avoided
by anyone whom God wants killed. I come from France and from
other countries, where I have carried out the order that God, Our
Lord, gave me. God did not forget the great shame, the grief and
the extraordinary loss caused by the Saracens. It is now sixty years*

*since they won the good city of Acres, where Christianity was
then based, with much bloodshed, killing many good Christians.
They contemptuously dragged the crucifixes which they found in
the churches through the mud along the roads, to the disgrace of
Jesus Christ. Christians should be ashamed of this. To his outrage,
God has not found an ally willing to take revenge. That is why
He punishes in all countries, and especially in France. Its king
is powerful and rich; he excels and, moreover, holds ecclesiastical
property throughout his country, which he should use to take revenge
for the harm that God has suffered. That is why Our Lord has
severely punished him and will shortly punish him even more, unless
he does noticeably better. Now I travel to England to do God's
desire.' At the same moment they lost sight of him and the vision
ended, they did not know how.*

Boendale identified Edward III as the penultimate king before the
coming of the Antichrist,[52] and the rider that brings the plague across
the sea evokes one of the four horsemen of the Apocalypse. Eerily,
apocalyptic motifs are here imagined in a familiar geography that readers
would have known from everyday life. Brielle was the main port for the
flourishing herring trade between England and the Low Countries.[53]
The anecdote serves as a reminder that the North Sea was a connection,
not a barrier, between England and the Dutch Low Countries, and that
its currents were continually being crossed by people, goods and, yes,
also diseases.

THE COURTRAI CHEST AND THE BATTLE OF THE GOLDEN SPURS

The most important goods crossing the North Sea were wool and cloth.
Wool was shipped from England to the Low Countries and turned into
cloth, which then went back the other way. The wool trade was vital
to the economies of both regions, and interventions that jeopardized it
invariably made history. The international significance accorded to the
Battle of Courtrai in 1302, also known as the Battle of the Golden Spurs,
should be seen in this context. What we know about it today owes much
to an accidental discovery made in Oxfordshire. In 1905 the warden of
New College, William Spooner (after whom spoonerisms are named),
was inspecting one of the college's tenements at Stanton St John, just

outside Oxford to the north-east. He came across an old wooden chest with an exquisitely carved front panel (fig. 1.6). The chest was taken to the college and soon identified as depicting the Battle of the Golden Spurs. The conflict was prompted by a political alliance between the count of Flanders, Guy de Dampierre, and King Edward I of England, which was forged to protect their mutual interests in the wool trade. This provoked King Philip of France into invading Flanders, but the cloth-making towns rose up in revolt against French rule and vanquished the French army on

1.6 Early fourteenth-century depiction of the Battle of the Golden Spurs (1302), which contains many accurate details of heraldry and weapons, such as the *goedendag* ('good day'), a cross between a club and a spear, used during the battle by Flemish townspeople. The Courtrai Chest, New College, Oxford. Courtesy of the Warden and Scholars of New College, Oxford / Bridgeman Images.

their home turf. The humiliation of the French army by burghers shook the world and its social foundations.[54] Some contemporaries describe an army of fully armed knights defeated by a rabble of townspeople armed with whatever tools they could find at home. Recent research, informed by the Oxford Courtrai Chest, has qualified this, pointing out that, while their victory was unexpected, the Flemings opposing the French army were well organized and well equipped.[55]

The battle resonated in England, too. English authors responded with gratification to the ignominious defeat of the French royal army. A Middle English poem about Courtrai, known as 'The Flemish Insurrection', was written shortly after the battle. It is preserved in a multilingual (Latin, Anglo-Norman French and English) collection of secular and religious lyrics from the 1330s, the famous Harley manuscript.[56] The poet delights in the humiliation of elite French *chevaliers* by a haphazardly assembled rabble of Flemish artisans. Interestingly, the poet clearly knew some Dutch and expected the same from his audience, as can be seen from the pun on the name of the Flemish rebels' leader, Peter Conyng (Pieter de Coninck). The pun involves playing off the Dutch meaning of the name *conyng* (king) against the French (and Middle English) meaning of *conyn(g)*, namely 'rabbit'. The French noblemen pointedly describe Peter 'Conyng' as an animal that must be hunted down and spit-roasted:

> 'Sir Rauf de nel,' sayþ þe earl of boloyne,
> 'nus ne lerrum en vie chanoun ne moyne,
> Wende we forþ anon riþt wiþoute eny assoygne,
>   Ne no lyves man.
> We shule flo þe Conyng, & make roste his loyne ...'[57]

> *'Sir Raoul of Nesle,' said the earl of Boulogne,*
> *'we are not going to leave alive canon or monk.*
> *Let us go forth at once without any delay*
> *   and let no living man stop us.*
> *We shall flay the Rabbit and roast his loin ...'*

But to the Flemish rebels 'Conyng' is, quite literally, the king, in pointed contrast to the French king who seeks to lord it over them without their consent:

Þe webbes ant þe fullaris assembleden hem alle, …
Token Peter Conyng huere kyng to calle,
        Ant beo huere cheveteyn.[58]

The weavers and the fullers met together
and agreed to call Peter Conyng their king,
        and to take him as their leader.

The linguistic logic is impeccable. Who better to call 'king' than the man who is already called 'king' by name? The political side you take as to whether Peter Conyng should be regarded as vermin or king depends here on the language you speak. From this perspective, it is interesting to note that the poet sided with the Flemish, and knew, as presumably did his audience, what *conyng* meant in Dutch. The historical context that accounts for the poet's pro-Flemish outlook is that the 'webbes ant þe fullaris' were buying English wool.

   Another British author who took a gleeful interest in the Battle of the Golden Spurs was Adam Usk, a lawyer and former teacher at the University of Oxford, who visited Flanders in 1406 on his return from Rome, where he had spent time in exile after stealing a horse.[59] While in Bruges, he remained at the abbey of Eekhout. In its library he found a curious account of the battle, written soon after it by a supporter of Pieter de Coninck. The account, which Usk included verbatim in the chronicle he had been writing, tells the story of the battle as a collage of quotations (a cento) from the Gospels. It is titled *Passio Francorum, secundum Flemingos* (*The Passion of the French, according to the Flemings*). When the commander of the French army, Robert of Artois, is thrown off his horse,

        clamavit comes voce magna dicens: 'Bayard, Bayard, ou es tu?
        Pur quey as moy refuse?' Hoc est: 'Equus meus, equus meus, ut
        quid me dereliquisti?' Et, hoc dicto, expiravit.[60]

        the earl cried out in a loud voice, saying: [in French] 'Bayard,
        Bayard [a common name for a brown horse], where are you? Why
        have you forsaken me?' That is: [in Latin] 'My horse, my horse, why
        have you forsaken me?' And, having said this, he died.

Robert's words echo Christ's on the cross: 'My God, my God, why have you forsaken me?' In the Gospels of Mark and Matthew, Christ's words are presented bilingually too, in Aramaic and Greek. The *Passio Francorum* was found so 'offensively profane' by the early twentieth-century editor of Usk's Latin chronicle that he chose to leave the account untranslated.[61]

Dendrochronology (tree-ring dating) and radiocarbon dating show that the planks of the Courtrai Chest came from trees felled between about 1240 and 1280. The original chest, therefore, like the *Passio Francorum, secundum Flemingos* and the 'Flemish Insurrection', is likely to have been made very soon after the battle.[62] The specificity of the details depicted also suggest this: the maker, probably a carver from Bruges, may well have participated in the battle – which would explain how he was able to reproduce in great detail the weapons used and the people and groups involved.[63] Sometime around the seventeenth century, the planks were taken from their original chest and reused for a new one. How the chest came to be in a home in a rural Oxfordshire parish is not known. Its North Sea crossing remains a mystery.

THE COUNTY OF HOLLAND AND THE DIOCESE OF UTRECHT: JAN BEKE

In 1346 Jan Beke, a Benedictine monk from Egmond, located behind the old sand dunes along the North Sea coast in North Holland, dedicated a new Latin chronicle of the region to Jan van Arkel, bishop of Utrecht, and William V of Bavaria, the newly ascended count of Holland. The work combines the history of the county of Holland with that of the archdiocese of Utrecht, which held ecclesiastical jurisdiction over Holland:

> Principes ergo Francorum, qui Karolingi dicti sunt,
> gubernantes longo tempore regnum et imperium, diviserunt
> totam Hollandiam, ut infra dicetur, in bypartitum dominium,
> videlicet in episcopatum et comitatum. Nam et Karolus
> Martellus dux et maior domus Francorum contulit ad ecclesiam
> Traiectensem primam donacionem, et Karolus Calvus rex et
> postmodum imperator Romanorum tradidit ad comitatum
> Hollandiensem primitivam dicionem. Ut ergo tam episcopatus
> Traiectensis quam eciam comitatus Hollandiensis primordiale
> cognoscamus inicium, profecto convenit quod ex gestis
> Anglorum principale proponamus exordium.[64]

The princes of France, who are called the Carolingians, for a long
time ruled the Roman Empire and France; they divided Holland,
as will be explained in more detail hereafter, into two principalities,
namely into a diocese and a county. For Charles, who is called
'Martel', who was a duke and principal lord of France, gave the first
donation to the church of Utrecht, and King Charles, who is called
'the Bald', and later became Roman Emperor, first created the county
of Holland. And in order to understand the very first origin of both
the diocese of Utrecht and the county of Holland, we ought to start
from the history of England.

By 'the history of England', Beke specifically meant Bede's *Ecclesiastical
History of the English People*, written in 731. After telling of the advent of
the Saxons, Angles and Jutes in Britain, their conversion to Christianity
and the establishment of the English church, Bede had given an account
of the missions of English churchmen to the Germanic-speaking peoples
of the Continent, including the Frisians. This included the travels of
St Willibrord, the founder and first bishop of Utrecht, and those of St
Boniface, who was famously killed during a mission to the Frisians.

Beke's account, however, replaces Bede's insular perspective with
a Continental one. Rather than telling the history of a people (the
English) and a religion (Roman Christianity) successively arriving on
British shores, Beke presents a story of a Continental people relocating to
England, converting to Christianity and introducing that religion to the
Continent on their return:

> Sicut Anglicana promit historia, Saxones inferiores, qui
> vulgo dicuntur Frisones, cum innumera classe Brittannicam
> expugnaverunt insulam, quos papa Gregorius doctor egregius
> per Augustinum et Mellitum, ut narrat Dialogus, revocavit ad
> baptismi graciam. Ex quibus quidem inferioris Frisie Saxonibus
> divino comitante presagio progenitus est quidam ingenuus puer,
> nomine Willibrordus.[65]

> *As the English history tells, the Lower Saxons, who are now*
> *commonly called Frisians, came with countless ships and conquered*
> *the British Isle. They were then converted by Pope Gregorius, an*
> *outstanding teacher, to the grace of baptism, through two instructors:*

one was called Augustine, and the other Mellitus, as is described in Dialogus. From these Lower Saxons (or rather Frisians) a child was born called Willibrord, accompanied by a divine portent.

This Willibrord, educated in the English church at Ripon in present-day North Yorkshire, was subsequently sent with companions to convert the peoples of the northern Low Countries, whose language they were able to speak because of the affinity between the English of Britain and the Saxons of the Continent. The early history of the Low Countries and England was narrated as one of currents and cross-currents, navigated by a people stretching along two shores of the North Sea.

HOLLAND: 'THE SHORT CHRONICLE OF GOUDA'

Around the turn of the fifteenth century, the counts of Holland increasingly asserted their political independence from the archbishops of Utrecht.[66] This had an effect on historical writing: Beke's chronicle remained the most important source on the history of Holland for subsequent chroniclers, but there were several attempts to disentangle the history of the county of Holland from that of the diocese of Utrecht, resulting in chronicles that are exclusively concerned with the county. In the process, the material concerning the foundation of the diocese of Utrecht – and thus the material from Bede's *Ecclesiastical History* – was omitted, thereby severing the ties between Holland's and England's histories. An apparent desire to maintain the links between the early history of the Dutch Low Countries and that of Britain, however, soon led to the development of a new origin story for the people of Holland. It took its cue from Geoffrey of Monmouth's *History of the Kings of Britain*, which told how Brutus and his companion Corineus (name-giver of Cornwall) found the island of Albion populated by a race of giants, whom they fought and expelled.[67]

The Dutch chronicle known as the 'Short Chronicle of Gouda', from its place of first publication in 1478, takes this story as a starting point:

> Soe toech Brutus mit sijn geselle Corineus ende mit sijn volc
> mit veel scepen, ende quamen an een groet eylant dat Albyoen
> hiet dat al bewoent was mit grote ruesen ende ruesinnen
> daer Brutus tegen street, ende hiet datmen die ruesen in die
> beenen soude houwen. Soe dat Brutus mit sijn volc verloech

ende verdreef alle die ander. Ende doe dede hi dat lant nae hem
selven hieten Brutangen. Ende Corineus die hadde dit lant van
Coruwaengen. Ende van desen groten volc dat Brutus verdreef
die quamen mit scepen over die zee ende landen inder wilder
Sassen lant, dat nu Vrieslant is ghehieten, ende setten hem te
striden teghen dat wrede volc. Mer die Sassen hebben der veel
versleghen ende verdreven. Des toghen si weder over stier, ende
sijn ghecomen daer nu Vlaerdinc staet, ende worpen hem daer
neder om daer te woenen om datten naest ten water was, ende
maecten daer een groet casteel dat Slavenburch hiet. Ende an dat
Slavenburch daer stont dat grote bosch dat daer nae over menich
jaer hiet dat Wilde Wout Sonder Ghenaden. Ende dit was dat
eerste begrijp van Hollant.[68]

*Brutus departed along with his companion Corineus, his people and
many ships. He came to a great island called Albion, which was already
inhabited by great giants and giantesses, against whom he fought.
Brutus ordered [his people] to slash the legs of the giants, and so he and
his people defeated and expelled all the others [on the island]. After this
he named the land Britain after himself, while Corineus had the land
of Cornwall. Some of these great people who were expelled by Brutus
crossed the sea in ships and landed in the territory of the wild Saxons,
which is now called Friesland. There they fought against that cruel
people, but the Saxons defeated many and expelled them. Hence they
returned to sea and, arriving at the place where Vlaardingen is now,
they came ashore to live there, because it was next to the water. They
made a great castle there called Slavs' Fortress; and next to that Slavs'
Fortress there was the great forest called the Merciless Forest. This was
the first origin of Holland.*

The story may seem fantastical to us, but it gained popularity at the time
and can be found in many chronicles of Holland in the fifteenth and
sixteenth centuries.[69] The opportunity to link the early history of the region
to that of Britain apparently long outweighed any scepticism historical
writers may have felt about the narrative.

While Holland's historical writers had been forced to look for different
sources for their earliest history, there continued to be much interest
in Bede's *Ecclesiastical History of the English People* in the Dutch Low

Countries, particularly in the fifteenth century.[70] In one manuscript in the Bibliothèque nationale de France, Bede's history is bound together with a chronicle of Flanders.[71] One Bodleian Library manuscript of Bede's text, Holkham misc. 7, was written in Flanders in the late fifteenth or early sixteenth century.[72] English readers similarly showed an interest in Jan Beke's history of Holland and Utrecht. One of the Bodleian Library's copies of the 1612 printed edition of Beke's work was owned by the prominent seventeenth-century English legal historian John Selden, and a manuscript of excerpts from the chronicle relating only to the diocese of Utrecht was owned by the antiquarian, historian and manuscript collector Sir Robert Cotton, in whose library Selden had been an amanuensis.[73] Beke's interest in English history had led to that interest being reciprocated by English readers.

ENGLAND: THE MIDDLE ENGLISH *BRUT* AND THE LONDON CHRONICLES

The relations between speakers of Dutch and English inevitably had an impact on recorded history, and chroniclers writing in the English vernacular also bear witness to the lives of the people they chronicled. The early fifteenth-century Middle English prose *Brut*, the most widespread English chronicle of the period, is not generally interested in affairs outside England that do not involve English participants, but brief mention is made of St Lidwina of Schiedam: 'an holy maid in Holand, called Lydwith, which lyved onely bi miracle, not etynge any mete'[74] ('a holy maid in Holland, named Lydwith [i.e. Lidwina], who lived only by miracle, not eating any food'). Dutch speakers are occasionally mentioned as inhabiting various parts of Britain, but their presence, like that of other peoples, is seen as a destabilizing factor, as in this passage about the barons' revolt against Edward II in 1321–22:

> And the land tho was withouten Law, for holy cherche tho hade nomore reverence than hit hade bene a bordel hous. And in that bataile was the fader ayeins the sone, and the uncle ayeins his nevew; for so miche unkyndenesse was never seyne bifore in Engeland amonges folc of on nacioun; for o kynrede had no more pite of that other, than an hundred wolfes haveth on o shepe; and hit was no wonder, for the grete lordes of Engeland were nought alle of o nacioun, but were mellede

with othere nacions, that is forto seyn, somme Britons, somme
Saxones, somme Danois, somme Peghtes, somme Frenchemen,
somme Normans, somme Spaignardes, somme Romayns, some
Henaudes, some Flemyngus, and of othere diverse naciouns,
the whiche nacions acorded nought to the kynde bloode of
Engeland.[75]

*And the land then was lawless, for the Holy Church was then treated
with no more reverence than if it had been a brothel. And during those
troubles father stood against son, and uncle against nephew. Such
enmity had never been seen in England among folk of one nation, as
one lineage showed less mercy to another than a hundred wolves show
one sheep. And this was no wonder, because the great lords of England
were not all from one nation, but were mixed with other nations, that
is to say, some Britons, some Saxons, some Danes, some Picts, some
Frenchmen, some Normans, some Spaniards, some Italians, some from
Hainault, some Flemings, and various other nations, which nations
were incompatible with the natural blood of England.*

At times of trouble, Dutch-speaking communities in England regularly
encountered violence. During the Peasants' Revolt of 1381, Flemish people
were singled out for attacks. In a single day thirty-five Dutch speakers
were dragged out of St Martin Vintry parish church and beheaded.[76] In one
London chronicle these events are referred to with a telling detail: 'many
Fflemynges loste here heedes at that tyme, and namely they that koude nat
say breede and chese but case and brode' ('many Flemings lost their heads
at that time, and namely those who could not say "bread" and "cheese" but
[instead said] "case" and "brode"').[77] That Dutch speakers had been part of
the population of London for as long as anyone could remember did not
prevent them from being marked as alien.

FROM BURGUNDY TO ENGLAND: WILLIAM CAXTON

While Dutch speakers were part of the cosmopolitan society of London,
English speakers likewise lived in Dutch towns and cities. One such
Englishman in the Netherlands was William Caxton, the first English
printer, who began his publishing career on the Continent. He published
his earliest books in English in the Low Countries, where he lived for some
thirty years. His choice for the first printed book in English, the *Recuyell*

Hus endeth the seconde book of the recule of the hiſ
torpes of Troyes/Whiche bookes were late tranſ
lated in to frenſhe out of latyn/by the labour of the vene
rable perſone raoul le feure preeſt as a fore is ſaid/And
by me Indigne and vnworthy tranſlated in to this rude
engliſſh/by the comandement of my ſaid redoubtid lady
duches of Bourgone: And for as moche as I ſuppoſe
the ſaid two bokes ben not had to fore this tyme in oure
engliſſh langage/therfore I had the better will to accom
pliſſhe this ſaid werke/whiche werke was begonne in
Brugis/ꝛ contynued in gaunt And fynyſſhid in Colepn
In the tyme of þͤ troublous world/ and of the grete deuy
ſions beyng and reygnyng as well in the royames of
englond and fraunce as in all other places vniuerſally
thurgh the world that is to wete the yere of our lord a
thouſand four honderd lxxi . And asfor the thirde book
whiche trteth of the generall ꝛ laſt deſtruccōn of Troye
Hit nedeth not to tranſlate hit in to engliſſh/ffor as mo
che as that worſhipfull ꝛ religyoꝰ man dan John lidgate
monke of Burye dide tranſlate hit but late/ after whoſ
werke I fere to take vpon me that am not worthy to bere
his penner ꝛ ynke horne after hym . to medle me in that
werke . But yet for as moche as I am bounde to con
templare my ſayd ladyes good grace and alſo that his
werke is in ryme/And as ferre as I knowe hit is not
had in proſe in our tonge/And alſo parauenture/he
tranſlated after ſome other Auctor than this is/And
yet for as moche as dyuerce men ben of dyuerce deſyres.
Some to rede in Ryme and metre . and ſome in proſe
And alſo be cauſe that I haue now good leyzer beyng in
Colepn And haue none other thynge to do at this tyme

of the Historyes of Troye, probably printed in Ghent (1473/4), may well have been motivated by the connection between Troy and the history of Britain and the Low Countries. The story of Troy was a foundation legend for the House of Burgundy (which by this time had accumulated the various principalities of the Low Countries), but it also formed part of the history of Britain: Brutus, the mythical founder and name-giver of Britain, was a descendant of Aeneas of Troy. Caxton dedicated the work to Margaret of York (fig. 1.7), sister of King Edward IV of England. In the dedication, however, Caxton addresses her not only as the king's sister, but also as 'Duchesse of Bourgoine, of Lotryk, of Brabant, of Lymburgh, and of Luxenburgh, Countes of Fflandres, of Artoys & of Bourgoine, Palatynee of Heynawd, of Holand, of Zeland, and of Namur, Marquesse of the Holy Empire, lady of Ffryse, of Salins, and of Mechlyn',[78] listing the extensive possessions she controlled as duchess.

In 1480, four years after returning to London and setting up his press in Westminster, Caxton published *The Cronycles of Englond*, a version of the popular Middle English *Brut* chronicle, as well as a historical description of Britain excerpted from John Trevisa's by then almost century-old translation of Ranulph Higden's *Polychronicon*.[79] Historical works in English evidently found a willing market. In 1482 Caxton, eager to meet this demand, published a complete version of the *Polychronicon*, updated with a continuation by Caxton himself.[80] In this work, following the practice first established by Alfred of Beverley, Flemings are listed as one of the 'nations' populating Britain, together with the Scots, the Britons (i.e. Celts), the Anglo-Normans and the English. There is an account of the Flemings' first arrival in England, following a flood in their country of origin during the reign of Henry I, which eroded much of the Flemish coastline and forced people to migrate in search of safety.[81] Gerald of Wales's story of the scapulimancy of the Flemings in Pembrokeshire is also briefly repeated.[82]

In the same year, Caxton printed a second edition of the *The Cronycles of Englond*. It became a bestseller. There were further editions in 1483 and 1485, and when Caxton died the Dutch printer Gerard Leeu took it up from Caxton's catalogue: an edition appeared in Antwerp in 1493 (fig. 1.8). Caxton's move from the Low Countries to Westminster did not put an end to the printing of English-language books in the Low Countries. For a long time to come, publishing in English, including histories of England, formed the business of printers on both sides of the North Sea.

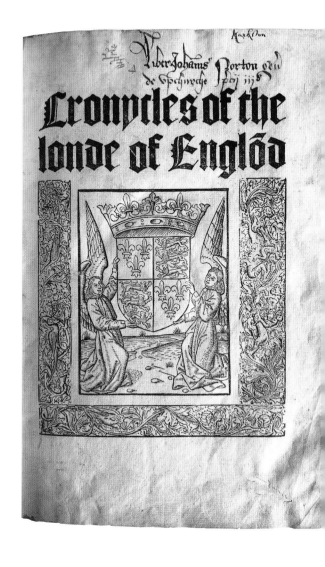

1.7 *opposite* William Caxton's *Recuyell of the Historyes of Troye*, printed in Ghent (1473/4), dedicated to Margaret of York, duchess of Burgundy. On the page shown here, Caxton states that he started the translation (from French) in Bruges, continued in Ghent, and finished in Cologne. Oxford, Bodleian Library, S.Seld. d.1, fol. 251v.

1.8 *above* Edition of the popular Middle English *Brut* chronicle, first printed in 1480 by William Caxton as *The Cronycles of Englond*. Soon after Caxton's death this version was produced in Antwerp (1493) by Gerard Leeu, who was killed shortly before its publication. Oxford, University College, [Br.] d. 1, title page. Courtesy of The Master and Fellows of University College Oxford.

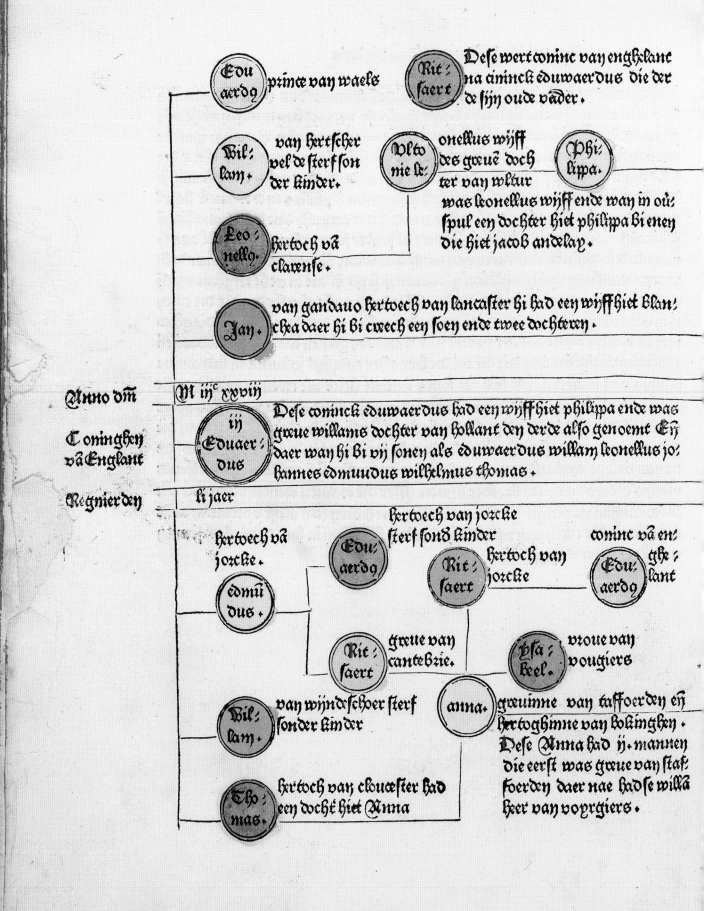

Edu aerdg — prince van waels

Rit saert — Dese wert coninc van enghelant na coninck eduwaerdus die der de sijn oude vader.

Wil lam — van hertscher vel de sterf son der kinder.

Ulto mie le — onellus wijff des greue doch ter van wltur

Phi lippa.

was leonellus wijff ende wan in ou spul een dochter hiet philippa bi enen die hiet jacob andelay.

Leo nellg — hertoch va clarense.

Jan — van gandauo hertoech van lancaster hi had een wijff hiet blancka daer hi bi cwech een soen ende twee dochteren.

Anno dm

Coninghen va Englant

Regnierden

M iiij c xxviij

iij Eduaer dus — Dese coninck eduwaerdus had een wijff hiet philippa ende was greue willams dochter van hollant den derde also genoemt En daer van hi bi vij sonen als eduwaerdus willam leonellus johannes edmundus wilhelmus thomas.

li jaer

hertoech va jorcke. edmü dus.

Edu aerdg — hertoech van jorcke sterf sond kinder

Rit saert — hertoch van jorcke

Edu aerdg — coninc va en ghe lant

Rit saert — greue van cantebrie.

Ysa beel — vroue van vougiers

Wil lam — van wijndischoer sterf sonder kinder

anna — gruuinne van taffoerden en hertoghinne van bokinghen. Dese Anna had ij mannen die eerst was greue van staffoerden daer nae hadse willa heer van voyrgiers.

Tho mas — hertoch van cloucester had een docht hiet Anna

ENGLISH HISTORY IN DUTCH: JOHAN VELDENER

The earliest complete chronicle of England in Dutch is found in a work published by Johan Veldener, who had been Caxton's business partner in the Low Countries.[83] Veldener had helped Caxton in his earliest printing experiment in Cologne by designing the type for Caxton's first printed edition of the medieval encyclopedia *De proprietatibus rerum* (*On the Properties of Things*) by Bartholomaeus Anglicus ('Bartholomew the Englishman') in 1472.[84] In 1474 there was a major breakthrough in printing in Cologne, with the publication of Werner Rolevinck's *Fasciculus temporum* (*Bundle of Times*). Manuscript versions of this Latin universal chronicle carried complex diagrams, and reproducing these in print was a feat of engineering in which Veldener may have been involved, not as publisher but as typographer. Aware of the shortcomings of the first *Fasciculus temporum*, in which text and image were not in perfect alignment, Veldener himself printed an improved version in Louvain. In 1480 he continued his engagement with the work in Utrecht, publishing a Dutch translation with a continuation consisting of a series of chronicles of England, France and the principalities of the Low Countries (fig. 1.9).[85]

The chronicle of England included in this work was not a direct translation from any existing chronicle, but an original compilation based on a combination of French, Latin and perhaps English materials. It was adapted for inclusion in the Dutch-language edition of *Fasciculus temporum*, and so English history was once again amalgamated with Dutch history. The migration of the giants of Albion to become the first inhabitants of Holland is mentioned,[86] and links between English royalty and Dutch rulers are emphasized, as in the (incorrect) identification of Maria, wife of William I of Holland, as the daughter of Edmund Crouchback, and the (correct) identification of Maud of Lancaster ('Mechtelt') as the wife of Count William V of Holland.[87] While it stayed close to the *Brut* chronicle tradition overall, the influence of Jacob van Maerlant can still be felt, even two centuries after his death, for the Saxon invaders of Britain are introduced as 'dese heydensche Enghelsche Sassen off Vriesen'[88] ('these heathen English Saxons or Frisians'). As with Maerlant's work, local concerns intersect with English affairs: the interest in links to Dutch history is paired with a very explicit political stance in support of the House of Lancaster. The entanglement of English and Dutch history is most evident at the end of the chronicle, which links the histories of England, Holland and Brabant. The final sentence reads: 'Ende hoe

I.9 Page from the chronicle of England in the Middle Dutch *Fasciculus temporum* (Utrecht, 1480), with roundels for genealogical relations. At the centre is the entry for Edward III, married to Philippa of Hainault, daughter of Count William III of Holland. Oxford, Bodleian Library, Auct. 2 Q 3.32, fol. 227v.

I.IO Woodcut used twice in the *Divisiekroniek* (*Division Chronicle*) of 1517 to illustrate the 'Slavenburch' and the 'burch van Britten'. The two dragons and the man with a wand show that it was originally made to illustrate the story of Merlin. Oxford, Bodleian Library, Vet. B1 d.9, fol. 17r.

coninck Eduwaert gheweken is uut Enghelant ende quam in Hollant te Tessel &cetera soecket in die cronijcke van Brabant CC ende xl blat ende ij^c ende xli blat'[89] ('On how King Edward [IV] fled from England and came into Holland at Texel, etc., see the chronicle of Brabant, page 240 and page 241'). For Jan Beke, the history of Holland had started in England; in Johan Veldener's Middle Dutch *Brut*, that of England concluded in the Netherlands.

HOLLAND: THE *DIVISIEKRONIEK*

The work that transmitted the medieval chronicle tradition of Holland to historians of the Netherlands in the later sixteenth and seventeenth centuries is named the *Divisiekroniek* (*Division Chronicle*, after its organization into 'divisions'). This anonymous chronicle of the county of Holland and its wider region, interlaced with a chronicle of the popes and emperors, was published in 1517 by the printer Jan Seversz in Leiden. In some respects this history marks an advance in historiography: it is the first vernacular chronicle of Holland to cite the Germanic tribe the Batavians as early inhabitants of the region (an innovation of late fifteenth-century humanists, appropriating Tacitus), but in other respects it holds firm to the medieval tradition, and reproduces the legend found in the 'Chronicle of Gouda' that the giants of Albion were Holland's founding fathers.

Woodcut illustrations enliven the historical narrative. Some were made specifically for the *Divisiekroniek*; others were printed from woodblocks that had originally been cut to illustrate other works altogether. The woodcut illustrating the 'Slavenburch' (the 'Slavs' Fortress' founded by the giants of Albion) was then used a second time to portray the 'burch van Britten' (the 'Fortress of Britten'),[90] so called because it faced Britain across the North Sea. This is one of those recycled images that was originally meant to accompany a very different text. What it depicts is in fact an episode from British history (fig. 1.10).[91] The woodcut shows a castle under construction, with a lake and two fighting dragons. Next to the lake stands a figure with a pointed hat and a magic wand. This is an illustration of an episode from Geoffrey of Monmouth's *History of the Kings of Britain*, where Merlin explains to the British king Vortigern why the foundations of his castle keep collapsing: underneath the castle was a lake with two dragons at war with each other. The ensuing interpretation of the dragons' antics was the occasion for Merlin's famous prophecies.

Merlin is never mentioned in the *Divisiekroniek*, but Geoffrey of Monmouth's *History* had earlier given historians of Holland the inspiration for the story of the giants of Albion. The woodcut is thought to have been cut originally in a Gouda workshop in the 1480s, and provides fascinating evidence for the existence of a printed Arthurian text from Holland, perhaps a history or perhaps a romance, of which not a single copy survives. Despite the wealth of surviving evidence of the impact of Anglo-Dutch relations on Dutch and English literary culture, it is clear that even more evidence once existed but is now lost.

THE DUTCH REVOLT AND ANGLO-DUTCH HISTORICAL WRITING IN ENGLAND

By the mid-sixteenth century the Burgundian Netherlands, having been inherited by Charles of Habsburg, had come to be ruled from Spain. The harsh repression of Protestant movements led to opposition and then rebellion against the king of Spain, from which the Dutch Republic was eventually born. There was much interest in the Dutch Revolt (1568–1648) in England, not least because the English crown supported the Protestant cause of the northern Netherlands. Pamphlets describing events in the late 1570s and early 1580s were published in English, and in 1583 – two years after the declaration of independence by the Seven United Provinces of the Netherlands, consisting of the northern principalities of the Dutch Low Countries – an influential collection of documents appeared, embedded in a chronicle of the revolt and the events leading up to it. A copy of this work in the Bodleian Library contains annotations from a sixteenth-century reader. These annotations shed light on how an English reader of that time perceived the Low Countries. In a description of the role played by the Low Countries in international trade, this reader underlined the phrase 'the Paragon of all trade' and indexed it in the margin: 'the lowe countries, the paragon of the world' (fig. 1.11).[92]

I.11 'The lowe countries, the paragon of the world': an early annotation in the margin of an English account of the early years of the Dutch Revolt, *A Tragicall Historie of the Troubles and Ciuile Warres of the Lowe Countries* (1583), translated from French by Thomas Stocker. Bodleian Library, Tanner 282, fol. 4r.

Anglo-Dutch relations were at the heart of the earliest historiography of the Dutch Revolt. Dutch-speaking communities in various places in England, such as London and Norwich, had been replenished by new migrants fleeing the religious persecutions of the middle of the century, and their members remained in contact with friends and family in the Low Countries. Emanuel van Meteren, the Dutch trade consul in London, corresponded regularly with his cousin Abraham Ortelius, the map-maker, who lived in Antwerp. Ortelius supplied him with news of current events, while he helped Ortelius sell his maps in England. The Continental news collected by van Meteren formed the basis of a new project: a complete documentary history of the Dutch Revolt. The experienced Ortelius advised him on how to deal with publishers.[93] Without van Meteren's knowledge, however, his history was published in Latin and in German, pirated from a manuscript copy he had shared with people on the Continent to get advice on how to shape the history. Van Meteren promptly followed these unauthorized versions with his Dutch edition, published in 1599 (fig. 1.12).

Van Meteren's history was eagerly taken up by English historians of the Dutch Revolt. It informed the first comprehensive English chronicle of the Dutch Low Countries, which also covered their medieval history, Edward Grimeston's *A Generall Historie of the Netherlands* (1608). Grimeston amalgamated all the sources he could lay his hands on. The resulting history was published in a large folio edition, adorned with engraved portraits of successive rulers of Holland: the counts of Holland, and those who carried the title after them, including the dukes of Burgundy and the Habsburg emperors, and finally the stadtholders in the early years of the Dutch Republic. It is here that we find, prominently, an image of Queen Elizabeth I (fig. 1.13), who is recorded as 'Elizabeth, Queene of England, France and Ireland, Defendresse of the Catholicke Faith, and Protectrix of the libertie of the united Provinces of the Netherlands'.[94]

Grimeston's book argues that the strong ties between the Dutch Low Countries and England, which positioned Queen Elizabeth for this role, had their roots in the relations between the two in the Middle Ages. Trouble in the Netherlands could not be ignored in England, given

> how much it concerned the kingdome of England, having beene long united to the Netherlands by many auncient contracts,

1.12 Emanuel van Meteren's first authorized edition of his history of the Dutch Revolt, *Memorien der Belgische ofte Nederlantsche Historie* (*Recollections of the Belgian or Dutch History*, 1599). Queen Elizabeth I is depicted at the top of the page, overseeing Dutch history. Oxford, Balliol College Library, 0705 f 02, title page.

MEMORIEN

Der

BELGISCHE

Ofte

Nederlantsche Historie,

Uan onsen tijden.

Inhoudende hoe de Nederlanden aenden anderen
ghehecht/ ende aen Spaengien ghecomen zijn: Met de oor=
saken der Inlantsche beroerten/ ende oorloghen der selver/ Oock de
veranderinghe van Princen/ van Regimenten ende van Religie/
mette scheuringhen/ verbontenissen ende vredehandelin=
ghen: Mede verbattende eenighe harer ghebueren
ende andere Landen handelinghen.

Meeft onder de regeeringhe van Philippus
de II. Coninc van Spaengien, tot synen doot, ende den
vvtgaenden Iare 1598.

Uerciert met een Caerte van alle de Nederlanden/ ende
aller Regeerders afbeeldinghe in Coper ghesneden.

Beschreven door EMANVEL VAN METEREN.

Eensdeels int Latijn ende Hoochduytsch stuckwijs in druck wtghegaen, maer nu by den
Autheur selve oversien, verbetert ende vermeerdert, wtghegeuen.

TOT DELF,

Ghedruct by Jacob Cornelisz Uennecool.

Anno M. D. XCIX.

1585 Elizabeth, Queene of England, France and Ireland, Defen-
dreſſe of the Catholicke Faith, and Protectrix of the libertie
of the vnited Prouinces of the Netherlands.

ELIZABETHA ANGLIÆ REGINA

When God by grace had me aduanc't vnto my regall ſtate,
(Which till this time I ruled haue in peace moſt fortunate)
To ſerue him, and my ſubiects good to ſeeke, it was my care:
And thoſe that forced were to flie by meanes of bloody warre,
'Gainſt them by Spaniards made, I did moſt willingly relieue,
And with a feruent zeale to them all aid and comfort giue,
And by what meanes I could deuiſe, my mind I alwaies bent,
Their imminent decay and danger great for to preuent.
And to that end protectrix of their countrey I became,
Defending them with all my power (to my eternall fame)
Wherein no feare of Spaniſh force ere could my courage quaile,
Nor in my reſolution good, make me in ought to faile.

The

A

B

THE XIII. BOOKE.

The Argument.

HE Queene of England hauing taken vpon her the protection of the vnited prouinces, sent the earle of Leicester to be her Lieutenant. They receiue him with pompe, and acknowledge him for gouernour. The Spaniards prosper in Friseland. Colonel Schencke ouerrunnes the countrie of Westphalia. Graue besieged and yeelded to the Spaniard. Iarre betwixt the Estates & the earle of Leicester, who is discontented, and they discontented with him. Nuys besieged by the Spaniard, and taken by assault, whilest they are in parle. The earle of Leicester recouers certaine places. Iealousie betwixt the noble men of the countrie and the English, by reason of gouernments that were giuen vnto the English, and they reiected, whereof the Estates complained vnto him going into England. A great dearth of corne in the yeare 1587. Deuenter sold vnto the Spaniard, with the great fort of Zutphen. Factions increase betwixt the Estates and the English. Scluse besieged, and in the end yeelded to the Spaniard. The towne of Guelder sold. The Estates labour to reconcile the earles of Leicester and Hohenlo. Apologies on either side. Leicester failes to seize vpon the towne of Leyden. Hee is called backe into England, and resignes his gouernment into the Estates hands. Bonne surprised by Schencke. The king of Spaine makes a counterfeit shewe to desire peace with England. Deputies on either side at Bourbrouc, who doe nothing, whilest the Spanish fleete aduanced. Prince Maurice takes his place in the gouernment after the earle of Leicester retreat. The Spanish fleet thinke to inuade England, and is dispersed. Geertruydenbergh sold to the Spaniards by the souldiers that were mutined without cause. The death of Colonel Schencke at an enterprise vpon Nymeghen. The death of Mœurs: Rhinberck yeelded to the Spaniards. The Estates sent succours of men and money vnto the French king. Breda happily surprised. The prince of Parma releeues Paris. Prince Maurice recouers many townes and places for the Estates. Groning straitly prest.

D

Ccording to the accord made betwixt the high & mighty princesse, *Elizabeth* Queene of England, and the Estates of the vnited prouinces of the Netherlands, her Maiestie sent certaine troopes of horse and foot, into the countries of Holland and Zeeland, vnder the command of sir *Iohn Norris* knight, a gallant souldier (who had long done seruice to the said Estates, and to the prince of Orange) who came to the *rendez vous* which was giuen them in Vtrecht, where hauing past musters, they were

E

presently imployed, and led by the earle of Mœurs before the fort of Isselloort, neere vnto the towne of Arnham, vpon the Veluwe, where the riuer of Issel comes out of the Rhin, which fort had beene taken by *Verdugo* for the Spaniard long before: the earle of Mœurs hearing that Colonel *Taxis* was gone forth the day before, made haste to besiege it, and to batter it, so as the besieged seeing no hope of succours, and fearing to be taken by assault, they yeelded vp the fort by composition, to depart with their liues and goods. Although this siege was not without the losse of some few men, yet the earle of Mœurs and the English were so incouraged, as passing the riuer of Rhin, they went to besiege the fort of Berchschooft in the higher Betuwe, in the which captaine *Turc* commanded for the prince of Parma: who notwithstanding the weakenes of the place, which was shewed him by his owne men, would needs endure the cannon, but the souldiers mutined against him, and deliuered him, with the fort, into the earle of Mœurs hands for the Estates.

F

Colonel

Isselloort yeelded to the Estates.

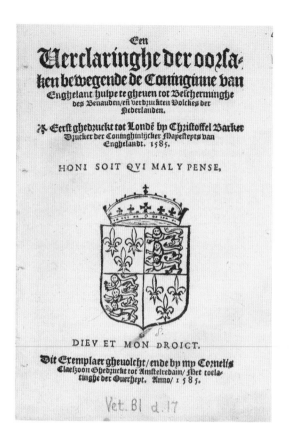

and bound to hold and maintain the same, in respect of the situations of both those countries, for that the Netherlands had many great rivers, and England an island lying right over against it, who being enemies, might doe great hurt one to the other, and being united together, might rule and have the soveraigntie of the great ocean sea, whereby they both get their livings, and without it could not maintaine themselves.[95]

England and the Netherlands, due to their proximity and their long-standing relations, would prosper in unity, but had the potential to destroy each other in discord. This argument had been attributed to Queen Elizabeth I herself, in a pamphlet of 1585 justifying her support for the rebellious provinces against Charles V, Holy Roman Emperor:

> First it is to be understoode (which percase is not perfectly knowen to a great nomber of persons) that there hath beene, time out of minde, even by the natural situation of those low Countreis and our Realme of Englande, one directly opposite to the other, and by reason of the ready crossing of the Seas, and multitude of large and commodious Havens respectively on both sides, a continuall traffique and commerce betwixt the people of Englande, and the Naturall people of these lowe Countries, ... wherby there hath beene in former ages many speciall alliances and confederations, not onely betwixt the Kinges of England our Progenitours and the Lordes of the said countries of Flanders, Holland, Zeland, and their adherentes: but also betwixt the very naturall subjectes of both Countries.[96]

The relations between England and the Netherlands are presented in familial terms. The bond is that of a felicitous marriage: 'this our realme of England and those countries have bene by common language of long time resembled and termed as man and wife'.[97] The pamphlet was published at the same time in English, French, Latin and Dutch by Christopher Barker, printer to the queen, for international distribution. Several Dutch and French editions were printed in the Netherlands (fig. 1.14), including an edition by the official printer for the States of Holland. The interests of the Dutch and English nations were harmoniously aligned.

1.13 *previous pages* Queen Elizabeth I, 'Protectrix of the libertie of the united Provinces of the Netherlands'. This is one engraving in a series of portraits of the rulers of Holland, starting from its earliest counts, in Edward Grimeston's *A Generall Historie of the Netherlands* (1608). Oxford, Bodleian Library, Vet. A2 c.16, pp. 904–5.

1.14 *above* Dutch translation of Elizabeth I's *Declaration* (1585), justifying her support for the United Provinces. This edition, authorized by the Dutch authorities, bears the English Royal Arms, and a reference to the printer of the English original, Christopher Barker, printer to the queen. Oxford, Bodleian Library, Vet. B1 d.17, title page.

1.15 *opposite* Richard Verstegan, *A Restitution of Decayed Intelligence in Antiquities* (1605), printed in Antwerp for sale in London. The Tower of Babel is presented as the 'origin of nations'; language affinity led Verstegan to argue that the Dutch and English peoples are related. Oxford, Bodleian Library, Mal. 749, title page.

RICHARD VERSTEGAN'S ANGLO-DUTCH HISTORICAL WRITING

The case for a genealogical relationship between the English and the Dutch was further developed by the truly Anglo-Dutch author Richard Verstegan. A descendant of a Dutch migrant to England, Verstegan fled to Antwerp as a Catholic refugee. There, in 1605, he published his English history for the English market, *A Restitution of Decayed Intelligence in Antiquities* (fig. 1.15). In this work Verstegan argued that the English were of Continental Germanic origin, thereby distancing himself from the British focus of much of English historical writing. Verstegan emphasized that the descendants of the Trojan Brutus were the Britons (identified as the ancestors of the Welsh and Cornish), and not the English. The latter, he posited, descended from the 'English-Saxon' people who first arrived in Britain under the leadership of the two brothers Hengist and Horsa.[98] He followed up the English *Restitution* with the Dutch *Nederlantsche antiquiteyten* (*Dutch Antiquities*) in 1613. The immediate occasion for this history of the Netherlands was the rebuilding of the Church of St Willibrord in Antwerp. As Verstegan explains in his introduction, echoing and amplifying Jan Beke, he made use of English history as a basis for his Dutch history because the two were intrinsically linked: the English people originally descended from the Dutch and, in turn, the Dutch people owed their Christianity to the English, since it was the English St Willibrord and his companions who had converted them. Verstegan was thus convinced that the ancestors of the English and the early inhabitants of the Low Countries owed their identities to their interrelations, just as he was himself half-Dutch and half-English.

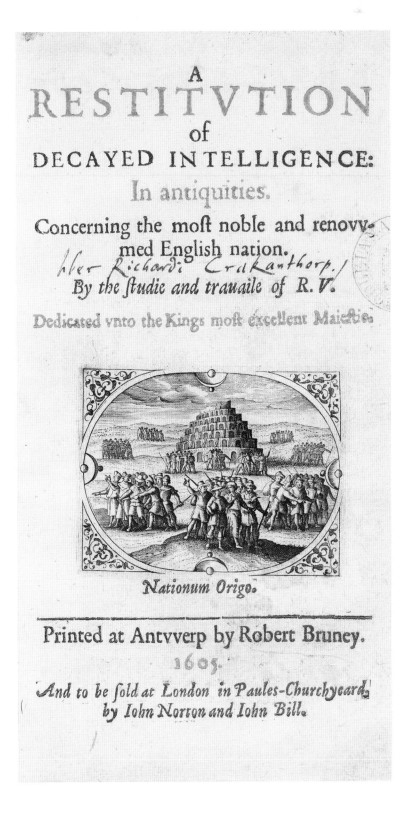

A
RESTITVTION
of
DECAYED INTELLIGENCE:
In antiquities.
Concerning the moſt noble and renovv-
med English nation.
By the ſtudie and trauaile of R. V.
Dedicated vnto the Kings moſt excellent Maieſtie.

Nationum Origo.

Printed at Antvverp by Robert Bruney.
1605.
And to be ſold at London in Paules-Churchyeard,
by Iohn Norton and Iohn Bill.

THE WARS OF THE SEVENTEENTH CENTURY

During the seventeenth century, English and Dutch history became ever more entwined. The English Civil Wars of the mid-seventeenth century led to an explosion of interest in British affairs in the Dutch Republic. Charles I was executed in 1649. The Dutch of course took notice, all the more so since the king's son, named after his father, had taken refuge in The Hague. The Dutch Republic, however, allied itself with the short-lived republic of Oliver Cromwell, and part of Charles II's later period of exile was spent in the southern Netherlands, which was under Spanish Habsburg rule, only to be concluded back in the Dutch Republic, from where he returned to England in 1660. Both the northern and the southern Netherlands evidently provided crucial audiences for English political propaganda, and in two decades, starting in 1639, nine new histories of Britain were produced by Dutch historians, in Dutch as well as English.[99] In addition, the *Chronicle of the Kings of England from the Time of the Romans' Government unto the raigne of our soueraigne Lord King Charles* by Richard Baker, first published in English in 1643, appeared in a Dutch translation in 1649.[100] The historiographical interest occasioned by the political upheavals of the mid-seventeenth century was significant and spilled over into literary genres,[101] most prominently in Joost van den Vondel's *Maria Stuart of Gemartelde majesteit* (*Mary Stuart, or, Tortured Majesty*) of 1646, a play about Elizabeth I and Mary, Queen of Scots. Vondel intended his play as a historical parable in defence of the beleaguered Charles I, and was fined by the Amsterdam authorities for expressing Royalist sympathies,[102] but his feelings were widely shared by his compatriots. Refusing to take orders from a Spanish tyrant, as the Dutch had done, was one thing; rising up against and killing one's own king was another. As far as the Dutch were concerned, regicide and peasants' revolts were crimes against the established order of things.[103]

In 1623 an incident occurred far from the North Sea that nevertheless affected Anglo-Dutch relations and attracted much attention in England. On Ambon Island, one of the Maluku Islands in the Banda Sea (in present-day Indonesia), twenty men, including ten from the English East India Company, were tortured and executed for treason by agents of the Dutch East India Company. These events soon sparked off a series of English pamphlets accusing the Dutch of cruelty. The pamphlets were printed in English for the home audience, and also in Dutch to counter Dutch pamphlets arguing for the necessity of the executions.

yet they saw, they could not make their reckoning
to any purpose, vnlesse they vtterly draue the English out of the trade of those parts; thereby to haue
the whole and sole traffick of the commodities of
the Indies in these parts of Europe, in their owne
hands; and so to make the price at their pleasure,
sufficient to maintain & promote their conquests,
and withall to yeeld them an ample benefit of their
trading. Which vnlesse they can, by this and the
like worrying and wearying of the English, bring
to passe, it is easie to be iudged by those that vnderstand any thing of the course and state of the trade
of those parts, that albeit their returnes heerafter
should proue as great continually, as of late extra-
ordinarily they haue happened to be, yet the maine
stock and estate of the Company must needs abate
and decay by some hundred thousands of pounds
yeerly. Thus, Reader, thou seest what hath made
vs vnprouided against such accidents, and what
now enforceth the Dutch East-India Company, or
their seruants in the Indies, against the common
Genius of their Nation, and the wonted firm af-
fection between these two Nations mutually, thus
to degenerate, and break out into such strange and
incredible outrages against their neerest allies and
best-deseruing friends. Farewell.

Hac ita corrige. Page 20.l.1. for three, r. fiue   p. 25 l. 15. dele all, p. 35. l. 3
r. sleeping in the watch. In the Answ. p. 12. l. 11. for him, r. them.   p. 21. l. 30
r. Price and M Towerson;

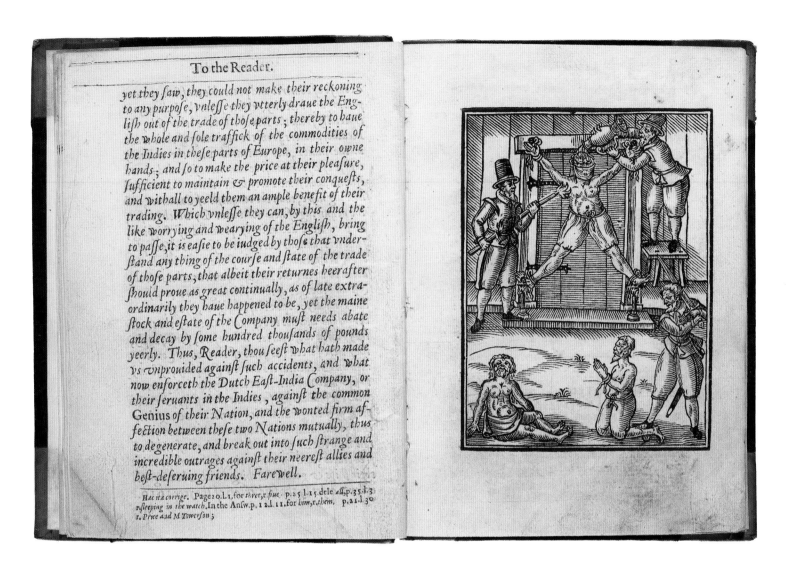

The disagreement over the Amboyna Massacre would long remain
unresolved: each of the three Anglo-Dutch Wars of the seventeenth century
(1652–54, 1665–67 and 1672–78), resulting from rivalry in naval trade,
occasioned new English pamphlets reminding readers of barbarous Dutch
cruelty (fig. 1.16).[104]

A reorientation of English views on Dutch history under the influence
of the Anglo-Dutch Wars of the 1650s to 1670s can also be detected in the
publication of Hugo Grotius's *Annales et historiae de rebus Belgicis* (*Annals
and History of the Netherlands*) in England. Grotius was well known in
England as a philosopher of maritime jurisdiction, and had been embroiled
in a controversy about this topic with English opponents in the early part of

1.16   Woodcut depicting torture, including
waterboarding, of English prisoners by agents of the
Dutch East India Company, from John Skinner's *A True
Relation of the Unjust, Cruell, and Barbarous Proceedings
against the English at Amboyna in the East-Indies* (1624).
Oxford, Bodleian Library, Crynes 831, sigs [A4]v–[A5]r.

I.17 King William III's entry into The Hague, as depicted on an engraving in Govard Bidloo, *Relation du voyage de sa majesté Britannique en Hollande* (1692). The king was welcomed by city magistrates at the Westeinderbrug, where a triumphal arch was erected. Oxford, Douce L subt. 12, between pp. 30 and 31.

the century. Early in his career, he had been commissioned by the States of Holland to write a history of the Dutch Revolt. The resulting *Annales* were largely completed in 1612 but published posthumously in 1657. An English translation appeared at the outset of the Second Anglo-Dutch War (1665–67), which presented clear instructions on how to interpret the Anglo-Dutch Wars: 'The annals, and history of the Low-Countrey-warrs wherein is manifested, that the United Netherlands, are indebted for the glory of their conquests, to the valour of the English.' This spin on the history of the Low Countries served to underline Dutch treachery: 'yet, notwithstanding their Preservation by the English Nation, so often acknowledged by Themselves; they, like the ungrateful Snake, endeavour to destroy their Foster-Father, forgetting all their Obligations to England'.[105] Yet it was not very long before English and Dutch history became more entangled than ever before.

THE 'GLORIOUS REVOLUTION' AND ANGLO-DUTCH HISTORIES

Members of the Nassau family had figured on the title pages of pamphlets describing recent events since the early days of the Dutch Revolt. William of Orange, and later his son Maurice, were each the subject of short works, describing single events or giving more comprehensive accounts of their military accomplishments, such as William Shute's *The Triumphs of Nassau* (1613), a translation into English from the French translation of a Dutch work.

In 1688, as William III of Orange readied himself to ascend the English throne, a different kind of text on the history of the House of Nassau appeared in England, which provided readers not only with an account of the deeds of its princes, but also with a genealogy of the family. *The History of the Most Illustrious William, Prince of Orange* was first published in 1688, and reprinted in 1689 and again in 1693; the latter year also saw the publication of *The History of the House of Orange* and *The Lives of all the Princes of Orange*. No longer were the ancient relations between the English-speaking and Dutch-speaking peoples, or their princes, the focus: the interest in these works is exclusively dynastic, aiming to highlight William of Nassau's illustrious ancestry.

The English fascination with the House of Orange does not appear to have been reciprocated in the Netherlands, where there was very little interest in the history of the English royal house. Accounts of

William's passage to England, however, were published widely, as were accounts of his visit, now as king of England, to the republic in 1691 (fig. 1.17). The publication history of one such description of William's visit to The Hague, *The Triumph-Royal*, shows how the figure of William of Orange could on occasion command an international readership. The title page of the English-language edition states that the account was 'first done in Dutch, then into French, and now into English'. New historical writing was occasioned only by the death of Queen Mary II in 1694, which inspired an outpouring of eulogies and other commemorative publications, including translations from English into Dutch.[106] Petrus Rabus's *Opkomst, geboorte, leven en dood van Maria Stuart* (*Rise, Birth, Life and Death of Mary Stuart*) is presented as a biography of Mary, but it also contains a genealogy of the Stuarts, as well as an account of the political and military history of England during the life of Mary II Stuart (fig. 1.18). It has a particular focus on Anglo-Dutch relations and covers both times of war and periods of alliance between the two countries, from 1662 to 1694. Mary, the work concludes, 'was een Princes, die met alle recht niet alleen de Kroon van Groot Britanje, maar ook van Nederland … genoemd mocht worden'[107] ('was a princess, who by right can be called the Crown not only of Great Britain, but also of the Netherlands'). When looking at history from an Anglo-Dutch perspective, the republican Dutch saw no contradiction in being English royalists.[108]

The reign of William and Mary brings us to the end of our period. Their ascension soon became known as the 'Glorious Revolution', but the histories we have examined in this chapter recognized that the cultural, political and economic exchanges between England and the Low Countries had always been intense. The 'Glorious Revolution' had in fact been an evolution.

1.18 Illustration by Jan Luyken for Petrus Rabus's *Opkomst, geboorte, leven en dood van Maria Stuart*, depicting Mary II's deathbed. William III looks on from the doorway; his reign continued until his own death in 1702. Amsterdam, Rijksmuseum, RP-P-1896-A-19368-1022, frontispiece.

In pr... ...

probatio penne sibona fit
probatio in cauxti sibonu in

S... ...

pbonis ... sit xensibomi fit
astmmmmo
quinonu noseragono quoq: seno
aper...o.muno

Iobe...r parer nicolae vium dñ n
thin...r impieranbus nril deposce
Scribere qui cupiunt sensum ds augea illis
Ordare modulos papigamus nobils modol.
singula dulcisonu verco: discrimina uocu
Sellonis resono tenuir... di...scere plet tro
re fl dilcreiles melius formare timora
dicentissi grauis noster moderando suauis
Apurimi... exyrys fideterrehelo canora
Nunc more modo c...gentel
lanc...s superne a fil...lutu ...quid sepertunui uo
...bent ...cularis nidos ...capris nisi ego & tu
...Herbban olla uirtut nostri agunnan busale in
...ula ura ur... ...nba dur... e na
...ser uri nos cuus ir ur dignar uoi sal...

agera precer ...gut emies ...

batio penne sibona fir

Ad Putter, Elisabeth van Houts, Moreed Arbabzadah and Kathleen E. Kennedy

Hebban olla uogala nestas hagunnan hinase hic
enda thu uuat unbidan uue nu
Abent omnes uolucres nidos inceptos nisi ego et
tu quid expectamus nu(nc)

*All birds have begun their nests, except me and you
– what are we waiting for now?*

OXFORD, BODLEIAN LIBRARY, MS. BODL. 340, FOL. 169v

The histories told by medieval and early modern chroniclers give us insights into the social lives of people, but books themselves also have histories and social lives. The materials and technologies underpinning the production of books; the ability to read them and the means to acquire them; the trends and fashions that make specific types of books popular with different audiences and at different times; the market conditions that create possibilities for import, export or local production; the changing fortunes and transformations of books as they move between owners and annotators, and travel from one country to another: all these aspects of book production and book consumption also have histories. In this chapter and the following chapter (on early printing), we explore some of the ways in which Anglo-Dutch relations shaped both the history of book production in general and the histories of individual books in particular. As elsewhere in this book, we proceed on the basis of a selection of examples from the Bodleian Library that illustrate the story of Anglo-Dutch relations.

THE BOOKS OF THE MONASTERY

Before the invention of printing, books were manuscripts, handwritten volumes laboriously copied by scribes. Until the thirteenth century,

2.1 Back of the final leaf of a manuscript of Ælfric's *Catholic Homilies*, with pen trials, including (centre right) two lines of Old Dutch verse, with Latin translation above. The Old English text on the other side of the page can be seen showing through the vellum. Oxford, Bodleian Library, MS. Bodl. 340, fol. 169v.

these scribes were mostly monks who had been trained to use a quill and ink produced from gall or carbon on parchment, made of animal skin. Parchment, ink and quills were expensive, meaning that only rich monasteries or wealthy individuals could act as patrons of books. To provide the reading material required by the Rule of St Benedict, most monasteries had a scriptorium, where monks would copy books for their library. Essential books were the Bible, liturgical books, works of the church fathers such as St Augustine and St Jerome, and the lives of saints venerated at the monastery. Manuscripts could, of course, be donated to the monastery or purchased from elsewhere, but mostly they were produced in the monastery's scriptorium.[1]

In 1933 Kenneth Sisam published what he called 'by far the earliest scrap of Netherlandish that has been recorded in England'.[2] This medieval Dutch scrap consists of thirteen words written in the late eleventh century on the back of the final leaf of a manuscript of Ælfric's Old English *Catholic Homilies* (Oxford, Bodleian Library, MS. Bodl. 340, fol. 169v; fig. 2.1), one of a set of two manuscripts containing the homilies (the other being MS. Bodl. 342). The two volumes were kept together as a set for much of their lives, before being erroneously separated, resulting in the non-sequential numbering.

The Dutch on the final leaf of MS. Bodl. 340 was probably written by a scribe at Rochester's scriptorium in order to test a newly cut pen.[3] A quill pen had to be recut frequently (as often as twice per folio), and each time the scribe had to check that the new nib worked by writing with it. Such scribbles are called pen trials, pen tests or pen probes. In this manuscript, the Dutch scribe has tested the pen and ink by writing the Latin phrases *probatio pennae* ('test of the pen') and *probatio incauxti* ('test of the ink'; usually spelled *incausti* or *encausti*). Pen trials were frequently more elaborate and sometimes included verses commenting on what it was like to work as a scribe.[4] At these times, scribes occasionally revealed their native script, even when they had otherwise abandoned it in favour of the style of the monastery to which they had moved.[5] This is perhaps the case with the pen trials in MSS. Bodl. 340 and 342. The scribes of the pen trials reveal traits that suggest they had learned to write in the eleventh century in the Low Countries, Germany and Italy,[6] but these handwriting styles are not present in any surviving Rochester manuscripts. The scribes must have adopted the local writing style and used it for manuscript production, confining their native hands to pen trials.[7] The Low Countries script of the *Hebban olla* pen trial therefore corroborates claims that the words are Old Dutch musings by a scribe who was trained in the Low Countries.[8] As we have seen in Chapter 1, the monasteries in England were not necessarily monolingual environments. Monks from Dutch-speaking areas (like Goscelin) were active in English monasteries, so it is no surprise to find this indirect evidence of their presence. Reading Old English texts like Ælfric's *Catholic Homilies* may have encouraged them to scribble a few words in their own vernacular. Anglo-Dutch contact clearly persisted for a long time at Rochester: another scribe provided some glosses above words at the beginning of the manuscript, and one of these glosses is the Dutch *keysere* above the Old English *casere* ('caesar', 'emperor'), perhaps an observation on the similarity between the two languages as much as a translation. Another gloss is in Middle English and the rest are Latin translations of the Old English words.[9]

The many hands that left their mark on MSS. Bodl. 340 and 342 attest to the active lives of the manuscripts in question over the course of centuries and the international character of their users. A book was not necessarily static in either its location or its form. The movement of books and people in the Middle Ages is easily underestimated. It is true that the majority of people were likely to be born, to live and to die within the same area, but some subsets of the population were far more mobile. MSS. Bodl. 340 and 342 are not the only example of a scribe from the Low Countries in England: another such scribe was active at Salisbury at the same time as the Rochester scribe (*c.*1075–1100).[10] The Norman Conquest stimulated the movement of people and therefore also of books: some English took refuge in Flanders and carried their English books with them. Glosses and marginalia can attest to the continued use of these manuscripts in Flanders, but their absence is also telling. A manuscript given by Abbot Saewold of Bath to Saint-Vaast in Arras contains the lives of several English saints (St Cuthbert, St Guthlac and St Dunstan) alongside those of two French saints (St Philibert and St Aichard). A later reader has added corrections and chapter numbers to the life of St Philibert, but nothing for the English saints. The efforts of this reader suggest that at Saint-Vaast less use was made of the 'English' parts of the book, because of either a lack of interest or a lack of relevant material (e.g. another life of St Cuthbert with which to compare this one).[11]

It is not only books written in England that bear witness to Anglo-Dutch relations in manuscript production. Bergues, Bibliothèque Municipale, MS. 19 contains a collection of saints' lives and was copied in the twelfth century at Saint-Winnoc in Flanders, a daughter house of Saint-Bertin at Saint-Omer. It celebrates the relics of the abbey's patron saint, St Winnoc, a seventh-century saint from Brittany, and the relics of two English saints, St Oswald (d.642), a Saxon royal martyr, and St Lewinna.[12] In 1058 the English relics of the previously unknown St Lewinna were 'stolen' from *Sevordt* (Bishopstone in England) by the Dutch-speaking monk Balger, whose adventures were recorded by Drogo of Saint-Winnoc. Drogo noted that Balger only knew the identity of the saint from scraps of parchment written in Old English characters, which were attached to the walls around her shrine and which he could not understand without the help of a local. According to Drogo, it was Countess Adela of Flanders who had prompted the search for information and relics of St Lewinna.[13] The Bergues manuscript is probably a copy of Drogo's own manuscript, which Drogo wrote between 1058 and 1075, and is well known for its illuminations of saints Winnoc, Oswald and Lewinna (fig. 2.2).[14]

The drawings are older than the manuscript and may come from Drogo's original manuscript. The inclusion of exactly three illuminations in this manuscript, one devoted to each saint, pays homage to the liturgical tradition that developed at Saint-Winnoc, where these three saints were invoked in worship of the Holy Trinity:[15]

> Hi sunt tres aeternitatis columnae,
> Quos Trinitas huic providit ecclesiae:
> Winnocus, Oswaldus, cum Levinna,
> Quorum nos salvent suffragia.

> *These are the three pillars of eternity, whom the Trinity provides for this church: Winnoc, Oswald, and Lewinna, whose suffrages [prayers for help addressed to particular saints] save us.*

These manuscripts from England and the Low Countries thus reflect the complex web of connections involving cross-cultural patronage, travel and production.

The international traffic in saintly relics provided the context for manuscript exchange between England and the Continent on more than one occasion. The relics of St Oswald arrived in Flanders via Judith (d.1094), the daughter of Count Baldwin IV of Flanders and wife of Earl Tostig (d.1066) of Northumberland. Forced to flee England in 1065, Earl Tostig and Judith went into exile in Saint-Omer. Two richly illuminated gospel books, probably made for Judith, now in New York (Pierpont Morgan Library, MSS. 708 and 709), accompanied the Oswald relics from England.[16] The stories behind St Lewinna and St Oswald's relics show how the patronage of the wife (Adela) and daughter (Judith) of counts of Flanders provided the money to commission texts and manuscripts from monks both in England and on the Continent.

Patronage was especially vital for the production of expensive illuminated manuscripts.[17] From the Carolingian period onwards, manuscripts were embellished with decorative elements and full illustrations of the text. Decorative elements could be added by a skilled calligrapher, but high-quality illustrations required more specialized expertise. This often entailed employing foreign, itinerant artists, whose travels, aided by the links between monasteries of the same monastic order, are the reason behind similarities in the illumination of manuscripts from regions that are not geographically close. Manuscript art attests to repeated waves of influence from the British Isles to the Continent, resulting in related artistic forms on both sides, and Continental art also influenced insular art. Carolingian manuscripts and monks from northern France were employed in England for the creation of new books, which gave rise to the Winchester style. At the beginning of our period, England was an exporter of excellence that influenced manuscript illumination on the Continent.[18]

2.2 The English martyr St Lewinna being crowned in heaven. A monk, probably Drogo of Saint-Winnoc who wrote Lewinna's life and may have designed the portrait, is kneeling in worship. Bergues, Bibliothèque Municipale, MS. 19, fol. 112r.

In the late tenth century the scriptorium of Saint-Bertin in Flanders became one of the pre-eminent scriptoria in Europe.[19] English monks, aided by Saint-Bertin's connection with Winchester Abbey, arrived at the invitation of the abbot and produced manuscripts displaying Winchester traits, which led to Winchester influence on Continental styles.[20] Stephen Harding (c.1060–1134), an Englishman who founded the Cistercians, commissioned a book when he visited the abbey at Saint-Vaast,[21] and an English monk called Elias copied and decorated a manuscript at Saint-Bertin c.1145–52.[22] These movements of people thus created a tangled network of relationships that tightly bound together changes in manuscript production on the Continent and in Britain.

It is not just the physical books that bear witness to contact between England and the Low Countries; their contents too reflect these close cultural connections. More recent English saints were celebrated in Flanders, as seen in a copy of the life of St Anselm, archbishop of Canterbury from 1089 to 1109, by Eadmer, probably from Saint-Martin at Tournai, now at the J. Paul Getty Museum in Los Angeles; it is notable that the two illuminated full pages executed c.1140–50 do not show the portraits of the saint but of the author-scribe (fig. 2.3).[23] This is a lovely example of how monk-illuminators proudly visualized their trade as they copied texts.

While parchment was durable, other writing material was considered even more enduring. Monks therefore preferred inscriptions on stone and lead for tombs and burials. The tombstone with the Latin epitaph of the Flemish-born Gundrada of Warenne (d.1085) is now the oldest one for a woman in England,[24] while the lead burial plaque of the English noblewoman Gunhild (d.1087), sister of King Harold (d.1066), who died in exile in Flanders, contains her brief Latin biography.[25]

THE AGE OF COMMERCIAL BOOK PRODUCTION

While monasteries and religious houses continued to play an important part in handwritten book production (and also later in printing in the Low Countries), the thirteenth century ushered in the new era of commercial book production. The rise in literacy among the laity, which had its roots in urbanization, was an important factor in this development. It is no coincidence that the earliest centres of lay book production in western Europe were the larger cities. Paris was the largest, followed by the towns of the Low Countries. Modern readers

2.3 Portrait of Eadmer as author-scribe. This illumination is from a manuscript of his life of St Anselm, archbishop of Canterbury (1089–1109), and was executed c.1140–50, probably at the Abbey of Saint-Martin at Tournai. Los Angeles, J. Paul Getty Museum, MS. Ludwig XI 6, fol. 2v.

may be surprised to learn that around 1350, after the Black Death, the population of London (*c*.35,000) was significantly smaller than that of Bruges (*c*.46,000) and Ghent (*c*.64,000).[26]

The textile industry and the trade in luxury goods – and books *were* luxury goods – had led to the concentration of prosperous townspeople in a relatively small area. Outside Italy, Flanders was the most densely populated area in Europe, and the thriving cloth-making towns of the Low Countries were the envy of the world. Flemish cloth had the reputation of being the best, and so, when Geoffrey Chaucer extols the quality of the Wife of Bath's 'clooth-makynge' in *The Canterbury Tales*, he does so by saying that she 'passed hem [surpassed those] of Ypres and of Gaunt [Ghent]'.[27] The kings of England and Scotland both appreciated that the cloth trade was the key to prosperity at home. The Scottish 'staple', the single point of entry for wool exported from Scotland to Flanders, became established in Bruges in 1347 (the English also used Bruges but soon switched to Calais). King Edward III of England, who had travelled through the Low Countries as a young man, and his wife Philippa, daughter of the count of Holland and Hainault, were so impressed with the prosperity of the region that overtures were made to lure craftsmen to England. In 1331 a certain John Kempe, 'weaver of woollen cloths', was invited to bring his business and workforce over from Flanders, along with any dyers and fullers who wanted to join him, in a successful attempt to foster the same economic conditions for urban prosperity in England.[28] In 1356 Kempe joined the guild of native weavers and acquired citizenship.[29] Trade and industry also drove up literacy rates. To draw up a bill or a contract one needed to be able to read and write, and that practical literacy also enabled one, outside of work, to read books. So it was that, alongside the nobility and the clergy, there emerged a new class of readers.

The resulting demand for books made commercial book production viable. The *Livre des mestiers* (*Book of Trades*), originating in Bruges *c*.1340, provides a vivid insight into the early phase of the urban 'text industry'.[30] The *Livre* is a French–Flemish conversation manual that teaches the reader what to say to people of various trades. Among those singled out for attention are Gilbert the scribe, who 'can wel scriven chaertren, privilegen ende instrumenten' ('can expertly write charters, privileges and legal instruments'), and George the bookseller, who 'heeft meer bouken dan alle die vander stede, ende hi vercoopt gansepennen ende swanepennen, ende hi vercoept fransijn ende perkement' ('has more books than anyone else in town, and also sells quills made of goose-feathers and swan-feathers, and vellum and parchment').[31] The *Livre* went through several later versions, and the changes and additions show that the trade of the scribe and the bookseller were booming. A fifteenth-century version was translated by William Caxton, who encountered the work while he was stationed in Bruges as 'Governor of the English Nation' (that is, head of the corporation of English merchants trading in the Low Countries). In Caxton's French–English edition, the profession of scribe has become 'the most noble craft that is in the world',[32] and 'George the booke sellar' now sells all manner of books:

Be they stolen or enprinted	
Or othirwyse pourchaced	
He hath doctrinals catons	[*The Distichs of Cato*, a school text]
Oures of our lady	[books of hours]
Donettis partis accidents	[grammar books]
Sawters well enlumined	[psalters]
Bounden with claspes of silver	
Bookes of physike	[medical treatises]
Seven salmes kalenders	
Ynke and perchemyn	
Pennes of swannes	
Pennes of ghees	
Good portoses	[portable breviaries]
Whiche ben worth good money.[33]	

The bookseller caters to all tastes, and now sells printed as well as handwritten books. There was 'good money' in this business.

ENGLISH AND DUTCH ENCOUNTERS IN BOOKS OF HOURS

The 'Oures of our lady' mentioned by Caxton are what we now refer to as books of hours. At the heart of these books for private devotion was a series of prayers known as the Little Office of the Blessed Virgin Mary, organized according to the time of day in which the prayers should be said, and therefore more commonly known as the 'Hours of the Virgin'. In most books of hours, this office was preceded by a calendar of saints and

2.4 'How sweet are thy words unto my taste!' Page from a sumptuously decorated Psalter (*c.*1320), produced at Saint Peter's Abbey, Ghent. The illustration in the lower margin shows a courting couple. Oxford, Bodleian Library, MS. Douce 6, fol. 106v.

some selected gospel readings. Books of hours also usually contained the seven penitential psalms, the office of the dead, other devotional prayers (such as the Hours of the Cross and the Hours of the Holy Spirit) and suffrages (prayers to saints). Often sumptuously illustrated, these books made it possible for laypeople to imitate the clergy by participating in divine worship in their own homes or when they went to church, since their small size made them portable. They thus played a role in the gradual democratization of religion, though, being luxury goods, only the rich could afford them, and until the end of the fourteenth century they were in Latin.[34]

From the thirteenth century onwards there is evidence from Flanders of the commercial production of books of hours, and before that illuminated psalters, containing the complete Psalms. At this time the names of professional illustrators begin appearing in town records. For instance, 'Zegardus' and 'Hannekin' (1291), 'Theodericus illuminator' (1291), 'Odard den Verlichter' ('Odard the Illuminator', 1303) and 'Jan den Verlichter' ('Jan the Illuminator', 1305) were all active in Bruges.[35] A number of illuminated psalters from this period made in Flanders are now in the Bodleian Library, for example MSS. Auct. D. 4. 2 (c.1276) and Douce 5 and 6 (c.1320). In the thirteenth and fourteenth centuries, these psalters and books of hours were still intended primarily for local consumption by the urban elite, secular and religious, and the above-mentioned manuscripts bear this out. MS. Auct. D. 4. 2 has a

calendar to which the name 'Joras de Woser' was added, while MSS. Douce 5 and 6 display the arms of Saint Peter's Abbey in Ghent, where the manuscript was produced.[36]

The enduring attractiveness of these Gothic books from the Low Countries is shown by an illustrated leaf from MS. Douce 6 (fig. 2.4). Accompanying the sacred text, beginning 'Quam dulcia faucibus meis eloquentia tua; super mel ori meo' ('How sweet are thy words unto my taste! Yea sweeter than honey to my mouth', Psalm 118:103), is an illumination of a young man exchanging 'sweet words' with a young woman. Their courtship is a recurrent theme in the book's decorative scheme. Lines with verses from the Psalms are playfully filled with drolleries (illustrations of amusing, often grotesque, figures), and a rabbit dashes across the top line in the opposite direction to the reading eye. The branches growing from the decorated initials (here L in *Lucerna*) create a natural border around the text block in which birds can find a perch. This ludic and often irreverent border decoration is characteristic of the period.

Many books of hours were intended for women. A fine example is Bodleian Library, MS. Lat. liturg. f. 3, also known as the Hours of Anne of Bohemia, who as Richard II's wife became queen consort of England in 1382. This book still holds many mysteries. A key question for scholars is whether or not it was ever owned by Anne of Bohemia. The illumination on folio 65v, which shows a young lady giving her right hand to a crowned king while her left hand is raised in exactly the same gesture that Anne of Bohemia displays on the famous Wilton Diptych, has long been known to be a nineteenth-century forgery. But the same lady is shown again kneeling to the Virgin Mary (as owners of books of hours were often portrayed) in an illumination on folio 118r (fig. 2.5).

This is not a forgery, and it has been noted that it bears a strikingly close resemblance to the donor image found in a missal completed in Ghent in 1366, now at the Museum Meermanno – House of the Book in The Hague.[37] Moreover, the heraldic arms in the manuscript point to the arms of Anne of Bohemia as queen consort, though it should be noted that they are approximations rather than entirely accurate representations.[38] Thus the initial C on folio 40r of the manuscript shows the attributed arms of Edward the Confessor, five martlets and a cross, though that cross should really be gold and not white. The royal banners of Richard II had these arms from at least the 1380s, and around 1394 Richard adopted them on his shield, impaled with Edward III's arms,[39] which are also shown

2.5 Donor portrait of Anne of Bohemia kneeling to the Virgin Mary and Jesus, from the 'Hours of Anne of Bohemia', produced in Flanders in the 1340s and customized in 1381 for Anne of Bohemia, who was betrothed to Richard II of England. Oxford, Bodleian Library, MS. Lat. liturg. f. 3, fols 117v–118r.

in two initials in this manuscript. However, it is most unlikely that the book was originally made for Anne of Bohemia. The hand of the main illuminator has been identified in other manuscripts from Flanders from the 1340s.[40] The best explanation for this puzzle is that this book of hours was produced in different stages. In its original conception it was not a book of hours personalized for a particular owner. This was done a few decades later, again by a Flemish artist, who illuminated the donor page and painted in the heraldic initials. Why was this done? In 1381 Anne, who was betrothed to Richard II, travelled from her native Bohemia to England, where the two were to be married. She stayed first in Brussels with her uncle and aunt, Duke Wenceslas of Brabant and his wife Johanna, and also visited the count of Flanders, Louis de Male, in Bruges, where she stayed for three days and was presented with lavish gifts. It is probable that one of these gifts was this book of hours, and that it was hastily customized for her through the addition of her portrait, her own heraldic arms and those she would gain by marriage to Richard II.[41] The provenance of this book of hours in Flanders is confirmed by the text of the manuscript. As might be expected, the main language is Latin, but the scribe also added some notes in Dutch, explaining to the user, who may not have had much Latin, when various prayers should be said. There is just enough Middle Dutch to indicate a Flemish dialect.[42] Since Anne of Bohemia did not speak Dutch, the rubrics cannot have been written with her in mind.

The Hours of Anne of Bohemia provides an early indication that travellers passing through the Low Countries on their way back to England or Scotland might want a book of hours as a memento of their visit, but there is more evidence from the fifteenth century. For instance, the Dean Brown's Hours are named after Dean James Brown of Aberdeen Cathedral, who enjoyed a brief stay in the Low Countries after his return from ecclesiastical business in Rome in 1498. During his stay he commissioned a book of hours to his own specifications, with a calendar of Scottish saints and a donor image of himself, kneeling before the Virgin and Child.[43]

An important late medieval development in book history in Flanders and also in Utrecht, which established itself as a rival centre for commercial deluxe devotional books in the fifteenth century, was the 'mass production' of Netherlandish books for export to English and Scottish markets.[44] It is usually easy enough to tell books of hours imported from the Continent from those that were home produced. A useful diagnostic is the specification in Flemish books of hours intended for export to both England and Scotland that the book has been made 'secundum consuetudinem Anglie' or 'ad usum Anglie' ('for English use') or 'secundum usum et consuetudinem sarum' ('for the use and custom of Salisbury'), the Sarum liturgy being the prevalent one in England at that time. Other tell-tale signs are the names of the saints recorded in calendars and litanies. All towns and regions had their local saintly celebrities; conversely, saints famous in one part of the world were often unknown elsewhere. Because calendars in books of hours list saints' days and also mark the relative importance of saints by using red ink (or gilding) for the names of the top saints (a practice that has given us the phrase 'a red letter day'), calendars are excellent records of local biases. For instance, in a calendar from Bruges, whose patron saint was Donatian, we can expect Donatian's saint's day and the day of the translation of his relics to be marked as important holidays; in a calendar from Ghent the same will be true for St Bavo.

Of course, scribes producing books for an English market made accommodations for their intended readership, but some English saints were not well known and gave Netherlandish scribes trouble. Guthlac and Swithun caused further confusion on account of phonology and orthography. Dutch had no 'th' sound, and the letter thorn (þ), which was often used to represent 'th' and may have been encountered by Dutch scribes, would have been unfamiliar to them. Not surprisingly, therefore, in some Flemish calendars for English audiences these saints appear as 'Zwichin' and 'Gudhlac'. Nor is it surprising to see Flemish spelling habits reflected in the orthography of particular saints' names. Thus the habit of writing *gh* for *g* is sometimes reflected in spellings of Gertrude (*Gheertrudis*) and Agatha (*Aghathe*). An easy way of avoiding difficulties of this sort was to omit the calendar altogether, and so some Flemish producers left it to the English to add their own.

Some of these peculiarities can be seen in the Pudsay Hours, produced in Flanders for English readers. This book of hours (Bodleian Library, MS. Don. e. 120) was copied, illuminated and bound in the Low Countries in the 1460s, but it was always intended for English readers. Names of English saints that were not well known on the Continent were lost in translation: St Botolph appears as 'Botulp' and Alban has become 'Atan', presumably via 'Alan', which was the way Flemish scribes usually

made sense of 'Alban'. More curious still is the mysterious saint 'Walleparde', who appears in the litany (fig. 2.6) and whose identity is a mystery. No saint with this name seems to have existed, even though the name appears frequently in Anglo-Flemish books of hours (sometimes in the variant spelling 'Wallepaxtus'). This uniquely Anglo-Dutch saint may have come into existence as a conflation of 'Valentine' and 'Agapite',[45] unless the name is a garbled version of Walpurga/Walburga.

It is not just the Flemish connection that makes this manuscript interesting. Throughout the fifteenth and sixteenth centuries it was a treasured possession of the Pudsey family in Yorkshire, whose Lancastrian and Catholic allegiances can be traced in the additions to the book made by family members.[46] A movingly personal prayer to Henry VI in two rhyme-royal stanzas, beginning 'As far as hope will yn length', was added to the manuscript following a visit by the poet to Henry VI's shrine in Windsor, where in fact it may have been written: 'Of forgevness I aske the grace / Hope hathe me movyde to seke *this place*.'[47] Henry VIII's decree of 1538 forbidding worship of St Thomas Becket was ignored by the family. His name has not been crossed out in the calendar. One of the Pudseys paid the ultimate price for sticking to the old faith. Thomas Pudsey (*c.*1531–1576) is remembered in the book of hours as having 'died in Yorke prisoner for his conscience, a trewe confessor of the catholik faythe' (fol. 4v).

The production of devotional books for export to England became a highly professional operation, and, although we have so far mentioned saints' names and spellings as distinctive qualities of these Netherlandish books, it was of course the quality of the illuminations that made them

2.6 St 'Walleparde', in a list of saints of the litany in a book of hours produced in Flanders for the English market (1460s). The name appears on the penultimate line, between that of St Valentine and St Agapetus. Oxford, Bodleian Library, MS. Don. e. 120, fol. 49r.

special to English readers. When William Revelour, a chaplain in York, bequeathed his book of hours in 1446, he identified its Flemishness with reference to the pictures: 'unum primarium largum cum ymaginibus intus scriptis ad modum Flandr(ie)' ('a large primer with pictures inside drawn in the manner of Flanders').[48] Various facts and figures indicate the increasing professionalization of this industry. Some 200 Flemish books of hours made for England survive in libraries and museums today. Already in 1426 in Bruges 25 per cent of illuminators were working for English clients. Not long afterwards illuminators had become so numerous in Bruges that they set up their own guild.[49] 'Assembly line' methods were developed: single-leaf miniatures were imported from other centres, while Bruges miniatures were exported to book producers in other towns.

The quality of this work is apparent in another manuscript in the Bodleian Library: MS. Auct. D. inf. 2. 13, also known as 'Queen Mary's Psalter'. The alias is unfortunate for various reasons. First, it is not really a psalter but a 'psalter-hours', a book of hours including not just a selection of psalms but the complete set. Secondly, although the book was owned by Mary Tudor (1516–1558), it was not made for her, and a piece of moral advice in her hand (beginning 'Geate you such ryches') was written before she was queen, as shown by the fact that she signed it 'Your lovyng mistres, Marye Princesse'. Finally, it does not help that there exists another psalter given to the same Mary that is known by the same name (British Library, MS. Royal 2 B VII). So on this occasion it seems best to call the book Auct. D. inf. 2. 13.

While many books of hours were destroyed or defaced in the Reformation (especially in Scotland, where the survival rate of books of hours was much lower), Auct. D. inf. 2. 13 escaped mutilation. Mary Tudor was a Catholic and the things that offended reformers, such as the worship of St Thomas Becket, comforted her. When the book came into Protestant hands, however, it was saved by the quality of the illustrations and its association with royalty. Presenting the book to the Bodleian in 1615, Richard Connock stipulated (in an inscription on a flyleaf of the manuscript) that it should be 'kept, not for the Religion it contains, but for the Pictures and former Royall Owners sake'.

The pictures are indeed stunning. In the miniature depicting the murder of Thomas Becket in Canterbury Cathedral, the stillness of the saint, who has eyes only for Jesus, contrasts with the wild gestures of the three assassins (fig. 2.7). Equally dramatic is the effect of the colour

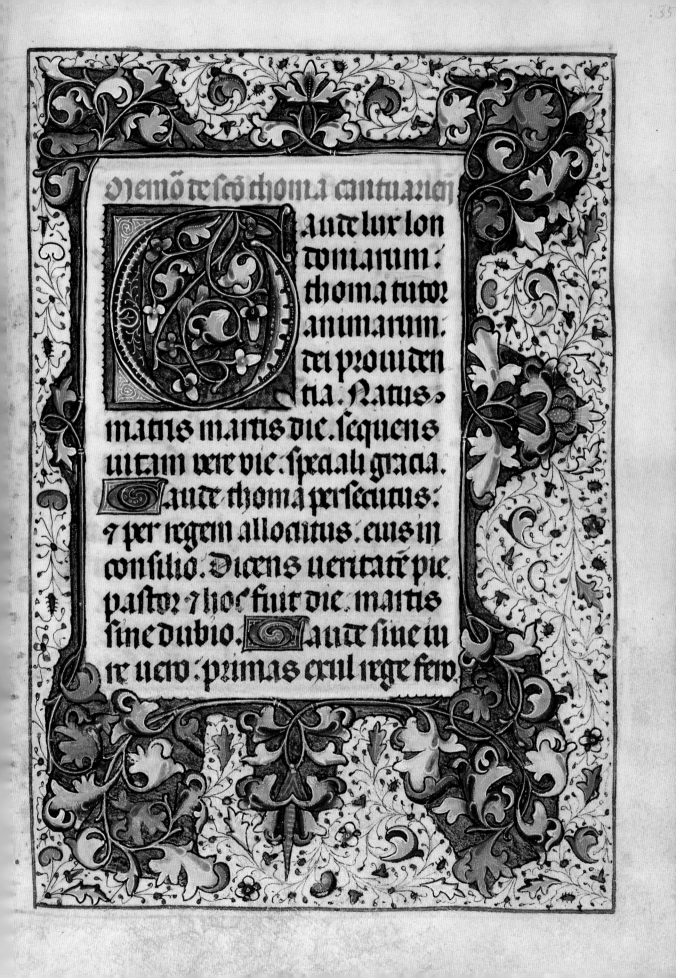

Memŏ te scŏ thoma cantuarien.

Auctelur lon
tomarum:
thoma tutor
animarum.
dei prouiden
tia. Natus.
matris martis die. sequens
uitam uere die. specali gracia.
Auctē thoma persecutus:
7 per regem allocutus. eius in
consilio. Dicens ueritatē pie
pastor 7 hoc fuit die. martis
sine dubio. Auctē sine in
re uerō. primas exul regē seuo.

scheme. Painted in a style known as demi-grisaille, the artist's palette is largely monochrome, in various shades of grey. This throws the use of colour into relief. The eye is drawn to the gold candelabra and communion vessels on the altar, and to the splendid brocaded curtain that closes off the chapel and so places us on the privileged side of the sacred space that is here being profaned. The vaulting above the curtain gives a sense of space and the coloured marble stones on the floor give this space the illusion of depth. The most chilling detail is the splodge of red. It marks the deadly wound of a saint whose identification with the crucified Christ becomes complete when he too is murdered. The same vivid splodges of red are used for Christ's wounds in the illustration of Christ's deposition from the cross.[50]

That Auct. D. inf. 2. 13 was produced in Bruges is almost certain. The incipit 'Hore beate Marie Virginis secundum consuetudinem Anglie'[51] ('Here begin the Hours of the Blessed Virgin Mary according to the custom of England') shows that it was made for export, and the litany, which includes the mysterious St Wallepaxtus, is of the type that came out of Bruges. The binding is modern but two panels of the original binding and the original silver clasps (minus the enamel miniatures that once adorned them) survive and look like the work of the Bruges binder Anthonis de Gavere, whose superb craftsmanship is preserved intact in a book of hours (*c.*1460) commissioned by the wealthy English merchant Thomas Browne (now Philadelphia Free Library, MS. Widener 3).[52] Since the historiated initials of Auct. D. inf. 2. 13 are probably by the same artist as that of the Browne Hours, a Bruges provenance is clearly indicated. Various details, however, point to a cosmopolitan production. One curiosity is that the twenty-five full-page miniatures (of which one is now missing) were not made by a local illuminator, but instead commissioned from an artist in Utrecht, known to art historians as the 'Master of Evert van Souldenbach'. Evert was a canon of Utrecht Cathedral from 1445 to 1503, and patron of a history (Vienna, Österreichische Nationalbibliothek, Cod. 2771) that was copied and illustrated in an important Utrecht workshop. The fame of the Master of Evert van Souldenbach had spread as far as Bruges. A cycle of miniatures was commissioned from him and supplied from Utrecht on loose sheets, which were then inserted. The versos of these pages are either blank or contain writing in a different ink. That they otherwise look like an organic part of the manuscript has everything to do with the work of the border artist, who filled in the

2.7 *previous pages* Miniature of the murder of Thomas Becket, from 'Queen Mary's Psalter', owned by Mary Tudor and produced in the fifteenth century and bound in Bruges (*c.*1460). The full-page miniatures were made in Utrecht, and the border decoration blends Flemish and English styles. Oxford, Bodleian Library, MS. Auct. D. inf. 2. 13, fols 34v–35r.

borders of the loose leaves and the fixed ones in a style that is a hybrid of Flemish and English. The acanthus leaves curling out from the inner borders are typically English, but the smaller motifs look more Flemish than English, showing that the artist had a command of both styles.

This border artist, who also worked on the borders in similar books of hours and psalter-hours,[53] is nicknamed 'the Englishman', but that name begs all kinds of questions. Was this an Englishman who plied his trade in Flanders? We know of many Flemish book-artists who went to England to work. One of the earliest examples is a Flemish illuminator who collaborated with English craftsmen on the Vienna Bohun Psalter (Österreichische Nationalbibliothek, Cod. 1826) in the 1350s. Was 'the Englishman' who painted the 'Anglo-Dutch' borders in Auct. D. inf. 2. 13 a migrant who went in the other direction? This would be unusual but not unprecedented. An English illuminator, 'Willam de Engelsman', is found in records from Utrecht in 1415, and is known to have collaborated on various book projects in Utrecht and Nijmegen.[54] It is equally possible that 'the Englishman' was a Fleming, who had learned English border style abroad or from English exemplars. In any case, this book of hours is profoundly hybrid: made in Bruges, with pictures from Utrecht, for an English patron, with a calendar made for use in Lincoln but with Flemish spellings (such as 'Adriaen' for the martyr Adrian in the entry for 4 March). The borders show the same cultural crossover: its styles of art are Flemish and English, and this transnational mix was apparently popular among a set of very wealthy English book patrons. Modern art historians tend to view late medieval English border art as deeply traditional and resistant to change compared to the dynamic styles preferred across the Continent. A border artist employing both an English and a Continental style, and wealthy patrons interested in this blend, remind us that medieval people themselves might have had other opinions on the matter.

THE ANGLO-BURGUNDIAN ALLIANCE

MS. Auct. D. inf. 2. 13 has brought us to the second half of the fifteenth century, and it is not possible to discuss Anglo-Dutch relations in manuscript book production in this period without considering the role of the dukes of Burgundy and their courtiers as patrons of literature and the arts.[55] The Burgundian era was officially inaugurated in 1369 when Philip the Bold, duke of Burgundy, married Margaret, the daughter of Louis de Male, count of Flanders, and thus brought Burgundy and Flanders and various territories on its border under Burgundian rule. For two generations the Burgundian dukes ruled the Low Countries remotely, from their palace in Dijon and their residence in Paris, and it was only under Philip the Bold's grandson, Philip the Good, that the Low Countries became the focus of Burgundian rule. Having acquired other principalities (Brabant and Limburg in 1430, and Hainault and Holland in 1433), Philip the Good moved his court between different cities in the Low Countries. Both Philip and his son Charles the Bold sought to project their political power through patronage of the arts: tapestry, architecture, painting and, last but not least, deluxe manuscripts. Philip the Good's library was the finest in western Europe, and his bibliophilia set a trend that noblemen at home and abroad were keen to follow.[56]

Scotland was no exception in this regard, and took pride in the close connections it enjoyed with the Burgundian empire. The marriage of Philip the Good's grand-niece Mary of Guelders and King James II of Scotland in 1449 inaugurated a period when the higher echelons of Scottish society looked to Burgundy for books, art and chivalric culture to enhance their prestige.[57] The most famous book that embodies Scottish–Flemish relations in the Burgundian era is the Hours of James IV of Scotland. It was commissioned as a wedding present for James IV's wife, Margaret Tudor, who in turn gave it to her sister Mary, as we know from an inscription: 'Madame, I pray your grace remember on me when ye loke upon thys book. Your lofyng syster Margaret.'[58] The occasion of a royal wedding required the finest book of hours that money could buy, and that book was ordered from a Flemish atelier (probably in Ghent). There are full-page illuminations of Margaret Tudor, already wearing her crown as queen of Scotland, and of King James IV, the latter's portrait so lifelike that art historians believe it must have been based on drawings sent to the Flemish artist now known as the Master of James IV of Scotland.[59]

Philip the Good of Burgundy had also allied himself with King Henry V of England against the French king, and this Anglo-Burgundian alliance enabled the dukes of Burgundy and the English crown to dominate France north of the Loire until the last quarter of the fifteenth century. There were certainly periods when the relationship broke down (most notably when Philip the Bold switched sides and besieged Calais in 1436), but the alliance was consolidated in 1468 by the marriage between Charles of Burgundy and Margaret of York, King Edward IV's sister. This was the celebrity marriage of the century and attracted hosts of English tourists. Sir John Paston II was in Bruges to see it and waxed lyrical about it in a letter to his father. In true Burgundian style, Margaret became the most important female patron of books of the fifteenth century. Twenty-six manuscripts are known to have been owned by her, and many of these were made especially for her.[60]

Most of these manuscripts are devotional and all are in French, which was the preferred language of the Burgundian court, though the dukes were astute enough to realize that they and their children needed to have Dutch in case the townspeople in Flanders insisted on their right to be governed in the medium of their vernacular language, as they did in times of political tension. Margaret of York, too, had excellent Dutch, for she gave lessons in the language to the emperor of Austria, Maximilian I, who married her stepdaughter, Mary of Burgundy.[61] Bodleian Library, MS. Douce 365 is a beautiful example of a manuscript commissioned by Margaret of York. It is one of a number of books produced in Ghent and copied by one of the leading scribes, David Aubert, who entered the service of Philip the Good and was responsible not only for the copying of books but also for commissioning the illustrations and bindings. After 1474 he was employed by Margaret of York, for whom he produced at least eight manuscripts, illustrated by the finest artists of the day, including the Master of Mary of Burgundy, who illustrated MS. Douce 365, and Simon Marmion.[62]

Some of the books produced for Margaret include portraits of her, and it is fitting that in MS. Douce 365 she is depicted with a devotional book (fig. 2.8). Margaret herself can be seen kneeling in a private chapel in front of a prie-dieu. She is accompanied by two ladies-in-waiting, one of whom also holds a book, probably a book of hours, wrapped in a protective leather chemise, the medieval equivalent of the dust jacket.[63] Behind the women stands a man who looks as if he has only just entered the church: the hat he has taken off is still in his right hand. While he watches them intently, the ladies are too intent on their devotions to have noticed his presence. The handsome male figure is none other than Charles the Bold himself. The artists who worked for Margaret had a habit of including him in the margins of their pictures in order to give tactful recognition to his influence 'behind the scenes'.[64] The demi-grisaille again throws the use of colour into relief and casts a flattering spotlight on Charles the Bold: the scarlet fabric and the gold chain signal his elevated status.

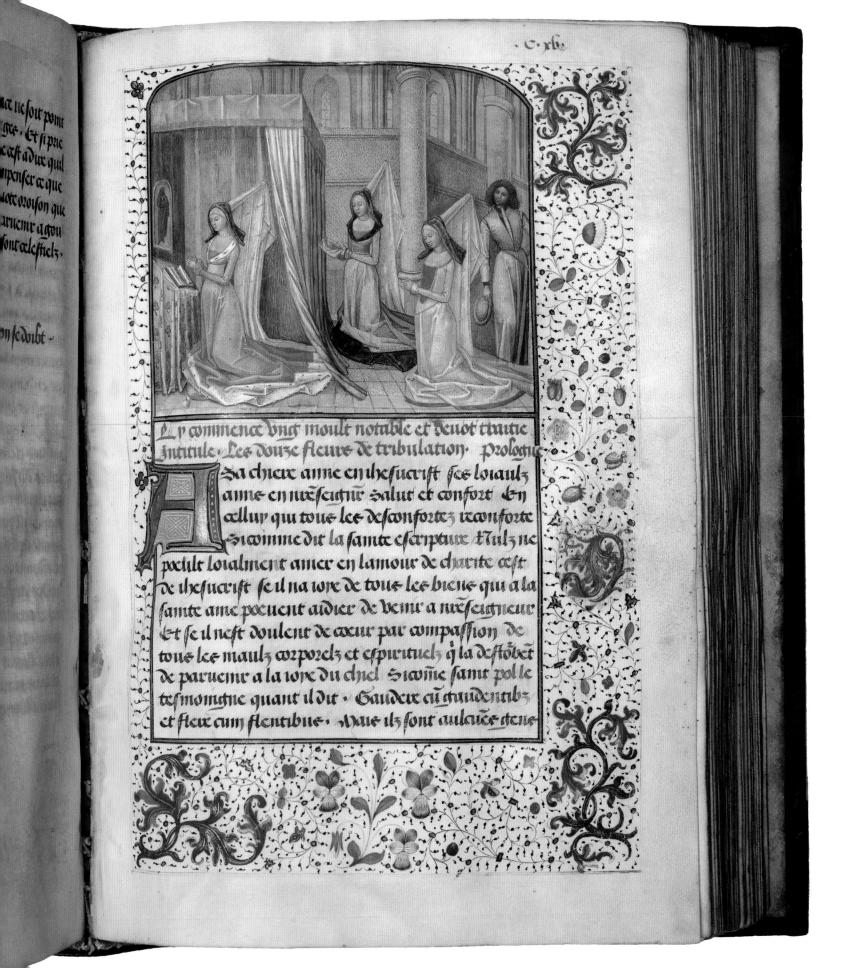

Ey commence vng moult notable et denot traitie
Intitule·Les douze fleurs de tribulation· Prologue

A ſa chiere ame en iheſucriſt ſes loiaulx
ame en nreſeigne ſalut et confort en
celluy qui tous les deſconfortez reconforte
Si comme dit la ſainte eſcripture Nulz ne
peult loialment amer en lamour de charite ceſt
de iheſucriſt ſe il na ioye de tous les biens qui a la
ſainte ame peuuent aidier de venir a nreſeigneur
et ſe il neſt doulent de cœur par compaſſion de
tous les maulx corporelz et eſpirituelz q̃ la deſtõbẽt
de paruenir a la ioye du ciel Si comme ſaint pol le
teſmoingne quant il dit · Gaudere cũ gaudentibz
et flere cũ flentibus· Mais ilz ſont aulcunes gens

For anyone interested in what England meant to the Burgundian Low Countries and vice versa, Jean de Wavrin's *Recueil des croniques et anchiennes istories de la Grant Bretaigne, à présent nommé Engleterre* (*Collection of Chronicles and Ancient Histories of Great Britain, Presently Called England*) and the history of its manuscripts are a goldmine of information. Jean de Wavrin (*c*.1400–*c*.1475) was from Lille, where French and Dutch were spoken, though the city was predominantly French speaking. He had Dutch-speaking relatives in Bruges, including a half-brother ('Jan Croset die men noemt de Wavrijn' – 'Jan Croset who is called Wavrijn') and an uncle ('Ianne de Wavriin').[65] His active service in the Anglo-Burgundian army kindled a lifelong interest in England, and when he retired as a diplomat, he indulged his Anglophilia by writing a history of England in order to show the joint destinies of France, England and Burgundy. He made friends with English noblemen such as John, duke of Bedford and regent of France, and Richard Neville, earl of Warwick, whom he visited personally in Calais (then an English colony) to glean reliable information that could perfect his history ('matieres veritables pur le parfait de mon euvre').[66] He visited England in person in 1467 in the company of Anthony, the 'Great Bastard of Burgundy' (he was the illegitimate son of Philip the Good), and there he saw the joust between the Great Bastard of Burgundy and Anthony Woodville. His adventures in England are briefly reported in the *Recueil des croniques*.

A first version of the *Croniques*, in four volumes, was issued by Wavrin around 1446. This begins with the mythical history of Britain based on Geoffrey of Monmouth and ends with the death of Henry IV, but Wavrin later decided to update it to the present. The result was a six-volume work, completed two years before he died. Expensively executed, lavish manuscripts of the *Croniques* were prized possessions. Louis de Gruuthuse, a personal acquaintance of Jean de Wavrin and, after Philip the Bold, the greatest collector of books (French, Dutch and Latin) in the period, owned a six-volume set.[67] Edward IV, who had taken refuge in Gruuthuse's palace in Bruges in 1470–71 and acquired from Gruuthuse a taste for expensive books, built up a royal collection of books from the Low Countries. Naturally, a manuscript of Wavrin's *Croniques* was part of it. This manuscript, now in the British Library, has a dedication addressed to Edward IV, and a donor illustration showing the author presenting the work to the king of England.[68]

2.8 Margaret of York, duchess of Burgundy, at prayer, from a compilation of French devotional texts (1475) commissioned by Margaret, written in Ghent by David Aubert and illuminated by the Master of Mary of Burgundy. Charles the Bold, Margaret's husband, makes a cameo appearance. Oxford, Bodleian Library, MS. Douce 365, fol. 115r.

Another set of manuscripts is associated with Dutch royalty: a copy of another version of the *Croniques* was owned by the House of Orange-Nassau, whose family members became stadtholders in the Netherlands and, in the nineteenth century, kings and queens of the nation. The volumes of this 'royal Dutch edition' that survive are now dispersed across different libraries: volume four is in the Walters Art Museum in Baltimore; volumes two, three and five are in the Royal Dutch Library in The Hague;[69] and ten illustrated leaves from volume two are now bound together in Oxford, Bodleian Library, MS. Laud Misc. 653. The value of these manuscripts is shown by their early history. They were produced in Bruges, in a workshop that was able to command the best talent from across the Low Countries.[70] The main illuminator, known as the Rambures Master after the patron of a different book of hours illuminated by him,[71] was active in Hesdin and Amiens but was then drawn to Bruges, where he collaborated with other artists on the decoration of Wavrin's chronicle. His illustration of the joust organized by Edward III in honour of the countess of Salisbury (fig. 2.9) captures the specific interests of Wavrin's *Croniques*: England is central to this chronicle, and more precisely the interactions between the Continental and the English 'flower of chivalry'. Edward III's jousts, attended, as Wavrin notes, by a whole host of international VIPs (prominent among them Duke William II of Hainault, count of Holland and Zeeland), deserve to be recorded and illustrated by the crème de la crème of scribes and illuminators, and what they produce in turn deserves the distinction of being owned by the greatest connoisseurs of expensive books.

The earliest owner of this particular copy is likely to have been Anthony of Burgundy, whose arms, partly painted over, can be seen on several pages of the second volume. But it soon came into the hands of another great bibliophile, Engelbert II, count of Nassau and lord of Breda, a long-standing friend and ally of Charles the Bold. From him, the set eventually passed down to William of Orange, leader of the Dutch independence revolt against the Spanish Habsburg Empire. When William's library, lodged in his castle in Breda, was confiscated by King Philip II of Spain, Philip sent his librarian to Breda with instructions to ship the finest books off to the Spanish royal library, the Escorial. The manuscripts of Wavrin's *Croniques* were part of the shipment. Soon after 1577, when the confiscation of William of Orange's goods was revoked, the manuscripts of Wavrin were taken back to the Netherlands.[72] The illuminations were so

2.9 Illustration of the tournament organized by Edward III in honour of the countess of Salisbury, from a copy of Wavrin's *Croniques* (fifteenth century, third quarter). Among the spectators at the tournament was Duke William II of Hainault, count of Holland and Zeeland. Oxford, Bodleian Library, MS. Laud Misc. 653, fol. 5r.

De la maniere et ordonnance de la grant feste et Joustes que le noble Roy dangleterre fist pour lamour de la Contesse de sallebrii/ le xlic chapitre.

Este feste fut grande noble et tres plentureuse sicque oncques parauant nauoit este veue la pareille ou royaulme dangleterre Et y vindrent le Conte guille de henault et messire Jehan son oncle auec eulx grant quantite baronnye et cheuallerie du pais de henault Et tant que a ceste plentureuse feste furent xij Contes viijS cheualliers et bS dames que damoiselles toutes

de grant et hault lignaige Laquelle feste fut bien Joustee et dansee par lespace de xv Joures mais vng Jeune et noble bacheler y fut tue au Jouster quy eut grant plainte Cest a scauoir messire Jehan aisne filz de messire henry Visconte de beaumont beau cheuallier et hardi quy sarmoit de azur seme de floure de lis a vng lion rampant en vng baston de gueules parmy lescu Toutes les dames et damoiselles furent

desirable, however, that someone cut out all the illustrated leaves from the second volume (the stubs are still visible). Ten leaves were recovered by Archbishop Laud, who bought them from sailors and donated them to the Bodleian.[73]

MIGRANT BOOK PRODUCERS

The economic boom in the Burgundian Low Countries that was reflected in the sumptuousness of Wavrin's manuscripts was not to last. The last Burgundian duke, Charles the Bold, died in 1477, and attempts by other countries to develop the cloth industry by emulation and by luring over enterprising 'strangers' proved successful.[74] The same strategy worked for the book industry. The political climate in England was generally hostile to foreign workers, but book producers were made to feel more welcome. Legislation passed in 1484 to restrict the freedom of migrant workers was drawn up with specific exemptions for craftsmen and merchants who imported or produced 'bokes wrytten or imprynted', or decided to reside 'within the said Realme for the same intent'.[75] Encouraged by these favourable conditions, a number of Netherlandish scribes and illuminators went to England to seek their fortunes, and in this final section we shall consider some outstanding examples.

The first is the Caxton Master, so called because his earliest known works were illustrations of William Caxton's English translation of the *Ovide Moralisé*, which Caxton himself entitled *The Book of Ovyde Named Metamorphose*.[76] We know Caxton as the man who introduced printing into England, and we will have more to say about his printing activities in the next chapter, but in this context it needs to be emphasized that book producers and booksellers in this period usually did not deal exclusively in printed books or exclusively in manuscripts, but instead in both. The 1484 legislation recognized this ('bokes writtyn or imprinted') and the stock of Caxton's 'George the booke sellar' also mixes up manuscripts with 'enprinted' books. Caxton also dealt in both types of books. The one surviving copy of his Ovid is in fact a manuscript, though it is likely he also had it printed. Caxton's translation probably dates from his time in the Low Countries (*c.*1446–76), because at some points in his translation (from a French text) Dutch words popped into his mind, such as *spyncop* (spider) and *bedwynge* (restrain).[77] To illustrate his Ovid, Caxton used a talented artist who specialized in pen drawings. The closest stylistic matches for these drawings are from Utrecht books

2.10 Avarice, personified as an old man clutching his coins, in an illustration by the 'Caxton Master' from the unique manuscript of *The Mirroure of the Worlde* (fifteenth century, third quarter), possibly made in William Caxton's commercial workshop. Oxford, Bodleian Library, MS. Bodl. 283, fol. 59r.

noon sholde seke in metys ne in oother thynges ./ to bodyly
delite ./ But men sholde & maye take siche as is nedeful
to the sustennce of the bodye ./ Soo that a man maye
serve prayse ./ & thanke his maker ./ And that a man ta
ke yt not with too greto ferventnes ./ ne in to grote qun
tite ./ And whoo soo taketh yt thus ./ yt is noo synne ./ but
yt is rather meede ./ Yet ther be som men that be goode
And mercyfull to oother ./ And cruel to theym selfe ./
And whoo soo be cruel to hym selfe ./ to whom is hee
goode ./ Seint Bernard seithe that a man sholde
not allweye troste to fylle his bely ./ And to doo alle
his wille ./ A man sholde rather governe yt ./ and re
freyne yt be reson ./

The b. heede vice is covetice ./ the
whiche regneth in the woorlde ./ that
nowe is ./ more than any oother
vice ./ Be the whiche yt shewith
that the woorlde ageth ./ and is
in his laste aage ./ ffor the woorl
de fareth as man ./ In a mannes yougthe ./ regneth more
jolynes and lecherye ./ than any oother vice ./ whan hee

of the 1460s,[78] and it is perhaps no coincidence that during this same period Caxton spent some years in Utrecht, where he may have met the Caxton Master.

The Mirroure of the Worlde in Oxford, Bodleian Library, MS. Bodl. 283, was also illustrated by the Caxton Master and probably came from Caxton's commercial workshop. The text is an English translation of Laurent d'Orléans's *Somme le roi* (*Survey for a King*). This moral treatise about vices and virtues, originally composed *c.*1279, was hardly shiny and new, but it enjoyed a new lease of life in the middle of the fifteenth century in lavishly illuminated manuscripts from Flanders (Margaret of York, for example, owned a copy, now in the Royal Library of Belgium).[79] MS. Bodl. 283 may well owe its existence to this Burgundian vogue for illustrated copies, here tailored to the interests of a merchant class: the Caxton Master's drawing shows Avarice, personified as an old man, clutching his coins, with his moneybox on the table and a moneybag hanging from his belt (fig. 2.10). His fixed expression is that of someone who has eyes only for his money. The manuscript was owned by, and perhaps commissioned for, Thomas Kippyng, a London draper. Once relocated to England, the Caxton Master started work in a commercial London workshop, and went on to illustrate more books for aristocratic patrons: *Writhe's Garter Book* (*c.*1480) and the *Beauchamp Pageant* (*c.*1485).

Netherlandish scribes also came to ply their trade in England.[80] The prolific scribe Theodoric Werken from Abbenbroek (near Rotterdam) was active in England in the second half of the fifteenth century. Most of his output is in Latin, an international language that presented no difficulties for anyone who was well educated, but he also penned text in English. In San Marino, Huntington Library, MS. HM 142, an English–Latin anthology containing works by John Lydgate and Richard Maidstone,[81] Werken was chiefly responsible for a set of Latin prayers, but he also wrote the rubric to these prayers and signed his name (fig. 2.11).

The English prose is perfectly understandable, but there are some oddities that show this is a Dutchman's English. The transcription of the English rubric reads:

> Who so wyl have hys desyr fulfyllyt in al godnes hi most say a
> .m.ᵗ ave Mari*a* in x dayys þat ys every day .c. wher þat ever he
> be havyng an almes in hys hond whyl dey ben a sayng & aftyr
> say þis oryson.

The superscript 't' after '.m.' (an abbreviation for Latin *mille*) makes more sense in Middle Dutch (where the normal form is *dusent*) than in English (where the word is usually spelled with a final 'd'),[82] and Werken lapses into the Dutch spelling of the pronoun 'hi', before recovering himself with 'he'. He was obviously familiar enough with English handwriting to know the standard ways of writing forms of the demonstrative pronouns 'that' and 'this' (thorn, þ, plus superscript 't' or 's'), but his thorn is indistinguishable from the 'y', which is abnormal except for northern scribes, and we see him make the same kind of mistake that we have encountered in Flemish books of hours when he writes 'd' for thorn in 'dey', duly corrected by a later hand to 'they'.[83] There is a hybridity in the scripts too. Werken was a master of new humanist *littera antiqua*, and his own name is in humanistic capitals, but for the Middle English and the Latin prayers that follow he adapted himself to the handwriting of the English scribe who copied Lydgate and Maidstone and settled for the more old-fashioned Gothic *textualis*, characterized by heavy vertical strokes and angular rather than rounded letters.

A fresh impetus for foreign book-artists was given by the Tudor kings Henry VII and Henry VIII, who embarked on a deliberate policy of internationalizing their courts. Artists and technicians of all kinds (painters, musicians, architects, map-makers and so on) from across the Continent (the Low Countries, Germany, Italy, etc.) were employed to raise the tone of English court fashion.[84] In the 1520s the first professional illuminators were employed at the Tudor court, and Henry VIII found the best: the Horenbout family from Ghent, consisting of Gerard Horenbout, previously on the payroll of Margaret of Austria, regent of the Habsburg Netherlands, and Gerard's children Susanna and Lucas, who both

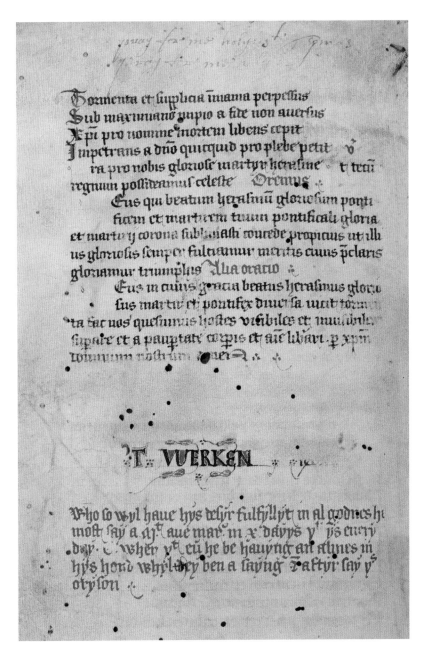

2.11 A Dutchman's English (1467): the Dutch scribe Theodoric Werken signs his name, and adds an English rubric to an anthology of English and Latin religious prose and verse, occasionally lapsing into Dutch habits (e.g. writing 'hi' for 'he'). San Marino, Huntington Library, MS. HM 142, fol. 60v.

followed in their father's footsteps to become painters, book decorators and portrait miniature artists.[85]

The Gospel lectionary of Cardinal Wolsey (Oxford, Magdalen College, MS. Lat. 223, *c.*1528), who was Lord Chancellor of England under Henry VII and Henry VIII before his fall from grace, shows the Horenbout family's work, and illustrates the stunning design of Flemish decoration from this period (fig. 2.12).[86] The plants are made to stand out against a coloured background and, by a *trompe l'œil* effect, look three-dimensional, as their flowers and leaves cast their shadows on it. Wolsey's coat of arms, including the red cardinal's hat, again looks as if it has been placed in front of the text block, because the top obscures our view of the frame. Readers will recognize in the historiated initial 'I' the scene of Thomas Becket's murder.

This manuscript was originally part of a pair: this one a lectionary of the Gospels, the other manuscript (now Oxford, Christ Church, MS. 101) a lectionary of the Epistles.[87] The scribe of both was another Netherlandish craftsman: Pieter Meghen, the most sought-after scribe in Tudor England, even decades after the introduction of print. The transition from manuscripts to printed books did not, of course, take place overnight, and in the late fifteenth century numerous manuscripts were even copied from printed books.[88] A friend of Erasmus (who called him 'Cyclops' because he had only one eye), Meghen also wrote books for Henry VIII and various other illustrious Englishmen, such as John Colet and John Fisher.[89] Key to his success was his perfection of the latest humanist script. As the illustration shows, this script broke away from traditional Gothic book hands in a self-conscious return to the handwriting of antiquity (though in fact *littera antiqua*, as this script is known, is modelled on early medieval Caroline minuscule, with elegantly rounded letters). The unusually generous spacing adopted by Meghen makes the reading experience a luxurious pleasure.

Manuscripts of this class were beyond the means of anyone except the super-rich, but a more modest manuscript too could be given a touch of class through the addition of a Flemish-style illustration. Oxford, Bodleian Library, MS. Ashmole 45, part 1 (*c.*1525), is nothing special. It is a paper book. Paper was first used for books in England in the second half of the fourteenth century, shortly after its adoption in the Low Countries, and had to be imported from the Continent, as England did not have a paper mill until late in the fifteenth century. The manuscript

2.12 The Gospel lectionary of Cardinal Wolsey, containing the readings from the Gospels to be read throughout the liturgical year. The manuscript was written by the scribe Pieter Meghen in a distinctly luxurious, spacious humanist script, and decorated by the Horenbout family. Oxford, Magdalen College, MS. Lat. 223, fol. 10v. Courtesy of The President and Fellows of Magdalen College, Oxford.

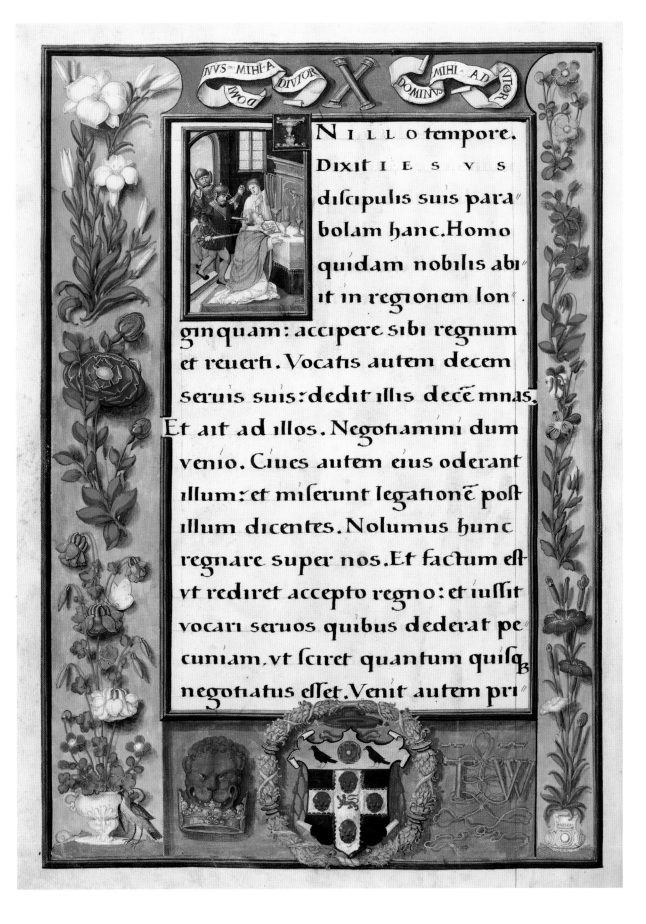

N ILLO tempore.
Dixit IESVS
discipulis suis para
bolam hanc. Homo
quidam nobilis abi
it in regionem lon
ginquam: accipere sibi regnum
et reuerti. Vocatis autem decem
seruis suis: dedit illis decē mnas.
Et ait ad illos. Negotiamini dum
venio. Ciues autem eius oderant
illum: et miserunt legationē post
illum dicentes. Nolumus hunc
regnare super nos. Et factum est
vt rediret accepto regno: et iussit
vocari seruos quibus dederat pe
cuniam, vt sciret quantum quisq̃
negotiatus esset. Venit autem pri

is written in a lower-grade cursive hand. The romance it contains, *The Erle of Tolous*, is the sensationalist tail-rhyme romance that Geoffrey Chaucer parodied in the Tale of Sir Thopas, and sophisticated readers of the time may have looked down on it. The scribe, who identifies himself as Morganus, has recently been recognized in a late fifteenth-century Chaucerian miscellany (Oxford, Christ Church, MS. 152).[90] But what lifts this book out of the ordinary is an illustrated donor page (fig. 2.13).

In this pen and colour-wash drawing, a fur-gowned gentleman presents a book (a proxy for the manuscript itself) to an equally finely dressed young lady, who can be identified by the rebus below as 'Maid Maria'. The drawing is Flemish in style, and there are close similarities with the portrait of Henry VIII, probably by one of the Horenbouts, in Wolsey's patent for Cardinal College (Kew, The National Archives, E 24/21/1),[91] which also has the same elaborate strapwork initials (here 'T' in 'The' at the top of the page). Written in humanistic capitals on the speech scroll are the words 'Prenes: en gre' ('Take this with pleasure'), a phrase that occurs frequently in the context of love lyrics and love gifts and suggests that this copy of the romance *The Erle of Tolous* was presented to Maria by a suitor.[92]

As MS. Ashmole 45 shows, the 'Flemish' style, perfected for the rich and powerful in the heyday of the Burgundian empire in the fifteenth century, became available in the sixteenth century to the aspirational classes. The invention of printing, the subject of our next chapter, was to make illustrated books even more widely accessible. Historians call it the 'Gutenberg revolution', but as we look back over six centuries of manuscript production on both sides of the North Sea, from the eleventh to the sixteenth centuries, we can also see revolutions in book history, such as the shift from monastic to urban centres of book manufacture, from bespoke production for a single patron to speculative 'assembly line' production for a larger market. Last but not least, this chapter has shown a complete revolution in Anglo-Dutch book relations. As we have seen, in the eleventh century the 'Winchester style' was coveted on the Continent and exported to the Low Countries; by the fifteenth century, however, it was the 'Flemish style' that held sway and was imported into England. The age of the manuscript thus needs to be recognized as a dynamic period, and the reversal of fashions reminds us that the cultural and commercial exchanges between England and the Low Countries were an important source of that dynamism.

2.13 Donor page of *The Erle of Tolous*: the drawing was probably done by the Horenbout studio, and the scripts range from elaborate strapwork initials and humanist capitals on the speech scroll, to decorative letters in the rebus, identifying the lady as 'Maid Maria'. Oxford, Bodleian Library, MS. Ashmole 45, fol. 2r.

I

Wm Browne

The Story of
the Kylo of Colone

PRENES ENGRE

MD & RIA

The foundation of all successe must be layd in
doing things well, and I am sure that will not
be don with English letters.

Bishop John Fell to Thomas Marshall, 1670

Nowhere are the close connections between England and the Low
Countries as conspicuous as in the early history of printing. The first
English-language book was printed by William Caxton in Flanders
*c.*1473, and the Low Countries continued thereafter to supply the English
market with English-language books. The earliest complete printed
English Bible, the 1535 Coverdale Bible, was produced in Antwerp and
printed either there or in Cologne, and many of the printers who were
active in England were Dutch-speaking migrants. The presence of
large numbers of these migrants in cities such as London and Norwich
encouraged local printers, English and Dutch, to publish texts in Dutch.
Established collaborations between printers and intellectuals in England
and the Low Countries also led to typographical innovations. It was type
founders in the Netherlands who refined the typeface needed to reproduce
Old English script. The equipment that was used to make it is kept in
the archives of Oxford University Press to this day, a memorial to the
contribution it made to the rise of this publishing house. In this chapter
we tell the story, starting in Germany, where printing in Europe began.

THE ORIGINS OF PRINTING

Leaving aside some fragmentary survivals, the first European book to
be printed using 'movable type' is the Gutenberg Bible (1455), produced
in Mainz and named after the printer Johann Gutenberg. Gutenberg
was a goldsmith by trade, and his skill was crucial in the development of
printing technology.[1] Printing was done with a hand press and involved
using frames set with lines of type to stamp ink on paper. Each line

Illustration from *A True Report and Description
of the Taking of the Iland and Towne of S. Maries,*
published in 1600 (detail of fig. 3.12)

consisted of individually cast pieces of metal for each letter, which could be used and reused to produce new lines and pages of text. A full set of pieces of type with a uniform appearance (but often including type of various sizes) is called a typeface.[2] From Germany the technique spread quickly, first to Italy and then to the Low Countries, where it arrived in the 1460s.

The earliest printers of the Low Countries who recorded their names in their books had learned their trade in Germany and/or Italy.[3] In the southern Netherlands these were Dirk Martens of Aalst and the German-born Johan van Westfalen. In Holland the pioneers were Nicolaes Ketelaer and Gerard van Leempt, whose first dated book is from 1473. The earliest books from the Low Countries were in Latin. It took a few more years for books to appear in the Dutch vernacular. The first dated book in Dutch (10 January 1477) is a Bible, published in Delft by Jacob Jacobszoon van der Meer and Mauricius Yemantszoon.[4]

This is now established history, but until the study of paper and typefaces was put on a solid footing, some believed that a Dutch printer from Haarlem – Laurens Janszoon Coster – invented printing. Legend has it that someone stole Coster's printing equipment and took it to Mainz: the German honour of having invented printing was thus glory stolen from the Dutch.[5] It is a great story and many people were ready to believe it, not just in Holland but also in Britain. John Spotswood, a Scottish professor who composed a fine preface to *The History of the Art of Printing*, printed by James Watson (Edinburgh, 1713), felt sure that printing was first invented in Haarlem, and concluded from this that it must have come to Scotland very soon too: 'we had printing very early here, nor could we miss being soon let into that Art, having, at the time of its invention, a close and constant trade with the Low Countries … And that we have it from Holland is clear from our cases and presses being all of the Dutch make, till of late years.'[6] In fact, Scotland did not have a printing press until 1507, and we now know the Coster legend to be an urban myth originating in a sixteenth-century attempt to glorify the achievements of the citizens of Haarlem.

However, alongside printing with movable type there flourished a different form of printing: block-book printing, which did originate in the Low Countries. Block-book printing involved cutting letters and pictures into wooden blocks. The blocks were coated in ink, and by pressing paper against them small picture books could be produced. An early reference

to the technology is found in court records from Louvain, where in 1452 the guild of carpenters sued a man named Jan van den Berghe for cutting 'letteren ende beeldeprynten' ('letters and images') into wood without being a member of their guild. Jan's defence was that his work was not comparable to other trades and that it served a religious purpose. He was

3.1 Scenes of the amorous children of Venus (left) and of the crafts of the children of Mercury (right). From an astrological treatise, *The Boke of Astronomy and off Philosophye* (fifteenth century, third quarter), copied (probably in Norwich) from a Dutch block book. Oxford, Bodleian Library, MS. Rawl. D. 1220, fols 31v–32r.

presumably a maker of blocks for devotional prints and/or block books, which were also predominantly religious in nature.[7] The earliest surviving block book, *c*.1450 if not earlier, is an illustrated Apocalypse, and is believed to originate from Haarlem, Laurens Coster's birthplace.[8]

Like other books, block books travelled. We can reconstruct the North Sea crossing of one particular block book: a 'planet book', with pictures of the seven planets of medieval cosmology and their 'children', the kinds of people thought susceptible to a particular planet's influence. We would now call it an astrological book, but contemporary readers made no distinction between astronomy and astrology and regarded both fields of enquiry as science. Originating in Holland, planet block books spread to Germany and Italy,[9] and one must have come to England. Perhaps it was in the luggage of one of the many Dutch speakers who settled in Norwich, because in the third quarter of the fifteenth century the pictures were replicated in a manuscript of an English astrological treatise, *The Boke of Astronomy and off Philosophye*,[10] which was probably copied in Norwich. An early owner of the manuscript was Nicholas Sywhat, alderman and mayor of Norwich (1535–36). One of its pages shows the manuscript illumination of 'children of Mercury' (fig. 3.1): painters, sculptors, clockmakers, organ builders, scribes and other craftsmen. The illustrator faithfully copied this and other pictures from a Netherlandish block book, a copy of which survives in the Statens Museum for Kunst, Copenhagen.[11]

CAXTON AS LOW COUNTRIES PRINTER

William Caxton is famous as the first English printer, but he also deserves to be ranked among the pioneers of printing in the Low Countries, where he spent the best part of his working life.[12] In his late teens he was apprenticed to Robert Large, the mayor of London. Sometime after Large's death in 1441, Caxton left England for Flanders, where he rose to become 'Governor of the English Nation' in 1462. In that role he directed the company of English merchants, the Merchant Adventurers, who had their headquarters in Bruges, the commercial centre of the cloth trade. In 1471–72 he was in the city of Cologne in Germany, where he got his first taste of printing by collaborating on an edition of the Latin encyclopedia *De proprietatibus rerum* (*On the Order of Things*) by Bartholomaeus Anglicus. Caxton's disciple, Wynkyn de Worde, remembered Caxton's first publishing venture in a four-line prayer for Caxton's soul at the end of his English-language edition of the same work (1495):

> And also of your charyte call to remembraunce
> The soule of William Caxton, first prynter of this boke
> In late tonge at Coleyn, hymself to avaunce,   [in Latin at Cologne]
> That every well disposyd man may theron loke.[13]

According to Wynkyn, Caxton's motive for printing this book was 'to advance himself', that is, to develop himself as a printer. In Cologne he was able to learn from the best, including the experienced printer Ulrich Zell and the master typographer Johan Veldener, who was to remain a close associate of Caxton's in years to come. Veldener developed the types for Caxton's earliest books, and followed Caxton to the Low Countries after his stay in Cologne, eventually setting up his own printing house in Louvain.[14]

We mentioned earlier that the first dated book printed with movable type from the Low Countries is from 1473. The date is worth repeating because it shows how precocious Caxton's earliest printed books are. After returning to the Low Countries, Caxton published the first printed book in English, *The Recuyell of the Historyes of Troye*, probably in Ghent *c.*1473. It was dedicated and presented to Margaret of York (wife of Charles the Bold, duke of Burgundy) who resided in Ghent for most of 1473 and early 1474. It was printed in a type produced by Veldener that was closely modelled on the handwriting of the Burgundian scribe David Aubert, who was also based in Ghent.[15] Also reminiscent of David Aubert's manuscripts is the engraved frontispiece of Caxton's *Recuyell*, which today survives uniquely in the Huntington Library copy of this book (fig. 3.2). The engraving portrays Caxton handing his book to Margaret of York, duchess of Burgundy.

The composition of the scene is strikingly similar to the portrait of Margaret of York in Oxford, Bodleian Library, MS. Douce 365, a devotional manuscript that was commissioned by her and copied by Aubert, which we discussed in the previous chapter (Chapter 2, fig. 2.8). In the miniature in the Douce manuscript Charles the Bold is at the back of the church (fig. 3.3), while in Caxton's frontispiece he is in the doorway. The motif of the male authority figure observing the scene from the margins has already been remarked upon by Lotte Hellinga.[16] No less

remarkable is the correspondence between the man in MS. Douce 365 and the courtier who stands by the window in the frontispiece: both hold their hat in their outstretched right arm, with their left hand placed on their hip. The atelier that produced MS. Douce 365 seems also to have been responsible for the engraving of Caxton's *Recuyell*.

The dating of Caxton's Low Countries editions is uncertain, but it seems that his next printed book was a French-language version of the same text: *Le receuil des hystoires troyennes* (Ghent, 1474?). Caxton's French *Receuil* is just as ground-breaking as his English version. Aside from a fragment of a translation of Donatus's *Ars Minor* (undated and unattributed, *c.*1470) printed in Holland, it is the earliest French book to be printed. The first dated French-language book from France is the *Legende doree*, printed in Lyon by Guillaume Leroy in 1476.[17] Caxton followed *Le receuil* with *The Game and Playe of the Chesse*, an allegory in which the various social responsibilities of people are compared to chess pieces and their functions in the game of chess. The book was published in Bruges in association with the Burgundian bookseller and publisher Colard Mansion.

The collaborative nature of Caxton's printing activities in the Low Countries was unavoidable. Book production, like all skilled trades, was strictly regulated in cities like Ghent and Bruges, and 'aliens' were not allowed to print books unless they teamed up with established guild members.[18] Making a virtue of this necessity, Caxton built up an excellent network of contacts, which he maintained after returning to England in 1476.

AFTER CAXTON: WYNKYN DE WORDE

Back in England, Caxton set up his printing shop next to Westminster Abbey. Some of his assistants in Flanders joined him in this new enterprise and took over the business when Caxton died in 1492. One of these, Wynkyn de Worde, deserves special mention. He is known above all as the man who brought the printing press to a broader public, diversifying his output to include popular romances, didactic books for children and devotional literature. His nickname, the 'Father of Fleet Street',[19] recognizes his status as the first printer on the famous street and also his work as a popularizer of literature. Together with

3.2 William Caxton presenting his Troy book to Margaret of York, duchess of Burgundy; standing in the doorway is her husband Charles the Bold. Engraved frontispiece of *The Recuyell of the Historyes of Troye*, printed by Caxton (1473/4), probably in Ghent. San Marino, Huntington Library, DeR 3.11, frontispiece.

another of Caxton's disciples, Richard Pynson (from Normandy), he left Westminster around 1496 to set up shop in London, which was then separate from Westminster. He was almost certainly a Dutchman. The suffix *-kyn* is a Dutch diminutive, and also very Dutch is the 'van' that occurs in some recorded forms of his name, such as 'Winandum van Worden'. 'Van Worden' or 'de Worde' suggests that he was born in Woerden, between Utrecht and Gouda. In the letter of denizenship, giving him the right to reside and work in England, he claimed to be from 'Lotharingia' (Lorraine), and 'Worde' has on that basis often been

3·3 [detail of fig. 2.8] Portrait of Margaret of York, duchess of Burgundy, with two ladies-in-waiting, and her husband, Duke Charles the Bold, in the background. From a compilation of devotional texts (1475), illuminated by the Master of Mary of Burgundy. Oxford, Bodleian Library, MS. Douce 365, fol. 115r.

taken to be Wörth in Alsace. However, Alsace is (and was) not Lorraine and it is in any case possible that Wynkyn used 'Lotharingia' with general reference to the Burgundian realm. The duke of Burgundy styled himself 'duke of Burgundy, Lotharingia, Brabant, etc.'.[20]

Wynkyn's close connections with the Low Countries book trade offer important clues to his provenance. As we shall see in Chapter 6, when he reprinted Caxton's *Reynard* around 1495, he embellished the original edition with woodcut illustrations modelled on those by the 'Haarlem Master'. In revising other Caxton editions, Wynkyn made changes that were similarly inspired by his reading of Dutch books.[21] For instance, for his new edition of the *Golden Legend* (1493), first published by Caxton some ten years earlier, he overhauled the typography and introduced some splendid woodcut initials, based on those first used in books printed in Gouda in 1486.

It is fitting that *The Chastising of God's Children*, probably Wynkyn's earliest publication and the first English book to be printed at Westminster with a title page,[22] has strong associations with the Low Countries. *The Chastising* is a Middle English religious compilation (*c.*1400) that brings together extracts from many different authorities, including the Brabant mystic Jan van Ruusbroec (d.1381). The Middle English author relied especially on Ruusbroec's *Geestelijke bruiloft* (*Spiritual Wedding*), which he knew in a Latin translation.[23] A scruffy fragment of this Middle English treatise, printed by Wynkyn around 1493, is now in the Bodleian Library (fig. 3.4).

As a witness to the original text, this fragment is of little value, not only because Wynkyn introduced various errors, but also because the modern restoration of the fragment has made it hard to read. The two pages that are conjoined in the fragment (the left-hand margin of the second page was cropped) do not actually go together. Comparing the text here with that of the standard edition,[24] it becomes clear that the first page is from a later chapter (chapter 25) than the second page (from chapter 24). However, the fragment comes into its own as a witness to Anglo-Dutch relations: it was recovered from the binding of an edition of Erasmus of Rotterdam's *Ecclesiastes* (a preaching manual), printed in Antwerp in 1539.[25] The edition was presumably acquired unbound by an English client, who had it bound in England, where pages from a copy of Wynkyn's *Chastising* that had fallen into disuse were used to reinforce the binding.

The first native Dutch speaker on the Continent to move into the English market for printed books was Gerard Leeu, the most important and prolific early printer of the Low Countries. At least ninety Dutch books can be attributed to him, the vast majority of these being first editions. Unusually for the time, he began printing in Dutch in 1477 and branched out into Latin books only later (in 1480).[26]

William Caxton, who had visited Gouda only a couple of years earlier,[27] may have met Leeu in Gouda, where he started his career before moving to Antwerp. Whatever their personal relationship, each kept a close watch on the other's professional activity. When Leeu published the beast epic of Reynard the Fox, *Reynaerts historie* (the first extant edition is from 1479), Caxton spotted its potential and brought out his own translation in 1481. When Caxton died in 1491, Leeu filled the gap in the market with a flurry of English-language books. Most of these were illustrated editions

3.4 Fragment from the earliest surviving edition of *The Chastising of God's Children*, printed by Wynkyn de Worde *c.*1493. Two leaves have been pasted together. The fragment was recovered from the binding of a copy of Erasmus's *Ecclesiastes*, printed in Antwerp in 1539. Oxford, Bodleian Library, Inc.e.E1.2

of Burgundian romances printed by Caxton, such as *The History of Jason* and *Paris and Vienne*. However, Leeu's *Salomon and Marcolph* (1492) is an exception. It survives in just a single copy, in the Bodleian Library, and is refreshingly unchivalric in tone.[28] In this debate between King Solomon and the peasant Marcolph, privilege and erudition are pitted against the low-brow proverbs and home truths offered by Marcolph, 'right rude and great of body ... but right subtyll & wyse of wyt'. The woodcut opening the text (fig. 3.5) captures the ideological battle beautifully: the ruler on his throne meets the churl, and his raised sceptre meets Marcolph's pitchfork. The same confrontation is present on the printed page, where the 'Bastarda' script associated with the deluxe illuminated manuscripts of the Burgundian rulers meets the cheap and cheerful format of the quarto edition.

Salomon and Marcolph was Leeu's swansong. He was killed in a violent brawl with his assistant and news of his death was announced to the world in a colophon to his *Chronicles of Englond* (1493, first printed by Caxton in 1480), which was posthumously printed by his assistants:

> Here ben endyd the Cronycles of the Reame of Englond with their apperteignaunces. Enprentyd In the Duchye of Braband in the towne of Andewarpe In the yere of our lord .M.cccc.xciij [1493], by mastir Gerard de Leew, a man of gret wysdom in all maner of kunnyng [knowledge], which nowe is from lyfe unto the deth, which is grete harme for many a poure man. On whos sowle God almyghty for hys hyghe grace have mercy.

So a book from Antwerp says goodbye in English to a Dutchman who died before he could bring his edition of an English history to completion.

Leeu passed on his mantle as the publisher of English bestsellers to another Antwerp printer, Jan van Doesborch, who apart from printing in English also moonlighted as a Dutch–English translator and worked as a 'stranger' in London for some years during the 1520s.[29] He seems to have had close business associations with London printers, and with Wynkyn de Worde in particular, because several of the books he printed in Dutch are translations and adaptations of Wynkyn's English books.[30] In English literary history, his claim to fame is that he introduced the English to the delights of the picaresque novel.[31] The heroes of this genre are disreputable rogues who have colourful adventures and amuse themselves (and us)

by playing pranks on their social betters. Examples are *Tijl Uilenspiegel*, which Doesborch published in 1519 as *Howleglas* (*Owl's Mirror*), and the *Parson of Kalenborowe* (1520), starring a thoroughly disreputable cleric. As a punishment for outrageous sins (like pretending he can fly and then selling foul wine to the parishioners who have come out to watch), the bishop orders the parson to assist him as he travels around the bishopric consecrating chapels. Preferring a life of ease, the parson bribes the bishop's lover to allow him access to his bedroom. He hides under the bed and, when the bishop and his lady make love, he interrupts proceedings by reassuring the bishop that he is always present when the bishop is 'consecrating a chapel' (fig. 3.6). The bishop immediately releases him from his obligations.

3.5 *Salomon and Marcolph*, printed in Antwerp by Gerard Leeu (1492). The woodcut shows King Solomon and the peasant Marcolph. The edition continues to use the deluxe typeface based on the scripts of Burgundian court scribes, but marks a move toward smaller, cheaper publications. Oxford, Bodleian Library, Tanner 178 (3), frontispiece and fol. 1r.

The internationalization fostered by the Gutenberg revolution meant that literature in Dutch began to exert a powerful influence on English literature. The Dutch play *Mariken van Nieumeghen* entered England through a prose translation, *Mary of Nemmegen*, by Doesborch, and the best-known Middle Dutch play *Elckerlijc* was translated into English as *Everyman*, and printed on at least four separate occasions. The earliest edition was printed by Pynson, *c.*1518–19, and survives in just two printed fragments,[32] one of them in the Bodleian Library (fig. 3.7).

PRINTING THE ENGLISH REFORMATION

In the last decades of the fifteenth century, printing had become concentrated in a handful of centres, most notably Venice, Paris and Basel. However, the Low Countries were also starting to play a more important role in the trade, and in the sixteenth century they punched significantly above their weight. Their publishing industry was larger than any other relative to the size of the local population. The Low Countries accounted for less than 4 per cent of Europe's population in the sixteenth century, but published around 10 per cent of its books.[33] While this industry in the Low Countries was initially relatively decentralized, by the 1520s Antwerp had become predominant, and England a chief market for Antwerp's output.[34] Over 400 books in English were printed in the Netherlands in the sixteenth century, making it the principal centre publishing English books outside England. Continental European news for the English market was one of Antwerp's early outputs for export markets, soon followed by clandestine vernacular English Protestant tracts during the reign of Henry VIII.[35] These were printed and exported in great numbers, in spite of such vernacular works for the local market, in Dutch, being suppressed by authorities in Antwerp from 1530 onwards.

The publication of vernacular bibles was not prohibited in the Low Countries, and bibles in French, Danish, English and Dutch, as well as

3.6 *Parson of Kalenborowe*, printed in Antwerp by Jan van Doesborch (1520). The woodcut depicts the parson under the bed of the bishop and his lady. Doesborch successfully introduced the picaresque novel to English audiences. Oxford, Bodleian Library, Douce K 94, sig. Ciir.

And now we frēdes let vs go without lenger tarȳꝫ
I thanke god that ye haue taryed so longe
Nowe [ ] eche of you on this rodde his honde
And shortly folowſ me
I go before there I wolde be
God be our guyde
¶ Euery man we wyll not fro you go
Tyll ye haue gone this vyage longe
¶ I discrecion wyll byde by you also
¶ And though this pilgrimage be neuer so strōge
I wyll neuer parte you fro
Euery man I wyll be as sure by the
As euer I dyde by Iudas machabee
¶ Alas I am so faynt I may not stonde
My lymmes vnder me do folde
Frendes let vs not turne agayne to this londe
Not for all the worldes golde
For in to this caue muste I crepe
And torne to the erthe and there to slepe
¶ What in to this graue alas
¶ Ye therof shall ye consume more and lesse
¶ And what sholde I smoder her
¶ Ye by my say and neuer more appere
In this worlde lyue no more we shall
But in heuen before the hyest lorde of all

Beaute goth faste awaye and hye
She promysed with me to lyue and dye
Euery man I wyll the also forsake a[ ]waye
[ ]game lyketh me not at all
[ ]v than ye wyll forsake me all
[ ]strength tary a lytell space
[ ] ꝑ by the rode of grace
I wyll hye me fro the faste
Though thou wepe tyll thy herte to braste
¶ Ye wolde euer byde by me ye sayd
¶ Ye I haue you ferre ynough conueyd
ye be olde ynough I vnderstonde
your pylgrymage to take on honde
I repente me that I hether came
¶ Strength you to displease I am to blame
Wyll ye breke promyse that is dette
¶ In fayth I care not
¶ Thou arte but a foole to complayne
[ ]our speche and waste your brayne
Go thr[ ]ye in to the grounde
¶ I had wen [ ]ter I sholde you haue founde
He that truste[ ]in his strength
She hym dece[ ]th at the length
Both strength and beaute forsaketh me
yet they promysed me fayre and louyngly

in Latin, were produced in Antwerp.[36] Even some of the Dutch bibles, however, betray the English links of their producers. Among the many books printed in Antwerp for the publisher and bookseller Peter Kaetz, for whom many liturgical books in Latin were printed,[37] is a Bible in Dutch, published in 1525, volumes of which conclude with a woodcut of the English Royal Arms (fig. 3.8).[38] Kaetz, himself originally from Antwerp,[39] had been based in London from 1522, but appears to have resettled in Delft in 1525.[40] The van Ruremunds, the same Antwerp printers who printed this bible for Kaetz, also produced news about England for Dutch readers,[41] and a phrase book that could be used by both Dutch and English speakers to pick up the basics of each other's language.[42] It is not clear why the printers chose to include the English Royal Arms as a device in these

3.7 One of only two surviving fragments of the first edition of the play *Everyman*, printed in London by Richard Pynson (*c*.1518–19), recovered from a binding. Names of the dramatis personae can be seen in the margin, partly cut off. Oxford, Bodleian Library, Douce Fragm. f.10, fols iiv–iiir.

3.8 Woodcut of the English Royal Arms, used as a device by printers of the van Ruremund family including Catherine van Ruremund, for both clandestine and authorized English and Dutch publications from the 1520s to the 1540s. Here used in a Dutch Bible (1525). Oxford, Bodleian Library, O.T. Dutch g.1 (d.3), sig. [Xviii]v.

Dutch-language bibles. Possibly they were included as a decoy, to imply a provenance outside the Netherlands and thus avoid scrutiny by local authorities wary of Lutheran Dutch output.

At least as common as book production in English was the production of books in Latin for the English market. It is often hard to identify whether a specific edition was intended for sale in England, and indeed many editions will have been meant for a market that stretched from Glasgow to Naples. Sometimes, however, the name of an English bookseller or publisher is included on the title page, as is the case with several editions of Latin school books printed by Dirk Martens of Antwerp for Judocus Pelgrim and Henricus Jacobi in London in 1507–8.[43] Occasionally English readers wrote their names in imported books. A curious example is a copy of the Latin moralized Aesop's *Fables*, published by Gerard Leeu in Antwerp in 1488, in which one naughty English schoolboy jotted down the cast list for a play to be performed by a group of five actors.[44] In other cases, such as books of hours which followed a particular liturgy, the content – 'Sarum', that is, following the liturgy of Salisbury – is a clear indicator that a book was meant for English readers.[45] The English market for liturgical books, which had previously been exploited by manuscript producers in the Low Countries, continued to be seen as an attractive one by sixteenth-century printers.

The early Reformation provided a new stimulus for books crossing the North Sea, since it drove not only migration but also a demand for religious texts. English Protestants fleeing to the Continent in the 1520s, when Henry VIII's dedication to Catholicism was still unwavering, developed relations with local publishers to print religious tracts for importation back into England. In these years, English books of William Tyndale and his Lutheran associates were printed by the Antwerp printer Merten de Keyser and furtively imported into England,[46] to circumvent the controls imposed on religious publications there. Antwerp itself, however, was ruled by the Catholic Charles V, and many of de Keyser's publications therefore carried false imprints in order to evade identification by the authorities.

The opportunities for the Dutch book trade in England were contingent on political developments: the suppression of the printing of Protestant ideas of the 1520s was followed by a period of relative freedom in the 1530s, to be followed in turn by intensified suppression of unauthorized religious publications from 1538.[47] Printers and publishers, driven in part by religious inclinations, but also always concerned with the commercial interest of their endeavours, were quick to take advantage of opportunities. And so, during a period of relative freedom to publish religious pamphlets in England itself, the sophisticated Antwerp industry took on an ambitious project that exceeded the capability of London printers at the time: in 1535 the first complete Bible in English was conceived in Antwerp. It was the work of Miles Coverdale, an English Protestant who had first fled England in 1528, and had eventually found refuge in Antwerp.[48] Coverdale had been working to complete Tyndale's project of translating the Bible into English. The publication of the resulting bible followed one month after the excommunication of King Henry VIII, and thus its producers could hope to find a receptive environment in England. Coverdale at this point (as he specified, 'whan I had translated this Bible'[49]) decided to dedicate the work to the king, whose portrait and arms graced the title page (fig. 3.9). The politically precarious circumstances of publication, however, led the publisher to omit an imprint from the title page. Anonymity would not have been seen as an unnecessary precaution: one of the Coverdale Bible's contributing authors, Tyndale, had that same year been arrested by local authorities in Antwerp at the request of the English crown, and was awaiting execution by strangulation and burning.[50]

The ploy was successful in confounding English censors and bibliographers alike, and the Coverdale Bible of 1535 is still often listed as printed in 'Zürich?'. To this day, the exact place of printing remains disputed. Dutch scholars, however, knew long ago that it was connected with Antwerp, and that Coverdale's work itself was financed by a Dutchman, Jacob van Meteren. They took this information from a short biography of Jacob's son, Emanuel van Meteren, appended to an early edition of the latter's history of the Netherlands. Here, Emanuel's biographer tells us:

> Sijn Vader in sijn Jeucht hadde gheleert die edele Conste van 't Letter setten, hy was begaeft met de kennisse van veelderley talen ende andere goede wetenschappen, wist van in die tijden t'licht t'onderscheyden van duysternisse, ende bethoonde sijnen bysonderen yver in 't becostighen vande oversettinghe ende Druck vanden Engelschen Bijbel binnen Antwerpen, daer toe ghebruyckende den dienst van een gheleert Student met namen Miles Coverdal, tot groote bevoorderinghe van het Rijcke Jesu Christi in Enghelandt.[51]

> *His father, in his youth, had learned the noble art of typesetting; he was gifted with knowledge of many languages and other disciplines, knew in those times how to distinguish the light from the darkness, and showed particular diligence in financing the translation and printing of the English Bible at Antwerp, using the services of a learned student named Miles Coverdale, to the great promotion of the Kingdom of Jesus Christ in England.*

3.9 The Coverdale Bible, the first complete printed English Bible, produced in Antwerp. The title is framed by scenes from the Old Testament (left) and New Testament (right), while the English Royal Arms and Henry VIII's portrait provide the impression of royal approval. Oxford, Bodleian Library, S.Seld c.9, title page (in facsimile).

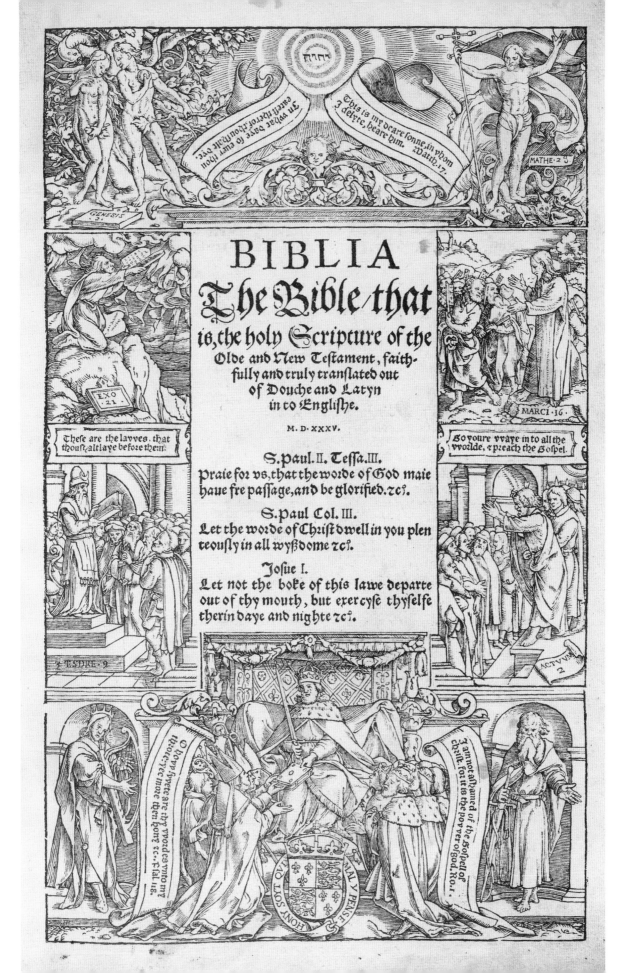

BIBLIA

The Bible, that

is, the holy Scripture of the
Olde and New Testament, faithfully and truly translated out
of Douche and Latyn
in to Englishe.

M. D. XXXV.

S. Paul. II. Tessa. III.
Praie for vs, that the worde of God maie
haue fre passage, and be glorified. &c.

S. Paul Col. III.
Let the worde of Christ dwell in you plen
teously in all wyssdome &c.

Josue I.
Let not the boke of this lawe departe
out of thy mouth, but exercyse thyselfe
therin daye and nighte &c.

It has since been argued that the work was also printed in Antwerp, possibly by Merten de Keyser, who had previously published many clandestine publications of Tyndale and his colleagues, though Cologne is maintained as another possibility.[52]

The title page of the Coverdale Bible presented it as 'faithfully and truly translated out of Douche and Latyn in to Englishe', where 'Douche' is probably German, not Dutch. In his introduction, Coverdale noted that, while compiling his English Bible,

> to help me herin, I have had sondrye translacions, not only in latyn, but also of the Douche interpreters: whom (because of their synguler gyftes & speciall diligence in the Bible) I have ben the more glad to follow for the most parte, accordynge as I was requyred.[53]

Later editions omit this information: direct translation from Hebrew and Greek would have been preferable; in the absence of direct translation, other languages could remain unmentioned, as they were no selling point for an increasingly sophisticated Protestant readership. Its demands soon led to further revised versions of the English Bible.[54] Two were printed in 1537, one of which was the work of another English Protestant refugee, John Rogers, who was also an associate of Jacob van Meteren. He returned to England with his family in 1548, but was burned at the stake in 1555, under Mary I.[55]

In 1539 an officially sanctioned version of the English Bible followed, the Great Bible, itself a revision of Coverdale's version.[56] At the same time, with the passing of the Act of Six Articles and the execution of Thomas Cromwell, the tide turned against the publication of Continental Protestant ideas in English. That English government control of the press stopped at the British North Sea coast provided a new impetus for Antwerp publishing houses to put out clandestine English works. A new generation of Antwerp printers took advantage of this commercial opportunity, while also motivated by the desire to propagate the new religion. Their publications were consistently protected by false imprints, alleging places of publication such as Geneva, Leipzig and Zurich. These claims were at least plausible, since some English works were in fact printed in these locations.

One of this generation of printers in Antwerp, actively printing English clandestine religious materials in the late 1530s and early 1540s, was Catherine van Ruremund, widow of Christoffel van Ruremund.[57] Christoffel had been a printer of liturgical books for the English market, and used his trade network to establish himself as the first Antwerp printer of English Protestant works, publishing William Tyndale's English New Testament in 1526. The trade of prohibited works to England, however, was evidently not without risk: Christoffel ended his life in prison in Westminster after being captured in 1530 during a journey selling copies of Tyndale's New Testament in London.[58] This left his widow Catherine in charge of the business in Antwerp. She was undeterred by her husband's death. An impressive sixty-seven English and Dutch editions issued between 1534 and 1546 either carry her imprint or can be attributed to her, covering a wide range of genres: English Bible translations, English religious prose,[59] an English almanac and prognostication,[60] works on Dutch current events, Dutch prognostications, a Dutch ballad,[61] proclamations by Emperor Charles V in Dutch and French and even a few proclamations by King Henry VIII in Dutch.[62] In her clandestine publications, Catherine continued to use the woodcut of the English Royal Arms that had earlier been used by her husband (fig. 3.8). While Catherine van Ruremund's Dutch output was mostly orthodox, the English output was almost exclusively dissenting, with one line of publication for an English readership forming a significant exception: in 1532 and again in 1541–45, Catherine published several Latin liturgical books for Sarum use.[63] Were these books simply an attractive commercial proposition or were they a cover under which to carry out the trade in banned books for the English market? Or did both motives apply?

The opportunities for Dutch printers to publish clandestine English religious works depended not only on the existence of a market, but also in part on the lack of opportunities for local English printers to service that market, given the dangers they would face. The production of English religious works in the Netherlands was therefore contingent on the fortunes of the new religion in England. Publishers, however, were typically flexible and opportunistic. Following the coronation of the staunchly Protestant Elizabeth I, printers in the Low Countries simply switched to publishing Catholic recusant books instead, followed towards the end of the sixteenth century by Puritan and other dissident Protestant works, while simultaneously servicing the Dutch market with translations of English and Scottish Puritan and devotional works.[64] Fake imprints, providing a certain level of security to publishers, would long remain a mainstay of this industry. In the 1570s, for example, the London printer William Carter printed recusant tracts in English under the false places of printing Douai and Bruges.[65] Imprints were also a form of branding, and apparently misleading imprints could therefore also have commercial rather than political motivations. In the 1580s the Londoner Thomas Purfoot printed books under the name of his Dutch business partner, Christophe Plantin, which was recognized as that of the most prestigious printing house of the age.[66]

DUTCH PRINTING IN ENGLAND

The increasing frequency of religious persecutions and the subsequent movement of religious refugees between countries made it inevitable that not only books, but eventually also their publishers and printers, crossed the North Sea. Jacob van Meteren, who had financed the Coverdale Bible, moved to London in the early 1550s. He and his wife met an unfortunate end during one North Sea crossing, just around the time their son, Emanuel van Meteren, was about to join them and the newly founded Protestant congregation of the Dutch Church of Austin Friars in London. The Dutch Church, founded in 1550, immediately became a hub for the rapidly growing Dutch community of London, and its existence also led to the establishment of Dutch printing activity in the city. Steven Mierdman, who in the 1540s had established himself as a printer of both Dutch and English religious tracts in Antwerp,[67] was one of its earliest members. In 1551 he serviced the early foundation with a Dutch summary of the church's teachings and a Dutch catechism for the children.[68] New versions were published a year later by Nicolaes van den Berghe,[69] a printer whose name was occasionally anglicized as Nicolas Hill.[70] The Dutch Reformed Church was suppressed by Queen Mary upon her accession in 1553. About 175 members promptly fled in two Danish ships that happened to be waiting in the Thames for a favourable wind. Following a tortuous journey, during which they were refused entry at several places, they resettled in the city of Emden in Lower Saxony,[71] where there was already a Dutch congregation;[72] others joined them over time. Van den Berghe and Mierdman continued to print in Emden. Among their publications were editions of both the catechism and the teachings of the Dutch Church in London. A successor continued to print regular editions in Emden into the 1560s.[73] Title pages of Emden editions of the Psalms noted that the Dutch lyrics were the ones 'diemen in de Duydtsche ghemeynte te Londen was ghebruyckende' ('that were customarily used in the Dutch congregation of London').[74] Others had as their place of printing 'buyten Londen' ('outside London').[75] In four short years, the London congregation of the Dutch Church had acquired for itself an identity that was inherently linked to the city, a diaspora community defined by its origins both in the Dutch Low Countries and in London.

After the accession of Elizabeth I in 1558, the Dutch Church of London was once again restored in 1560. Many of the Emden exiles returned, and the congregation was replenished with new arrivals from the Netherlands. The Dutch Church was not, however, re-established with the same privileges and independence it had previously enjoyed under Edward VI: under the Elizabethan settlement, it was made subject to the bishop of London.[76] The printing of texts required by the members of the Dutch Church was also now to be carried out by an established London printer. In 1561 its Dutch Psalms, catechism and core teachings were once again printed in London, but they were now published under the imprint of the prolific London publisher John Day rather than of a member of the congregation. The publications were a success, and demand was met by multiple reprints between 1561 and 1566 (fig. 3.10).[77] That year another Dutch printer, Garrat (Gerard) Dewes, made an attempt to capture the market for Dutch books servicing the Dutch congregation.[78] Yet another Dutch printer in London, Henry Bynneman, printed religious

3.10 *De Kleyne Catechismus* (*The Small Catechism*, 1566), printed in London by John Day. This was a reprint of the catechism for the Dutch Church of London printed by Dutch printers in London, and then in Emden, in the 1550s and 1560s. Oxford, Bodleian Library, Mason T 2, title page.

tracts in Dutch,[79] and subsequently also literature, publishing the second collection of Dutch poems by a London author, Jan van der Noot, in a collaboration with John Day, who had earlier published van der Noot's first collection.[80] Day's own origins are uncertain,[81] but early in his career he already had several Dutchmen living with and working for him,[82] and his name was listed as publisher on publications of local Dutch printers such as Steven Mierdman.[83] Considering Day's and Bynneman's collaboration on the publication of van der Noot's work, Bynneman may well have been involved in Day's Dutch publications from the early 1560s, ensuring the accuracy of the Dutch typography. By the late 1560s Day's dominance in the London market for Dutch works was complete.[84] This fact was widely recognized: a Dutch political pamphlet about English affairs in 1571 borrowed credibility by adopting his imprint, even though it was in fact the work of the Calvinist publisher Nicolaes Gevaertsz in Wesel.[85]

Soon Dutch Reformed congregations also existed in Sandwich, Thetford, Colchester, King's Lynn, Maidstone, Yarmouth, Ipswich, Canterbury, Southampton and, most prominently, Norwich.[86] Dutch communities formed significant minorities in several cities: by the 1580s, 20 per cent of the population of Colchester, and one third of the population of Norwich, originated from the Low Countries.[87] In 1567 a second centre for Dutch printing in England was established in Norwich, home of the second Dutch Reformed Church in England. Anthonius de Solempne, arriving from Brabant, established his press here – the very first printing press in Norwich.[88] Within three years de Solempne had published several works in Dutch, some of which were evidently meant for a local market: a psalter, a confession of faith and a calendar containing a range of historical and practical information especially useful to readers with interests on two sides of the North Sea (fig. 3.11).[89]

Norwich, with its strong mercantile ties to the Netherlands, was also a convenient place from which to service the Dutch market. The polemical Dutch works de Solempne published may well have been meant primarily for a readership in the Low Countries.[90] Likewise, some Dutch editions printed in London were meant for a Dutch-speaking readership in the Netherlands, not England: in 1581 Thomas Vautrollier printed one anti-Catholic pamphlet 'gheschreven aen alle inwooners onser goet-jonstighe vader-stadt S. Truyden' ('written to the inhabitants of our benevolent paternal city St Truiden'), in the Catholic southern Netherlands,[91] as well

October/Wijnmaent.

De tienste Maent heeft xxxi. daghe/de Mane xxx. By dē Hebreen THISRI, oft ETHANIM: ende is de achtste.

1	A	Remig. en
2	b	(Bauo
3	c	Candidus
4	d	Franciscus
5	e	
6	f	Fides
7	g	Marttijn pa.
8	A	
9	b	Dionisius
10	c	Victor
11	d	Gommar
12	e	Cypriaen
13	f	Son in scor.
14	g	Son op ten 7.
15	A	ond. ten 5.
16	b	Gallus abt
17	c	Florentius
18	d	Lucaseua
19	e	(gelijt
20	f	
21	g	Elf m.maec.
22	A	Seuerus
23	b	Seuerinus
24	c	Felix matt.
25	d	Crispijn en
26	e	(Crispiaen
27	f	
28	g	Symon en
29	A	(Iudas
30	b	Eusebius
31	c	

Den i. wert den Ioden de feest der Basuynen beuolen, Leui. 23.24.

Den derden vasteden de Ioden, en beschreydeden Godoliam. Ierem. 41.

Dé vi. wert Vlricus Zwinglius verslagen te Cappelle in Zwitserlant. Anno 1531.

Den xv. Begonste de Feeste der Loouerhutten, die seuen daghen duerder Leu. 23.24.

Op den seluen dach wert Soliman gedreuen vã het belech van Weenen in Oostenriick, door Philippũ Paltzgraue, en verloos acht duysent Turcken, Anno 1529.

Den xviii. (die den 150. was van het begin der Diluuie) ruste de Arcke op den Berch vã Ararat in Armenien. Ge.8,4.

Den 24. wept Titus drie duysent Ioden den wilden Beesten voor, in het Iaer na de geboorte Christi.73.

Den 31. begonste M. Luther teghen des Paus Aflaten questien te maken. 102. Iaer na dat Ioannis Hus verbrant was.

Iaermercten.

Dé 1.Arele/Audenaerde/vl. Harlinghen / Dochem / vri. Den 4.Breda/Cyndoué/vr. Rummerswale/Zee. Des maendaechs nae den eersten/Gorcum/hollant. Des later. daer na/Aelst/vl. Liere br. Amersfoort/Waelwijc/hol. Dé 6.S.Faes/ing. Dé 10.Doché/Francke/vri. Des woonsd. na dé 9. Dieft/bra. Sgrauensande. Schoohoué/hol.Dé 13. Meessen/vl bra.Dé 18.Brussel/br. Haerle/Dort.hol.Sottegem/vlaen.

November/Slachtmaent.

De elfste Maent heeft xxx. daghen. De Mane xxx. By den Hebreen MARESVAN, oft BVL, en is de neghende.

1	D	Alle hevil.
2	e	Alder sielen
3	f	Hubrecht
4	A	Modesta
5	b	Felix
6	b	Leonardus
7	c	Willeboort
8	D	De vier ge-
9	e	(croonde
10	f	Theodorus
11	g	Marttijn
12	A	Lebuijn
13	b	Brictius
14	c	Son in sagt.
15	D	Serapion
16	e	Secundus
17	f	
18	g	Autaen
19	A	Elizabeth
20	b	
21	c	Marie pres.
22	D	Cecilia
23	e	Son op te 8.
24	f	ond. te iiij.
25	g	Catharina
26	A	Petrus bss.
27	b	
28	c	Vitalis ma.
29	d	
30	e	Andries a.

Desen Feestdach vã alle Heyligen, is eerst ingeset van Bonifacio de iiij. om te vieren op dē xiij. Mey, anno.610. Daer na is hy herset op desen eersten Nouembris, van Gregorio de iiij. ontrent den Iare 840.

Den iiij. heeft ELIZABETH de ghenadige Coninginne van Enghelant den vreemdelingen vergunt de stadt Norwits, om aldaer te woonen: en den 24. December is de Duytsche Kercke open ghedaen, anno 1565.

Den xv. was de Feestdach die Ieroboam instelde tot Dan en Bethel, na dat hy de guldé Calueren dede oprichté. 1.Re.12.

Den 17. Werdt Elizabeth gecroont Coninginne van Engelandt Anno 1558.

Den xvij. als Titus de geboorte sijns vaders Vespasiani celebreerde, so wierp hy 3000. Ioden den wilden beeste voor, so als hy den 24. Octtober gedaen. int laetste van Nouember sijn Westmærlandt en Nordthomberlandt, in Engelant tegen de Coninginne opgestaen. 1569.

Iaermercten.

Den eerstē Troyé in Cham. Delft/hol.Warremarde/vri. Rouanen/bra. Bergen/he. Dé 2.Erfort/Wirtsburg/du. Des maé. na dé 2.Liere/br. Dé 3.Lios/br. dueré.3.we. Den 6.Bouin/lud. Den 9.Beueren/vla. Den 11.S.Lieuens Hauté/bla.Deuenter/hol. Dē 21.Briel/hol.Mierlo/br. Den 22.Arien/art. Dé 25.Estinghen/Duyt. Den 26.Priis/hen. Den 26.Vlissinghe/Zee. Sgrauenhaghe/hol. Den 19.Bracht/bra.

3.11 *Calendier historiael*, a calendar with historical notes, printed by Anthonius de Solempne in Norwich (1570). The title page bears the motto 'Godt bewaer de coninginne Elizabeth' ('God save the queen Elizabeth'); November marks her recognition of Norwich's Dutch Church. Oxford, Bodleian Library, Arch. A f.33 (1), 'October' and 'November'.

as a guide to learning French and English.[92] De Solempne's trade in wine must have done better than his publishing venture, however, because after a few years, including attempts to publish in French and English (as well as his more regular choice of Dutch), no new titles appear from the Solempne press.[93] His last offering, an apparent attempt to switch to the market of English readers, was a morning prayer to be said daily during a particularly cold winter.[94]

PRINTING THE NEWS

John Day's interest in servicing the Dutch community in London, meanwhile, expanded as a result of events in the Netherlands: in the 1560s the religious conflict between a growing Protestant population and a Catholic government led first to open revolt and then to the establishment of a fledgling republic. John Day printed English translations of several of the declarations by William of Orange, the leader of the revolt.[95] In addition, Day printed both Latin and English editions of the Netherlands' appeal to the Imperial Diet in 1570, all for an English readership.[96] While restrictions were imposed on printing about matters pertaining to the state and the church in England, current events abroad were an unrestricted subject, which publishers gratefully explored – and which foreign agents targeted to push their version of events.[97] From the very start of the conflict that would become known as the Dutch Revolt, England provided a target audience for propagandistic publications. Translations of significant documents, generally without further explanation (though framed in such a way that they justified the opposition to the Spanish monarchy) appeared in English in London from 1566,[98] and English pamphlets about current events in the Low Countries, often translated from Dutch or French, were published in London within two weeks of the events to which they related.[99]

The increasingly central role that Elizabeth's government played as a supporter of the Dutch Republic soon led to this English interest in Dutch affairs being reciprocated on the other side of the North Sea. A flurry of Dutch pamphlets about English affairs in the 1580s bears witness to the perceived significance of Anglo-Dutch relations in the period. The defeat of the Spanish Armada, for example, was widely celebrated.[100] Meanwhile, one London printer found it necessary to counter in Dutch the malicious rumours about Queen Elizabeth's governor in the Netherlands, Peregrine Bertie, Baron Willoughby de

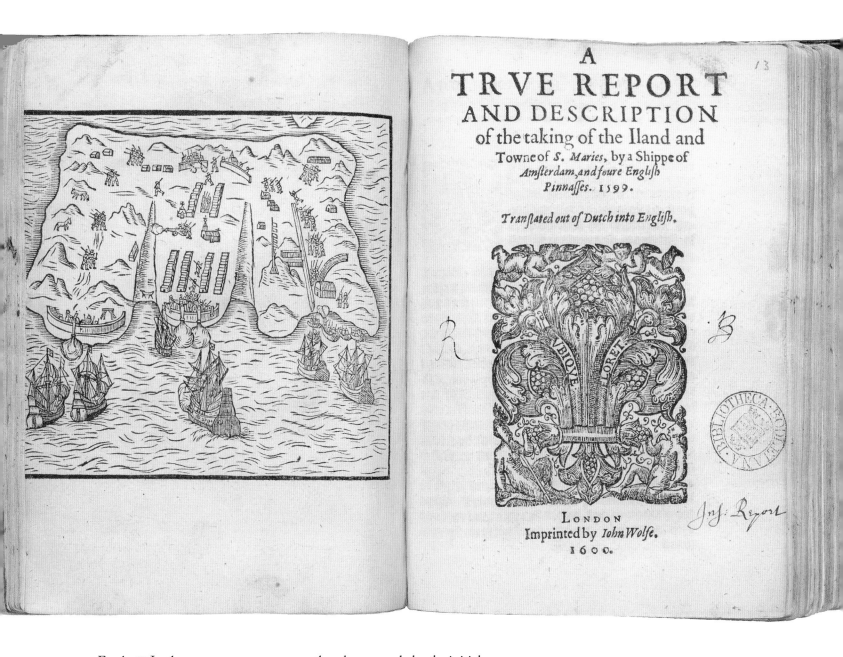

A

TRVE REPORT

AND DESCRIPTION

of the taking of the Iland and
Towne of *S. Maries*, by a Shippe of
*Amfterdam, and foure Englifh
Pinnaffes.* 1599.

Tranflated out of Dutch into Englifh.

VBIQVE FLORET

LONDON
Imprinted by *Iohn Wolfe.*
1600.

Eresby.[101] In the 1590s an anonymous author, known only by the initials 'H.W.', translated polemical pamphlets from Dutch into English for publication by John Wolfe in London, aiming to encourage English support for the political cause of the Republic.[102] Many such publications, while generally supportive of the Protestant Dutch cause, cannot with certainty be ascribed to patronage from a particular political source, but such patronage certainly existed. Charles Sylvius of Delft, for example,

3.12   Anglo-Dutch news from the Atlantic Ocean off the West African coast: *A True Report and Description of the Taking of the Iland and Towne of S. Maries*, 'translated out of Dutch into English', published in London by John Wolfe (1600). Oxford, Bodleian Library, 4° L 70(13) Art., frontispiece and title page.

was commissioned by the States of Holland to publish works by William of Orange in Latin, French, Dutch, German and English.[103]

The protracted conflict between the Netherlands and Spain led to the arrival of contingents of English soldiers in the Low Countries. Among them were authors such as George Gascoigne, Thomas Churchyard and Henry Hexham, all of whom published eyewitness accounts from the times they had spent on military campaigns across the North Sea.[104] At the same time a stream of pamphlets was printed highlighting the role of English troops in the Continental conflict or, in some cases, correcting previous accounts in which (according to the English pamphleteers) the Dutch had underplayed the English role.[105] Over time, the continual output of news about the Low Countries from English presses led to the development of a new genre of newsprint, as publications of short tracts describing single events were replaced by pamphlets collecting unrelated news reports from different sources and places. The pioneer of this genre, the precursor of the modern newspaper, was the London printer John Wolfe, who published collections of unrelated news reports about recent Continental (as well as intercontinental) events, primarily collected from Dutch sources, in the 1590s (fig. 3.12). The English 'corantos', regularly printed weekly newsbooks of twenty-four pages, which became the preferred format in the 1620s, were imitations of Antwerp's first newspaper, the *Nieuwe tijdinghen* (*New Tidings*), and likewise mostly reproduced translated Dutch materials.[106] The early history of newsprint in Dutch and English, growing out of the early decades of the Dutch Revolt, was Anglo-Dutch, playing out around the shores of the North Sea.

An especially prominent role in the Anglo-Dutch printing industry in this period was played by Richard Schilders in Middelburg. Originally from Hainault, Schilders had trained as a printer in London from 1567, before returning to the Low Countries in 1579, when he established Middelburg's first printing press. He printed controversial works in both Dutch and English, becoming one of the two principal publishers specializing in works by English and Scottish critics of the Anglican establishment.[107] Among his many publications was also a Dutch translation of King James VI of Scotland's *The Battle of Lepanto* (1591). The Dutch translation, printed in 1593, was by Abraham van der Myl, a minister and poet from Flushing (Vlissingen),[108] which was at the time one of three coastal towns handed over by the Dutch to the English queen to secure English military support ahead of a financial settlement. Garrisoned by English soldiers, Flushing was governed by Sir Robert Sidney. Schilders's publication of James's work was connected to the printer's interest in Scottish Puritanism; Dutch interest in James was further stimulated in 1603, when he succeeded to the English throne as King James I. The prominent Amsterdam publisher Cornelis Claesz was particularly well placed to meet the ensuing demand for the king's works in Dutch: he had for several years had contact with the Scottish publisher Andrew Hart, and had printed several works for him, in Latin and English, promoting the House of Stuart to both an English and a wider European audience. Claesz commissioned and published Dutch translations of James's works *Basilikon Doron*, *Meditation upon the Chronicles*, *Daemonologie* and *Ane Frvitfvll Meditatioun*, in a collaboration with his neighbour, the printer Laurens Jacobsz.[109] Reframed by introductory materials to promote international Protestant solidarity, the works were translated by two Dutch remigrants from Norwich. Vincent Meusevoet had grown up in Norwich and had previously translated works by the Cambridge Puritan William Perkins. After the translations of James's works, he continued to make English news accessible to Dutch readers, through translations of pamphlets about current events, including the Gunpowder Plot. The Dutch translation of *Ane Frvitfvll Meditatioun* came from Meusevoet's older contemporary in Norwich, Michiel Panneel. After returning to the Netherlands, Panneel had previously translated a treatise on Revelation by the Scottish mathematician and theologian John Napier, *A Plaine Discouery of the whole Reuelation of Saint Iohn*.[110] Both translators, who had each learned their English in East Anglia, evidently had some problems with the Scottish words in their sources, even though much had already been ironed out in the English editions that they relied on. For instance, the word 'marrow' meaning 'companion' (still current in present-day Scots) was confused with 'marrow' meaning 'bone marrow', so that the Scottish idiom 'the halfe marrow [marriage partner] in his bed' was translated as ''t halve merch [i.e. bone marrow] in zijn bedde'.[111]

PHRASE BOOKS AND DICTIONARIES

Regular North Sea crossings of soldiers and diplomats, as well as of merchants and students, demanded reciprocal understanding – and while some of that communication could be carried out in French and Latin, many English speakers had to learn Dutch, and Dutch speakers English.

Vernacular language learning in the late Middle Ages was informal. No schools offered instruction in languages such as Dutch and English. School and university learning took place through the medium of Latin. Learners acquired a new language principally by immersion, but some instructional materials were available, particularly for merchants: vocabularies and phrase books were among the genres of text that soon made the transition from manuscript to print. In Chapter 2 we encountered the French–English phrase book published by William Caxton, translated (probably by Caxton himself) from a French–Dutch one, the *Livre des mestiers*.[112] Gerard Leeu's *Gemmula vocabulorum* (*Little Gem of Vocabulary*), printed in Antwerp in 1484, made Dutch accessible through Latin. The multilingualism of the early modern city, with its international population of traders and refugees, evidently inspired thinking about vernacular languages.[113] It is therefore less surprising than might appear at first glance that the oldest known grammar of the Dutch language was written in London. This work, which remained unpublished at the time but survives in an original manuscript, *Voorreden vanden noodich ende nutticheit der Nederduytscher taelkunste* (*Argument about the Need and Utility of the Dutch Grammar*, 1568), was written by a member of the Dutch community of London, Johannes Radermacher.[114]

The presence of English soldiers and dignitaries in the Netherlands from 1585, when Robert Dudley, earl of Leicester arrived with 6,000 troops to support the States General in their fight against Spain, provided the impetus for the production of more language-learning materials, and for new thinking about the relationship between Dutch and English. The first Anglo-Dutch grammatical treatise, which was based on a similar work about Dutch and French, was published shortly after the arrival of English troops in the Netherlands: *The Conjugations in English and Netherdutche* presents the basic verbal conjugations in both languages with some useful vocabulary and a list of adverbs.[115] A more practical, applied approach to language learning was provided the same year by Jacob Walraven's bilingual edition of George Whetstone's *The Honourable Reputation of a Souldier*, similarly published by the Englishman Thomas Basson in Leiden. In his Dutch introduction, Walraven describes in detail how he had learned English without ever having visited England, despite the fact that no schools in the Netherlands offered instruction.[116] He had picked up some of the language fifteen years earlier in cosmopolitan Antwerp, but had then started daily one-hour conversation classes with several friends, led by a native English speaker who had moved to the Netherlands. This Englishman was Walraven's publisher, Thomas Basson, who had been a book merchant trading with Plantin, worked for Elzevier and then became a prolific publisher and bookseller in Leiden, becoming University Printer in the 1590s.[117] His publications were mostly in Latin, but he occasionally printed for a wider Dutch readership, as well as for the English market.[118] Walraven had thus learned the language through reading and conversation, and he urged his readers to do the same: 'hy, die beneffens t' Duytsch, oock Latijn ende Françoys verstaet, kan (kennende pronunceren) al spelende leeren: immer veel al van zelf wel verstaen' ('he who in addition to Dutch, knows Latin and French, can (presuming knowledge of pronunciation) learn while playing, as he already understands much by himself').[119] To help the reader with the 'knowledge of pronunciation', he produced a short pronunciation guide, *English Pronunciation, or, A Shorte Introduction and Waye into the English Speache, very fitte for all those that intende to learne the same.*[120] This was appended to a Dutch–English bilingual version of *The Honourable Reputation of a Souldier.* Better help with pronunciation, however, would be provided by a native speaker,

> tzy dan van Schoolmeester, ofte binnen u deur (hebdyse) eenich Joncker, Dienaer oft Engelsch Soldaet, die u zo wel het A, b, c. als ooc al de reste te voren pronunceert, om zo by u strax na gebootst, metter tijt aengewent te werden: Dit doen zy zelf gaern, bevandt het noch op staende voet van twee Edel-luyden by my t'huys, mits dat ick haer ooc het Duytsch pronunceerde, waer na zy begeerich haken. Dits met d'een d'ander hant gewasschen.[121]

> *whether from a schoolmaster, or at home from any young man, servant or English soldier (if you have them), who pronounces the A B C and all the rest for you, so that by imitating him immediately afterwards you can eventually learn it. They do this happily, as I myself recently experienced with two noblemen at my home, if I also pronounced the Dutch to them, which they eagerly pursue. Thus one hand washed the other.*

Learning English, Walraven argued, was especially important now that the court, the army and garrisons included so many English speakers. The inability to speak a few words in English may cause tradesmen of every description, 'Backer, Brouwer, Visscher, Vleys-houwer' ('baker, brewer, fisherman, butcher'), to miss out on commercial opportunities; but, more fundamentally, 'Ist niet verdrietich, met open, beyde mont ende ooren, te moeten stom ende doof zijn?' ('Is it not sad, while having both mouth and ears open, to be dumb and deaf?'). And while interpreters might offer help at important meetings, for example with foreign dignitaries such as the earl of Leicester, what if none was at hand or, worse, what if the translation was selective and the language barrier used to manipulate the outcome of negotiations? 'Waert dan niet best zelf wat gheleert? zo niet perfect, doch om te verstaen.'[122] ('Would it then not be best if you learned some yourself? If not perfect, enough to understand'). To make his bilingual text suitable for language learning, Walraven placed the English text and its Dutch translation in parallel columns, and the Dutch translation follows the English verbatim. Where Walraven found following the exact word order impossible, he used superscript numbers in the Dutch text to indicate the original word order (fig. 3.13). Walraven concluded with further reading suggestions: a vocabulary published by Jan Paedts,[123] *The Conjugations in English and Netherdutche* of Thomas Basson, and books, such as a New Testament and Psalms, that were available in both languages for easy comparison. The presence of English speakers must have led local booksellers to stock English titles, for Walraven recommended 'ooc cleyne historikens crijchdy nu hier haest int Engels wel te coop, ende tegens tduytsch over gelezen, zal u uyter maten veel vorderen'[124] ('also small histories in English you can probably now easily find for sale here, and reading them alongside the Dutch you will very quickly advance').

The language-learning tool that was still missing, however, was an English–Dutch/Dutch–English dictionary. English readers of Dutch had to rely on the Dutch–Latin dictionary of Cornelis Kiliaan, printed in successively enlarged editions between 1574 and 1599; Thomas Marshall, for example, owned a copy.[125] But vocabularies offering Dutch and English rarely exceeded 5,000 words, until Henry Hexham published his dictionary, with 31,000 entries. Hexham, who had been born in Lincolnshire *c.*1595, spent most of his adult life in Holland as a soldier fighting for the United Provinces. He developed into a translator, rendering religious works from English into Dutch.

OF THE HOVNO-RABLE REPVTA-tion of a Souldier, vvith a Morall Report of the Vertues, Offices, and (by abuse) the disgrace of his Profession.

VANDE EERVVEER-DIGHE ACHTBAER-heyt des Soldeners, met een Stich-tich verhael der Deuchden, Amp-ten, ende (by misbruyck) d'On-tucht Zijnder Beroe-pinghe.

A T what time, Ambition, the Impe of miscreate Enuy, vpon desire of Soueraigntie, begat Warre: Necessitie, Inuêtresse of all Pollicies, Artes, and Mecanicall Craftes, deuised many Engines for Warre.: the vse whereof, gaue first reputation vnto the Souldier, who euer since hath bene honorably esteemed.

And although for difference of Aucthorities and Offices, requisit in Martiall gouernmêt: There is Generall, Lieutenāt, Coronell, Captaine, Ensigne, Corporall, &c. Yet the hyest to the lowest, only glorieth in the name of a Souldier.

ALEXANDER, CÆSAR, and the greatest Monarques, vsually cal'de the meanest Souldiers, Companions, Fellowes, and alwayes greeted them by such like familiar salutations.

CÆSAR, would thus vsually incouradge his Souldiers: Companions, & Frends, saue that (by

TE vvat tijde, Eer-giericheyt, de Spruyt des wanschapen Af-gunsts, op begheerte van Hoocheyt, voort bracht het Oorloch: 4Verdacht 1de 2Noot (3Vindersse vā alle policie, kū-sté, en hādtwercké) 5menich Krijchs-gereetschap: t'gebruyck wāer af, gaf aldereerst Achtbaerheyt aē dē Solde-naer, wie altijt zedert heeft 2eerweer-dichlick 3geacht 1gheweest.

Ende al hoe wel, door onderscheyt van Auctoriteytē ende officien (noo-dich int Krijchs-regiment) daer is, Overste, Lieutenant, Coronel, Capi-teyn, Vaendrich, Corporal, &c. Noch-tans de hoochste totte leechste toe, 2beroemt sick 1alleé inde naem van een Soldener.

ALEXANDER, CÆSAR, ende de grootste Monarchen, 2noemden 1gewoonlijck den minsten Soldena-ré, Mee-maets, Maggers, ende 2groe-tede 3hemluyden 1altoos by dierghe-lijcke gemeenzame groetenissen.

CÆSAR wilde 2gewoonlic 1aldus 4zijné 5Soldenaré 3verstouten; Met-geセelle en vriēdē, behoudēs dat 2Ic(1by

D   luy-

He contributed to an expanded version of the Dutch translation of Foxe's *Book of Martyrs*, providing a translation of Foxe's treatise on the tyranny of the popes, and later also translated the Latin version of Mercator's *Atlas* into English, published by Hendrik Hondius in Amsterdam. In 1647 Hexham published his English–Dutch dictionary, which was reissued in

3.13 Jacob Walraven's bilingual edition of George Whetstone's *The Honourable Reputation of a Souldier* (Leiden, 1586). To facilitate comparison for the purpose of language learning, superscript numbers are used in the Dutch text to indicate the word order in the original English. San Marino, Huntington Library, 69799, p. 25.

1648 in a new edition, expanded with a Dutch–English section.[126] Each part of the dictionary concludes with a grammar: a Dutch grammar of the English language for the English–Dutch part,[127] and an English grammar of the Dutch language for the Dutch–English part.[128] Hexham notes about his Dutch–English/English–Dutch dictionary that it 'may be usefull unto all sorts of men, Especially, considering the Love, Correspondencie, Traffick, and Trading which is betweene our two Nations'.[129] In his Dutch dedication he added: 'ende bysonderlick, omdat het behulpigh, vorderlick, ende dienstigh mach zijn voor Studenten, Kooplieden, Fattoors, ende alle de ghene van onse Engelschen die begeerigh zijn om de Nederduytsche Spraecke te leeren'[130] ('and especially, because it may be of help, advancement, and service for students, merchants, agents, and every one of our English who desire to learn the Dutch language'). The grammars emphasize the closeness of the two languages: the way Dutch links two nouns by putting one in the genitive (e.g. 'Davids psalmen') 'agrees with our English'.[131]

FRANCISCUS JUNIUS

The similarity between the two languages, which Walraven had noted as a factor facilitating the easy acquisition of English by Dutch speakers, and which Hexham emphasized in his grammars, was also noted by scholars with an interest in historical linguistics. Consequently, the early history of printing Old English (the English language as written until *c.*1150), like the study of the language itself, has a history that involves several North Sea crossings. Old English had characters not used in ordinary printed Latin alphabets, such as specific forms of g, r and s, as well as þ (thorn), ð (eth) and ƿ (wynn) (fig. 3.14).

Producing such letters involved considerable skill. To make type, a metal stamp, or punch, would be carved by a punch cutter. To produce sufficient type for printing entire pages, this punch would be used to stamp an impression of the letter in copper, the matrix. This matrix could then be used by the type founder as a mould to cast as much type as was required, using a melted mixture of lead, tin and antimony.[132] To be able to print Old English in addition to the regular Latin alphabet, new punches had to be carved, new matrices struck and new type cast.

The first typeface with which Old English could be printed had been made for Archbishop Matthew Parker in 1566, for an edition of Old English sermons printed by publisher John Day.[133] This typeface was subsequently used for the early editions of William Camden's *Britannia* too.[134] The works of the legal and historical scholar John Selden, who from 1611 onwards published studies in which Old English was regularly cited, demanded the production of new founts of type. Selden's *Mare clausum*, a work first published in London in 1635, was an intervention in the Anglo-Dutch conflict over the law of the sea, including fishing rights in the North Sea; it included citations of historical documents written in Old English. When planning their own editions of this work, Dutch publishers decided to source their own Old English type. In a letter to Selden, now kept in the Bodleian Library,[135] the publishers Bonaventura and Abraham Elzevier justified their publication (1636) of a pirated edition of Selden's work by saying that the supply of copies did not meet demand, and that the English edition was too lavish, and therefore too expensive.[136] While cutting costs by reducing the size of paper, the Elzeviers did not compromise on Selden's linguistic prowess, and they had Old English type made specifically for this edition. The resulting typeface, however, was rather crude. A much better Old English typeface was made for Joan Blaeu's *Atlas* of *c*.1645, which included historical descriptions of Britain based on William Camden's work. The Old English letters were produced by a punch cutter and type founder with the wonderful name of Reinier Voskens ('Reynard son of Little Fox'), or his

3.14 Example of the 'Pica Saxon' Old English typeface, given to the press of the University of Oxford by Franciscus Junius. From *A Specimen of the Several Sorts of Letter Given to the University by Dr. John Fell* (1693). Oxford, Bodleian Library, Vet. A3 c.244 (1), sig. d2r.

Pica Saxon.

ABCDEFGHIKLMNOPRSTÐUÞXYZ
abcðeꝼghiklmnopꝓrꞇꝺþuꝑxẏz ꝫ

Fæðeɲ uɲe þu þe eaɲꞇ on heoꝼenum. Ꝺi þin nama ᵹehalᵹoð:. To-become þin ꝑice:. Ᵹepuɲꝺe þin ꝑilla on eoɲꝺan. ꝼꝓa ꝼꝓa on heoꝼenum:. Uɲne ꝺæᵹhꝑamlican hlaꝼ ꞅẏle uꞅ ꞇo ꝺæᵹ:. Anꝺ ꝼoɲᵹẏꝼ uꞅ uɲe ᵹẏlꞇaꞅ. ꝼꝓa ꝼꝓa ꝑe ꝼoɲᵹiꝼað uꝑum ᵹẏlꞇenꝺum:. Anꝺ ne ᵹelæꝺꝺe þu uꞅ on coꝓꞇnunᵹe. ac alẏꞅ uꞅ oꝼ ẏꝼele:. ꝺoðlice:.

brother.[137] Thus by the middle of the seventeenth century typographers in the Netherlands had become so expert in making Old English type that, when the historical linguist Franciscus Junius required such type, he was able to commission it in Amsterdam.[138]

Franciscus Junius had grown up and been educated in Leiden.[139] At school he became friends with Gerardus Johannes Vossius, who would later marry Franciscus's half-sister Elisabeth. Vossius soon emerged as one of the foremost classical scholars of his generation. He had many admirers and several patrons in England. His regular travels to England were continued by his son Isaac Vossius, who lived in England during the final two decades of his life. He accumulated a large library of manuscripts, expanding the collection he had inherited from his father. This library he kept in Windsor, where he was canon of the Royal Chapel. On Isaac's death in 1689, the library was sold, with the University of Leiden outbidding that of Oxford.[140] So the manuscripts crossed the North Sea to the Netherlands, but one important manuscript, the 'Codex Vossianus', a tenth-century Latin psalter with Old English glosses, did make it to the Bodleian Library, through the hands of Isaac's uncle Franciscus Junius: it is now MS. Junius 27. Like his father before him, Isaac had been primarily interested in classical literature. It was Junius's passion for Old English that made the 'Codex Vossianus' of specific interest to him.

While Gerardus Johannes Vossius was establishing himself as a philologist in the Netherlands, Junius had gone to England, where he became tutor to the son, and later the grandsons, of Thomas Howard, earl of Arundel, as well as to Arundel's protégé Aubrey de Vere, earl of Oxford.[141] For Arundel, Junius produced a work on the theory of art, *De pictura veterum* (*On the Painting of the Ancients*, 1637), which was dedicated to King Charles I and printed in Amsterdam under the supervision of Vossius.[142] Junius himself subsequently translated the work into English and Dutch. When de Vere entered the service of Frederick Henry of Orange in 1644, Junius moved to the Netherlands with his charge;[143] thus his return to the Netherlands was itself an English affair. Back in the Netherlands, Junius devoted himself to studying the origins of the Dutch language, which led to the study of several older Germanic languages: the relative scarcity of survivals of Old Dutch made him turn to related languages, including Gothic, Old English and Middle English.[144] These linguistic interests led to his commissioning typefaces, including one to print Old English, for his study (1655) of the Old Dutch version of

3.15 Opening page of the Old English *Genesis A*, the first poem of the 'Cædmon Manuscript', written *c.*1000. The manuscript, given to Franciscus Junius by James Ussher, archbishop of Armagh, was part of Junius's gift to the University of Oxford in 1677. Oxford, Bodleian Library, MS. Junius 11, fol. 1r.

US IS RIHT MICEL ÐÆT

we rodera weard, wereda wuldorcining,
wordum herigen, modum lufien. he is mægna
sped, heafod ealra heah gesceafta, frea ælmihtig.
næs him fruma æfre, or geworden, ne nu ende cymþ
ecean drihtnes, ac he bið a rice ofer heofenstolas.
heagum þrymmum. soðfæst and swiðfeorm sweglbosmas
maran healde. þa wæron gesette wide and side
þurh geweald godes wuldres bearnum, gasta weardum.
hæfdon gleam and dream, and heora ord fruman, engla
þreatas, beorhte blisse. wæs heora blæd micel.
þegnas þrymfæste þeoden heredon, sægdon lus
tum lof, heora liffrean demdon, drihtenes duge
þum wæron swiðe gesælige. synna ne cuþon. fir
ena fremman, ac hie on friðe lifdon, ece mid
heora aldor. elles ne ongunnon ræran on rode
rum. nymþe riht and soþ, ærdon engla weard, for
oferhygde dæl on gedwilde. noldon dreogan leng
heora selfra ræd, ac hie of siblufan godes a
hwurfon. hæfdon gielp micel þæt hie wið drihtne
dælan meahton, wuldorfæstan wic, werodes
þrymme, sid and swegltorht. him þær sar gelamp,
æfst ofer hygd, and þæs engles mod, þe þone unræd
ongan ærest fremman, wefan and weccan, þa he
worde cwæð, niþes ofþyrsted, þæt he on norðdæle.

the 'Willeram', a commentary on the Song of Songs originally written in Old High German; his linguistic commentary also drew parallels between Old Dutch and Old English.[145] Before using the type for his edition, Junius had it checked by John Selden, whose own work *Mare clausum* had occasioned the first production of Old English type in the Netherlands. He wrote to Selden:

> In the meane while have I here Anglo-Saxonick types (I know not whether you call them Punchons) a cutting, and hope they will be matriculated, and cast within the space of seven or eight weeks at the furthest. As soon as they come to my hands, I will send you some little specimen of them, to the end I might know how they will be liked in England.[146]

Around this time, Junius received the manuscript that is now Oxford, Bodleian Library, MS. Junius 11 (fig. 3.15),[147] from James Ussher, archbishop of Armagh – possibly because Ussher had heard of Junius's Old English type, which made it possible for him to produce a printed edition of the manuscript. MS. Junius 11 was written in the second half of the tenth century, probably in Canterbury, and contained Old English poetic paraphrases and retellings of biblical narratives. In 1655 Junius used the Old English typeface produced for his 'Willeram' commentary to print the texts of this manuscript, attributing them to a poet called 'Cædmon'.[148] This attribution was suggested to him by Bede's *Ecclesiastical History*, which tells the story of Cædmon, a lay brother of Whitby Abbey who received divine poetic inspiration.[149] From Junius's printed edition of the texts of this manuscript, it came to be called the 'Cædmon Manuscript'. Junius's edition was the first published work of Old English poetry.[150] The edition consisted simply of a diplomatic transcription, though Junius planned a fuller edition with a linguistic commentary. To this end, he annotated his own copy of his printed text (fig. 3.16).[151] This personal copy (now Oxford, Bodleian Library, MS. Junius 73) and the original medieval manuscript entered the Bodleian Library collections in 1677, when Junius gave his entire collection to the university four months before his death. His books, however, were not the only benefaction he left to Oxford: he also gifted to its press the ability to print Old English, through the donation of the punches and matrices from which Old English type could be produced.

3.16 Opening page of the Old English *Genesis A* from the 'Cædmon Manuscript' in the edition by Franciscus Junius (1655), printed using his own Old English typeface. This copy contains notes by Junius himself, in preparation for a never completed annotated edition. Oxford, Bodleian Library, MS. Junius 73, p. 1.

CÆDMONIS
Paraphrasis poëtica,
Genesios ac præcipuarum sacræ paginæ historiarum.

(marginal note) roðer, Firmamentum; Ælfr. gloss.
hroðor, Æther; Gloss. R. pag. 94.
4,20. 46,17.   3,15. 4,18. 74.

U r ir riht micel. ðæt ƿe roðena ƿearð. ƿereða ƿulðor

cining. ƿorðum herigen:. moðum lufien:. he ir mæg

na rpeð. heafoð ealra heah gerceafta: frea ælmih-   3,18. 4,10 & 22.
21,10. 32,2

tig:. Næf him fruma æfre. on geƿorðen. ne nu enðe   78,1.

22,23. 3,16. 33,8. 41,25.

5 cymþ. ecean ðrihtner. ac he bið á ƿice. ofer heofen

rtolar. heagum þrymmum. roðrfæft j rƿið fenom. rƿegl-bormar heolð:.

þa ƿæron gerette. ƿiðe j riðe. þurh geƿealð goðer. ƿulðer beafnum.   3,19.

2,3.

garta peanðum:. Hæfðon gleam j ðfeam. j heofa onðfuman. engla   42,12.

þfeatar. beophte blirre. þær heofa blæð micel. þegnar þrymfæfte.
2,23. 3,5.   43,8.   34,8.   21,18.   ic deme ſ arme̅ze,
Cenſeo; Ælfr. gramm.

10 þeoðen heneðon. rægðon lurtum lof. heofa lif-ffean. ðemðon ðfihte-
10,22.   60,16.

ner ðugeþum. þæfon rƿiðe gerælige. rynna ne cuþon. firena ffemman:.

ac hie on ffiðe lifðon. ece mið heofa alðof. eller ne ongunnon. ƿæfan

on ƿoðefum. nymþe fiht j foð. æfðon engla ƿeafð. fof ofeƿhygðe.   44,18.

43,1.

ðæl on geðƿilðe: nolðon ðfeogan leng. heofa relfa fæð. ac hie of ffiblu-

15 fan. goðef ahƿuffon:. Hæfðon gielp micel. þ hie ƿið ðfihtne. ðælan
48,5. 71,6.   3,6.

meahton. ƿulðorfæftan ƿic. ƿenoðef þfymme. firð j rƿegl-topht. him

24,3.   8,17.   17,19. 38,1.

þæf raf gelamp. æfft j ofeƿhygð. j þæf engler moð. þe þone unfæð.

60,16.

ongan æfeft ffemman. ƿefan j peccean. þa he ƿofðe cƿæð. niþef of
96,7.

þyfteð. þ he on nofð ðæle. (2) ham j heahretl. heofena fiver.
8,25. 18,18.   10,18.   27,7.

20 agan ƿolðe:. Þa ƿeafð yffe goð. j þam ƿefoðe ƿfað. þe he æf þuf ðoðe.

A   plite

JOHN FELL'S PRESS OF THE UNIVERSITY OF OXFORD

From the late 1660s John Fell, bishop of Oxford, after a stint as vice-chancellor of the university, dedicated himself to establishing a printing press for it, to be placed in the Sheldonian Theatre, which had been built under his vice-chancellorship. Printing had first been established in Oxford in 1478, but had always remained in the hands of private entrepreneurs, who were often officially sanctioned and occasionally commissioned by the university, and from the 1580s licensed.[152] From the 1630s the university had aimed to establish its own press, but such attempts remained largely fruitless until Bishop Fell was put in charge of the enterprise in the 1660s.[153] To ensure a stable basis for printing by the university, Fell decided to acquire sets of typeface, including the punches and matrices from which further type could be cast when required. He did not, however, believe that any English type-cutter was up to the task: 'The foundation of all successe must be layd in doing things well, and I am sure that will not be don with English letters',[154] he wrote in 1670 to Thomas Marshall, commissioning him to search for good-quality materials in the Netherlands.[155] Following study at Oxford, Marshall had lived in Holland as a Royalist refugee from 1648, and as chaplain to the Merchant Adventurers from 1650 to 1672. In Holland he had

met Isaac Vossius and studied with Franciscus Junius, and had collaborated with the latter on an edition of the Gothic and Old English Gospels (Dordrecht, 1665).[156] He bequeathed his impressive library, containing manuscripts in Middle Dutch and Frisian as well as Old English, to the Bodleian Library. Marshall had good Dutch: he was capable of translating Dutch into English in a letter to Fell.[157] He spent much time sourcing typefaces for Fell from Amsterdam between 1669 and 1672, acquiring and sending over materials, as well as on occasion personnel:

he arranged for the move to Oxford of two Dutch type founders.[158] Marshall returned to England in 1672. Four years later his friend Franciscus Junius followed him, moving to Oxford to pursue the study of Germanic languages.[159] He took with him his printing materials and, having learned from Marshall the needs of the burgeoning university press, donated to it his types, punches and matrices (fig. 3.17).[160] Thus several typefaces for ancient languages, including Old English, Gothic and Runic, became available to the Oxford University Press.[161] The Old English typeface would continue to be used for several works printed by the university press, including a posthumous publication of one of Junius's own works in 1743.[162] The materials themselves – the punches and matrices for the production of Old English typeface made for Junius in Amsterdam – are preserved in the archives of the press to this day. The printing of Old English at the early Oxford University Press was thus made possible by the scholarly interest of a Dutchman with an Anglo-Dutch life, by his ideas about the affinity between Old English, Old Dutch and other Germanic languages, and by the skills of Dutch craftsmen who were working in an established tradition of printing Old English in the Netherlands.

For centuries after the introduction of print, English printing, which had originated in the Low Countries, retained its ties with the Netherlands in a variety of ways: Dutch craftsmen and traders set up presses in England, and publishers and printers in the Netherlands served English audiences. Texts in Dutch were printed in England to serve the local Dutch-speaking market and to a lesser extent the market on the Continent. Dutch specialists in printing technologies, particularly punch-cutters and type founders, became highly prized in England and were sought out for their products as well as their skills. Dutch publishers of clandestine books for the English market repeatedly crossed the North Sea, risking life and limb to sell their books. Their regular presence in London supported the establishment and survival of a community of Dutch faithful in the city. Meanwhile, the officially sanctioned trade in printed materials between the Low Countries and England flourished too. An increasingly central place in that trade was taken up by the publishing of engraved maps, itself the product of an international exchange of knowledge, skills, craft and artistic ability. The role of Anglo-Dutch relations in the development of maps and map-making is the topic of our next chapter.

3.17 *opposite and above* Matrices of the Old English and punches of the Gothic typeface made in Amsterdam for Franciscus Junius. The punches were used to make impressions in the matrices, which were then used as moulds to cast new metal type for printing letters. Oxford, Oxford University Press Archives.

Sjoerd Levelt and Anne Louise Avery

De Duytse Kerck is blijven staen.

The Dutch Church is still standing.

DUTCH ACCOUNT OF THE GREAT FIRE OF LONDON, 1666

Anglo-Dutch relations had a particularly significant impact on map-making, both as an art and as an industry, in the sixteenth and seventeenth centuries. By nature a collaborative endeavour involving scholars, artists, engravers, printers and publishers, the business of map-making also became an inherently international one, involving not only maps but also people repeatedly making North Sea crossings. This chapter will survey panoramas of London and depictions of Britain, the Low Countries and the North Sea, all of which were created as a result of reciprocal relations between people from England and the Netherlands.

Maps in the Middle Ages were sometimes rich in detail – containing pictorial elements such as mythical creatures, as well as information about routes gleaned from pilgrims, merchants and crusaders – but were generally poor in spatial specificity. Broadly speaking, medieval map-making can be divided into *mappae mundi* (world maps), regional maps including itineraries, and portolan charts.[1] Cartography, moreover, was never understood to be merely pictorial: a *mappa* could indeed be a drawn map, but it could also be a textual description: 'chorography' entailed the description and/or depiction of a region, whereas 'geography' dealt with the whole known world. When Ptolemy's *Geography* was studied by Italian humanists *c.*1400, a Latin translation of the Greek text was disseminated without any maps; such was also the case in its first printed edition, of 1475.[2]

The entire world could be rendered graphically in a *mappa mundi*, known as a T-O map for its customary form, an O divided into three sections by a T drawn inside it; the upper half for Asia, and the lower quarters for Europe and Africa respectively; their purpose was primarily didactic

Part of a panorama of London from the broadsheet
*A True Pourtraict with a Brief Description of the
Deplorable Fire of London …* (detail of fig. 4.13)

and moralizing.[3] Itineraries listed the places one would pass when travelling between two locations, often simply in writing, sometimes laid out as a strip, but also occasionally as a map of a region.[4] The first maps of individual European countries appeared in the thirteenth century. The English chronicler Matthew Paris's map of Britain from the 1250s, which has at its core an itinerary from Newcastle upon Tyne to Dover, is believed to be the earliest.[5] Such maps, while indicating sequential relations between geographical locations, were not drawn to scale; direction and distance were not the primary preoccupations of their makers.[6] This was in contrast to the 'portolan charts', maps specifically created for sea journeys, initially covering the Mediterranean and the Black Sea in particular, which technological innovations such as the compass allowed to be drawn to scale.[7] These marine charts had increasingly accurate depictions of coastlines and provided a means of determining distance and position. They were used primarily for planning journeys and weighing the geopolitical and commercial environments along a route. Only occasionally were they used for determining a ship's location during a journey, since experienced pilots usually did this without resorting to maps.[8] Over the fourteenth and fifteenth centuries, the portolan charts' precision started to influence expectations of the kind of information a map should be able to provide.[9]

Already in the earliest maps of Britain, its proximity to the Dutch Low Countries is on clear display: Britain is depicted in its relation not only to the surrounding sea, but also to the lands across it. In the right margin

of Paris's map, the principalities across the North Sea are listed: Holland, Brabant and Flanders. Similarly, the Gough Map (Bodleian Library, MS. Gough Gen. Top. 16) from *c.*1400[10] marks the harbours Sluis (Sluys) and Grevelingen (Gravelines) – frequent points of transit on journeys to and from the Continent – across the water from Essex and Suffolk along the Flemish coast (fig. 4.1); Calais is a little further south, opposite Kent.

4.1 East–west oriented depiction of Norfolk, Suffolk, Essex and Kent; Sluys, Gravelines and Calais face the English coast to the east across the North Sea. Detail from the Gough Map, a map of Britain, probably made around 1400. Bodleian Library, MS. Gough Gen. Top. 16.

The oldest extant map of Flanders likewise marks the main harbours and estuaries along the south-eastern English coast, just outside the frame that surrounds the map.[11]

In response to an increasing demand from European populations interested in an ever-expanding known world, the sixteenth and seventeenth centuries saw rapid developments in map-making techniques, methodologies, skills and knowledge. These developments were stimulated by international collaborations involving scholars, artists and craftspeople, and accelerated by the maturing of printing both as a technology and as an industry. A number of survivals suggest an early role for Dutch artists in English map-making in the Tudor period. One early map of the south coast of England, for example, uses a Flemish unit of measurement, the 'kenning', and has been identified as the work of a Fleming for that reason;[12] but, while the word was indeed probably borrowed into English from Dutch, we find it attested in earlier English sources,[13] and therefore it may well have been part of a shared North Sea culture rather than evidence of specific influence. One important Tudor artist who can be identified is Anthony Anthony, a brewer of Flemish origin, who rose through the ranks from gunner to clerk at the Tower of London. His name is forever associated with the 'Anthony roll', a depiction of the royal fleet presented to Henry VIII in 1546.[14] He also drew several maps: one shows a route proposed for the Channel crossing of Anne of Cleves from the Continent to England, to join her husband Henry VIII in 1539; another depicts the North Sea and the Dutch and English coasts, though in this case his contribution appears to have been primarily artistic, adding ships to a map drawn by someone else.[15]

As we have seen in the previous chapter, Dutch specialists played a significant role in the development of printing books in England, and so it is not surprising that they also contributed to advances in the printing of maps. The earliest printing in England of a wall map of Britain and Ireland was by the Flemish engraver Thomas Gemini (though the map was not his original composition, but a copy of an Italian engraving of a map drawn by the Englishman George Lily).[16] There was Dutch involvement too in the earliest atlases (not yet known by that name) published in England. When Christopher Saxton, with royal backing, produced his collection of thirty-five county maps of England and Wales between 1574 and 1579, Dutch craftsmen played such prominent roles in the project that one of Saxton's engravers signed his work 'Augustinus

Ryther Anglus' (Augustine Ryther the Englishman) to distinguish himself from his foreign colleagues.[17] The second atlas published in England was a translation of a Dutch work, Lucas Jansz Waghenaer's *Spieghel der Zeevaert* (1584), published as *The Mariners Mirrour* in 1588, translated and adapted for an English readership by Anthony Ashley, clerk to the Privy Council.

The story of the development of map-making in the period, however, is not merely one of increasing precision and accuracy, since 'truthfulness' was just one of a range of epistemologies that played a part in making and reading maps. Early modern maps were produced to be not copies of reality but interpretations of it. They had to be informative in a variety of ways and thus also included, for example, ethnographic knowledge. Conditioned as we are to read maps as a representation of the spatial dimensions of the landscape, scaled to size, the maps of this period often contain details that may seem to us the product of ignorance or fabrication.[18]

ANTON VAN DEN WYNGAERDE'S PANORAMA OF LONDON

Modern maps are often drawn from an imaginary viewpoint looking straight down at the depicted area, but geographical areas can also be captured from different angles, with an illusion of three-dimensionality. Map-makers' artistry came to the fore in such pictorial maps. Bird's-eye views of cities had been a feature of Flemish painting from the early fifteenth century that had already been introduced to England,[19] and cities under siege drawn from a human perspective were an early and much favoured topic for so-called *ad vivum* drawings. The fashion, in which artists from the Netherlands played a prominent role, in turn encouraged the pictorial mapping of cities more generally.[20]

A renowned exponent of the art was Anton van den Wyngaerde, a native of Antwerp. In the early 1540s, while he was still at the beginning of a remarkable career that would see him move to Spain and work for a king and emperor, he visited London. Crossing through the city and its surroundings from neighbourhood to neighbourhood, he regularly took out his sketch paper and chalk to record the features of significant buildings. He would then attempt to gain access to a nearby building to make a second drawing from a more elevated position. Then, finding a location on a nearby hill or other elevation in order to view the same

4.2a London Bridge, on one of the panels of Anton van den Wyngaerde's *Panorama of London*. Van den Wyngaerde apparently had not been able to get an unobstructed view of the gate at the southern end of the bridge. © Ashmolean Museum, University of Oxford, WA1950.206.7.

tobes of haly bez

grea

angnsen

S Antoni

S michil in Cornell

peter in Cornell

S andreas

S margretta

Stat

Stator

S Batulfe Gybila

Stat

grooto strepa

S Thomas apostel

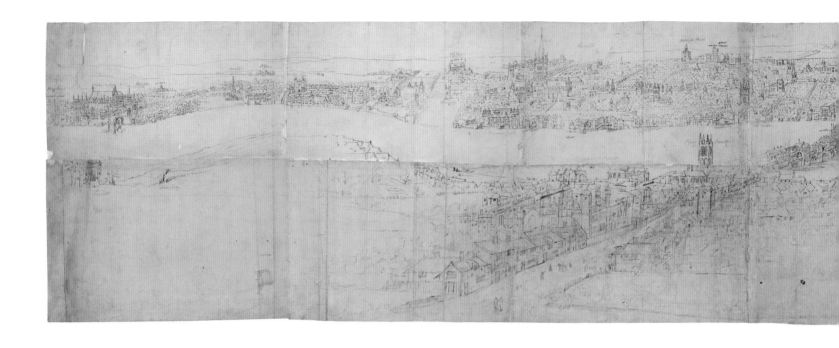

building in its urban context, he would draw it again. He ended up with detailed studies of many London landmarks, some of which are still familiar today, such as Westminster Abbey and the Tower of London. Many, however, such as the old St Paul's Cathedral (before the Great Fire of London) and London Bridge, with its gates and many buildings (fig. 4.2a), are now long lost.[21]

Once he had recorded views of significant buildings in neighbourhoods from Westminster to Greenwich and from Southwark to Spitalfields, van den Wyngaerde redrew the materials that he had gathered together in a single vision. He left open only those areas (e.g. Whitehall and the south end of London Bridge) that he had not yet been able to draw from observation or a second-hand source. He thus created a panorama of London as seen from the south, over three metres long and the earliest surviving of its kind (fig. 4.2b).[22]

Cityscapes developed into a thriving genre of pictorial art in the sixteenth century, from woodcut inserts in printed books and single-sheet engravings to wall-covering paintings. Rich patrons commissioned depictions of cities they were associated with or those they ruled.[23] Akin to cartography, such panoramas aimed to provide a true likeness of the landscape, based on survey in situ. Like early modern cartography, panoramas also presented more than mere representations of the

4.2b *above* Anton van den Wyngaerde's *Panorama of London*. The city is presented from a vantage point on the south bank of the Thames opposite the Tower of London. Southwark High Street (leading off London Bridge), which had a significant Dutch population, can be seen in the foreground. © Ashmolean Museum, University of Oxford, WA1950.206.

4.2c *opposite* The church of Austin Friars, with its distinctive steeple, on Anton van den Wyngaerde's *Panorama of London*. The friary was dissolved in 1538, but its church was repurposed for the Dutch Reformed congregation in 1550. The tower collapsed in the early 1600s. © Ashmolean Museum, University of Oxford, WA1950.206.7, detail.

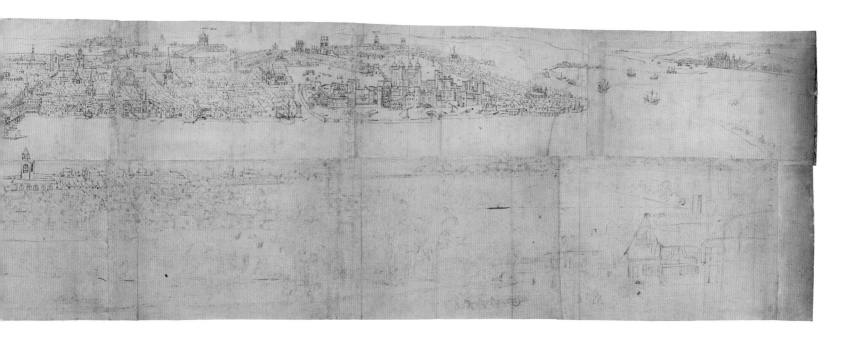

landscape. They could serve the ideological programmes of their patrons by exaggerating the size of some buildings and omitting others, and told narratives by including not only permanent but also ephemeral features of the landscape, such as ships, people and farm animals.

One of the many buildings van den Wyngaerde surveyed for his panorama of London was the church of Austin Friars (fig. 4.2c), a former Augustinian priory in the city, less than a mile east of St Paul's Cathedral. Its characteristic steeple was much loved and so, in spite of the dissolution of the monasteries, it survived into the reign of King James I.[24] Only a few years after it was drawn by van den Wyngaerde, in 1550, the church would become the focus of the community of Londoners who shared his origins and language, if not his religion, when it became the site of the Dutch Reformed Church of London, which we discussed in the previous chapter.

It is not known where the London panorama of van den Wyngaerde was until its acquisition in the early nineteenth century by the Ashmolean Museum of the University of Oxford.[25] In the 1550s van den Wyngaerde came to be employed by Philip II, king of Spain (r.1556–98), who through his marriage to Queen Mary I was king of England from 1554 to 1558. In this capacity van den Wyngaerde revisited London, making new drawings of several London landmarks – topographic artistry in the service of political power.

THE TAIL OF THE *LEO BELGICUS*

Topography could also be in the service of politics without being under direct political patronage. Such is the case with the most iconic map of the early modern Low Countries, the *Leo Belgicus* (fig. 4.3a). The use of the word 'Belgicus' for the entirety of the Netherlands was justified by reference to classical literature, where the Belgae were a federation of tribes described by Julius Caesar as inhabiting the region near the North Sea coast south-west of the Rhine. While in Caesar's description they occupied a much smaller region, as a federation the Belgae appeared ideally suited to become the classical representation of the burgeoning collection of seventeen Netherlandish provinces – roughly corresponding to today's Benelux (Belgium, the Netherlands and Luxembourg) – that had come under unified control first under Austrian Habsburg and subsequently Spanish Habsburg rule. *Leo Belgicus*, then, can perhaps best be translated as the 'Lion of the Low Countries'. In 1579 the seven northernmost provinces had declared independence, disrupting the union between the northern and southern Netherlands. When in 1583 the Austrian cartographer Michael Aitzinger described all seventeen provinces of the Netherlands as the 'Belgian Lion', taking the zoomorphic metaphor from the presence of lions in the arms of many of the individual provinces and using it as an allegory for force and bravery, he did so not to represent a political reality, but from a wish to see a previous (imaginary) unity 'restored'.[26] Aitzinger's vision of the Netherlands, expounded in a book describing the region's recent history, was illustrated by the map, representing the entirety of the seventeen provinces as a lion, reminiscent of heraldic representations. The lion as depicted on the map is a cross between a lion rampant (standing erect with forepaws raised) and a lion passant (walking, with its back oriented horizontally, one front paw raised, the others on the ground). The *Leo Belgicus* was the first map representing the Netherlands as a political unity, even though that unity had disintegrated in the split between the Protestant north and the Catholic south.

The *Leo Belgicus*, however, originated not only in the author's imagination, but also in that of its engraver, Frans Hogenberg, and we see his personal biography reflected in some of its details. Hogenberg was born in Mechelen, near Antwerp, *c.*1540. Following in his father's footsteps, he trained as an engraver. He became an associate and friend of the map-maker Abraham Ortelius in Antwerp.[27] Hogenberg appears

4.3a *Leo Belgicus* (*Lion of the Low Countries*), engraving by Frans Hogenberg for the Austrian cartographer Michael Aitzinger (1583). The depiction of the Low Countries as a lion, inspired by the heraldry of the region's principalities, was much emulated in the seventeenth century. Oxford, Bodleian Library, Douce A subt. 35, fold-out.

to have lived in England in the 1560s, as one of many new arrivals fleeing religious persecution in the southern Low Countries. In any case, his family had strong Anglo-Dutch ties: from 1573 his brother Remigius Hogenberg, also an engraver, worked for Matthew Parker, archbishop of Canterbury, living at Lambeth Palace in London. By 1570, however, Frans Hogenberg himself lived in Cologne, where he engraved maps for Ortelius's atlas, the *Theatrum orbis terrarum* (*Theatre of the World*), printed in Antwerp.[28] Later, on Ortelius's recommendation, he provided engravings for the history of the Netherlands that had been written by the Dutch Londoner Emanuel van Meteren.[29] The *Leo Belgicus* with its tail embodies the connection between the Netherlands and England (fig. 4.3b): the lion's tail crosses the sea at the northern edge of the English Channel between Grevelingen (Gravelines) and Dover; it then straddles Kent, looping back into the North Sea and coming back ashore in Lincolnshire's Holland; it subsequently crosses through Norfolk, which had a sizable population of Dutch speakers; its tassel finally reaches down south to brush London, where Hogenberg himself may have lived, and where his brother still lived. While many of the arms of the provinces contain lions rampant, the lion passant guardant (often designated 'leopard' in heraldic terminology but a lion all the same) is prominently featured three times in the Royal Arms of England.

Although the *Leo Belgicus* has a basis in cartography, accurately locating topographical names and geographical features, it is evidently also something else: a symbolic representation of what its creators thought the Low Countries were (or should be) like, and how they saw their connection with neighbouring countries. It should be situated in a tradition of chorography ('writing about places'), a genre that combined topography and history, and could be expressed in maps or text or a combination of the two. Whereas geography prioritized mathematical projection, chorography focused on depiction. It was particularly current among early modern historians, which had a significant impact on the production of maps in the sixteenth and seventeenth centuries. Like the *Leo Belgicus*, maps produced for various types of chorography regularly emphasized the proximity of England and the Dutch Low Countries, and the function of the North Sea as connecting, not dividing, them. In addition, as in the case of Hogenberg, the maps discussed in this chapter have layered Anglo-Dutch histories, whether in the lives of their makers or in the circumstances of their production and dissemination.

As the *Leo Belgicus* became a meme, repeatedly reproduced by engravers in the Low Countries, it was adjusted to the political wishes of successive artists, in one version, for example, depicting only the province of Holland.[30] One detail of Hogenberg's Anglo-Dutch vision was quickly lost in all subsequent versions: the lion's tail, which crossed the Channel and embraced parts of the North Sea and south-east England towards London, did still cross the sea to England in many of the later versions, but then swept aimlessly into the North Sea instead.

ABRAHAM ORTELIUS

During a low tide in 1520, on the North Sea coast near Katwijk in South Holland, the ruins of historical walls were exposed in the sand. It was not long before the structure was identified as the Brittenburg, the fortress known from medieval chronicles, which in the 1517 *Divisiekroniek* had been depicted by a woodcut of Merlin at Vortigern's castle (see Chapter 1, fig. 1.10). The walls were soon submerged again, but over the next half-century the structure was occasionally exposed, and the interest of historians was piqued by each sighting. When the walls re-emerged from the sea in 1562, Abraham Ortelius of Antwerp inspected the site. Abraham's father had died when the boy was eleven, after which he had been raised and educated by his uncle Jacob van Meteren, an Antwerp merchant whose trade focused primarily on London; we have previously encountered him as the instigator of the Coverdale Bible. Abraham's stepbrother Emanuel lived most of his adult life in London, as did Abraham's sister Elizabeth, who in November 1562 married Jacob Cool, originally probably also from Antwerp. Cool already had five children from a previous marriage in London and had a further three with Elizabeth, including a favourite of Abraham's, Jacob Cool Jr.[31] Abraham Ortelius himself, though he regularly travelled throughout Europe for his trade,[32] always remained resident in Antwerp.

When the Brittenburg emerged from the waves of the North Sea in 1562, Ortelius was primarily a dealer in maps. His trade consisted of buying multiple copies of individual maps, colouring them in and reselling

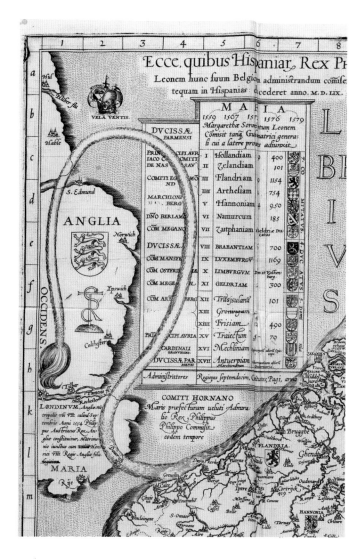

4.3b The tail of the Lion of the Low Countries, reaching across the English Channel, looping into the North Sea, and curling back through East Anglia towards London. From the *Leo Belgicus* map (1583) by Frans Hogenberg, whose brother lived in London. Oxford, Bodleian Library, Douce A subt. 35, fold-out, detail.

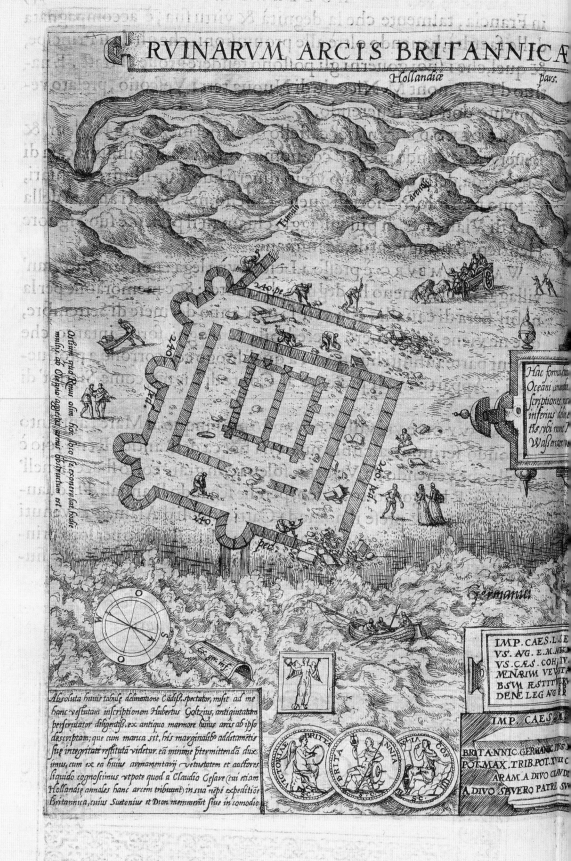

RVINARVM ARCIS BRITANNICAE

Hollandiæ pars.

Haec forma...
Oceani...
scriptiones...
inferius adm...
tis, vbi nunc...
Wassenaer...

Germania

IMP. CAES. L...
VS. AVG. E. M...
VS. CAES. COH...
MENARVM VE...
BSVM RSTIT...
DENE LEG AG...

IMP. CAES. A...

BRITANNIC. GERMANIC. I...
POT. MAX. TRIB. POT. XVII C...
ARAM. A DIVO CLAV...
A DIVO SEVERO PATRE S...

Absoluta huius tabulæ delineatione Cadisti spectator, misit ad me
hanc vetustam inscriptionem Hubertus Goltzius, antiquitatum
perscrutator diligentiss. ex antiquo marmore huius arcis ab ipso
descriptam; quæ cum manca sit, his marginalibus additamentis
siue integritate restituta videtur. eã minime ptermittenda dux-
imus, cum ex ea huius armamentarij vetustatem et auctores
liquido cognoscimus, vtpote quod à Claudio Cesare (cui etiam
Hollandiæ annales hanc arcem tribuunt) in sua nempe expeditiõe
Britannica, cuius Suetonius et Dion memmerũt siue in comodio.

them. Forty years later, in 1603, his friend, the Dutch Londoner Johannes Radermacher, reminisced in a letter to Abraham's favourite nephew Jacob Cool Jr:

In hac mentio nonnunquam facta est Abrahami, quem se cognatum habere Meteranus dicebat, literarum artiumque bonarum amore flagrantissimum, sed eadem fere qua nos iniquitate fortunae restrictum: quod etsi liber, nulliusque servitute devinctus, matrem tamen viduam, et sorores duas adolescentulas, in rei familiaris angustia, sua opera iuvare mallet, quam scholasticis in se impensis gravare. Iste cum ad historias intelligendas delectaretur inprimis studio Geographico, ex comparatione undecunque haberi possent optimarum chartarum geographicarum, hac ratione victum tam honeste quam iucunde quaerere tentavit, ut eas opera sororum mappis concinne munitas, sua vero coloribus; distinctius elegantiusque quam alius cuiusquam, illustratas distraheret: in Italiam usque (quam pulchra hac occasione saepius lustravit) transferens factas in Belgio, inde ac aliunde referret peregrinas.[33]

Abraham Ortelius was often spoken of in this way. Van Meteren said that Ortelius was his relative and burned with a passion for literature and the liberal arts, but was hampered by almost the same iniquity of fortune as we were. Although he was free and not bound by servitude to anyone, he nevertheless preferred to use his wealth to help his widowed mother and two adolescent sisters, who were in financial straits, rather than burdening himself with spending on his own education. Since in addition to studying history he enjoyed especially geography, he thus attempted to make an honest and pleasant living by acquiring the best maps from wherever they could be obtained in order that he might sell maps which, once suitably mounted on linen by his sisters and coloured by him, would be more clearly and elegantly illustrated than anyone else's. He took maps made in Belgium all the way to Italy (which, for this pleasant reason, he rather often explored) so that he might bring back foreign maps from Italy and elsewhere.

4.4 *previous pages* Study of the 'Brittenburg' by Abraham Ortelius (1568), as included in Lodovico Guicciardini's *Descrittione di tutti i Paesi Bassi* (*Description of all the Low Countries*). The walls' foundations can be seen exposed in the sand by low water. Oxford, Bodleian Library, F 2.7 Art., pp. 344–5.

But in the early 1560s, while his sister Anne lived with him and continued the colouring business, Abraham's interests expanded into publishing maps himself.[34] Over the following years, Ortelius eagerly discussed the findings at the Brittenburg site with learned friends.[35] The result of these discussions was a depiction of the site and a description of its remains, published in 1568 (fig. 4.4). It appears to have drawn interest particularly from Ortelius's Anglo-Dutch circle. In 1568 Johannes Radermacher wrote to Ortelius to tell him that he had bought a copy in London; in 1572 the English diplomat Daniel Rogers wrote to Ortelius to request a copy to add to Ortelius's atlas, the *Theatrum orbis terrarum*, which had first appeared in print in 1570.[36]

The atlas went through many supplements and enlarged editions within Ortelius's lifetime, expanding from the original 69 to 222 maps.[37] The *Theatrum* was an innovative work, and constituted a transformative step in establishing the early modern genre of the atlas. It comprised maps of the entire known world, brought together from the work of many cartographers but each presented according to a regular specification,[38] with accompanying descriptive texts about the regions depicted on the maps. Such atlases were chorographical as well as topographical. Maps, Ortelius wrote in his introduction, primarily served the study of history:

> the reading of *Histories* doeth both seeme to be much more pleasant, and in deed so it is, when the Mappe being layed before our eyes, we may behold things done, or places where they were done, as if they were at this time present and in doing. … Which things being so, how much those which are students and lovers of *Histories* are combred, hindred and stayd, yea, & many times, even while they are in their race and continued course, drawne backe, it is an easie matter to conceive, when either the description of all countreys cannot be gotten, or if they may be gotten, they are dearer then that every mans money will reach and attaine unto especially those that are but poore, or none of the wealthiest.

Ortelius (here in the English edition of 1608) described how maps were often too expensive, and were customarily printed in a size too large for convenient consultation in smaller lodgings. Unrolling or unfolding maps could be cumbersome, and in order to hang them on one's wall, 'a Princes

4.5 *following pages* Map of England and Wales (1573), based on information sent to Abraham Ortelius by Humphrey Llwyd. From Ortelius's *The Theatre of the Whole World* (1608), with maps printed by the Antwerp Plantin press, and English text printed by the Londoner John Norton. Oxford, Bodleian Library, Douce O subt. 15, after p. xlii.

SEP[T...]

Scotiæ pars.

ANGLIAE
REGNI FLO,
RENTISSIMI
NOVA DESCRIP,
TIO, AVCTORE
HVMFREDO
LHVYD DEN,
BYGIENSE
15 · 73

Cum Priuilegio.

OCCIDENS.

Hiberniæ pars.

MARE HIBERNICVM

WALLIS.

Sorlinges insulæ.

CORNWALL

OCEANVS BRITANNICVS

MERI

Scala miliarium Anglicorum.

OCEANVS GER
MANICVS

ORIENS.

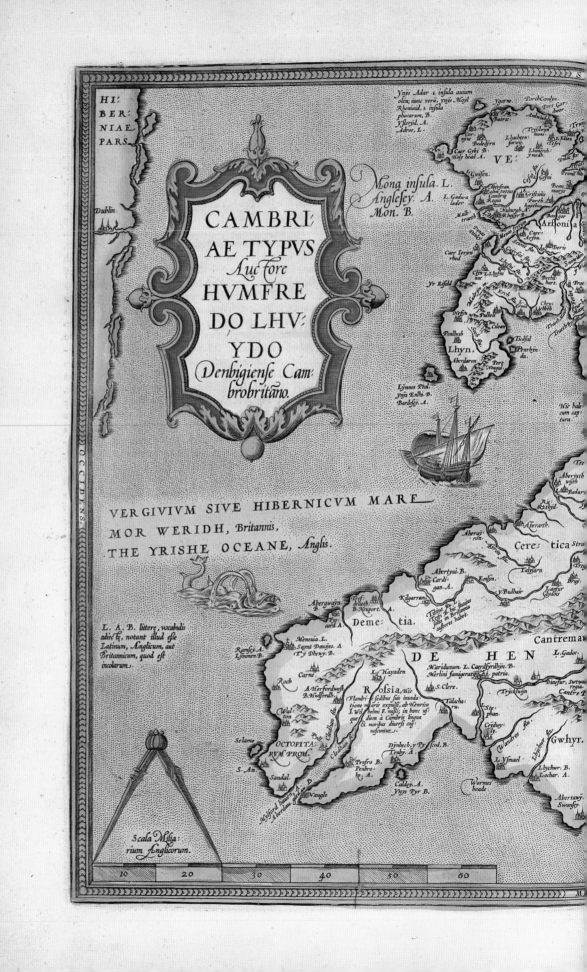

HI:
BER:
NIAE
PARS.

Dublin

Ynys Adar i. insula auium
olim; nunc verò, yuys Moyl
Rhoniaid, i insula
phocarum, B.
Yssleryd. A.
Adror, L.

Ygarne
PorthComlyn.
Port Gar:
wor.

Mona insula. L.
Anglesey. A.
Mon. B.

VE

CAMBRI
AE TYPVS
Auctore
HVMFRE
DO LHV:
YDO
Denbigiense Cam:
brobritano.

Lhyn.
Aberdaron
Port Vougai

Lynnos Ptol.
Ynys Enlhi. B.
Bardsey. A.

Arsonia

Penllech
Aberyst
wyth
Badarn

VERGIVIVM SIVE HIBERNICVM MARE

MOR WERIDH, Britannis,

THE YRISHE OCEANE, Anglis.

Cere tica

L. A. B. litterę, vocabulis
adiectę, notant illud esse
Latinum, Anglicum, aut
Britannicum, quod est
incolarum.

Abergwayn
Tref
drūth.
B. Newport. A.
Tyr
card. A.
Deme tia.

Cardi
gan. A.
Emlyn
y Bulhair
Lanfur
Glydois

DE HEN
L. Gadoc

Meneuia. L.
Saynt Dauses. A.
Ty Dhewy. B.

L. Hayaden
Maridunum. L. Caerfyrdhyn. B.
Merlini famigeratissi patria.

Dinefur Sutywoto
regia.
Cantre

Ramsey. A.
Lynnen. B.

Roch
Carne
A Herfordwest.
B. Hwsfordh.

Trykhuin

Croydey:
ly.

Stephan

S. Clere

Roslia, Wi:
Flandri se sedibus suis inunda
tione maris expulsi, ab Henrico
I Whilhelmi F. missi; in hunc us
que diem à Cambris lingua
& moribus diuersi cog
noscuntur.

Talacha
ru.

Gwhyr.

Wal
ton
Selame

OCTOPITA:
RVM PROM.

S. An:
Sandal.

Djnbech, y Pryscod. B.
Tenby. A.

Penfro B.
Penbro:
ke, A.

Caldey. A.
Ynys Pyr B.

Wormes
heade
L. Ysmael

Lhychwr. B.
Lochar. A.

Abertawy
Swansey.

Mylford hauen
Aberdawgledheu

Ningle

Scala Milia:
rium Anglicorum.

| 10 | 20 | 30 | 40 | 50 | 60 |

Ljrpol.

Waringthon Merse flu

Cilguri. B. Wyrral. A.

Frodshau

Aliquod Regionum huius tractus synonyma, prout Latinè, Britannicè & Anglicè etiamnum appellantur.

Cambria, L.
Cambry, B.
Wales, A.

Ceretica, L.
Ceredigion B.
Cardigan, A.

Venedotia, L.
Gwynedhia, B.
Northwales, A.

Pouisia, L.
Powijs, B.

Demetia, L.
Dyfet, B.
Westwales, A.

Dehenbart, B.
Sutwales, A.

ANGLIAE
PARS
olim
LHOEGRIA
appellata

Brangonia olim, nunc Vigornia L.
Caer fraugo, B.
Worcestre, A.

Claudia, & Glouernia L.
Caer Glofi, et Caer Loÿw, B.
Glocestre, A.

Danica sylua.
Dean forest.

Cum Priuilegio

Venta Belgarum L.
Caer oder yn nant bathon. B.
Brightstowe A.

ORIENS.

gallery or spacious Theater' was required. His atlas, then, would provide such a theatre within the dimensions of a book:

> This I having oft made triall of, I began to bethinke my selfe, what meanes might be found to redresse these discommodities, which I have spoken of, and either to make them somewhat lesse, or, if possibly it might bee, to take them all cleane away. And at length me thought it might be done by that meanes which we have observed and set downe in this our booke, to which I earnestly wish that every student would affoord a place in his Library, amongst the rest of his bookes.[39]

The atlas that provided a similar all-world view, Ptolemy's *Geographia*, had been subject of study in the West since the late fourteenth century, and was reproduced in many printed editions from 1477 (after its initial edition without maps of 1475).[40] Though it did lay out maps of the known world, the accompanying texts were limited to explication of the projection methods and coordinates of places noted on the maps. The chorographical method of Ortelius, combining geographical with historical information, provided a vision of the world more suited to the needs of the modern student. Those needs were also kept in mind when considering the scope and size, and consequently the affordability, of the work.

Family and business ties ensured that Ortelius had an interest in England from early on, but his interest in history led to him becoming the centre of a burgeoning Anglo-Dutch intellectual network.[41] This development started, however, with a meeting with a Welshman, Humphrey Llwyd, an antiquarian historian and map-maker from Denbigh, who after graduating from the University of Oxford entered the service of the earl of Arundel. Ortelius possibly met Llwyd when the latter travelled through Antwerp in 1567.[42] At this time Llwyd was preoccupied with defending legendary British history from the challenge posed to it by the Italian humanist Polydore Virgil, who had questioned the historicity of King Arthur. Following conversations between the two men in Antwerp, Llwyd sent Ortelius historical materials on Britain when he returned home. These included a treatise on Anglesey, work on the origins of the name 'Brittenburg' and maps of England (fig. 4.5) and Wales (fig. 4.6),[43] which Ortelius subsequently printed as part of his

4.6 *previous pages* Map of Wales (1573), from Abraham Ortelius's *The Theatre of the Whole World* (1608). It was the first map of Wales alone to appear in print, and was based on information sent to Ortelius by Humphrey Llwyd. Oxford, Bodleian Library, Douce O subt. 15, after p. 13.

4.7 *opposite* 'The Lowe Countries', from *The Mirror of the Worlde* (1598), translated from the French version of Abraham Ortelius's *Theatre* by the teenager Elizabeth Tanfield (later Elizabeth Cary). Oxford, Bodleian Library, Dep. d. 817, fol. 18v.

The lowe Countries

This table containeth but 17 prouinces w'th th'Emperour Charles of
good memorie gave to his sonne king Philippe of Spaine namely
the Duchie of BRABANTE, GVILDERLAND LIMBOVRGE
and LVXIMBOVRGE, the Earldom of FLAVNDERS AR
TOIS, HENAVLE HOLLANDE ZELANDE, NAMVRE, &
ZVTPHEN The Marquisate of the holy Empire the Lordshippes
of FRISELANDE, MALINS, VTRVKE, OVERISSIL and
GROININGE, which Countries are all well inhabited in such sorte
that Lewes Guicciardine in his perticular description of the low Countries that there are 208 and 8 walled townes compassed with ditches
and more then 6300 villages w'ch have churches and Parishes, besides
Castles and greate lords houses of which there is an infinite mul-
titude. Strangers as Spaniards, Italians & French men call the
countrie of one common name Flaunders, and the Inhabitants
Flemmings: in which they committ a greate errour, taking a part for
the whole, for Flaunders is but a parte of all this Countrie. Even
as one meaning Spaine should name Castilia or Andalusia, or if
one speakinge of all Italy should name Tuscaine or Lombardie
likewise if one readinge of Normandy or Gascony should thinke he
hard of all the Realme of Fraunce. This errour Ortelius a wyse
man and very curiouse in such searches saith haith bene bredd by
the traffick of the low cuntries which is done at Bruges, and noe
where els in all this Countrie soe that this towne only causeth the
freguentacion of strange nations, and this towne beinge seated
in Flaunders, all comes from Flaunders, all goes to Flaunders, &
hearing no other bruite but Flaunders, they thought the name of
all the Countrie to be soe.

atlas *Theatrum orbis terrarum*. The map of Wales was the first of its kind to appear in print.[44] Llwyd died before Ortelius received his materials, but the Dutch geographer – soon appointed royal geographer to King Philip II of Spain,[45] and as such a powerful patron in his own right – ensured the further publication of Llwyd's notes on British history, *Commentarioli Britannicae descriptionis fragmentum* (Cologne, 1572; published in English in 1573 as *The Breviary of Britain*).[46] The work was a catalyst for further Dutch perceptions of Britain: the Dutch artist Lucas de Heere compiled a Dutch description of the British Isles in 1573–75 in which he referred to Llwyd's Latin 'copieux boucxkin' ('copious little book') as one of his authorities on British antiquities.[47]

Ortelius's goal for his atlas, which was the provision of a source of cultural knowledge, was evidently achieved. This can be seen, for example, in the work of Christopher Marlowe, who had a copy of the *Theatrum* open on his desk as he composed his play *Tamburlaine the Great* (first printed in 1590). 'Give me a map,' Tamburlaine calls towards the end of the play, 'then let me see how much / Is left for me to conquer all the world.'[48] Not only lists of geographical names, but also visual details from Ortelius's maps, appear in Marlowe's play: the ships dotting the Mediterranean with slaves 'That naked row about the Terrene Sea';[49] 'A Turkish galley of my royal fleet';[50] and a depiction of 'fair Europe, mounted on her bull, / Trapped with the wealth and riches of the world, / … wear[ing] a woeful mourning weed'.[51]

ELIZABETH CARY'S *THE MIRROR OF THE WORLDE* [52]

Another early reader of Ortelius's atlas was the young Elizabeth Tanfield (*c*.1585–1639), who translated its French version into English when she was eleven or twelve years old (fig. 4.7). The act of translation was educational: Elizabeth was being tutored in multiple languages, including Latin, French, Hebrew and Spanish, after mastering the fundamentals 'without a teacher' in early childhood.[53] Her linguistic brilliance attracted rare praise from the grumpily misogynistic poet Michael Drayton in two dedications in his *Englands Heroicall Epistles* in 1597, when she was only twelve, and he may have been employed as one of her tutors. Her Ortelius manuscript, now Oxford, Bodleian Library, Dep. d. 817, is written in her own hand, constituting a rare woman's voice within the chorographical world.[54]

In 1602 Elizabeth married Sir Henry Cary, Lord Falkland, an unhappy union eventually fractured through their theological differences and her

4.8 Portrait of Elizabeth Cary (*c*.1620) by Paul van Somer. Van Somer, originally from Antwerp, lived in London from 1616. Sarah Campbell Blaffer Foundation, Houston, BF.1985.20.

conversion to Catholicism in 1626. The first years of Elizabeth Cary's married life were shaped by Anglo-Dutch relations. Her husband promptly left for the Netherlands as a soldier in the Protestant war against Spain, only to return to England after three years in Spanish captivity from 1605.[55] During this period Cary took up original composition, becoming the first known female author of original drama in English with a now lost play set in Syracuse, followed by *The Tragedy of Mariam* (1613), based on Josephus's account of Mariam's desperately unhappy marriage to Herod the Great.[56]

Around 1620 she sat for a flamboyant portrait with artist Paul van Somer (fig. 4.8), a painter from Antwerp, who had also spent periods in Leiden and Brussels. Somer lived in London from 1616, where he painted a series of portraits commissioned by courtiers and royals. He died in 1622 and was buried at St Martin-in-the-Fields.[57] His image of Elizabeth blazes with solar imagery and, in contrast to her pious effigy in the Church of St John the Baptist, Burford, kneeling at the head of her father's tomb, seems to evoke her difficult but self-determined path away from parental, marital, gender and religious norms.

The manuscript of Elizabeth's *Mirror* entered the collections of the Bodleian Library only relatively recently. In the early twentieth century it was owned by the antiquary Harold Lee-Dillon, seventeenth Viscount Dillon. He gave it to Burford parish in 1925, where it was deposited in a safe in St John the Baptist Church. It was rediscovered in the 1970s and loaned to the Bodleian Library.

WILLIAM CAMDEN AND JOHN SPEED

Through his friendship with Humphrey Llwyd, Abraham Ortelius became passionate about British antiquities. This interest had far-reaching consequences. During a visit to England he shared his enthusiasm with his friend William Camden, urging him to devote his energies to the same topic – as Camden reminisced in the introduction to the work that resulted from that encouragement, *Britannia*:

> Eximius veteris geographiae restaurator Abrahamus Ortelius ante annum tricensimum mecum pluribus egit ut Britanniam nostram, antiquam illam illustrarerem: hoc est, ut Britanniae antiquitatem et suae antiquitati Britanniam restituerem, ut vetustis novitatem, obscuris lucem, dubiis fidem adderem; et

ut veritatem in rebus nostris, quam vel scriptorum securitas vel vulgi credulitas proscripserant, quoad fieri posset, postliminio revocarem.[58]

Abraham Ortelius the worthy restorer of Ancient Geographie, arriving heere in England above thirty foure yeares past, dealt earnestly with me that I would illustrate this Ile of Britaine, or (as he said) that I would restore antiquity to Britaine, and Britaine to his antiquity; which was as I understood, that I would renew ancientrie, enlighten obscuritie, cleare doubts, and recall home veritie by way of recovery, which the negligence of writers and credulitie of the common sort had in a manner proscribed and utterly banished from amongst us.[59]

4.9 Terrestrial globe (1592) by Emery Molyneux, the first to be made in England, with maps engraved by Jodocus Hondius. Molyneux and Hondius soon both moved to Amsterdam, then the burgeoning centre for map-making. National Trust inv. 486024, Petworth House, West Sussex. Photo © NTPL / John Hammond.

Ortelius and Camden engaged in a lively correspondence, of which several letters are preserved in the Bodleian Library.[60] In 1586 the first edition of the resulting study, *Britannia*, appeared, followed by five successively enlarged editions under Camden's direction over two decades and an English translation in 1610. The work was a sweeping survey of Britain's history according to its geography, moving through the island (with a supplement for Ireland) from region to region. By the early seventeenth century the study of British antiquities, which Camden had commenced at Ortelius's urging, had long outgrown its original ambition. The sixth Latin edition (1607) saw an updating that may have been inspired by Ortelius's atlas *Theatrum*: the first edition of *Britannia* had contained a single map of England and Wales, but in Camden's final revision of 1607 Britain was split into regions, each covered by a different map. The division into regions corresponded with Camden's knowledge of the different tribes of Britain described in Roman sources. These maps, based on recent surveys, were engraved by William Hole, an Englishman, and by William Kip, who was originally from Utrecht.[61] As in Ortelius's atlas, the maps of Camden's *Britannia* were printed with text on the reverse of the page.

The example of Ortelius's *Theatrum* may also lie behind the title of the work that set a new standard for the topographical depiction of Britain: John Speed's *The Theatre of the Empire of Great Britaine* (1611/12). Whereas Ortelius's *Theatrum* was an intangible influence, William Camden's contribution to Speed's work was material: it was he who introduced the author to the engraver Jodocus Hondius. Hondius led the principal firm of map engravers in

4.10 Map of Oxfordshire, with inset street map of Oxford. The map was engraved by Jodocus Hondius in Amsterdam. The copper plate was then sent to London for use in John Speed's *The Theatre of the Empire of Great Britaine* (1612). Oxford, Bodleian Library, J. Maps 224 [10], recto.

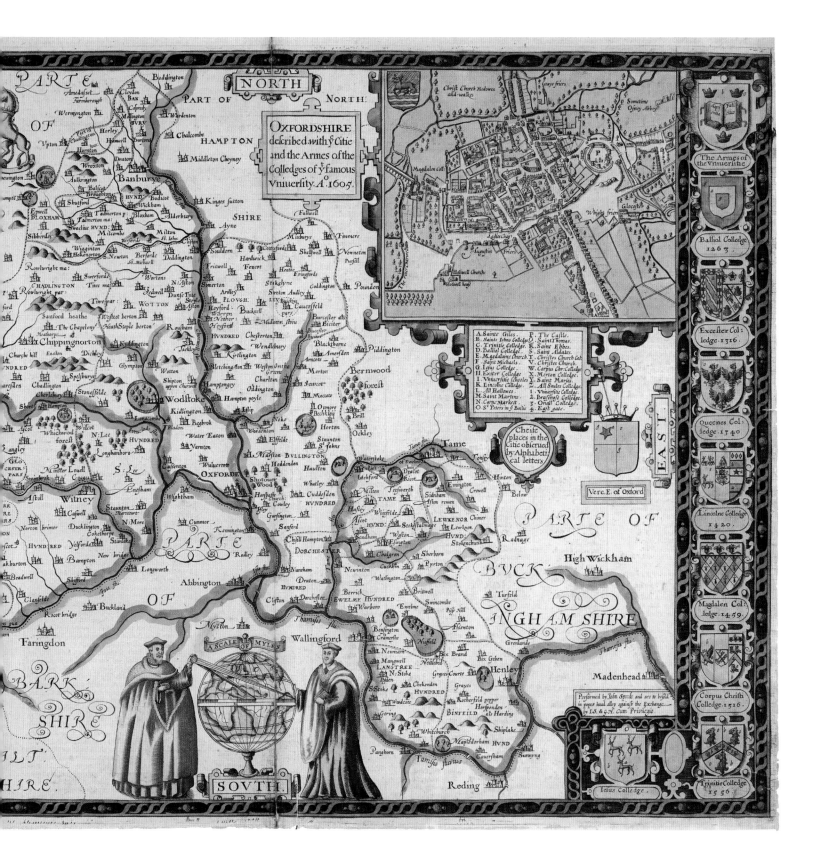

Amsterdam, and had himself lived in London between 1584 and 1593 after fleeing religious troubles in his native Ghent. In London, Hondius engraved the gores for the globes of Emery Molyneux, based on a world map incorporating Sir Francis Drake's circumnavigation of the earth. These are the oldest surviving globes published in England (fig. 4.9). In the 1590s Hondius returned to the Netherlands, but to Holland instead of the south; he was soon followed by Molyneux himself, who required his expert engraver in order to continue producing globes.[62] Through Camden's introduction of Hondius to Speed, the maps of Speed's *Theatre* came to be engraved in Amsterdam while the text was being prepared for printing in London at the same time. Printed proofs of the maps were sent from Amsterdam to London; once checked, the engraved copper plates made their own North Sea crossing to England. They were used for editions in London throughout the seventeenth century, being passed from printer to printer and surviving even the Great Fire of London. They were last used for an edition of Speed's *Theatre* in 1676, and were still used for the printing of individual maps as late as 1795.[63] Even when the text that originally accompanied the maps is omitted, the chorographical vision of Speed's and Hondius's cartography speaks clearly from the maps: the map of Oxfordshire, for example, includes an inset of a bird's-eye view of Oxford and (in the margins) the arms of the university and its constituent colleges, as well as those of the earl of Oxford and the university's legendary founder, King Alfred (fig. 4.10).

CLAES JANSZ VISSCHER'S *PANORAMA OF LONDON*

Jodocus Hondius also played a part in what is probably the most famous depiction of London in the seventeenth century. The *Panorama of London* by the Amsterdam engraver Claes Jansz Visscher (fig. 4.11) was published in 1616 by Hondius's heirs – nominally his young son, Ludovicus, but in reality his widow, Collette.[64] It is similar in set-up to Anton van den Wyngaerde's earlier panorama, but depicts the city from a somewhat different vantage point, west instead of east of London Bridge. Its four plates together constitute an image two metres long. Van den Wyngaerde's panorama was never disseminated and survives only in its single hand-drawn copy. Visscher's engraved panorama, however, was often reproduced. Its depiction of the old St Paul's Cathedral towering above its surroundings has become the iconic image of the London skyline before the Great Fire.

Unlike van den Wyngaerde who surveyed the city in person, however, Visscher in all likelihood never visited London. He may have worked from a recent survey, perhaps one made by Jodocus Hondius or by Hondius's brother-in-law Pieter van den Keere, both of whom had lived in London. In the same year van den Keere produced a similar panorama of Constantinople, and he later created a series of maps of the counties of England that were then used for a reissue of Camden's *Britannia*. They became known as the 'Miniature Speeds' when they were subsequently used for a pocket edition of John Speed's *Theatre*. Drawings of London made by Hondius or van den Keere could have come to Visscher through Colette Hondius, who had taken over the publishing business after the death of her husband in 1612. Many details of Visscher's panorama, however, are erroneous. Some evidently rely on previous sources, not even necessarily related to London: the ships on the Thames, for example, are drawn from Visscher's own earlier depiction of the Armada.[65] The steeple of Austin Friars, still prominently marked, had recently collapsed. Despite its detailed and realistic appearance, Visscher's panorama of London was not that of an eyewitness, but an imagined depiction of what the city should look like.

THE ATLASES OF HONDIUS AND BLAEU

While Abraham Ortelius was developing his atlas, his friend Gerard Mercator, originally from Flanders but in exile in Duisburg from 1552, developed himself as the time's most expert map-maker, focusing in particular on globes and wall maps. He shared several of Ortelius's English contacts, including the mathematician and geographer John Dee, and gathered details on the geography both of the Arctic and of Britain from them, while they, in turn, were inspired by his theories on improving compass observations. Among Mercator's most famous productions was a giant wall map of Britain and Ireland, of 1564, published by Christophe Plantin in Antwerp; records of sales of copies of this map to customers in London survive.[66] Eventually, following in the footsteps of Ortelius, who had published his first atlas in Antwerp in 1570, Mercator's own complete *Atlas* was published posthumously in Duisburg in 1595, a year after his death (two parts had been published by him in 1585 and 1589). The copperplate engravings produced for this atlas were subsequently obtained by Jodocus Hondius. Following Jodocus's death in 1612, this acquisition helped establish the Amsterdam publishing house of the Hondius family as the principal publisher of maps and atlases in the 1620s.

4.11 *following four pages* Claes Jansz Visscher's *Panorama of London*, first published in Amsterdam in 1616 by Collette Hondius. The octagonal depictions of the theatres in the foreground are erroneous, but other details, such as the Dutch eel ships mooring in the Thames, are accurate. Oxford, Bodleian Library, Douce Prints a.53 (2), recto.

Londinum, antiqua olim regia Britannia
Urbs, et qua notrev̇ides clariṡima ſecle
Quas tua templa canet ſublimibus alta columnis
Ac vi/q, domus, magnique Palatia, Regni,
Quas refert hantc̄ Francine in ſacra Capita
Dextras et oyes, et crebre ſernire Pontem
Splendidaq, et nitidi tu ſub ſtibudine, ſinh.
Imperium Regina truce. das Iura Britannia
Londinum.

Burly houſe   Harrow on the hill

The Swan

Vißcher Delineavit

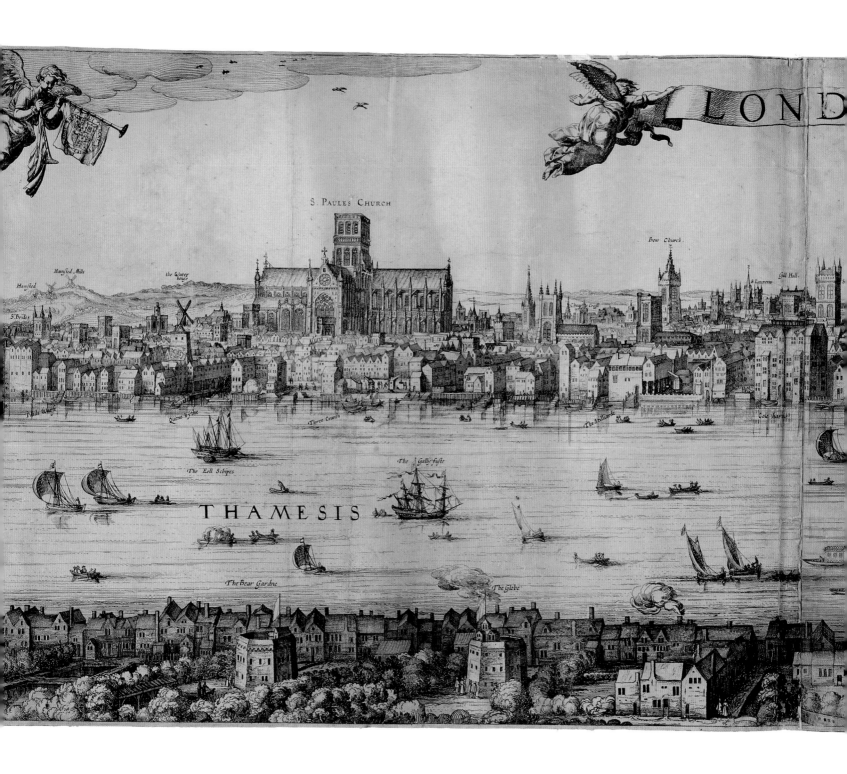

S. PAULES CHURCH

LOND

Hamsted Mills

the Water house

Bow Church

S. Brides

Hamsted

Gill Hall

S Laurens

Powle Wharfe

Quene hythe

Three Cranes

The Stilliarde

Cole harbar

The Eell Schipes

The Galy fuste

THAMESIS

The Bear Gardne

The Globe

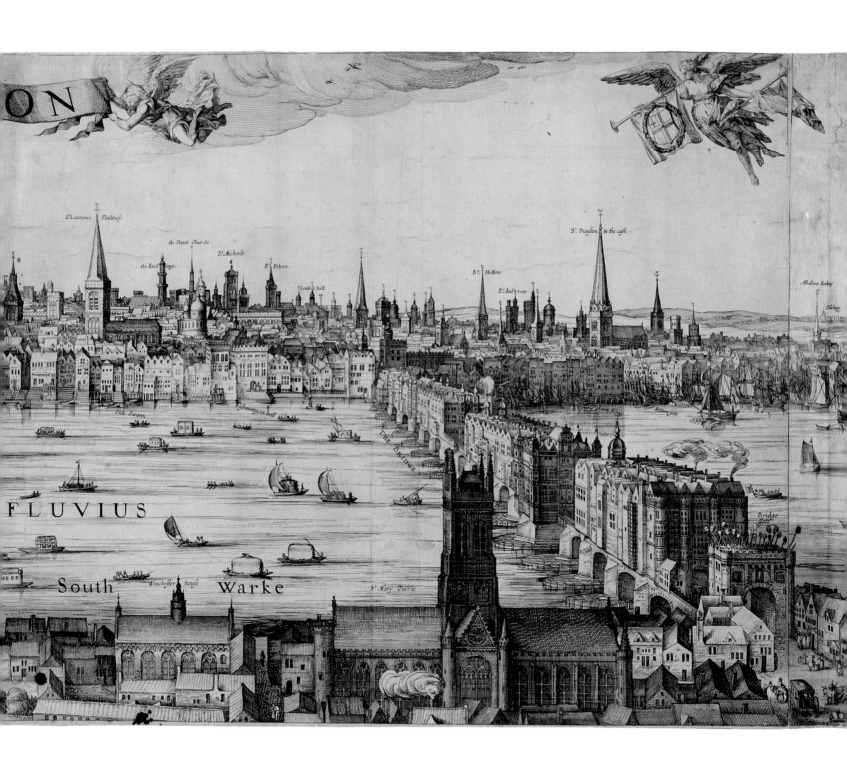

ON

St Laurence Pountney.

the Dutch Churche.

the Exchange.   St Michaels.

St Peters.

Leaden hall

St Dunston in the east

St Hellen.

St Andrew

Alhallowes Barking

Old Swann

Fishmongers hall

THE BRIDGE

Lion Key

Billingsgate

FLUVIUS

Bridge Gate

South   Winchester house   Warke

St Mary Overs

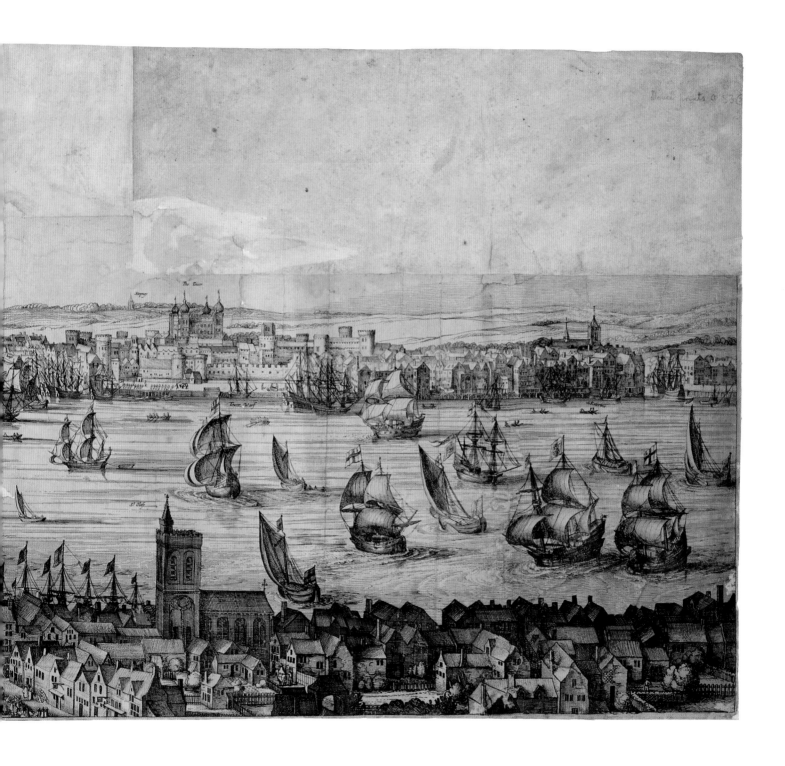

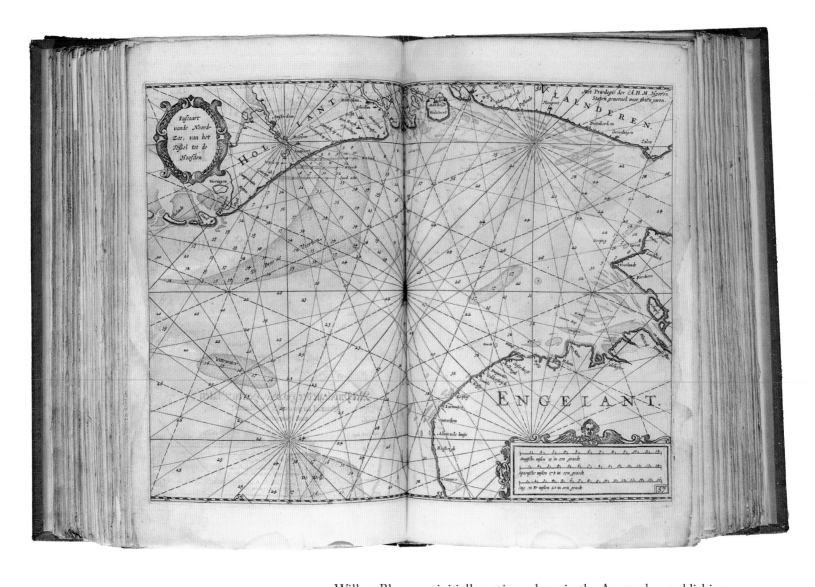

4.12 Portolan chart of the North Sea between England, Holland and Flanders. From the pilot guide *Zeespiegel* (*The Sea-Mirrour*), first published by Willem Janszoon Blaeu in 1623, and in English translation in 1625. Oxford, Bodleian Library, Map. Res. 98 (1639), vol. 3, after the title page.

Willem Blaeu was initially a minor player in the Amsterdam publishing market, having started his career as a maker of globes. By the 1620s Blaeu was principally focused on the niche market of portolan charts, aided by his son Joan Blaeu. These charts aimed to accurately depict the seas and coasts for navigational uses (fig. 4.12). The Hondius firm's plagiarism of one of their works appears to have been the catalyst for a series of remarkable publications, which were among the most lavishly produced and expensive books of their time. From the 1630s onwards, both publishing houses dedicated their efforts to producing ever more elaborate atlases of the known world. In retaliation for the Hondius family's plagiarism, the Blaeu family embarked on producing their own atlas, which led to intense competition between the two houses, as each publisher created their own ever-expanding series of volumes.[67]

In 1645 both houses published volumes covering England; both paired copies of the county maps of John Speed's *Theatre* with text taken from Camden's *Britannia*. Speed's maps, as noted above, had been engraved by Jodocus Hondius, who had been introduced to Speed by Camden. Camden's *Britannia* had been inspired by the urging of Abraham Ortelius. In the English volumes of the great atlases of the Blaeu and Hondius publishing houses, this intricate history of reciprocal Anglo-Dutch influences in chorography reached its culmination. Evidently, the publishers further anticipated markets both in Britain and on the Continent which were eager for detailed information about the islands of the North Atlantic. England, together with Scotland and Ireland in a later volume, occupied a disproportionate place in the eventual complete set of volumes of Blaeu's world atlas: a total of 113 maps, which together constitute almost a third of the work.[68]

PANORAMA OF THE GREAT FIRE OF LONDON

While Blaeu and Hondius were producing their massive sets of volumes, other Amsterdam publishers devoted themselves to the other end of the market: printed ephemera. Over the course of the seventeenth century, Amsterdam had established itself as the centre of news publishing in western Europe. Publishers served international, polyglot audiences with cheap, up-to-date accounts of current events. Accompanied by engravings, the equivalent of today's journalistic photography, broadsheet accounts of important political events and natural disasters were published to answer an insatiable demand for news. They were rapidly distributed to both local and international audiences. When a fire destroyed the greater part of London in September 1666, Amsterdam printers were quick to publish accounts of the event. That England and the United Provinces were at war – the Second Anglo-Dutch War had been raging for a year and a half – only served to heighten the salience of the disaster that had struck England's capital. It also helped bring the conclusion of the conflict closer, because England was forced to divert its energy and revenue to restoring the destroyed city. A spectacular engraving, depicting a panorama of London engulfed in flames and billowing clouds, was soon printed in Amsterdam, made by an anonymous engraver for publisher Marcus Willemsz Doornick (fig. 4.13).[69]

LONDON

Withe Hall · THAMESIS. FLUVIUS · South Warke.

Afbeelding, en kort-bondige Beschrijving,

Van den verschrickelijcken

BRANDT der Stadt LONDON.

Op den 12, 13, 14, 15 en 16 Septemb. Anno 1666.

Van verscheyde schadelijcke Branden / waer door heele Steden zijn t'onder gebracht / getuygen d'oude en nieuwe Historien; maer van dese vernielende en gruwelijcken Brandt / in de Stadt Londen, op den 12 Septemb. begonnen / heeftmen in eenige Eeuwen niet gelesen. Want d'oude Stadt / daer de meeste rijckdom te vinden was / is bijna t'eenemael in asch en puyn verstoven en nedergevallen. Sy is dan ontsteecken op Sondagh morgen / ten 2 uuren / in Puddinglane, streckende die Lane of Steegh na de Brugge van den Towr, by de nieuwe Vis-straet, in een Backers Huys, door wat toeval weetmen niet; maer dit wel / dat de sleynachtinge van desen Brandt / by soo overhevigen stijven windt uyt den Oosten / voorsaeck is ghe-

den van Marcklane, en tot den Towrdock: Alduis is het grootste en beste gedeelte / zijnde het binnenste van dese Stadt vernielt / wel een uur gaens of meer / wesende de uythoeken maer blijven staen / so dat van den Tempel tot des Towrs Magazijnen by na niet is over gebleven / uytgenomen van Ledenhal tot Aldergate, en na Bis-schops Gate-straet, en van die deelen na Cripplegate, en van Aldersgate tot Smijt-field. Buyten de Poorten is de grootste schade geschiet in Fleet-street, en van Hol-borne tot Fleedbridge. Wat Huysen in 't geheel zijn verbrandt / kan men niet wel seggen; maer men gist 20 duysent Huysen / en van 98 Kercken zijn maer 11 onge-schent gebleven / soo dat 'er 87 zijn verbrandt / daer onder de seer beroemde St. Pau-lus Kerck, daer van men seyt dat voor Christi Geboorte gebouwt geweest is. Wat elende in dese Brandt is gheweest / is niet om uyt te spreecken / veele brachten haer goet van 't een in 't ander Huys / en dat verbrande daer na wederom / die in 't open Veldt vluchten hebben 't best gehadt; doch hoe jammerlijck de luyden haer daer hebben moeten behelpen / kan men gissen. Daer herbergen 10 of 12 Huys-gesinnen in een Huys / en noch moeten veele op 't open Velt blijven; weshalven sijn Majesteyt heeft geordonneert / aen de omleggende Plaetsen en Dorpen / de be-schadighde te ontfangen in haer Kercken / Kapellen en Gods-huysen; en oock / dat de Bevelhebbers die by de Inwoonders sullen doen in-legeren. Den Towr heeft mede groot perijckel geloopen: in-voegen / dat / soo men de Huysen daer om-trent niet om ter hadde geholpen / het was daer mede aengegaen / also de Brant al in de Poorten was: doch elders heeftmen wel de Huysen neergestaelt / maer de windt soo stijf zijnde / heeft de blam over de neergehaelde Huysen heen geset. Op Woensdagh dede den Koning groote naerstigheyt / besonder by Templebare, om het

Pourt

De l'hor

VILLE

Le 12, 13, 1

E 12 S
s'estant p
au Pont
tellemen
estoit to
possible
de maison
tier-la e

M. le Duc d'Yorck monter
exemple à travailler à l'extin
pour y couper chemin, mais

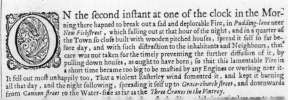

t & Defcription,

embrafement de Feu, dans la

e LONDRES.

& 16 Septembre, l'an 1666.

nbre, a deux heures apres minuit, le feu
maifon d'un Boulanger, dans la ruë qui va de la Tour
voifins ayant negligé d'aider à l'éteindre, il accreut
violence du vent d'Ooft, qu'à la pointe du jour il
embrafé dans les maifons des environs, qu'il fut im-
indre quel remede qu'on y apportaft par abbatement
par le jet des eaux, la plûpart des maifons de ce quar-
bois & de plâtre & les ruës fort étroites. Le Roy &
eval pour exhorter le Maire & tous les autres par leur
l'embrafement, & firent fauter quantité de maifons

A true Pourtraict with a Brief Defcription

Of that deplorable

FIRE of LONDON.

Befallen the 12, 13, 14, 15 *and* 16 Sept. 1666.

ON the fecond inftant at one of the clock in the Mor-
ning there hapned to break out a fad and deplorable Fire, in *Pudding-lane* neer
New Fifhftreet , which falling out at that hour of the night , and in a quarter of
the Town fo clofe built with wooden pitched houfes , fpread it felf fo far before day , and with fuch diftraction to the inhabitants and Neighbours, that
care was not taken for the timely preventing the further diffufion of it , by
pulling down houfes, as ought to have been ; fo that this lamentable Fire in
a fhort time became too big to be mafted by any Engines or working neer it.
It fell out moft unhappily too , That a violent Eafterley wind fomented it , and kept it burning
all that day , and the night following , fpreading it felf up to *Grace-church ftreet* , and downwards
from *Cannon ftreet* to the Water-fide as far as the *Three Cranes in the Vintrey*.

4.13 Panorama of London from the broadsheet
*A True Pourtraict with a Brief Description of that Deplorable
Fire of London Befallen the 12, 13, 14, 15 and 16 Sept. 1666,*
published by Marcus Willemsz Doornick in Amsterdam
very soon after the event. Oxford, Bodleian Library, Firth
a.3 (f.23), recto.

In the political climate of the Second Anglo-Dutch War, it was natural to blame foreigners for this catastrophe. John Dryden, in his *Annus mirabilis* (1667), a poem commemorating the events of the Second Anglo-Dutch War, blamed winds of Dutch origin: 'from the east, a *Belgian* wind / His hostile breath through the dry rafters sent'.[70] The broadsheet of the Great Fire also apportions blame. As figure 4.13 shows, the engraving was accompanied by brief narrative accounts of the Great Fire in Dutch, French and English, each differing from the other in some interesting details. The Dutch and French newsprint reports that, after the fire, a Flemish baker in Westminster was found lighting his oven and was beaten to within an inch of his life. The baker was rescued by the duke of York, but his house was ransacked. All three accounts mention that several Hollanders and Frenchmen were imprisoned on suspicion of causing the fire. The English account asserts that the disaster was a consequence of human, even specifically English, sin: 'the wole was an effect of an unhappy chance, or to speak better, the heavy hand of God upon us for our sins shewing us the terrour of his Judgment'. The political context appears to speak through these words: if England had not pursued its war against the Netherlands, it might have been spared God's wrath. The Dutch account, too, concludes with an apparent divine judgement, but by contrast, strikes a positive note about one particular London community – 'Nu men wat begint te bedaren, spreeckt men van weder te willen herbouwen' – and concludes: 'de *Duytse Kerck* is blijven staen' ('Now people are calming down somewhat, they're talking of wanting to rebuild. … The Dutch Church is still standing'). Indeed, the steeple of the church of Austin Friars, first depicted in the panorama of London by Anton van den Wyngaerde, is visible through the billowing clouds of the Great Fire, even if in reality it was no longer standing, having fallen into disrepair in the early 1600s.

The engraving, evidently, was not an eyewitness depiction of the fire. Details of the engraving all point towards one source for its depiction of London: Claes Jansz Visscher's *Panorama of London* of 1616. Thus, for example, the south bank theatres are depicted as hexagonal as they were there, and geographical details are copied almost exactly. A pair of ships on the Thames (between the Beargarden theatre in Southwark and Queenhithe on the north bank) are labelled 'The Eells Schipes' on Visscher's panorama: Dutch eel ships were a regular sight on the Thames, as they had special permission to moor mid-river to sell their fish.[71]

A single ship in the same location is marked as 'The eells Schipes' on Doornick's plate; its details suggest that the engraver conflated the two ships of Visscher into a single one. The war between England and the Netherlands, however, meant that Dutch eel ships had been barred from the Thames in February 1666, and were not allowed to return until 1681.[72] They could therefore not have been seen moored in the Thames during the Great Fire. The panorama of the Great Fire of London is in fact a copy. It was made by an artist who may well never have seen the city, and was based on a previous panorama made by an engraver who also probably never saw London. To depict the Great Fire of London, the engraver working for Doornick took Visscher's idealized panorama of England's capital and enveloped it in flames.

Between van den Wyngaerde and Doornick's panoramas lies a century and a quarter in which map-makers were inspired by the proximity of England and the Low Countries, as well as by an interest in each other's history and geography. Their work was made possible not only by the opportunities for intellectual contact between the two, but also by convenient trade links, which allowed them to send back and forth information, printing proofs, copper plates and printed works. Dutch producers of maps imagined that they inhabited a country shaped like a lion, with a tail crossing the North Sea to England. Their study of the landscape was inspired by an imagined past in which links with Britain provided the names of the earliest built structures. Commercial affairs and the production of maps and books were also always personal, so it is to the people that we turn in the next chapter.

**Sjoerd Levelt, Robyn Adams, Jack Avery
and Edward Holberton**

Ey, meet in uw gepeys, hoe na uw Britsche stranden
Sich strecken over zee tot onse Nederlanden

O measure in your thoughts how closely your British beaches
Stretch over sea to our Netherlands.

JACOB CATS, 1660

Anglo-Dutch relations shaped not only histories, trade and industries, but also human lives and institutions. Contacts between Dutch and English people, and the experiences English people had in the Netherlands and vice versa, inspired them to write new works of scholarship and literature and to create establishments in which the heritage of these contacts could be preserved and nurtured. The library of the University of Oxford was founded not just once but twice in its history by men whose lives were entangled in the politics of the Low Countries. In the seventeenth century the impact of three Anglo-Dutch Wars paradoxically led to a shared marketplace of ideas, while repeated North Sea crossings by courtiers and artists gave rise to the development of a shared court culture, ultimately culminating in the coronation of a Dutchman, William of Orange, as king of England, Scotland and Ireland.

DUKE HUMFREY, JACQUELINE OF HAINAULT, AND THE EARLY LIBRARY OF THE UNIVERSITY OF OXFORD

A little book in the Bodleian Library collections, MS. Duke Humfrey d. 2, carries on its binding a glossy miniature portrait on enamel of a modestly dressed young woman, surrounded by a caption: 'Jacqueline Dutchess of Bavaria Countess of Holland Zealand & Henault, Wife to Humphrey Duke of Glocester 1427' (fig. 5.1). The book, at first glance, seems to tell a straightforward narrative: Humfrey, duke of Gloucester

Illustration from Edmund Spenser's English translation of
Jan van der Noot's *The Theatre* (detail of fig. 5.6)

(1390–1447), was the youngest son of King Henry IV and husband of Jacqueline, duchess of Bavaria and countess of Hainault, Holland and Zeeland. He was a prominent early benefactor of the library of the University of Oxford. His gifts to the library helped re-establish an institution that had, according to legend, once been founded by King Alfred in the ninth century; according to the historical record, however, it had been established on the basis of a bequest from Thomas Cobham, bishop of Worcester, in the early fourteenth century. Duke Humfrey gave about 300 books to the university. A new room was built to house his and others' donations, and it was called 'Duke Humfrey's Library'. Manuscripts in the Bodleian Library that were once in Duke Humfrey's possession are now classified under the shelf-mark 'MS Duke Humfrey'.

While none of the details above are incorrect, the full story is a much more complicated tale of false starts and dead ends, of Renaissance self-fashioning and posthumous mythologizing.[1] The text contained in MS. Duke Humfrey d. 2, a classicizing Middle English poem *On Husbondrie*, translated from the Late Antique agricultural writer Palladius, was indeed written for Humfrey, but not during his first marriage, to Jacqueline of Hainault. Instead it was composed during his second marriage, to Eleanor Cobham, Jacqueline's lady-in-waiting.[2] When Jacqueline had first arrived in England in 1421, as a guest of King Henry V, she was fleeing her uncle John III of Holland, who had challenged her succession to the county. Her presence in England had been welcomed as an opportunity for a renewed alliance between England and the Low Countries. A union between Humfrey and Jacqueline, in the words of poet John Lydgate, would be

> … a wey wherby we may atteyne
> Þat Duchye of Holand by hool affeccoun
> May beo allyed with Brutus Albyoun.[3]

> … *a way through which we can ensure*
> *that the Duchy of Holland may with wholehearted affection*
> *be allied with Brutus's Albion [i.e. Britain].*

The marriage in 1423, however, rather than promoting a harmonious North Sea alliance, led to Humfrey becoming embroiled in the intractable partisan wars that marked the Dutch Low Countries in the fifteenth century. An expedition across the North Sea ended in disaster, and, while

5.1 Enamel portrait of a lady, identified as 'Jacqueline Dutchess of Bavaria Countess of Holland Zealand & Henault, Wife to Humphrey Duke of Glocester 1427', added to the binding of a book formerly owned by Duke Humfrey. Bodleian Library, MS. Duke Humfrey d. 2, front board.

JAQUELINE DUTCHESS OF BAVARIA COUNTESS OF
HOLLAND ZEALAND & HENAULT, WIFE TO
HUMPHREY DUKE OF GLOCESTER 1427.

Humfrey extracted himself from the Continent, Jacqueline stayed behind. On the urging of Philip the Good, duke of Burgundy, the marriage was annulled in 1428, leaving Humfrey free to marry Eleanor Cobham, even though he did formally continue to claim the noble titles of his first wife.[4] *On Husbondrie* was written a decade later.[5]

MS. Duke Humfrey d. 2 was made for and owned by Humfrey himself, but the portrait on the binding was added at a much later date. A later owner, obviously drawn to the union between Humfrey and Jacqueline more than to that of the duke and Eleanor Cobham, which had ended in Eleanor's conviction for sorcery, chose to highlight the former marriage through the addition of the enamel portrait and its caption. Almost none of the books owned by Humfrey that are now in the Bodleian Library were part of the duke's original gifts to the university library. The library room built to house Humfrey's gifts soon fell into decline and closed around the middle of the sixteenth century, with none of the duke's books remaining. As we shall see below, it took another Englishman entangled in Low Countries politics to finally establish the university library that has an unbroken history up to the present day. Humfrey's manuscript of *On Husbondrie* was not given to the university library by the duke, but was instead handed over to the Bodleian Library in 1984 in lieu of taxes due from its previous owner, the Earl Fitzwilliam, of Wentworth Woodhouse.[6] That the portrait was added to the manuscript when it was no longer owned by the duke shows that Humfrey's Anglo-Dutch vision of himself, as both duke of Gloucester and by marriage count of Holland, Zeeland and Hainault, was accepted and perpetuated by the later owners of the manuscript, who were keen to emphasize its link not only to the duke but also to his illustrious spouse.

DESIDERIUS ERASMUS AND THOMAS MORE

Self-fashioning also played an important part in the life of the Dutch humanist scholar and philosopher Erasmus of Rotterdam.[7] In his case, too, that self-fashioning was transnational. 'Toties iam provocor tuis sororumque tuarum literis, optima Margareta,' he wrote in Latin on Christmas Day, 1523, from Basel to London, 'tam sanis, tam argutis, tam modestis, tam candidis, tam amicis, ut etiam si quis titulos detrahat, Thomae Mori γνήσια τέκνα possim agnoscere'[8] ('I have been put on my mettle so often lately, my dearest Margaret, by letters from you and your sisters, such sensible, well-written, modest, forthright, friendly letters –

that even if someone were to cut off the headings I should be able to recognize the "offspring true-born" of Thomas More').[9] His addressee, Margaret, and her sisters were daughters of his friend Thomas More. To repay them for their letters, Erasmus had composed for them a Latin commentary on Prudentius's hymns for Christmas and Epiphany: 'Bene vale, non infimum aevi Britanniaeque tuae decus, et totum istum chorum mihi saluta diligenter'[10] ('Farewell, not least among the glories of your generation and your native Britain, and mind you give my greetings to all the members of your choir')[11]). Margaret, nineteen years old, repaid Erasmus, too: within a year, she translated into English Erasmus's recently published treatise on the Lord's Prayer (*Precatio Dominica*, 1523); this translation was printed in London in 1526 as *A Devoute Treatise upon the Pater noster*.[12] It was accompanied by an eleven-page treatise championing the humanist education of young women, written by another humanist scholar and translator, and friend of Thomas More, Richard Hyrde. The publication had as its frontispiece a woodcut depicting not the male author, but the female translator of his work (fig. 5.2). It was one of the earliest translations into English of humanist scholarship.[13] Its association with Thomas More, at the time private secretary to Henry VIII, also lent Erasmus the implied seal of English royal approval.[14] Such approval was especially important, as the moderate reformer's works were receiving scrutiny at a time of increasing religious tensions in the early years of the Reformation. Thus Margaret occupied a pivotal place in the network of people in northern Europe propagating Renaissance humanism,[15] the intellectual and educational reform movement focused on the *studia humanitatis*, the study of classical Latin and Greek language and literature.[16] Women played a particularly significant role in the early dissemination of Erasmus's works in English during the Reformation, and in creating the perception that they were sanctioned by the English crown: in the same year that *A Devoute Treatise* came off the press,

5.2 Woodcut portrait of Margaret More, translator and daughter of Thomas More, showing her sitting at a desk surrounded by books. From *A Devoute Treatise upon the Pater noster* (1526), Margaret More's translation of a Latin treatise by Erasmus. London, British Library, C.37.e.6 (1), title page. © British Library Board. All Rights Reserved / Bridgeman Images.

A Sermon of the Excedynge Great Mercy of God was published, translated from Erasmus's Latin into English 'at the request of the moste honorable and vertuous lady, the lady Margaret Countese of Salisbury' (Margaret Pole) and printed by Thomas Berthelet, the King's Printer.[17]

Erasmus's acquaintance with England had first been made in quieter times, in 1499, when he visited as a tutor of the courtier William Blount, Lord Mountjoy. Born in Gouda, Erasmus was educated at the Latin school in Deventer, after which he entered the monastery of Stein near Gouda. He had become a tutor of young noblemen while studying in Paris, where he shared lodgings with several Englishmen, including Lord Mountjoy, with whom he developed a friendship.[18] In 1499, during the first of his repeated visits to England, Erasmus met Thomas More, then a rising star in court circles in London. The two struck up a lifelong friendship, which sparked some of the two authors' most well-known publications. As a tutor, Erasmus also developed close acquaintances with high-status English speakers in Scotland: in 1508–9 Alexander and James Stewart, sons of King James IV of Scotland, were his charges in Italy. Erasmus took to Alexander, in particular. When Alexander was killed with his father at the Battle of Flodden in 1513, Erasmus felt his loss personally: 'Periit et nostrarum rerum nonnihil: nempe quod in erudiendo te sumpsimus operae quodque mea partum industria mihi in te vindico' ('Something of mine was lost there too: the pains I had devoted to teaching you, and so much of you as was made by my efforts, I claim as my share in you').[19] As he later wrote in a letter (1530) to another Scottish friend, the chronicler Hector Boece (principal of King's College, Aberdeen, the forerunner of the University of Aberdeen), the consolation was that his efforts to educate the Scottish royal family had not been in vain, but had contributed to a cultural renaissance in Scotland:

> Nec mihi mediocrem attulit voluptatem, quod intelligo Scotiae regnum, vt aliis pluribus ornamentis, ita liberalium artium studiis indies magis ac magis expoliri. Hoc nomine semper amaui Iacobum Regem, quod ditionem suam non tam proferre studuerit quam exornare.[20]

> *I also found no small cause for delight in the knowledge that the kingdom of Scotland, among many other distinctions, is daily becoming more cultivated through its interest in the liberal arts.*

It is on this account that I always loved King James, for it was his ambition not so much to extend his kingdom as to enhance it.[21]

Proud of his own connection with these developments, Erasmus goes on to regale Boece with his happy memories of tutoring King James's two boys in Siena.

Following his stay in Italy, a decade after his first visit to England, Erasmus returned to stay with Thomas More in 1509. The More household was expanding: Margaret More was little older than a toddler. During this stay, Erasmus wrote the Latin work for which he is today best known, *In Praise of Folly*. Its Latinized Greek title, *Moriae encomium*, punned on the name 'More': 'I resolv'd to make some sport with The Praise of Folly,' Erasmus wrote to his friend: 'But who the Devil put that in thy head? you'l say; The first thing, was your sirname, of More, which comes so near the word Moriae (Folly) as you are far from the thing.'[22] The work is presented as spoken by the goddess Folly and presents a satirical treatment of the evils of European society.

Thomas More started writing his answer to *In Praise of Folly*, the work that would establish him as a major force in European humanist circles, during a stay in the Dutch Low Countries in 1515. 'Britanniam suam nunquam egressus est, nisi semel atque iterum, Principis sui nomine legatione fungens apud Flandros'[23] ('He has never gone out of his native Britain, save once or twice, when acting as ambassador for his sovereign in the Netherlands'[24]), wrote Erasmus about More in a letter recommending More's work to the publisher John Froben in Louvain in 1517. The work, *Utopia*, which Erasmus himself had brought to press in 1516, was soon reprinted by Froben. In its introduction More tells how, while staying at Bruges during a diplomatic mission to the Dutch Low Countries for Henry VIII, he was introduced to a certain Raphael Hythloday by Peter Giles, humanist, printer and friend of both Erasmus and More. Hythloday, a traveller, had spent time in the faraway country Utopia. Hythloday's description of the country Utopia forms the bulk of More's book. Where Folly in Erasmus's *In Praise of Folly* had ruthlessly exposed the foolishness of European Christian society, the book *Utopia* performed the function of the court jester telling uncomfortable truths: 'fictione qua velut melle circunlitum suaviuscule influeret in animos verum' ('[through] a fiction whereby the truth, as if smeared with honey, might a little more pleasantly slide into men's minds'),[25] as More describes it. He mirrored

Erasmus's carnivalesque satirical analysis with a vision of an ideal society in which all of the customary certainties of his own society were turned upside down. Each of their most famous works was inspired by their friendship, growing out of the challenge posed to both scholars by each other's erudition and wit. The friendship of More and Erasmus would continue to flourish, both in presence and in absence – Erasmus last left England in 1517, but it appears to have been no exaggeration when in August 1535, following More's execution the month before, Erasmus wrote that 'In Moro mihi videor extinctus, adeo μία ψυχὴ iuxta Pythagoram duobus erat'[26] ('in More I seem to have died, so much did we have one soul, as Pythagoras said'[27]).

The connection to Erasmus ensured that *Utopia* made an impression in the Netherlands. The name 'Utopia' would regularly be used as a fictitious place of printing for clandestine publications in the seventeenth century throughout Europe, but Dutch printers had already established the practice in the sixteenth century, within a few years of the work's first publication. The earliest titles to appear with Utopia as the place of printing were, appropriately, connected to Erasmus: the first was *Dialogus festivus sane ac elegans* (*A Merry and Elegant Dialogue*), a satire ascribed to Erasmus, bearing the imprint 'Amauroti, in insula Utopia' ('Amaurot, on the island of Utopia' – Amaurot being Utopia's capital city in More's text), and printed in 1518, though no copy survives today. The second work with a Utopian imprint was *Acta Academie Lovaniensis contra Lutherum* (*Acts of the Louvain Academy against Luther*), a tract condemning early persecutions of Lutheran scholars in the Netherlands, thought to have been written by Erasmus.[28] It was published in 1520 by Jan Seversz, whom we encountered in Chapter 1 as the printer of the *Divisiekroniek* (*Division Chronicle*) of 1517, now hiding under the pseudonym 'H.M. Civis Utopiensis' ('H.M., citizen of Utopia').[29] He was soon followed by the printer Simon Cover, a schoolmaster in Zwolle and an old friend of Erasmus, who used 'Utopia' as the fictitious place of printing for a clandestine Protestant publication.[30] The use of Utopia as a place of printing first moved out of the direct circle of Erasmus in the colophon to another clandestine tract, this time in Dutch, printed in Leiden in 1526.[31] In Protestant England, Erasmus became one of only a few Catholic authors who were still read for their religious teachings. His critiques of abuses in the church were appreciated by Protestant readers: *In Praise of Folly* was read in schools, was widely cited by authors[32] and appeared in English translation in 1549 (fig. 5.3).[33]

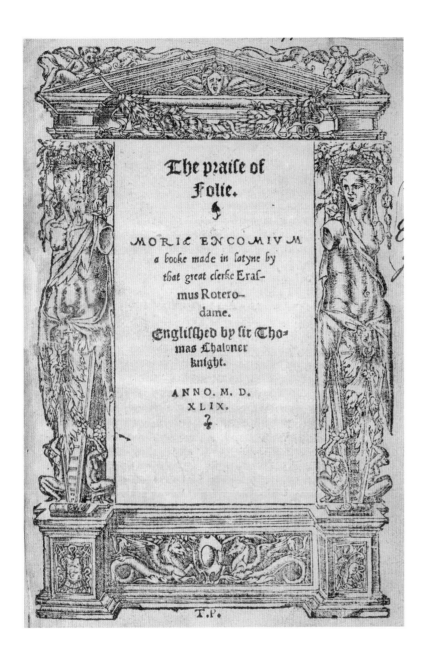

The praise of
Folie.

MORIÆ ENCOMIVM
a booke made in latyne by
that great clerke Eraſ-
mus Rotero-
dame.

Engliſhed by ſir Tho-
mas Chaloner
knight.

ANNO. M. D.
XLIX.

T.P.

THE *DUTCH CHURCH LIBEL*

Early modern cities depended on a continuous replenishment of their population with immigrants for their economic growth and prosperity. Already in the later Middle Ages, Dutch speakers were part of the fabric of the city of London, and their language part of its polyglot soundscape. The anonymous fifteenth-century poem *London Lickpenny* describes a scene outside Westminster Hall:

A libell fixte vpon the French Church Wall, in London. Anno 1593.

Ye strangers y doe inhabite in this lande
Note this same writing doe it vnderstand
Conceit it well for safegard of your lyves
Your goods, your children, & your dearest wives
Your Machiavellian Marchant spoyles the state,
Your vsery doth leave vs all for deade
Your Artifex, & craftesman works our fate
And like the Jewes, you eate vs vp as bread
The Marchant doth ingross all kinde of wares
Forestalls the markets, wheresoere he goe's
Sends forth his wares, by pedlers to the faires,
Retayles at home, & with his horrible showes: Doe toth thoursandes
In Baskets your wares trott vp & doWne
Carried the streets by the country nation,
You are intelligencers to the state & croWne
And in your harts doe wish an alteracion,
You transport goods, & bring vs gaWds good store
Our leade, our vittaile, our ordenance & what nott
That Egipts plagues, vext not the Egyptians more
Then you doe vs; then death shall be your lotte
Noe prize comes in but you make claime thereto
And every marchant hath three trades at least,
And Cutthrotes like in selling you vndoe
vs all, & with our store, continnally you feast: We cannot suffer long
Our poore artificers doe starve & dye
For y they cannot now be sett on worke
And for your worke more curious to the ey
In Chambers, twenty in one house will lurke,
Raysing of rents, was never knoWne before
Liking farre better then at native home
And our poore soules, are cleane thrust out of dore
And to the wanes are sent abroade to rome,
To fight it out for Fraunce & Belgia,
And dy like dogges as sacrifice for you
Expect you therefore such a fatall day
Shortly on you & yours for to ensewe: as never was seene
Since words nor threates nor any other thinge
canne make you to avoyd this certaine ill
Weele cutt your throtes, in your temples praying
Not Paris massacre so much blood did spill
As we will doe iust vengeance on you all
In counterfeitinge religion for your flight
When t'is well knoWne, you are loth, for to be thrall
your coyne, & you as countryes cause to flight
With Spanish gold, you all are infected
And with y gould our Nobles Winck at feats
Nobles said I? nay men to be reiected
Vpstarts y enioy the noblest seates
That wound their countries brest, for lucres sake
And Wrong our gracious Queen & subiects good
By letting strangers make our harts to ake
For Which our swords are whet, to shedd their blood
And for a truth let it be vnderstoode / Fly, Flye, & never returne.

L. Tamberlaine.

Not Paris massacre so much blood did spill
As we will doe our vengeance on you all
In counterfeitinge religion for your flight
When 'tis well knowne, you are loth, for to be thrall
your coyne, & you as counterfeyts cause to flight
With Spanish gold, you all are infected
And with y[ou]r gotts our Nobles winck at feats
Nobles said I? nay men to be rejected
Upstarts y[a]t enioy the noblest seats
That wound their Countries brest, for lucres sake
And wrong our gracious Queen & Subiects good
By letting Strangers make our harts to ake
For which our swords are whet, to shedd their blood
And for a truth let it be understoode / Fly, Flye, & never returne.

p. Tamberlaine.

Without the dores were Flemings grete woon;   [a large group]
Upon me fast they gan to cry
And sayd, 'Mastar, what will ye copen or by –   [buy]
Fine felt hatts, spectacles for to rede?'[34]

The Flemings of London evidently spoke an English peppered with their own native words, for the word *copen* is authentically Dutch. That the poet himself glosses it with 'or by' ('or buy') implies that he did not expect everyone to know it, but later attestations of it show that the word was borrowed into early modern English and Scots, before disappearing again from the language (with the exception of some dialects).[35]

Religious persecutions in various parts of Europe (in Britain as well as on the Continent) at times led to significant additional migration in and out of England. New communities replenished old and ensured new routes of communication to their areas of origin. Recent arrivals wrote to those they had left behind, trying to convince them to undertake the journey. Clais van Wervekin wrote to his wife in Flemish Ypres from Norwich on 21 August 1567:

ghy ne soudt nemmermeer ghelooven, hoe vriendelick dat tvolk tsaemen es, ende oock de Ynghelschen, hoe minsaemich zy tot onser natie vallen, zoo, dat ghy hier waert met half ons goedt, ghy ne soudt nemmermeer peinsen om in Vlaenderen te commen woonen.[36]

5.4a, 5.4b *opposite and above* Transcription of the *Dutch Church Libel* (1593) copied by John Mansell, who later became president of Queens' College, Cambridge. Its title notes that it is 'A Libell, fixte upon the French Church Wall, in London', mistaking Austin Friars for nearby St Anthony's. Oxford, Bodleian Library, MS. Don. d. 152, fol. 4v.

*You would never believe how friendly and supportive of each other
the [Flemish] people here are, and also the English; with what
care they treat our people, so that if you were here with half our
possessions, you would never consider returning to live in Flanders.*

Norwich was the most populous city in England after London, so it is not
surprising that it also had the second largest community of Dutch speakers
in the country. New migrants preparing to make the North Sea crossing
knew that they would find a community to which they already belonged:
'ic wylde wel dat ghy my sondt byden eersten boode', one wrote back home
while at an unspecified location on the Continent preparing to embark on
his journey to Norwich, 'den boom van de afcompste van Coornelys van
Schoere, die ic u eens gheleent hebbe, emmers de copie tot de kinderen
van Pieter Bladelincx toe, ons moeder en huer zuusters; want ic hope daer
jae vele van ons maerschyp te vynden'[37] ('I want to ask you to send me
by the first messenger the family tree of Cornelis van Schoere, which I
once lent you, or at least a copy down to Pieter Bladelincx's children, our
mother and her sisters, for I hope to find many of our relatives there').

Immigrants in the early modern city, like those of the medieval
or present-day city, occasionally met with xenophobia and political
exploitation of perceived differences between communities.[38] Dutch
migrants were no exception to this rule. As we have already seen, they
were targeted in the ethnic violence of the Peasants' Revolt of 1381. The
political climate again turned nasty for Dutch speakers in the aftermath of
the Treaty of Arras in 1435, when Philip of Burgundy switched sides and
made peace with France, banished English merchants and merchandise
from Flanders, and added insult to injury by laying siege to the English
colony of Calais (1436–37) with the aid of local troops. The betrayal caused
outrage and fuelled a number of anti-Dutch poems.[39] One copy of the
Middle English prose *Brut* chronicle includes a verse diatribe known as
the *Mockery of the Flemings*, and the chronicler notes that many similar
rhymes were circulating: 'Wherefore amonges Englisshmen were made
many rymes of þe Flemmynges; among the which, one is here sette for a
remembraunce'.[40] Another manuscript of the chronicle includes *A Ballade
in Despyte of the Flemynges*.[41] Both poems mock the Flemings for their
failure to capture Calais.

Written in the aftermath of the Siege of Calais, *The Libelle of Englyshe
Polycye* clearly reflects this hostile mood. The 'little book' ('libelle') was

influential and popular, surviving in multiple manuscripts, the earliest of which is Oxford, Bodleian Library, MS. Laud Misc. 704. The author decries the conciliatory English economic and military policy towards its Continental neighbours, arguing that Flanders needs to be met with trade sanctions and a show of strength. As a hub of international trade, Flanders is dependent on its trade partners, and on England in particular:

> The grate substaunce of youre cloothe at the fulle
> Ye wot ye make hit of oure Englissh wolle.[42]

So if England imposes a trade embargo by controlling the North Sea, it follows that

> Flaundres of nede muste wyth us have pease
> Or ellis he is distroyde wythowghten lees.[43]

In short – and conveniently ignoring that Duke Philip governed an empire rather than the county alone – Flanders needs peace with England more than England needs peace with Flanders:

> Thus muste Flaundres for nede have unite
> And pease wyth us, it woll none other bee.[44]

The *Libelle*'s aim was to influence foreign policy,[45] and indeed it was read as a serious political treatise for a long time: in the seventeenth century, the legal scholar and historian John Selden cited the work in his tract about the law of the sea (and, in particular, the North Sea), *Mare clausum*.[46] But it also sought to fan the flames of ethnic prejudice by stereotyping the Flemish as drunken louts.[47] *The Mockery of the Flemings* exclaims: 'to compare with Englisshmen, ye aught to be ashamed!'[48] In this volatile climate, a backlash again Flemish migrants living in England was inevitable. Rumours began to circulate that they were enemy spies and were poisoning local beer.[49] Threats, abuse and sometimes violence ensued, and royal letters of protection for them were issued during the heightened tensions following Burgundy's betrayal.[50]

The history of ethnic violence, reflected in hostile verse, repeated itself in the later sixteenth century. On 5 May 1593 the crowded neighbourhood of Austin Friars (between St Paul's Cathedral and the Tower of London) was thrown into turmoil by a sheet of paper that had been affixed to the wall of the church. On it was a poem targeting the sense of community, prosperity and stability that Clais van Wervekin had mentioned in his letter to his wife. It commenced:

> Ye strangers þat doe inhabite in this land,
>   Note this same writing doe it understand
> Conceit it well for savegard of your lyves
>   Your goods, your children, & your dearest wives.[51]

The neighbourhood was full of immigrant families: French, German, Dutch and Danish were all spoken in these streets, in addition to English. The church of Austin Friars, still known under its pre-Reformation name (when it had been a friary of the Augustinian order), was now the principal church of the Dutch Reformed community in London. We saw in Chapter 3 how its foundation in 1550 was followed by suppression in 1553 under Mary I; after its restoration by Elizabeth I,[52] however, the church became – and still is today – a centre for the Dutch community and its religion in London. Its establishment led to the Dutch speakers of London, who had previously lived primarily outside the city walls, moving into the city. This raised awareness of their presence and increased hostility towards them.[53] Addressing this community in particular, the poem, known as the *Dutch Church Libel* (fig. 5.4a), continued:

> Your Machiavellian Marchant spoyles the state,
>   Your usery doth leave us all for deade
> Your Artifex, & craftesman works our fate,
>   And like the Jewes, you eate us up as bread.

The accusations of usury and cannibalism ('you eate us up as bread') associate the Dutch with the Jews, who had been accused not only of desecrating the host but also of murdering Christians and drinking their blood. Jews were a rare sight in London: since their expulsion under Edward I in 1290, there had been no Jewish communities in England. Many of the people targeted by the anonymous poem, 'Ye strangers þat doe inhabite in this land', however, had come to England as religious refugees from cities that did contain thriving Jewish populations. As many of these newcomers in London were involved in international trade, they would have noticed the absence of Jews in London, a stark reminder of the city's previous history of ethnic cleansing.

The doggerel poem continues with a litany of complaints about the foreigners: their unfair trade practices, their espionage for foreign powers, their duplicity, the overpopulation of their lodgings, the increase in rents due to their presence and the heavy price that Englishmen have to pay for international politics. While the Dutch 'strangers' grow fat, the English are sent abroad to fight the wars of France and the Netherlands, to 'dy like dogges as sacrifice for you':

> Expect you therefore such a fatall day
> Shortly on you, & yours for to ensewe: as never was seene.
>   Since words nor threates nor any other thinge
> canne make you to avoyd this certaine ill
>   Weele cutte your throtes, in your temples praying   [We'll]
> Not paris massacre so much blood did spill
>   As we will doe just vengeance on you all.[54]

The slaughter of 'aliens' during worship was certainly not an imaginary threat. The poem refers to the 1572 St Bartholomew's Day Massacre in Paris, but Dutch speakers in London had famously been the target of such an attack long ago, the memory of which still lingered. The story of the massacre of Flemings during the Peasants' Revolt of 1381, when they had been dragged out of their churches and killed, was still being told and retold in histories such as John Stow's chronicles, which had been repeatedly republished and revised since 1565. In 1594, just a year after the appearance of the *Dutch Church Libel*, the massacre was even the subject of a scene in a stage play.[55]

The poem continues by asserting that the aliens were not true Protestant refugees, but feigned religion in the pursuit of money. These 'strangers' are not worth 'our' care (fig. 5.4b):

> … our swords are whet, to shedd their blood
> And for a truth let it be understoode / Fly, Flye, & never returne.[56]

Understandably, considering the poem's rhetorical violence, its appearance on the wall of the Dutch Church caused much consternation. It led to the arrest of the poet Christopher Marlowe, because it explicitly invoked

Marlowe's ruthless killer Tamburlaine.[57] It is sadly ironic that Marlowe's *Tamburlaine* should have been dragged into the *Dutch Church Libel*. The play was heavily reliant on Abraham Ortelius's atlas, which prominently imagined a shared and unifying European identity on its title page.[58] Perversely, Marlowe's play was appropriated in the *Dutch Church Libel* to attack London's Dutch migrant community, to which so many of Ortelius's family members belonged.[59] Marlowe was released, but he was stabbed to death ten days later. Except for a few lines cited in the eighteenth century, the poem was lost until in 1973 a contemporary transcription was identified in a collection of letters that had recently been acquired by the Bodleian Library (fig. 5.4a).

EMANUEL VAN METEREN

The *Dutch Church Libel* told the Dutch 'strangers' of London to 'Fly, Flye, & never returne', but for many London was where they had built their nests. This was certainly the case for Emanuel van Meteren, who had been born in Antwerp in 1535, the son of the merchant Jacob van Meteren. We saw in Chapter 3 how Jacob had been involved in the book trade, specifically the export of Protestant books from the Continent to England. From his earliest years Emanuel's life had been shaped by the persecution of the new religion. His contemporary and biographer, Simeon Ruytinck, wrote about Emanuel's mother, Odille Ortels:

> 't Is gebeurt (haren man om sijnen handel na Engelant
> gereyst zijnde) sose swanger was van desen Sone, dat men
> van d'Overheyts-wege haer huys is komen besoeken, om
> Leonard Ortels haren Oom, die daer plagh t'huys te liggen,
> te vangen, om 't punct van de Religie, en met een te sien of'er
> geen verboden Boeken te vinden waren; de wreetheyt van
> dese ondersoeckers beweeghde de goede Juffrou den Heere
> vierighlijck te bidden, op datse deselve niet vonden, 't welk ook
> also gebeurt is, al was 't datse verscheydemael de handen op de
> kist leyden daer de boecken in waren, Godes genadige hulpe
> en beschermingh daer in speurende, heeft belooft (sose een
> Sone baerde) den selven *Emanuel* te noemen, day is, *God met
> ons*, welke belofte sy oock volbrocht. Hier uyt heeft *Emanuel*
> oorsaeck genomen, tot sijn manlijck verstant gekomen zijnde,
> by 't woort Emanuel gemeenlijck te voegen, *Quis contra nos? Is*

Godt met ons, wie is tegen ons? om aen die vorighe weldaet te beter
te gedencken, en in alle gevaer op den Heere te betrouwen.[60]

*Once, while her husband had travelled to England for business, the
authorities visited her house when she was pregnant with this son,
in order to arrest her uncle Leonard Ortels, who often stayed there,
on grounds of religion, and simultaneously to see whether they could
not find any forbidden books there. The cruelty of these inquisitors
moved the good lady to fervently pray the Lord that they would not
find them – which happened accordingly, even though they repeatedly
put their hands on the chest which contained the books. Sensing God's
merciful assistance, she promised, if she would deliver a son, to call him
Emanuel, meaning 'God with us', which promise she fulfilled. This
inspired Emanuel, when he had become a grown man, to customarily
add to the word 'Emanuel': Quis contra nos?, that is, 'When God is
with us, who is against us?' – the better to commemorate past blessings
and to rely on the Lord when in peril.*

'Emanuel' ('God is with us') was the name that the prophet Isaiah foretold
for the Messiah, which according to the Gospel of Matthew had been
fulfilled in the giving of the name 'Jesus' ('the Lord saves'). Similarly,
in Ruytinck's telling the anecdote concerning Emanuel's name-giving
foreshadowed van Meteren's life. The episode was marked by Anglo-Dutch
relations – by the trade, books and religion that formed the essence of daily
life for the van Meteren family – just as Emanuel van Meteren's own life
would be from that day on.

Emanuel's father Jacob, who shuttled back and forth between Antwerp
and London for trade, was among the founders of the Dutch Church in
London in 1550, and from that moment he chose to remain in the city. After
a basic humanist education, Emanuel was asked by his father to join him
in London. Given the choice of either continuing his studies or devoting
himself to trade, Emanuel chose the latter, becoming an apprentice to the
Antwerp merchant Sebastiaan Danckaerts. Both his parents died soon
after, drowning during a North Sea crossing – a stark reminder of the perils
of even the narrow stretch of water between England and the Dutch Low
Countries. Van Meteren's apprenticeship with Danckaerts was spent between
Antwerp and London, and in 1560, having completed his apprenticeship, he
settled permanently in London, where he lived until his death in 1612.

Emanuel van Meteren's Anglo-Dutch identity was more complex than the simple dichotomy suggested by the *Dutch Church Libel*. Rather than being one of 'Ye strangers þat doe inhabite in this land', Emanuel was an Englishman, yet also identified as a citizen of Antwerp. His Englishness was connected to his identity as a Protestant, as he said himself, recounting his experience of a visit to Antwerp in 1575, where he was arrested by the local Spanish authorities. The execution of a fellow prisoner was the occasion for a Catholic mass, which the Protestant Emanuel refused to join:

> 's Middaghs daer na seyden my d'andere ghevangenen dat den Cipier te Hove en al-om verbreydt had, dat ick geen Misse had willen hooren, en also d'occasie daer toe weder voorviel, seyde ick den Cipier, dat ick geen Misse mocht hooren, dewijle ick een Engelsman was, en dat sulcks in Engelandt de breucke van 100 marck onderworpen was, &c. Den Cipier nam sulcks aen, en quelde my niet meer.[61]

> *The following afternoon, the other prisoners said that the jailer had spread the story at court and elsewhere that I had not wanted to attend mass, and when there was occasion I told the jailer that I could not attend mass, because I was an Englishman, and in England this was subject to a penalty of 100 marks, etc. The jailer accepted this and tormented me no longer.*

At other times, however, Emanuel considered whether it might be more expedient to use his status as a citizen of Antwerp:

> ick kon niet wel resolveren of ick my als Poorter van Antwerpen wilde defenderen of als Engels, met dese ghedachten my bekommerende, quam de dochter van den ondersluyter stillekens aen 't slot van mijn deure roepen: Engelsman, Engelsman. Ick vraeghde wat sy wilde. Sy seyde: Ick soude my als een Engelsman verantwoorden, en dat ick dien dagh van de Raets-Heer Boone sou ge-examineert worden, maer 't soude wel zijn.[62]

> *I could not easily decide whether I wanted to prosecute my defence as a citizen of Antwerp or as English. While I was occupied with these thoughts, the daughter of the guard quietly called through the keyhole of*

my door: 'Englishman, Englishman.' I asked her what she meant. She said that I should defend myself as an Englishman, and that I would be examined by councillor Boone that day, but it would be well.

Emanuel was indeed released and allowed to return to England. His personal effects, however, were confiscated by the Spanish authorities, including his *album amicorum* ('book of friends'). Back in England he started his second, and now only surviving, album.[63] The keeping of albums was a custom originating among international students. They were collections of inscriptions by acquaintances, acquired over periods of time. The inscriptions range from simple acknowledgements to elaborate emblems and poetry. Not all individual entries in an album were the result of personal, face-to-face meetings. Emanuel's album, for example, was once carried across the North Sea by a friend to the Antwerp magistrate Joannes Woverius for signing.[64] Nevertheless, Emanuel's album provides a snapshot of the thriving intellectual and artistic community straddling both sides of the North Sea. Emanuel personally brought many of the people involved in this network together: through his agency Janus Dousa Pater ('the Father', to distinguish him from his son, Janus Dousa Filius), the first curator of Leiden's university library, arranged to meet William Camden and Sir Robert Cotton, the great English antiquarian historians and collectors, in London. It was also through van Meteren that Cotton acquired several Dutch medieval manuscripts for his collection, which ultimately became one of the foundational collections of the British Library.[65]

Emanuel's network as recorded in his album contains a wide range of people from England and the Low Countries: merchants, church officials, diplomats, statesmen, local administrators, jurists, scholars, scientists, physicians and theologians. The most prominent English and Dutch historians and philologists of his time, not only William Camden, Robert Cotton and Janus Dousa Pater and Filius, but also Justus Lipsius, Pieter Cornelius Bockenberg and Paulus Merula, were among his contacts. Emanuel also connected England and the Dutch Low Countries through familial ties: through his mother Odille Ortels, he was related to the English diplomat Daniel Rogers, the grandson of Odille's sister Anne, as well as to the famous map-maker Abraham Ortelius, who was a son of Odille's brother Leonard (Abraham Latinized the Dutch name Ortels, as was customary within intellectual circles of the day). Through his second wife, Hester van den Corput, Emanuel further expanded this familial network to include luminaries such as Janus Gruterus, Nicolaas Utenhove, Franciscus Junius and (through Junius's half-sister Elisabeth) Gerardus Johannes Vossius.[66]

ARTISTS AND POETS

Emanuel van Meteren's album also includes inscriptions from a number of artists in Antwerp and from Dutch artists who visited him in England, such as Lucas de Heere (1534–1584). Born in Ghent, Lucas established himself as a prominent court artist in France. He came to London in the mid-1560s, fleeing religious persecution. He travelled widely in England and Wales. In his record of these travels, he describes visiting south-west Wales, where Gerald of Wales had described the presence of a Flemish community in the late twelfth century. The Flemings were still there, de Heere wrote: 'Ick hebbe oock med eenighe ghesproken die noch goed vlaemsch spraken, tzelfde aen haer ouders ende als van vader tot kinde gheleert hebbende'[67] ('I have also spoken with some who still spoke Flemish well, which they learned from their parents and from father to child'). De Heere lived in London until he moved back to Ghent in 1576, when a temporary truce had been established that allowed many Protestant refugees to return to the Netherlands. Shortly before his departure from London, he added to van Meteren's album a pen drawing of a siren and a Dutch sonnet (fig. 5.5). Van Meteren himself had commenced the album with two Dutch sonnets, including one addressed to his friends, inviting contributions to the album.

The Dutch sonnet, as a form of poetry, was itself a product of this particular Anglo-Dutch group of intellectuals. The first Dutch sonnets to appear in print were published by Lucas de Heere himself, based on French models, shortly before his departure for London, though some were originally written in Antwerp almost a decade earlier.[68] Although those written by Emanuel van Meteren in his album are his only surviving sonnets, they show a degree of expertise and maturity that suggests he had more experience with the verse form than de Heere.[69] The suppression of Protestant unrest in Antwerp in March 1567 brought a new wave of refugees from the southern Netherlands to London. Among the new arrivals was Jan van der Noot, originally from Antwerp, who within two years of arriving in London had published a collection of poetry – Dutch translations of sonnets by Petrarch and Joachim du Bellay as well as four original sonnets. It was printed, in Dutch, by John Day, as *Het theatre* (*The Theatre*). It includes introductory verses by Lucas de Heere and copperplate engravings by Marcus Gheeraerts, himself a recent immigrant from Bruges.[70]

While a number of Dutch books containing catechisms and Psalms had been printed earlier for use by the Dutch congregation in London, van der Noot's *Het theatre* was the first Dutch publication in London written for a market in the Low Countries. Nevertheless, van der Noot also had English readers in mind: in a Dutch preface, he dedicated the work to Sir Roger Martyn, lord mayor of London, and called to mind the harrowing events on account of which he had fled Antwerp eighteen months earlier:

> Het zijn nu 18. maanden Eerweerdighe Heere,
> dat ick verlatende mijns Vaders Lant in Engeland
> gekomen ben om te schouwen de besmettelycke
> ende verdoemelycke grouwelen des Ro. Antichrists
> die in Brabant ende over al de Nederlanden nu
> wederom met groot gewelt opghericht waren:
> ende oock om t' ontvlieden de onredelycke,
> onmenschelycke, noyt gehoorde ende on-
> wtsprekelycke moorderijen ende tyrannyen die
> sijn lidtmaten, dienaers ende beulen aenrechten
> ende ghebruycken over de ghene die heur tot
> sijne schandelycke superstitien, insettinghen ende
> ordonnantien niet en willen begheven. Tsynts
> welcken tijt ick my in dese Stadt van Londen
> ghehouden hebbe.[71]

Honourable sir, it has been eighteen months since
I arrived in England after leaving my fatherland, to escape the
infectious and damning horrors of the Roman antichrist which were
now again carried out in Brabant and throughout the Netherlands:
and also to flee the irrational, inhuman, unheard-of and unspeakable
massacres and tyrannies which its members, servants and torturers
carry out and use against those who refuse to give in to their shameful
superstitions, decrees and ordinances. Since this time I have resided in
this City of London.

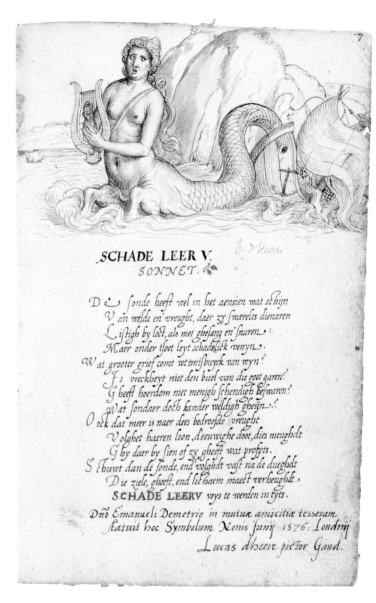

5.5 Drawing of a siren and a Dutch sonnet, made in London in 1576 by the artist Lucas de Heere, from Emanuel van Meteren's *album amicorum*. Shortly after, de Heere returned to the Low Countries after a decade in London as a religious refugee. Oxford, Bodleian Library, MS. Douce 68, fol. 7r.

Van der Noot offered the Dutch work to Martyn in gratitude for his hospitality to Protestant refugees, 'op dat sy sonder eenighe beroerte, des Heeren woort vryelyck moghen hooren, ende daer na leven' ('so that they, without being troubled, can freely hear the word of the Lord, and live accordingly').

Van der Noot's work was published by Day simultaneously in Dutch and French editions in 1568. An English translation of the French edition (fig. 5.6) was published in London a year later by the Dutch printer Henry Bynneman.[72] This translation was the first published work of the poet Edmund Spenser, predating his next work, *The Shepheardes Calender*, by ten years.[73] The young Spenser, aged seventeen, appears to have been assisted by van der Noot himself, as the translation, which is based principally on the French, nevertheless shows some signs of influence from the Dutch original.[74] Having paid Spenser for his labour, the author felt no need to acknowledge the young poet's role in the translation. Instead he claimed to have translated the poems himself: 'I have out of the Brabants speache, turned them into the Englishe tongue'[75] ('I have translated them out of Dutch into English'[76]).

The ties between the literary circles of the Netherlands and England were further tightened in the mid-1580s, when the burgeoning Dutch Republic, in the aftermath of the assassination of William the Silent in 1584, made overtures to the English monarchy attempting to persuade Elizabeth I to become its sovereign. Janus Dousa Pater, just appointed official historiographer of Holland and librarian of the University of Leiden (founded in 1575), visited England on a diplomatic mission. In his entourage was a group of Dutch poets, including Dousa's son Janus Dousa Filius, who found time to translate an English sonnet by Henry Constable into Latin and Dutch (he had been part of the group of friends of Jacob Walraven who had learned English together in Leiden). In London the two Dousas were hosted by the poet, scholar and soldier Sir Philip Sidney. The diplomatic mission of Janus Dousa Pater resulted in the appointment of Robert Dudley, earl of Leicester, as governor general and commander of the English forces in the Netherlands. He arrived in The Hague in early 1586, together with his nephew, Sir Philip. Sidney briefly lived among the intellectuals of the young University of Leiden, cementing the relations that had been shaped by successive reciprocal North Sea crossings since the 1570s.[77] The university itself, meanwhile, had become a magnet for young scholars from England, who engaged in a

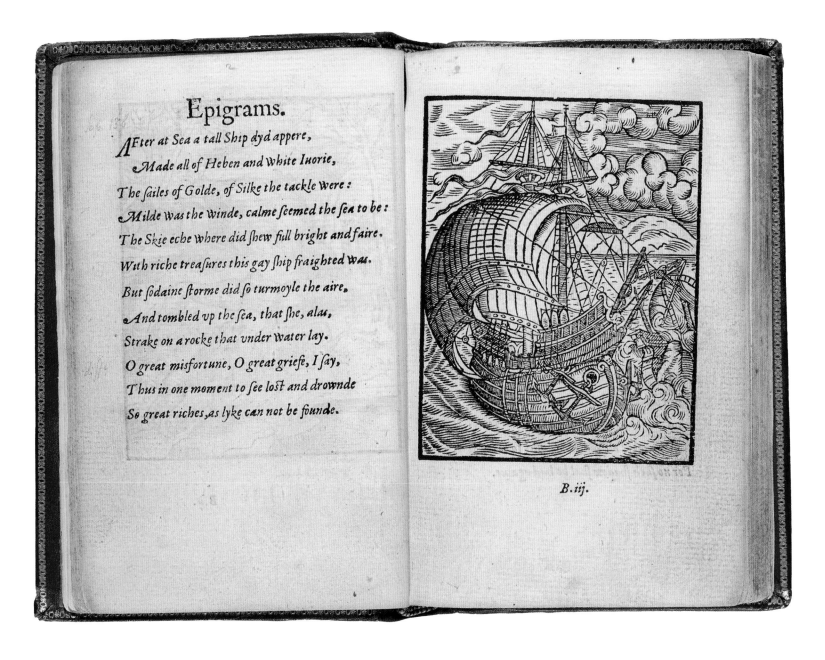

Epigrams.

AFter at Sea a tall Ship dyd appere,
Made all of Heben and White Iuorie,
The ſailes of Golde, of Silke the tackle were :
Milde was the winde, calme ſeemed the ſea to be :
The Skie eche where did ſhew full bright and faire.
With riche treaſures this gay ſhip fraighted was.
But ſodaine ſtorme did ſo turmoyle the aire,
And tombled vp the ſea, that ſhe, alas,
Strake on a rocke that vnder water lay.
O great misfortune, O great griefe, I ſay,
Thus in one moment to ſee loſt and drownde
So great riches, as lyke can not be founde.

B.iij.

range of literary activities, from translation between Dutch and English to the local publication of linguistic aids and poetry in English.[78] Sidney was appointed governor of Flushing (Vlissingen), but was injured in a military skirmish and died soon after. However, the basis for a new chapter in the history of intellectual relations between England and the Netherlands had been laid, the chapter in which the Bodleian Library was to come into existence.

5.6 Woodcut and a sonnet from Jan van der Noot's *The Theatre* (1569), a collection of poetry published in its original Dutch version by John Day in London. It was translated into English, via French, by the young Edmund Spenser. Oxford, Bodleian Library, Douce N 36, sigs B.ijv–B.iijr.

SIR THOMAS BODLEY AND THE FOUNDATION OF THE BODLEIAN LIBRARY[79]

In 1602, after having been in disuse for almost half a century, the library of the University of Oxford reopened its doors, refurnished and supplied with thousands of new books. Thomas Bodley's re-foundation of the library at Oxford followed a lengthy period of diplomatic service in the Low Countries. He was one of two English representatives appointed by Elizabeth I to serve on the Dutch Council of State. The majority of his time abroad between 1588 and 1597 was spent in The Hague. While there he negotiated the terms of the military and financial assistance provided by England, writing letters to the Privy Council and leading political figures to report on the progress of these negotiations. During this period he dealt with numerous figures associated with the Dutch Revolt, including Jan van Oldenbarnevelt, Land's Advocate for Holland, and Paul Buys, the former curator of the University of Leiden. In addition, Bodley's circle of correspondents and associates included military men (such as Sir Francis Vere and Sir John Norreys), members of the political elite leading the English negotiations (like Lord Buckhurst), and the powerful intelligencing bureaux of William Cecil, Sir Francis Walsingham and the earl of Essex. More minor figures feature in his correspondence, suggesting a strong network of family and patronage connections, including Bodley's old Oxford friend, the physician William Gent, and Michael Dormer, a shared friend of John Chamberlain, the notable letter writer. Many individuals who feature in Bodley's correspondence from this decade later appear in the donors' lists of the Bodleian.

It is tempting to consider the proximity of Leiden to The Hague (half a day's ride by horse), where Bodley lived, when thinking about the influence that the newly formed Protestant University of Leiden and the institution of its library (fig. 5.7) may have had on Bodley's future plans for the library at Oxford. Bodley was himself a celebrated scholar, who was widely recognized as gifted in Greek and Hebrew. During his Marian exile on the Continent he received his education at the hands of Theodore Beza and others in Geneva, according to his autobiography.[80] It is therefore likely that his proximity to the celebrated humanist scholars in Leiden (including Justus Lipsius and Joseph Justus Scaliger) sparked in Bodley an interest in restocking the library at Oxford for the benefit of its students. Scholars have long sought to trace the connections between the two institutions. Although a definitive and direct line of influence has not

yet been confirmed, there are some persuasive features that are suggestive of inspiration, if not emulation.

The university library at Leiden did not formally take shape until 1587. Even then, the number of titles was relatively modest, though strongly humanist in scope, containing around 442 titles in 525 volumes.[81] The first printed catalogue, entitled *Nomenclator* (a name given to many enumerative works at the time), was issued in 1595, while Bodley was still in the Netherlands. Later imprints included a list of donors. The *Nomenclator* was the very first printed catalogue of an institutional library and followed a shelf-list, rather than alphabetical, format. Nine years later the first printed catalogue of the Bodleian was issued in a similar shelf-list format. A later librarian at Leiden was Paulus Merula, who joined just as Bodley was concluding his diplomatic service. He was a professor at the University of Leiden and, like Bodley, a former pupil of Beza. Merula and his predecessor Janus Dousa Filius both appear in the portrait frieze in the Gallery (now the Upper Reading Room) of the Bodleian

5·7 The Library of the University of Leiden, as it was housed from 1595, two years before Thomas Bodley's return to England from The Hague. From Johannes Meursius's *Athenæ Batavæ* (*The Batavian Athens*, 1625), copied after an engraving from 1610. Oxford, Bodleian Library, 4° M 60 Art., p. 36.

Library, along with 200 other notable scholars (fig. 5.8).[82] Janus Dousa Filius had succeeded his father in the post and was in office during Bodley's residence in The Hague, where in the early 1590s Bodley lived on the same street as Dousa Pater. Dousa Filius had already been part of Bodley's extended network: in England in the 1580s he had associated with Bodley's friends and contacts, Sir Robert Sidney, Sir Philip Sidney and William Camden.[83] So there is circumstantial rather than tangible evidence that Leiden's university library influenced Bodley and his vision for the refurbishment of Oxford's library. Nevertheless, there are some compelling synergies between the two institutions that suggest Leiden was a background influence on the Bodleian and part of the humanist programme pulsing through bibliographical activity at the time. Sharing this humanist energy, although motivated by an extreme Protestant vigour, was the Bodleian's first Librarian, Thomas James. He was co-responsible for creating the first printed catalogue and the portrait frieze in the Picture Gallery, whose 'heads' fused the book-collecting habits of Bodley with the religious ideals of James.

There are a handful of individuals who shared direct links to Bodley, both during his legation to the Low Countries in the last years of the sixteenth century and during his withdrawal from state service at the turn of the seventeenth century. He also had an extended network of family, friends and political contacts.[84] Bodley's associates on the Continent who are named in his correspondence mostly gave books rather than financial donations, with the exception of some wealthy donors, such as Sir Thomas Sackville (Lord Buckhurst) and Sir Robert Sidney, who each gave £100 (about 2,000 days' wages for a skilled tradesman at the time),[85] and Sir Edmund Uvedale (listed in the Benefactors' Register as 'Udall'), who gave £50.[86] Uvedale was the marshal of Flushing, under the supervision of Sidney in his capacity as governor of Flushing, and both had been correspondents of Bodley. Flushing was one of the 'cautionary towns' given to Elizabeth I and garrisoned by the English as part of the Treaty of Nonsuch in 1585. By contrast William Borlas, appointed temporary lieutenant governor of Flushing in 1589, donated one book in 1601, a detailed volume of royal European genealogies.

The most outstanding donor in terms of scale was also one of the earliest, the Staffordshire physician William Gent, who had acted for Bodley as a carrier of government correspondence between England and the Low Countries in the early 1590s. In 1600 Gent gave 344 books,

mostly of a scientific and medical nature. He was generally known to be impecunious, so this was an extremely generous gesture. A soldier, Michael Dormer, donated sixty-nine items in 1603. Dormer had found patronage at the hands of Bodley while a cavalry officer in the Low Countries serving under Sir Robert Sidney in 1588. His donation is a remarkable collection of mid-sixteenth-century Italian literature and later sixteenth-century military and scientific treatises. Another notable donor connected to Bodley's time in the Low Countries was Charles Howard, Baron Effingham, who gave thirty-four books and seventeen manuscripts, among them impressive folio volumes of Erasmus's editions of the church fathers, including St Augustine, St Jerome and St John Chrysostom. During his stay in the Netherlands Bodley had been a regular correspondent with Howard, who was a member of the Privy Council.

Finally, mention must be made of a figure who does not feature by name in Bodley's correspondence during his time in the Low Countries, but who we know was with Bodley. His brother Josias, a military surveyor, donated in 1601 a set of brass surveying instruments, including an armillary sphere previously owned by Henry Percy, ninth earl of Northumberland (also a donor to the library).[87] Part of Thomas Bodley's

5.8 Portrait of Janus Dousa Filius in the Upper Reading Room, part of the Old Schools Quadrangle, Sir Thomas Bodley's final extension of the Bodleian Library, opened posthumously in 1624. The Upper Reading Room frieze has portraits of 202 Protestant reformers and earlier writers. Oxford, Bodleian Library, Upper Reading Room frieze.

brief as a representative on the Council of State was to send back intelligence to the figures running the machinery of state, in particular Sir William Cecil, who was especially interested in maps. Josias and Thomas Bodley collaborated in the creation of a set of maps of Groningen in 1594,[88] perhaps using the instruments that Josias later donated (fig. 5.9).[89]

The diplomatic correspondence, Bodley's own account of his negotiations in the Low Countries (fig. 5.10), the Bodleian Library records and Bodley's autobiography all combine to create a detailed picture of the friendships and connections forged amid war and diplomatic wrangling. A humanist education, a short (though successful) career at Oxford and a period spent abroad travelling and gaining experience together formed the basis for both a competent embassy in the Dutch Republic and a scholarly retreat to prepare the library at Oxford.

HOLLAND'S LEAGUER

In 1603, one year after the opening of Bodley's library, another institution grounded in Anglo-Dutch relations was established in London. Holland's Leaguer was founded on the Thames's south bank, in close proximity to the Hope, Swan and Globe theatres, as a high-end entertainment establishment for a clientele that reportedly included King James I himself. It was also the location for many an Anglo-Dutch meeting: the proprietor, Bess Holland, led a community of prostitutes who were primarily of Dutch origin.[90] Dutch women were already playing a prominent role in London prostitution in the fourteenth century,[91] and in the minds of early modern Londoners prostitution was intrinsically linked to Dutch identity.[92] In an allegorical account, a contrived commentary on the state of the English church,[93] and with a nod to the Anglo-Dutch history behind Thomas More's *Utopia*, Bess Holland was fictionalized as the Utopian madam Britanica Hollandia, so named by her parents 'by reason of some neere allyances betwixt them and the Neather-lands'.[94] The union of two peoples, which had been eulogized by Lydgate in the context of the marital union between Duke Humfrey and Jacqueline of Hainault, was now personified in London's most famous madam, and Lydgate's register of marital fidelity was replaced with that of a different type of alliance.

In the treaty
of Accord between her Queenes Matie
and the Provinces vnited wherevnto they
obteined her royall assent, the 10 day of
August in the yeare 85 it was constituted
first for them that during their
troubles they should be supported
with 5000 ffoote and a 1000 horse
at the charges of her highnesse
and then for her selfe that her monies
so consumed should be faithfully
restored when the state of the
country was brought to tranquillity
And for the sufficient assurance
as well of that reimbursment, as
of their further trustie dealinge
they condistended to deliuer the
townes of fflushinge in Zealand
with the Castle of Ramekins, to
be kept with a garrison of 700 men
English souldiers and the towne of
the Brill in Holland with the fforte
adioyning to be kept in like manner
with 3 English ensigns each of

them

5.10 Sir Thomas Bodley's first-hand account of
negotiations in the Netherlands in 1595–96, copied by a
professional scribe. Bodley notes that the negotiations
took place in the context of the alliance between
Elizabeth and the United Provinces of 1585. Oxford,
Bodleian Library, MS. Eng. hist. c. 46, fol. 1r.

Holland's Leaguer was surrounded by a moat with a drawbridge and included a walled garden for the convenience of the clientele (fig. 5.11). It soon became one of London's most famous brothels, but it also became the focus of scandal. In 1632 King Charles I ordered it closed down, at which time its moat and drawbridge were reported to have fulfilled their purpose: the soldiers besieging the building were led onto the bridge, which was then let down. Having fallen into the moat, the soldiers were then pelted from the building with the contents of the prostitutes' chamber pots. The siege was also described in a ballad which drew parallels between the events in London and siege warfare in the Low Countries. The memories of the generation of Sir Philip Sidney still coloured English perceptions of the Dutch, though the language of martial prowess, again in parallel with Lydgate's earlier description of Anglo-Dutch relations, is infused with not so subtle double entendres:

> The draw-bridge being
> up taken they durst to,
>   Stand to push of pike
> and give a thrust too:
>   Those that gave onset
> sometimes got th' worst ont,
>   And at their parting
> most dearly have curst ont
>   But however it is spoken
> that Hollands Leager
> Up lately is broken.[95]

THE ANGLO-DUTCH WARS AND ANGLO-DUTCH COURT CULTURE[96]

In the mid-seventeenth century England and the Netherlands went to war three times, all within the space of twenty years. It has often been asked how two countries that shared such deep and extensive relations could come to blows repeatedly. The answer has frequently been found in that very closeness. Once the Dutch had achieved independence from Spanish rule, they and the English found their similarities and ties to be problematic. The two states competed to play similar roles as Protestant maritime powers on Europe's north-western coast, and their political and religious crises became increasingly entangled. The English republicans and Cromwellians, who ruled for a decade following the execution of Charles I in 1649, feared the influence in the Netherlands of supporters of the House of Orange. Conversely, supporters of the restored Charles II and the Anglican church after 1660 felt threatened by Dutch republicans and their culture of religious tolerance, which became a magnet for English and Scottish dissenters.[97] The English frequently took a paternalistic attitude to a country which, they argued, would not have gained independence had it not been for English support in the previous century. As the seventeenth century's languages of politics changed, and concepts of 'the national interest' became more important, the sense of rivalry only intensified: the English and Dutch increasingly saw one another as economic competitors, not only in Europe but also further abroad in Africa, the Americas and East Asia.

At various moments the solution to this competition appeared, to the English at least, to be to incorporate 'the natural Frontier of *England*', the Low Countries, into a closer union.[98] Union in exchange for aid had been proposed to Elizabeth I during the Eighty Years War. This idea was revived by the English republican government after the execution of Charles I. In 1651 the ambassadors Oliver St John and Walter Strickland set out on a grand embassy to the United Provinces with proposals for 'a more real and intimate alliance' between the new English Commonwealth and its Protestant republican neighbour, which would consolidate – so the English government assumed – the ideological convergence between the two states, now that they were both godly republics.[99] But the ambassadors were taken aback by the strength of Dutch antipathy to the English regicide and the vigour of the ongoing popular support, especially in the Dutch provinces, for the House of Orange. William II of Orange had recently died and left an heir too young to take up the quasi-hereditary office of stadtholder, but the Orangists remained a force in Dutch politics and maintained close ties to the Stuarts.[100]

Political relationships across the North Sea were further complicated by the fact that the Netherlands had long-standing military connections with Scotland and hosted communities of Scottish emigres and exiles,

5.11 *above Hollands Leaguer* (1632). The woodcut shows the brothel with its moat and drawbridge, and its walled garden. The building was the old manor house of Paris Garden Manor on Bankside, at the location that is still called Holland Street today. Oxford, Bodleian Library, Douce GG 16, frontispiece and title page.

5.12 Oliver Cromwell as 'staartman' ('tail-man'), by an anonymous engraver (1652). A Hollander and a Zeelander are making an attempt to cut off the tail, assisted by an Irishman, a Scot, a Frisian and Prince Rupert of the Rhine, the Royalist commander. Amsterdam, Rijksmuseum, RP-P-OB-79.497.

who became well integrated into Dutch society. Some of the viewpoints that emerged from this diaspora can be glimpsed in the writing of the Scottish soldier and poet George Lauder, who served in Danish, Swedish and Dutch armies during the mid-seventeenth century, and developed political and literary affiliations with the House of Orange. Lauder wrote proudly of Scotland's contribution to the Continental Protestant cause during the Thirty Years War (1618–48). His verse represents the religious tensions of early Stuart and Interregnum Britain from a distinct perspective, which combines a Scotland-centred and militantly Protestant vision of Britain's destiny with an acute sense of how those tensions were shaped by European wars and horizons.[101] He attacks Charles I's attempts to impose the Prayer Book on Scotland, yet in a later poem written in

English, but printed in Delft, he laments Charles's execution in 1649 as a Westminster-hatched treason that had pulled down 'that Crown that stood / Vpon old Fergus stock, glu'd with the blood / Of Pictes and Romanes, Danes'. 'True Britaines' must take revenge on the 'Sacrilegious Sectaries and Knaves' of the English republican regime.[102] The cultural and political relationships between England, Scotland and the Netherlands in this period have been compared to a triangle of mutually shaping and disrupting forces.[103]

Not for the last time, the English misjudged the plurality of Dutch opinion, and the 1651 embassy ended in diplomatic failure. The stage was set for military confrontation between England and the United Provinces, which was hastened by the English Parliament's punitive 'Navigation Act' excluding Dutch shipping from English trade. But because this war was prosecuted in search of a closer union, some of the more insightful writing about the war is marked by a strong sense of what the combatants share.[104] The poet and polemicist Andrew Marvell, who would draw on his family background in the Netherlands-facing port of Hull to become an important figure in Anglo-Dutch politics of the later seventeenth century, wrote 'The Character of Holland', which satirizes the Dutch, but also emphasizes the combatants' geographical and cultural continuities. The poem alludes to contemporary geographical theories, such as that proposed by Richard Verstegan, that Holland had once been connected to Britain: 'Holland, that scarce deserves the name of land, / As but th'off-scowring of the British Sand'.[105] Building on the theories of linguists such as Verstegan, Franciscus Junius, Jacob Walraven and Henry Hexham, Marvell employs a series of Anglo-Dutch linguistic puns to highlight how the languages have common roots and continue to borrow from one another: 'How fit a title, clothes their governors, / Themselves the hogs as all their subjects boars!' runs one couplet,[106] punning on the Dutch title 'Hoog-mogenden' ('high and mighty') and the Dutch word 'boers', which here suggests the English 'boars' and perhaps also 'boors'.[107] In Marvell's war-time poem, Dutch republicanism as it now stands is a debased version of Protestant liberty, which the English can help to restore, if the Dutch will only let them: 'For these Half-anders, half wet, and half dry, / Nor bear strict service nor pure liberty' (ll. 53–4). 'Half-anders' is a macaronic pun, combining English 'half' with Dutch 'anders' ('other', 'different'), linguistically embodying the very idea that the Dutch and the English are both different and the same.[108]

5.13 The sun breaking out from behind the clouds, illuminating the three crowns of England and Wales, Scotland, and Ireland. From a manuscript with works by Jan van Vliet for Charles II, written during his stay in Breda prior to returning to England (1660). Oxford, Bodleian Library, MS. Rawl. poet. 6, fol. 3v.

The First Anglo-Dutch War (1652–54) consolidated sympathy in the Netherlands for the exiled Stuarts. Recent scholarship has emphasized the extent and influence of this Dutch 'royalism', which developed in tension with the republicanism of Holland.[109] Scatological Dutch popular prints represented Oliver Cromwell as a particularly devilish version of the 'staartman' ('tail-man'), the animalistic Englishman whose tail, emblematic of his unrestrained ambition, had to be pruned by the Dutch (fig. 5.12).[110] As we shall see in the next chapter, the tail of the Englishman was a literary trope as old as Reynard the Fox, traceable to at least the twelfth century.

After the Commonwealth regime began to collapse in 1659, the future Charles II travelled to the Netherlands to negotiate the Restoration. Along the way he was greeted with panegyrics and triumphal addresses. The Bodleian has a beautiful manuscript of Latin poems, with an emblem and a song, which was assembled in Breda at this time and which features work by the poet, diplomat and philologist Jan van Vliet. The poems commemorate Charles I, executed a decade before in 1649, and describe him as a holy martyr. They suggest that the Stuarts' enemies, who are described as tyrants and rebels, may shortly be defeated, and hint at a possible restoration. The visual emblem shows the sun breaking out from behind clouds to illuminate the three crowns of England and Wales, Scotland, and Ireland (fig. 5.13). The emblem's meaning is developed by an accompanying Latin song for three voices with a bass accompaniment.[111] Van Vliet later accompanied Charles II on his 1660 voyage from Breda back to London. During his subsequent stay in England, he collected books and consulted with scholars who shared his interest in medieval English literature and the common origins of Old English and other Germanic languages, including Franciscus Junius.

As this example shows, the Restoration was another occasion when the entanglement of English and Dutch cultures became evident. It is telling that another Dutch poet, Jacob Cats, in a poem written as Charles II passed through the Netherlands, stressed the same points about shared geography and shared language that had appeared in Marvell's satire on the Dutch a few years earlier:

> Ey, meet in uw gepeys, hoe na uw Britsche stranden
> Sich strecken over zee tot onse Nederlanden;
>   De taele die 'er vloeyt uyt uw bespraeckten mont,
>   Is Hollands even selfs, of heeft den eygen gront.

De godtsdienst, die men pleeght in al uw koninckrijken,
Die mach men wel te recht met d'onse vergelijcken;
  Dit's recht een Hemels werck, een onverbroken bant,
  Die vast te samen voeght het een en 't ander landt.[112]

5.14 Portrait of Sir Henry de Vic, English ambassador to Brussels for Charles I. He accompanied Charles II in exile in the Low Countries. This portrait was drawn on the occasion of the Restoration (1660) by the Dutch artist Peter Lely, the leading painter of Charles II's court. © Ashmolean Museum, University of Oxford, W.A.Suth.B.2.722.1.

O measure in your thoughts how closely your British beaches
Stretch over sea to our Netherlands;
　The tongue that flows from your eloquent mouth,
　Is equal to Holland's itself, or has the same ground.
The Religion which men follow in all your kingdoms,
One might rightfully compare with ours;
　This is a right heavenly work, an unbroken bond,
　That tightly binds together the one and the other Land.

Cats hoped that the shared culture, history and geography of the two countries was enough to override constitutional differences. Ascendant royalists constructed a spiritual basis for this relationship – the 'right Heavenly work' – which incorporated Anglo-Dutch amity into the providential interpretation of the Restoration.

Dutch painters had been prominent at the court of Charles I: Peter Paul Rubens and Gerrit van Honthorst received commissions, before Anthony van Dyck brought to England the elegant portraiture that came to define the Caroline court's visual style. One might have thought that the vibrant traffic between the visual cultures of the Netherlands and England would have been disrupted by the conflicts of the Civil War period, but that was not the case. The English republican regime put the royal collection up for sale to pay the king's debts, but the grandees and officials of Cromwellian England also provided a new market for portrait painters, including the Dutch-born portraitist Peter Lely, who worked in London but maintained close ties with The Hague during the 1650s.[113] At the same time Royalist exiles in the Netherlands developed a taste for the latest styles in Dutch portraiture and landscape painting, and brought these back to England in the 1660s. Artistic tastes and practices on both sides of the North Sea were 'strenuously entwined', writes Lisa Jardine, and Lely seized the opportunity to take up van Dyck's former position as principal court painter.[114] The returning Royalists celebrated the Restoration by commissioning new portraits of their families (and sometimes of their mistresses too). Lely's drawing of Sir Henry de Vic (fig. 5.14), who had stayed with Charles II during his exile, is part of a series of drawings of Knights of the Garter, which were perhaps commissioned with a view to a larger scheme of tapestries that went unrealized.[115] Lely also painted the most glamorous courtiers of the day and marked the turn away from Cromwellian plainness when

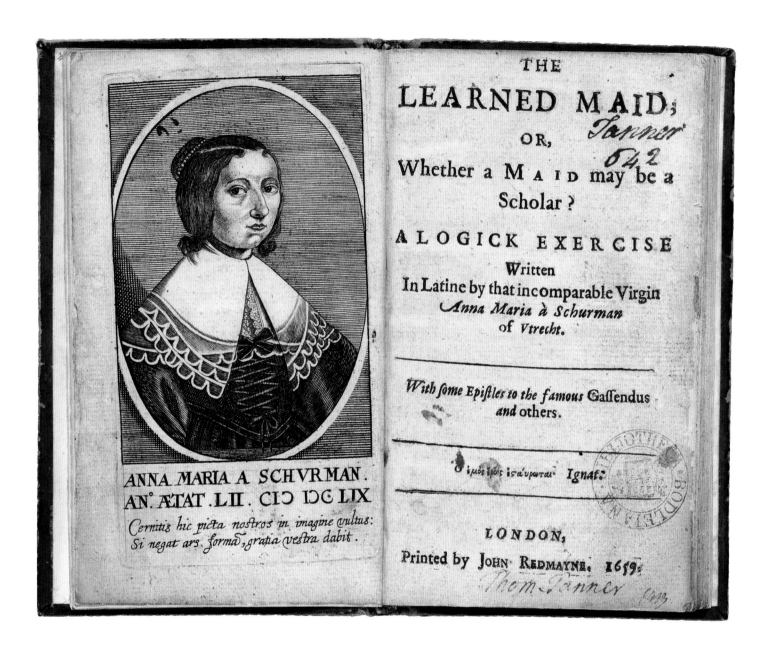

THE

LEARNED MAID;

OR,

Whether a M A I D may be a
Scholar ?

A L O G I C K E X E R C I S E
Written
In Latine by that incomparable Virgin
Anna Maria à Schurman
of *Vtrecht.*

With some Epistles to the famous Gassendus
and others.

LONDON,
Printed by JOHN REDMAYNE. 1659.

he was commissioned by the duchess of York to paint a series of sensual
and glamorous portraits of the most beautiful women of the court, the
'Windsor Beauties', in the early 1660s.

Anglo-Dutch debates and conversations continued to be powerful
influences on the two states' cultures of learning during the later
seventeenth century. English and Dutch scholars exchanged and
translated ideas and books in spite of the wars and political contests

5.15 Portrait of Anna Maria van Schurman, from *The
Learned Maid, or, Whether a Maid may be a Scholar?* (1659),
translated from her Latin defence of the education of
women. Schurman attended university lectures behind
a screen, so as not to be visible. Oxford, Bodleian Library,
Tanner 642, frontispiece and title page.

between their states. The year 1659 saw the publication of an English translation of a treatise on women's education by Anna Maria van Schurman (1607–1678), a renowned Dutch scholar and poet who was the first female student at a Dutch university (fig. 5.15).[116] Van Schurman spoke fourteen languages, including English, and corresponded with men and women throughout Europe, including, in England, the educationalist Bathsua Makin, to whom van Schurman wrote in Greek, and the member of parliament (MP) and historian Simonds D'Ewes, who wrote van Schurman English letters including citations from Old English.[117] Anglo-Dutch exchanges were also technological. The flourishing scientific culture of Restoration England was centred on the Royal Society, which maintained close correspondences with Dutch experts, and regularly discussed their experiments, botanical gardens and advances in instrument making.[118]

Within a few years of the Restoration, however, the two states were at war again. Until the First Anglo-Dutch War, the Netherlands had been the pre-eminent naval power in Europe. To defeat them, the English republic had embarked on a rapid ship-building programme and assembled its own powerful navy. Now England and the Netherlands were maritime rivals, and the two states competed to dominate the trade routes of northern Europe and the Atlantic. In Charles II's reign, this sense of rivalry twice combined with diplomatic and ideological frictions (the 'Cavalier' parliament and English court resented the oligarchic republicanism dominant in the Netherlands during the 1660s) to spark new naval wars.

From an English point of view, the Second Anglo-Dutch War began well, with a victory off Lowestoft in 1665, but their advantage slipped over the next two years. A lack of money and bungled opportunities, foreshadowed by a failure after Lowestoft to chase down the opposing fleet, culminated in a daring Dutch raid up the Medway and into the English dockyards. The public intellectual John Evelyn, who in a panic had evacuated his valuables from his Deptford house, drew a map of the attack from a hill above Gillingham, which he sent to his fellow diarist Samuel Pepys: 'a Dreadfull Spectacle as ever any English men saw, and a dishonour never to be wiped off' (fig. 5.16).[119] It illustrates the key locations of the week-long incursion, including the Dutch capture of Sheerness, the breaching of the iron chain across the Medway, and the attack on Chatham itself. Much of the English fleet was burned and

the flagship *The Royal Charles*, the same ship that had sailed Charles II
from the Netherlands to England at the Restoration, was towed away to
the Netherlands, where it became a tourist attraction: its stern carving
remains at the Rijksmuseum.

With little left to celebrate, the war was marked in English memory
through the 'Painter' satires of Andrew Marvell. In these, any Dutch
threat is secondary to that of an incompetent and corrupt domestic
administration. Marvell did not allow the galling fact that the Medway
raid had only been possible as an Anglo-Dutch enterprise to escape
notice: 'An English pilot too (O Shame, O sin!) / Cheated of pay, was
he that showed them in'.[120] However, the Dutch sense of triumph was
tempered by apprehension of French expansionism, which was felt by
English writers and readers too. In one manuscript miscellany of the time,
the enormous volume in the Bodleian Library compiled by the English
courtier William Haward, MS. Don. b. 8, Marvell's biting satires rubbed
shoulders with the translation of a Dutch tract that weighed the benefits
and hazards of an alliance between England and the Netherlands. It
judged an alliance inadvisable, given England's tendency to interfere in
Dutch politics, 'except a Defensive one against France'.[121] In the peace deal
that concluded the Second Anglo-Dutch War, the English were given
generous terms and swapped colonial holdings in South America for a fur
town in North America, once called Nieuw Amsterdam, now known as
New York.

Yet within a few years, the alliance broke, and the two nations were
at war again. In the Third Anglo-Dutch War (1672–74), both sides
experienced setbacks that had far-reaching political consequences, setting
in motion events that would eventually bring about the dynastic union
of England and the Netherlands under William and Mary in 1688. The
French king, Louis XIV, had previously been allied with the Dutch, but
in the 1670 Treaty of Dover he made a strategic alliance with Charles II of
England. In 1672 Louis invaded the Spanish Netherlands, while England
engineered a series of messy pretexts (petty disputes over the salutes due
to English flags, which embarrassed even English contemporaries) to
begin a new naval war with the Dutch. The start of the French land war
in 1672 was so disastrous for the Dutch that it is commonly referred to as
the 'Rampjaar', or year of disasters, where only the deliberate defensive
flooding of Holland prevented the French from marching on Amsterdam.
The humiliation suffered by Dutch armies caused a political revolution

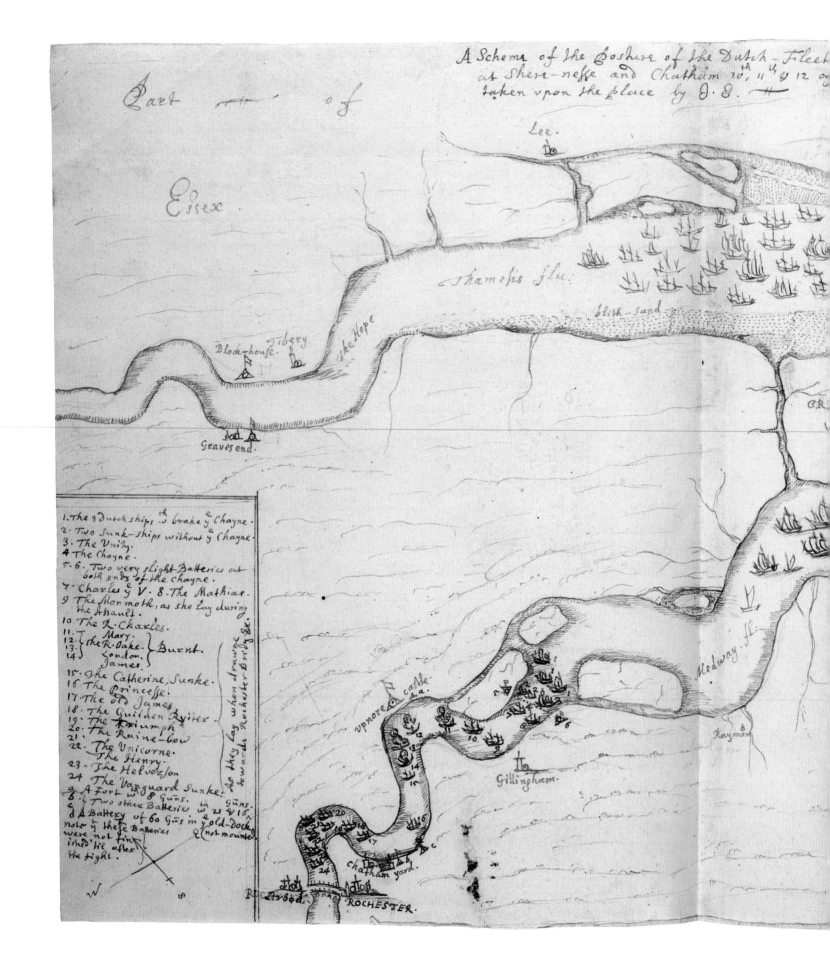

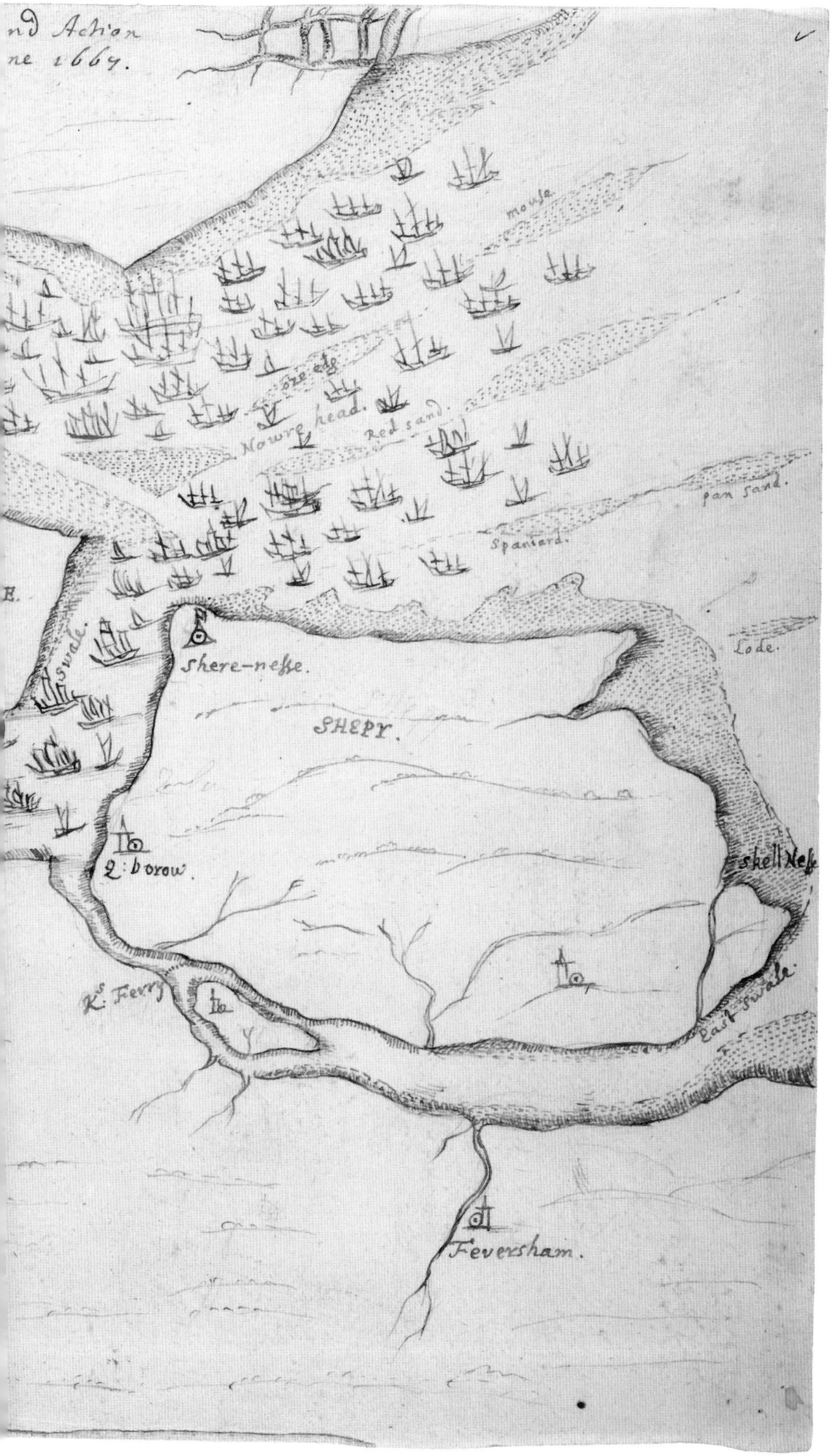

nd Action
ne 1667.
mouse.
oze edg.
Nowre head.
Red sand.
pan sand.
Spaniard.
Swale.
Shere-nesse.
SHEPY.
Lode.
Q: borow.
skell Nesse
Ks Ferry
East Swale.
Feversham.

5.16 Sketch of the Dutch raid on the River Medway (1667). It was drawn by John Evelyn for the diarist Samuel Pepys, who was an administrator for the Royal Navy, and sent to him one week after the event. Oxford, Bodleian Library, MS. Rawl. A. 195A, fol. 78.

at home, as Orangists overthrew the Dutch republican leadership, and William III of Orange took command of the Dutch war efforts. At sea the war proved less decisive and English public opinion began to turn against it. Widespread disappointment at a series of naval setbacks was exacerbated by public anger at the tendency of England's erstwhile French allies to refrain from actual combat.

The growing public discontent with the war was also fuelled and exploited by a clever Dutch propaganda campaign. A series of pro-Dutch political pamphlets were written with the help of political dissidents in Holland, including Pierre Du Moulin's influential *England's Appeal from the Private Cabal at Whitehall to the Great Council of the Nation* (1673). They were then smuggled into England by a clandestine intelligence network and widely circulated. A series of opposition figures and MPs, including Marvell, were also connected with this network, which aimed to pressure Parliament into withholding funding for the war and thus to compel Charles to negotiate a peace. To do this, the campaign urged MPs to recognize a connection between Charles II's divisive religious policies at home and his foreign alliance with France. They presented the war in religious terms, as an attempt by the Catholic Louis XIV to divide and conquer by setting Europe's leading Protestant states against one another. Parliament eventually forced Charles to the negotiating table to end the war, but the rising tide of anti-Catholicism and suspicion of the court's designs did not stop there. Soon a constitutional crisis enveloped both Charles and his Catholic brother and heir, the duke of York, who would later become King James II. Opposition pamphlets such as Marvell's influential *An Account of the Growth of Popery and Arbitrary Government* argued that the court's recent diplomatic, religious and parliamentary policies were part of a continuing conspiracy between the court and Louis XIV to bring Catholicism and absolutism to England: 'There has now for divers Years, a design been carried on, to change the Lawful Government of England into an Absolute Tyranny, and to convert the established Protestant Religion into down-right Popery.'[122]

Marvell's book retells the history of Charles II's dealings with France, the Netherlands and his parliament as a devious, corrupting court conspiracy. The book was printed anonymously and the publishers included on the title page a false place of publication: Amsterdam. In other words, the pamphlet was disguised as one of the subversive publications that had been brought in from abroad by the Dutch propaganda networks. Evidently, and revealingly, the publishers thought that this would not harm the book's commercial fortunes at all.

The Third Anglo-Dutch War had now ended. William of Orange played a double game: he secretly kept up contacts with the English opposition, but also tried to develop closer diplomatic ties with his uncle Charles. In 1677 William married Mary Stuart, the daughter of Charles's brother, James. The next few years witnessed the Exclusion Crisis: as it became clear that Charles would have no legitimate male children and that the successor to the crown would be his Catholic brother James, the political opposition, led by the earl of Shaftesbury, intrigued and campaigned to make Parliament pass laws that would exclude James from the succession in favour of a Protestant candidate. The opposition exploited an ugly public mood of anti-Catholicism. Marvell's warnings in *An Account of the Growth of Popery* seemed to be coming true when the preacher and conspiracy theorist Titus Oates reported the existence of a 'popish plot' to kill Charles II so that James could take over and return England to Catholicism. The plot was eventually exposed as a fiction, but many believed it to be true, and a number of people were executed. Meanwhile, William's balancing act became ever more delicate: his wife Mary was in the line of succession, and, because she was a Protestant, was widely regarded as a better prospect than her Catholic father. But William's strategic priority was to make Charles II support the Netherlands more actively in foreign policy, either by persuasion or by the threat of further intrigues with the English opposition. The Netherlands had often afforded refuge to exiles of one kind or another from across the North Sea, but, as political and religious divisions became more violent in the Stuart kingdoms during the 1670s and 1680s, a number of high-profile English and Scottish political dissidents, including the earl of Shaftesbury and his collaborator and friend the philosopher John Locke, fled to cities in Holland. James II succeeded to the throne in 1685, but through his autocratic political instincts and ill-advised religious policies, he soon alienated many of his subjects, including some who had hitherto been loyal supporters of the crown. The final straw came when his wife Mary of Modena gave birth to a son in June 1688, which presented England with the prospect of a perpetual Catholic succession. On the other side of the North Sea, William feared another French military offensive, which could be catastrophic for the Netherlands if it was supported by James's navy. After diplomacy with

James stalled, William accepted an 'invitation' to intervene in English affairs, which was sent by seven English peers. He rapidly gathered a huge naval task force, which set sail in October and landed in Torbay on 5 November. James II soon fled to France.

William's arrival and march to London were very carefully stage-managed to suggest not a foreign invasion but William coming to the aid of his wife's people. As in the Medway raid, the presence of English and Scottish 'volunteers' amid the Dutch force was conspicuous, their appearance carefully managed by William. Sympathetic eyewitnesses compared his arrival in London, amid cheering crowds, to the Restoration of Charles II. As he marched, William's intelligence networks in England distributed a *Declaration* on his behalf which pledged to restore English, Scottish and Irish rights and religion. It had been drafted by William's chief minister Gaspar Fagal and translated by the Scottish bishop-in-exile Gilbert Burnet. However, William himself is presented as speaking of his bond to his English spouse, Mary Stuart, and of his bond to the English nation and to English people of all classes:

> And since our Dearest and most Entirely Beloved Consort, the Princesse, and likewise wee Our Selves, have so great an Interest in this Matter, and such a Right, as all the world knows, to the Succession to the Crown, Since also the English did in the year 1672. when the States Generall of the *United Provinces*, were Invaded, in a most Injust warre, use their uttermost Endeavours to put an end to that Warre, and that in opposition to those who were then in the Government: and by their so doing, they run the hasard, of losing, both the favour of the Court, and their Imployments. And since the English Nation has ever testified a most particular Affection and Esteem, both to our Dearest Consort the Princesse, and to Our selves, WEE cannot excuse our selves from espousing their Interests, in a matter of such high Consequence, and from Contributing all that lies in us, for the Maintaining both of the Protestant Religion, and of the Lawes and Liberties of those Kingdomes, and for the Securing to them, the Continual Enjoyment of all their just Rights. To the doing of which, wee are most

Earnestly Solicited by a Great many Lords, both Spirituall and Temporall, and by many Gentlemen and other subjects of all Ranks.[123]

The *Declaration* is a consummate piece of propaganda, which drew on the extensive cultural exchanges of the previous decades in order to resonate with political attitudes on both sides of the North Sea.[124] It presents William's intervention as a defence of English, Protestant Irish and Scottish religion and sovereignty, and an act of assistance that gratefully reciprocates the resistance of Parliament in 1672–74, when the English people forced Charles II to halt his war with the Netherlands and his military assistance to Louis XIV.

The history of cultural institutions in Britain has never been played out exclusively within the circumference of Britain's shores. The court of the English monarchs relocated to the Continent on several occasions. Edward III stayed in Antwerp in 1339–40 (see Chapter 1); Edward IV was in Bruges in 1470–71; and Charles II stayed in the Netherlands during much of his exile. The eventual relocation of the court to England was always accompanied by a transfer of culture. Edward IV was inspired by his Dutch host Louis de Gruuthuse to establish a new collection of books, the eventual basis for the Royal Collection of the British Library. In this chapter, we have seen the influence of Dutch culture at the courts of Charles II and, of course, William III. Meanwhile, contacts between intellectuals from both sides of the North Sea, and repeated crossings between the Low Countries and England, created transnational networks through which information was exchanged, new ideas thrived and books were given, lent and traded. Like other English cultural institutions, the Bodleian Library of the University of Oxford was a beneficiary of such exchanges. Not only was the university library founded twice by men who had played significant roles at the highest levels of politics of the Low Countries, but its collections were repeatedly replenished by gifts from others who were leading Anglo-Dutch lives. It is for these reasons that the books held in the Bodleian Library collections are particularly suited to telling the story of Anglo-Dutch relations and their impact on Dutch and English literary culture in the Middle Ages and the early modern period.

6 *Reynard the Fox*

**Ad Putter, Moreed Arbabzadah
and Elisabeth van Houts**

Nec, si forte roges, comitamur cantibus Anglos.

*And we don't, if by chance you were to ask, follow
the English in our singing.*

YSENGRIMUS, *c.*1148

The literary heritage of Anglo-Dutch relations consists of chronicles,
manuscripts, printed books, maps and biographical records, but of course
it also includes Literature with a capital L. This chapter considers the
literature about Reynard the Fox as an example of how contacts and
travel between Britain and the Low Countries contributed to imaginative
fiction and helped it to evolve and to attract new audiences.

The stories of Reynard the Fox are 'beast epics', a genre based on an
ingenious transformation of simple animal fables. In fables, predictable
events in the animal world (for example, a wolf eats a lamb) form the
basis for moralization relevant to the human world (the powerful exploit
the weak). In beast epics, however, animals behave and reason like
humans: *they* do the moralizing, which thus becomes part of the fictional
entertainment.[1] Reynard in beast epics is especially given to moralization,
not to educate but to get his way: he is cast as a clever trickster, a smooth
talker, a rapist and sadist, but also a devoted family man; and what
makes him ideal for our case study is that he is one of the few literary
characters to have enjoyed an unbroken life in art and literature from
the Middle Ages to the present day. He made his first appearance in the
Latin *Ysengrimus* (*c.*1148) and may now be more famous on the Continent
than in England, but in the medieval and early modern period his
notoriety in England was huge, and his descendants, such as Roald Dahl's
Fantastic Mr Fox and Walt Disney's foxy *Robin Hood*, are still popular
today. England's first printer, William Caxton, personally translated a
Middle Dutch prose version of the story of Reynard, *Reynaerts historie*,

A fox plays dead, in an illustration from the thirteenth-
century 'Ashmole Bestiary' (detail of fig. 6.2)

into English, and published this translation in 1481 under the title *The Historye of Reynart the Foxe*. Caxton's edition was reprinted many times in the fifteenth and early sixteenth centuries and made the fox prominent in the world of books.[2] Reynard's presence in the visual arts across Britain, from Kent all the way up to Montrose in Scotland, is even more remarkable.[3] He can be found, for instance, in wood carvings, in stained-glass windows, in the margins of medieval manuscripts and also in the woodcut illustrations and engravings of printed editions.[4]

The reason for Reynard's popularity on both sides of the North Sea is easy to see. Always smart and quick to capitalize on the greed and gullibility of his victims, he triumphs against the odds. He is perpetually in trouble with the law, but gleefully hoodwinks the 'establishment' (represented by the court of King Noble the Lion), persisting in his life of crime (stealing capons, devouring hens) while ensuring that fools and enemies – Ysengrim the Wolf, Tibert the Cat, Bruin the Bear – get punished, whereas he himself escapes scot-free. In the medieval period only the Scottish poet Robert Henryson (1460–1500) invented a sticky end for the fox ('tod' in Scots), who is named Lawrence in the three Reynard stories that form part of his *Fables*: he dies as a convicted criminal on the gallows.[5] The key to his survival in the other Reynard stories is that he knows what outward appearances are likely to inspire respect and confidence – the robes of monks and friars, the guise of the devout pilgrim – and when he adopts these appearances to dupe his fellows, he confirms what we know from bitter experience, that 'holy looks' are often deceiving and that many wolves go disguised in sheep's clothing. This irreverent and satirical streak in the Reynard saga repeatedly earned printed Reynard books a place on the list of banned books (*Index librorum prohibitorum*) issued and reissued by the Catholic church from the sixteenth century onwards.[6]

Reynard's complex literary history has been expertly discussed by others and it is not our purpose to rehearse that information here.[7] Our aim is rather to focus attention on a more neglected aspect of that literary history, which is the way in which the stories and representations of Reynard in literature and art were shaped by the cultural relations between England and the Low Countries.

REYNARD AND THE *YSENGRIMUS*

Anglo-Dutch relations were a force in the development of the Reynard story from the start. The *Ysengrimus* (sometimes spelled Ysengrinus, Isengrimus or Isengrinus)[8] is a mid-twelfth-century Latin poem written in Flanders, probably in Ghent.[9] It is an epic narrative about a wolf called Ysengrim and his enemy Reynard the Fox (in Latin 'Reinardus'), who together with other animals constitute an anthropomorphic community. The anonymous author uses the animals to satirize and ridicule the contemporary nobility and clergy in Flemish society. The poem was probably written by a young cleric who was either a monk or at least a member of the monastic community of Saint Peter's or Saint Bavo's of Ghent, and who was in search of patronage from a bishop or abbot.[10] The author was clearly a well-educated man: his mastery of Latin is amply displayed over approximately 6,500 lines of elegiac couplets that reveal an impressive knowledge of classical and early medieval literature.[11] The text also displays a wealth of contemporary observations and material from folklore.

The *Ysengrimus* was not, of course, composed in a vacuum. Some individual episodes can be traced back to fables (many attributed to Aesop) and other works of the medieval and Carolingian periods.[12] *Ysengrimus* was not even the first literary work centred on animals as the main protagonists, since it follows in the footsteps of the so-called *Ecbasis captivi* (*The Escape of a Captive*), a tenth- or eleventh-century Latin animal epic.[13] Yet the differences between the *Ecbasis captivi* and the *Ysengrimus* should not be underestimated: for example, the *Ecbasis captivi* lacks the biting satire of the Flemish *Ysengrimus*; furthermore, the *Ysengrimus* differs in giving the animals names, thereby individualizing them in a way that makes them more than stock characters.[14] The name 'Ysengrimus' was already familiar in northern France, as we know from Abbot Guibert of Nogent's autobiography (*c.*1114). There Guibert reports that Waldric (also called Gaudry, bishop of Laon from 1106 until his death in 1112) prophetically described one of his murderers:

> Solebat autem episcopus eum Isengrinum irridendo vocare propter lupinam scilicet speciem: sic enim aliqui solent appellare lupos.

> *Now, as a joke, the bishop used to call this man Isengrin, because he had the look of a wolf and that is what some people commonly call wolves.*[15]

Bishop Waldric came from England,[16] so his comment shows that the name Ysengrim and its identification with a wolf were already current on both sides of the Channel and the North Sea.

The *Ysengrimus* is also an important but neglected source for Flemish ideas about the English.[17] The author's satirical comments about English people can sometimes be explained by the contemporary context. In the middle of the twelfth century, England and Flanders were closely connected through political, trade and cultural networks.[18] If the poem's completion, as is thought, can be dated to sometime between early 1148 and August 1149,[19] then it was composed at a time when King Stephen of England (r.1135–54), who married Matilda of Boulogne (d.1152), was a neighbour of Thierry of Elzas, count of Flanders (1128–1168).[20] In previous years Flemish mercenaries had provided military support both to King Stephen and to his cousin and enemy Empress Matilda, who contested Stephen's right to the English throne. Peace returned to England after Matilda had retired from England to Normandy in 1148.[21] Stephen's son Eustace became count of Boulogne, and the Flemish William of Ypres, Stephen's kinsman and military adviser, remained on the king's side.[22] The Flemish mercenaries have been shown on the whole to have been of a lower social status than the Flemish noblemen in England, who had arrived in 1066 as wealthy landowners thanks to William the Conqueror's gifts of land as a reward for their military support.[23] How, then, did the author of the *Ysengrimus* react to his English neighbours?

First, there is some evidence that he considered the English socially inferior to the Flemish. In book VII, which covers the death of Ysengrim and his funeral, an important role is played by Baltero the Pig, who is described as 'Anglicus ybris' ('the English hybrid').[24] The phrase has been understood as describing Baltero as the 'offspring of a domestic sow and a wild boar',[25] but this explanation ignores the important adjective 'Anglicus'. The point here is that Baltero is the son of an Anglo-Flemish couple, a remark that provides evidence for sexual encounters between English and Flemish people, something that is hardly surprising given the presence of Flemish mercenaries in England. Yet neither historians nor literary scholars have paid much attention to this topic.[26] Around 1200 Lambert of Ardres noted that in the previous century Flemish men regularly travelled to England and fathered children with English women. Count Arnold the Old (1098–1138) of Ardres apparently had three sons by three different women in England.[27] We do not know whether

Baltero was born from such a union or under similar circumstances. The poet places him in the company of people whose liturgical singing at a funeral was emphatically not that of the English: 'Nec, si forte roges, comitamur cantibus Anglos' ('And we don't, if by chance you were to ask, follow the English in our singing').[28] The ethnic distinction clearly reflects cultural tension between Flanders and England.[29]

Much better known is the author's satirical take on Englishmen with tails. At one point he refers to a 'certain redhead' who is 'more vicious than a tail-bearing Englishman' ('pravior Angligena caudato'), showing that an Englishman was stereotypically considered *pravus* ('vicious/wicked/depraved').[30] Elsewhere, an Englishman is mentioned who is also called 'Ysengrimus', but this English Ysengrim has a tail (*cauda*),[31] unlike our eponymous hero, who had been tricked into losing his tail while fishing. It has been suggested that *caudatus* means 'cowardly' rather than 'tailed', even though the latter would be the expected meaning.[32]

The potential explanation of 'caudatus' as 'cowardly' seems plausible, particularly given that a *cauda* can mean both the tail of an animal and a human hairstyle in which the hair is worn long. Cowardice seems to have been associated with long hair, which at the time connoted femininity and therefore powerlessness.[33] It is clear from the Bayeux Tapestry's depiction of the Norman conquest of England that the long hair of the English contrasted with the hairstyles of the Continental invaders. William of Poitiers, William the Conqueror's biographer, reports that when William returned to Normandy and held court at Fécamp the Norman and French noblemen were astonished at the long hair of the English hostages he had brought with him:

> Curiosi hi cum Normannis cernebant crinigeros alumnus plagae Aquilonalis: quorum pulchritudini Galliae comatae formosissimi iuvenes inviderent. Nec enim puellari venustati cedebant.

> *These men, like the Normans, looked with curiosity at the long-haired sons of the northern lands, whose beauty the most handsome youths of 'long-haired Gaul' might have envied; nor did they yield anything to the beauty of girls.*[34]

Later, during the first half of the twelfth century, the Conqueror's son, King William Rufus, was attacked by contemporary monastic chroniclers like William of Malmesbury for having courtiers with long hair, who wore luxurious clothes and long, pointed shoes:

> Tunc fluxus crinium, tunc luxus vestium, tunc usus calceorum cum arcuatis aculeis inventus; mollitie corporis certare cum feminis, gressum frangere, gestu soluto et latere nudo incedere adolescentium specimen erat.

> *Long flowing hair, luxurious garments, shoes with curved and pointed tips became the fashion. Softness of body rivalling the weaker sex, a mincing gait, effeminate gestures and a liberal display of the person as they went along, such was the ideal fashion of the younger men.*[35]

Orderic Vitalis similarly railed against the long hair and other shameful practices at the court of William Rufus.[36] The English (and Norman) men were thus characterized as effeminate and morally repulsive. It is significant that around the middle of the twelfth century the Flemish poet of the *Ysengrimus* still recognized this stereotype of the English, even though by *c.*1148 (the time of the poem's composition) the process of assimilation between the Normans and the English was well under way.[37]

Negative attitudes to the English are clearly evident from the earliest part of the work: in book I, Ysengrim tells Reynard that on a previous night, when Ysengrim was given the 'Sclava potio' ('Slavic drink') at Reynard's hearth, Reynard was a Brabantian, whereas now Reynard will be an Englishman, unless Satan swallows him up.[38] The 'Slavic drink' has been explained as a metaphor for a savage beating,[39] and the reference to Brabantians therefore draws on their association with lawlessness and cruelty. Clearly a contrast between the English and the Brabantians is implied.[40] In one manuscript 'Brabas' (Brabantian) is glossed with 'superbus' ('arrogant') and 'Anglus' ('Englishman') is glossed with 'coactus, patiens, humilis' ('submissive, passive, lowly').[41] This Flemish characterization of the English was not original, but it is important to understand that it was still deemed appropriate. The Flemish author undoubtedly felt superior to both Brabantians and Englishmen.

REYNARD IN BESTIARIES

The Flemish *Ysengrimus* had a well-known influence on vernacular beast literature in Flanders, France, Germany and Italy from the middle of the twelfth century onwards, as each country produced its own Reynard (English), Reynaert (Dutch), Renart/Renard (French), Rainardo (Italian), Reinhart (German), and so on.[42] Yet the later influence of the Reynard

6.1 Fox carrying a goose, from a Latin bestiary from early fifteenth-century England. Unlike the fox playing dead that is commonly seen in bestiaries, this iconography seems to reflect the Reynard stories. In the sixteenth century the name 'Anne Walshe' was written repeatedly in the manuscript. Copenhagen, Det Kongelige Bibliotek, Gl. kgl. S. 1633 4°, fol. 16r.

tales on medieval bestiaries in England is less well known. Bestiaries were collections of descriptions of animals, real and imagined, often accompanied by vivid illustrations. They were popular in England, although some were produced on the Continent. The height of their popularity was in the twelfth and thirteenth centuries, though the earliest record is perhaps of a tenth-century English bestiary. Vernacular versions for a secular audience began to appear as early as the twelfth century, when Philippe de Thaon produced his Anglo-Norman *Bestiaire*.[43] One manuscript copy, now held by Merton College, Oxford, contains a dedication from the author to Queen Adeliza of Louvain, the Brabantian wife of King Henry I.[44] Though not identical copies of a single text, bestiaries tended to have broadly similar descriptions and depictions of various animals. A bestiary from early fifteenth-century England is unusual for its secular motifs and allusions.[45] The fox is depicted carrying a goose (fig. 6.1), an image that seems to recall the Reynard cycle and that differs from the fox playing dead, which is the image usually found in bestiaries.[46] Compare the fox carrying the goose with a typical example of the devious fox lying on its back so that birds think it is dead, found in the early thirteenth-century English manuscript Oxford, Bodleian Library, MS. Ashmole 1511 (fig. 6.2). It is unsurprising that the famous Reynard of the beast epics influenced illustrations of foxes in some later bestiaries. It is also possible that the early bestiaries, which consistently associated certain character traits with particular animals, themselves influenced the *Ysengrimus* and the Reynard cycle.[47]

NIGEL OF WHITEACRE'S *SPECULUM STULTORUM*

Not long after the appearance of the *Ysengrimus* in Flanders, a beast epic appeared in England. The work, almost 4,000 lines of elegiac couplets, is called the *Speculum stultorum* (*Mirror of Fools*), and opens with a dedication that identifies the author as Nigel, whom we know from other sources to have been a monk of Christ Church, Canterbury. He has variously been called Nigel of Longchamp(s), Nigel (of) Whiteacre, Nigel of Canterbury and (erroneously) Nigel Wireker.[48] The connection with Canterbury is uncontroversial and therefore 'Nigel of Canterbury' and 'of Whiteacre' are both acceptable. The internal evidence suggests that the *Speculum stultorum* was composed in the last two decades of the twelfth century.[49] Instead of focusing on a fox and a wolf, the poem centres around a donkey called Burnellus (or Brunellus), who wishes he had a

6.2   Usual iconography of a fox, from the 'Ashmole Bestiary', a Latin bestiary from early thirteenth-century England. The fox is lying on its back so that birds think it is dead and try to pick at its remains; when they get close enough, the fox strikes. Oxford, Bodleian Library, MS. Ashmole 1511, fol. 23r.

uoce tanquam sibila. ut unittet modulos tistularum;
humanas carnes auidissime affectat. pedibz sic unget.
saltibz sic p̄.ut morari eam nec extentissima spacia pos
sit nec obstacula latissima; DE PARAND.

Ethiopia mittit bestiā
parandrum nomine.
boum magnitudine. ibico
uestigio. ramosis cornibz.
capite ceruino. ursi colore.
ꝓparit uallo pfundo, he
parandrum affirmant
habitum metu ūe ꝶ ꝶ
reliquescat fieri adsimili
tudinem cuicūq; rei ꝑꝑ mauerit. siue illa saxo alba
sit. seu fruttecto uirens siue quem alium modum ꝑferat;

DE WLP
Ulpis dr̄ q̄si
uolupis; est enī
uolubilis pedi
bus ꝶ nūquā in
recto itinere. s;
tortuosis an fiac
tibz currit; est
ꝶ fraudulentū
animal ingenio
sum; cum esurit
ꝶ inuenit quod
manducet. in
uoluit se in rubea tra ut appareat quasi cruentata ipietꝶ
se in terram. retinetꝶ; flatum suum tra ut penit ñ spiret;
Auel ū uidentes eam ñ flautem. ꝶ q̄si cruentatam. linguāq;

longer tail. In a marginal drawing from an early fifteenth-century manuscript, Burnellus is depicted with a mitre above his head (fig. 6.3), a reference to his dreams of being a bishop.

It is striking that the genre of the Latin beast epic suddenly appeared in England so soon after the *Ysengrimus* marked its invention, but this could, of course, have been pure coincidence – a second, independent innovation. Canterbury was, however, connected with the Low Countries in numerous ways: the monastery of Christ Church, for example, was in confraternity with the monastery of Saint-Bertin at Saint-Omer. Given the ties between Canterbury and the Low Countries, it is certainly possible that Nigel knew the *Ysengrimus* and was influenced by it.[50] Both poets portray animals rhetorically moralizing,[51] and there are also several possible parallels, but none provides conclusive evidence that Nigel was influenced by the *Ysengrimus*. For example, in the *Speculum stultorum* (ll. 1531–8) Burnellus decides to stay with the English students at the University of Paris, since he hopes that he will be able to get a bigger tail via this exposure to the English.

6.3 The donkey Burnellus (or Brunellus) imagines himself becoming a bishop; above his head is a bishop's mitre. Early fifteenth-century manuscript of the late twelfth-century *Speculum stultorum* (*Mirror of Fools*), copied by John Streech, Augustinian canon of Kenilworth (Warwickshire). London, British Library, Add. MS. 38665, fol. 114v. © British Library Board. All Rights Reserved / Bridgeman Images.

Hinc comes Angligenis prudens desiderat esse,
  Possit ut illorum conditione frui.
Est in eis etiam quiddam (ceu publica fama
  Somniat) adjungi cur magis optet eis,
Si de convictu mores formantur eidem,
  Cur nihil accrescat si comes esse queat?
Si quid eis praeter sortem natura ministrat,
  Ante retrove bonum cur nihil inde ferat?[52]

Hence wise was he in his desire to join
The Englishmen, to share their way of life.
Another reason too he had to wish
To join with them, for talk is but a dream.
If those who live together learn like ways,
Why not unite with them if possible?
If nature gives to them a better lot,
Why not derive from it some benefit? [53]

This is an oblique reference to the idea of Englishmen having tails:[54] nature gives the English 'a better lot' by endowing them with longer tails than Burnellus. It has been noted above that such claims about the English were commonplace in the Middle Ages, but the *Ysengrimus* may nevertheless have provided some inspiration for this passage. In the work of an author as original as Nigel,[55] capable of writing almost 4,000 lines of Latin poetry, examples of inspiration from a text like the *Ysengrimus* cannot be clearly distinguished from similarities that resulted from the authors operating in similar intellectual contexts.

REYNARD IN VERNACULAR LITERATURE AND ART

From Latin the Reynard stories were taken over into Old French in the *Roman de Renart*,[56] a cycle of verse episodes about the fox and his wiles, of which the oldest 'branch' (episode), *c.*1175, is the story, adapted from *Ysengrimus*, of how Reynard tricks Chauntecler the Rooster into letting his guard down. Reynard plays on Chauntecler's vanity. 'What a fine singer you are,' he says. 'How you remind me of your father, who abandoned himself to music to such an extent that he closed his eyes while singing.' When Chauntecler, eyes closed, bursts into song to show he can outperform his late father, Reynard snatches him, but he is in turn outwitted by the rooster. Chased by the villagers, Reynard is persuaded by Chauntecler to defy them, and when he opens his mouth to taunt his pursuers, Chauntecler flies away to safety. Anyone familiar with Geoffrey Chaucer's *Canterbury Tales* will recognize this as the plot of the Nun's Priest's Tale. Chaucer names the fox Russell rather than Reynard, but was obviously familiar with the Reynard cycle, for he mentions 'Renard' in another poem, *The Legend of Good Women.*[57]

Like *Ysengrimus*, the *Roman de Renart* occasionally pokes fun at Englishmen. In the first branch, Reynard disguises himself as a minstrel in order to escape the attentions of Ysengrim, who is out to kill him. To perfect the disguise he speaks a variety of French that is clearly meant to caricature the dialect of Anglo-Norman, that is, the French language as it was spoken by the English. For comic effect, the poet lards the bastardized French with English exclamations such as 'iai, iai' (yea, yea) and 'goditouet' (God knows, literally 'God it wot'). In *Ysengrimus*, Baltero the Pig is the 'Anglicus ybris'; in this episode of the *Roman de Renart*, the role is assumed by Reynard, as he turns himself into a hybrid of a French and an English speaker.[58]

While the story of Reynard gained wider popularity in French, the lingua franca of the courtly classes in the West, it never lost its roots in Dutch-speaking lands.[59] *Ysengrimus* was from Ghent; the oldest branches of the *Roman de Renart* are from northern France, some of which was Dutch speaking, while other branches are from Flanders, which was bilingual. The *Couronnement de Renard*, a later thirteenth-century beast epic inspired by the *Roman de Renart*, was dedicated to the memory of the count of Flanders, William of Dampierre, the second husband of Margaret II, countess of Flanders from 1244 to 1278. Also from Flanders are the earliest two Dutch Reynard histories, *Van den vos Reynaerde*, by a thirteenth-century Dutch poet who called himself 'Willem', and *Reynaerts historie* (probably fifteenth century).[60]

The popularity of Reynard the Fox is also evident in the visual arts from the Low Countries. He often peeks at us from the margins of medieval manuscripts. A stunning example comes from the beautifully illustrated *Roman d'Alexandre*, Oxford, Bodleian Library, MS. Bodl. 264, one of the greatest treasures of the Bodleian. The early history of the manuscript is itself enmeshed in Anglo-Dutch relations.[61] Work on the manuscript was begun in Tournai in the 1330s, probably on the initiative of the chronicler and bibliophile abbot of St Martin, Gilles li Muisis. A scribal colophon on folio 208r tells us that the writing of the Alexander cycle was completed in December 1338. By this time Tournai (Doornik in Dutch) was predominantly French speaking, but it was close to the French–Dutch language border and Dutch clearly continued to have currency there. For instance, in 1455 the prestigious Tournai theatre prize was won by a group from Ypres who performed 'en flamenghe' ('in Flemish').[62] Since the diocese of Tournai included the towns of Bruges and Ghent, which, as we saw in Chapter 2, were notable centres of book production in this period, it could draw on some of the finest artists from the Low Countries. At least two of these, Pierart dou Tielt (presumably from Tielt in West Flanders) and Jehan de Grise (whose family name points to Bruges), were employed to decorate the text. From a second colophon written by Jehan de Grise (also on folio 208r), it appears that they did not set to work immediately after the text had been copied but after an interval of some six years: a second colophon states that Jehan de Grise completed his work in April 1344.

War was the probable cause for the delay. In 1340 Tournai was besieged by Edward III, as it had sided with France rather than England in the Hundred Years War (1337–1453). By the fifteenth century, however, the manuscript was certainly in England. The reason it ended up there may again have been war. The manuscript may have been intended for or acquired by John II, king of France (r.1350–64). When John was captured by the English at the Battle of Poitiers in 1356, manuscripts in his possession were also seized, as we know from an inscription in another illuminated manuscript taken as war booty, London, British Library, MS. Royal 19 D III (an illuminated biblical history). The inscription reads:

> Cest livre fust pris oue le roy de Fraunce a la bataille de Peyters et le bon counte de Saresbirs William Montagu la [*sic*] achata pur cent mars et le dona a sa compaigne Elizabeth la bone countesse.

> *This book was taken along with the King of France at the Battle of Poitiers and the good count of Salisbury William Montague bought it for a hundred marks and gave it to his companion Elizabeth the good countess.*[63]

Whether or not this was also how MS. Bodl. 264 came to England, it must have been in London by the early fifteenth century. Here the *Roman d'Alexandre* was supplemented by the *Travels of Marco Polo* in French, and by the Middle English *Alexander and Dindimus*, an alliterative Alexander romance that relates the correspondence of Alexander with the Brahmins of India. The addition of the English text was based on a misunderstanding caused by a clash of cultures. In England, the Alexander legend was almost exclusively known in versions based on the *Historia de preliis Alexandri Magni* (*The History of the Battles of Alexander the Great*), which contained the episode of Alexander's exchange of letters

6.4a *following pages* Opening from a manuscript of the *Roman d'Alexandre*, written in Tournai (Doornik) in the 1330s and decorated to the highest standard of fourteenth-century book design by Flemish artists c.1344. The manuscript was already in England by the fifteenth century. Oxford, Bodleian Library, MS. Bodl. 264, fols 79v–80r.

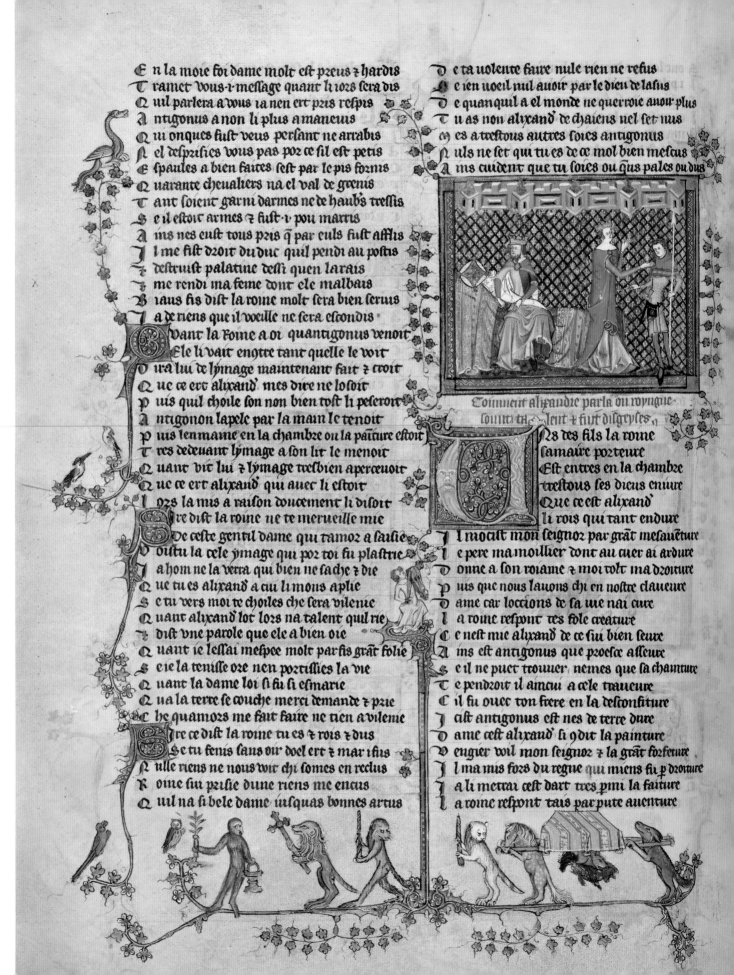

E n la moie foi dame molt est preus ⁊ hardis
T ramet vous ·i· message quant li iorz sera dis
Q uil parlera a vous ia nen ert pris respis
A ntigonus a non li plus amaneis
Q ui onques fust veus persant ne arrabis
S el desprisies vous pas por ce sil est petis
E spaules a bien faites cest par le pis fornis
Q uarante cheualiers na el val de grenis
T ant soient garni darmes ne de haubs treslis
S e il estoit armes ⁊ fust ·i· pou marris
A ins nes eust tous pris q par euls fust afflis
I l me fist droit du duc quil pendi au postis
⁊ destruist palatine desfi quen la rais
m e rendi ma feme dont ele malbais
B iaus fis dist la roine molt sera bien seruis
A de riens que il voeille ne sera escondis

Q uant la roine a oi quantigonus venoit
E le li vait enqtre tant quelle le voit
O ira lui de lymage maintenant fait ⁊ croit
Q ue ce ert alixand̄ mes dire ne losoit
P uis quil choile son non bien tost li peseroit
A ntigonon lapele par la main le tenoit
p uis lenmaine en la chambre ou la painture estoit
T res dedeuant lymage a son lit le menoit
Q uant vit lui ⁊ lymage tresbien aperceuoit
Q ue ce ert alixand̄ qui auec li estoit
L ors la mis a raison doucement li disoit

S ire dist la roine ne te merueille mie
D e ceste gentil dame qui tamoz a saisie
O oistu la cele ymage qui por toi fu plastrie
I a hom ne la verra qui bien ne sache ⁊ die
Q ue tu es alixand̄ a cui li mons aplie
S e tu vers moi te choiles che sera vilenie
Q uant alixand̄ lot lors na talent quil rie
⁊ dist vne parole que ele a bien oie
Q uant ie lessai mespee molt parfis grat folie
S eie la tenusse ore nen portissies la vie
Q uant la dame loi si fu si esmarie
Q ua la terre se couche merci demande ⁊ prie
C he quamors me fait faire ne tien a vileine

S ire ce dist la roine tu es ⁊ rois ⁊ dus
S e tu fenis sans oir doel ert ⁊ marrisus
S ulle riens ne nous voit chi somes en reclus
R oine sui prisie dune riens me encus
Q uil na si bele dame iusquas bonnes artus

D e ta uolente faire nule rien ne refus
⁊ ien uoeil nul auoir par le dieu de lasus
D e quanquil a el monde ne querroie auoir plus
T u as non alixand̄ de chaiens nel set nus
⁊ es a trestous autres soies antigonus
N uls ne set qui tu es de ce mol bien mescus
A ins cuident que tu soies ou gus pales ou dus

C omment alixand̄ parla ou royngue
soute th̄ eleut ⁊ fist disgreyses

O ns des fils la roine
s amaire porteure
E st entres en la chambre
t restous ses dieus eniure
Q ue ce est alixand̄
li rois qui tant endure
I mocist mon seignor par grat mesauture
I e pere ma moillier dont au cuer ai ardure
D onne a son roiame ⁊ moi tolt ma droiture
P uis que nous lauons chi en nostre claueure
P ame car loccions de sa uie nai cure
L a roine respont tes fole creature
C e nest mie alixand̄ de ce sui bien seure
A ins est antigonus que proesce asseure
S e il ne puet trouuer nemes que sa chainture
T e pendroit il aincui a cele traueure
C il fu ouec ton frere en la desconfiture
I ist antigonus est nes de terre dure
D ame cest alixand̄ si gdit la painture
V enguer vueil mon seignor ⁊ la grat forfeiture
I l ma mis fors du regne qui miens fu p droiture
I a li metrai cest dart tres pmi la faiture
L a roine respont tais par pute auenture

a nauras point de sens fols seras p nature
p oz ce quil le resamble en sa cheueleure
c uides que ce soit il de cors z de faiture
a ins sous le monde dieu nauint tele auenture
q ue diex a itel home donnast du mot la cure
e men chaut dist li enfes se ce est il ou non
c ar tout ai en talent voirement locciron
v enrons nous de cestui quant celui ne poon
s i saura bien li rois que de riens ne lamion
v oire ce dit la dame a dieu maleiçon
l i rois le ma tramis sen ferai traison
f u toi gars densus moi nai soing de ta tençon
l es dens te pechoiasse se ieusse un baston
d e sa paume li doune droiste le menton
d ensus soi le bouta sel hurte a lescalon
p lorant ist de la chambre z hors de la meson

P ensiue est la roine z en molt grant freoz
d el Roy qui se marist de son fil menoz
m oteusement li prie o larmes z o ploz
u vallet qua oi li pardint la foloz
c ar se il nel faisoit il seroit en erroz
q uant li rois vit les larmes i poi ot de tendroz
z dist a la roine qui fu de grant valoz
s e il mauoit plus dit z fait honte greignoz
t out li est pardone dame por nostre amoz
l a roine sapuie de deles laumaçoz
t ant doucement lembrace quil senti la chaloz
g rant ioie font ensamble p bien z p amoz
d essus i lit pare gisent demi un ioz
p uis issent de la chambre sus el palais hautoz
q nes i aperchoiue la li fait double hounoz
t ant g puent porter xxx mul ambleoz
i done doz molu gme a empereoz
c pailes de biterne trestous dune coloz
l i a fait aporter a i sien vauassoz
a ntigonus fait ele ce donras ton seignoz
z tu qui es messages auras por seue amoz
i. mantel sebelin de paile paint a floz
t uit ti gpaignon seront por toi meilloz
c hascuns aura ij pailes dynde superioz
d e cha uenir a moi ne se mete en laboz
n i porroie parler car el chief ai dloz
a lixand respont dit de losengeoz
s e messires li rois vous auoit a oistoz
m iex auoit esploitie que tuit si ancisoz

l ors apris le congie torne sen a baudoz
c andeolus le guie les plains de ual greignoz
s el rendi thom le hardi poigneoz
q ue il tenoit encor a roi macedonoz
a donc a pris congie si se mist retoz
s on demaine tref est li rois descendus
d eparti sont li paile z le bon oz molus
q ue ele li donna quil ne fust cogneus
o z aproche li mois z li tans est venus
q ue babilone ert prise z li palais rendus
o u il sera destruis z ses los abatus
c onsaus de nesun home nen puet estre creus
p ar nesun de ses homes nen puet estre tenus
p oz aler a sa mort est par matin meus

A ins que li rois meust si a fait sorison
d edens son tref demaine dont doz sot li roion
l es forches dedens z defors li pellon
l i rois en apela tholomer z cliton
o ces ij sont venu li xij compaignon
s eignoz dist alixand entendes ma raison
p riue estes demoi z bien de ma maison
o nques de uos gsaus ne me uint se bien non
c ar par uous tieng ie quite terre promission
l a seignozie en ai iusque a capharnaon
z tant g dure terre z mer clot enuiron
f ors seule babilone ne sai se ia lauron
d ieu merci z les nos nest sires se ie non
h ui est uenus li iours quen aurois guerredon
o z enuenes auant ia uous ferai gent don
a chascun i royaume sans ire z sans tençon
z sen aurois les rentes que nous en receuon
i e uous couronnerai a la loi que tenon
a lons en babilone le matin imouuon
u ne rien uous promet se prendre la poon
i e uous ferai tous riches doz quit z de maigon
i e tresoz lamirant uous metrai abandon
s emes la poure gent z les borgois gardon
q ue ia par nous ni perdent uaillant i esperon
s e la cites est nostre por quoi la destruiron
d es eues plenteiues nous uienent li poisson
d es fores qui sont larges aurons la uenoison
u ne piece de tans nous i seiozneron
s ire dient si home por dieu car ialon
f aites uostre plesir z nous tuit lotroion
C ar les herberges mainent grant ioie z grant deduit

a li metrai ceft dart tres pmi la faiture
a roine refpont tais par pute auenture

6.4b The funeral procession of Reynard the Fox. Decoration in the lower border of the *Roman d'Alexandre* illustrated *c.*1344. The bier is carried by the wolf and the horse, but Reynard is ready to jump out, having snatched the rooster. Oxford, Bodleian Library, MS. Bodl. 264, fol. 79v, detail.

with the Brahmins. The French *Roman d'Alexandre* in MS. Bodl. 264, however, was based on a different version of the Alexander legend. And when this French text was read in England, it was naturally assumed that an episode was missing, and *Alexander and Dindimus* was added to it to make good the perceived lack.[64] The manuscript was still in London (or back in London) in 1466 when it was purchased by Richard Woodville, Earl Rivers, who wrote an ownership note on folio 274r.

What made (and makes) the manuscript so precious are the illuminations. The pages from the *Roman d'Alexandre* show the latest developments in fourteenth-century book design, as seen on the pages reproduced here (fig. 6.4a). Colourful tendrils sprout from the decorated initials and provide a quasi-natural border for the two text columns. In the miniature illustrating the text we see Alexander, disguised as King Antigonus, with Queen Candace, who colludes in Alexander's deception in front of her servant. In addition, drolleries appear in the lower margin of the page. This style of illustration is first seen in devotional books from the second half of the thirteenth century; only at the turn of that century did it spread to secular romances and legal works.[65] In the border of this particular page the artist, perhaps prompted by the act of deception described in the *Roman d'Alexandre* and the miniature, celebrated the wily hero, Reynard the Fox (fig. 6.4b). In what is supposed to be Reynard's funeral procession, his bier is borne by the wolf Ysengrim and Ferrant the Horse (whose name means 'carrying', so he does his name justice). Leading the procession are various other animals carrying candles, the cross and the aspergillum for sprinkling holy water. The joke is that Reynard is not dead at all: his head can be seen sticking out from underneath the canopy, with Chauntecler the Rooster in his mouth. The image is loosely based on branch XVII of the *Roman de Renart*, which recounts how Reynard is carried in solemn procession to be buried, only to jump out of his grave and dash off with Chauntecler. The illustrator must have read this episode in a manuscript, for the image is closely modelled on depictions of Reynard's funeral in illustrated *Roman de Renart* manuscripts.[66] An especially close parallel is the miniature of Reynard's bier and funeral procession in one such manuscript from the second quarter of the fifteenth century in the Bibliothèque Nationale de France.[67]

REYNARD IN ENGLAND

Reynard stories and motifs did not take long to cross the North Sea to England. The story of the Fox and the Well, from branch IV of the *Roman de Renart*, was translated into English early in the thirteenth century. *Of the Vox and the Wolf* now survives in just a single manuscript, Oxford, Bodleian Library, MS. Digby 86, a trilingual Latin–French–English miscellany. The manuscript was copied in the west of England, but the language of the poem suggests that it was originally composed in the south-east.[68] The story tells how Reynard gets stuck at the bottom of a well in a bucket. He persuades Sigrim (Ysengrim) to lower himself into the well in the second bucket by declaring that he is in fact in paradise. As Sigrim's bucket plunges down, Reynard's bucket rises up. And so Reynard makes his escape at Sigrim's expense, though of course not without some personal insults as he passes Sigrim on his way down.

miacvis tius. propterea vnor
vir te deus in eternum · ad · an · a.

6.5 The fox and the stork at dinner. The fable, originally from Aesop, pitting two tricksters against each other, became associated with the Reynard story. From the 'Hours of Anne of Bohemia', produced in Flanders in the 1340s. Oxford, Bodleian Library, MS. Lat. liturg. f. 3, fol 128v.

In English art, the trickster fox appears even earlier, though he is initially to be identified not with Reynard but with the fox of Aesop's fable of the Fox and the Stork. The story is that the fox invites the stork for dinner but serves his food in a shallow dish that makes it impossible for the stork to eat anything. In return the stork invites the fox over, serving the food in a steep jar so that only the stork's long beak can get at it. 'One bad turn deserves another' is the moral of this tale. The scene showing the fox trying to drink out of the jar is depicted on an early twelfth-century memorial slab in Bridlington Priory in Yorkshire. What makes this slab so remarkable is the direct connection with Flanders: it was of Flemish manufacture.[69] It is made of Tournai marble, which, as we know from Scottish sources, was imported into Flemish cities to be turned into grave slabs;[70] and the person it commemorates is Walter of Ghent, earl of Lincoln (died c.1139), whose father had come over from Flanders with William the Conqueror and had been rewarded by the king with lands in Bridlington. Walter founded the Augustinian priory and endowed it with lands.

The spread of artistic motifs from Flanders to England can be traced in manuscripts too. The fable of the Fox and the Stork, which soon got

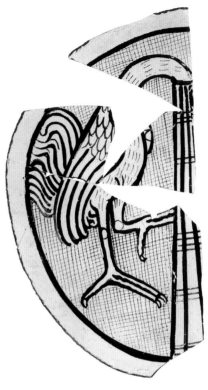

mixed up with the Reynard story,[71] had a special place in Flemish book art. It is illustrated (fig. 6.5) in the bottom margin of a page of Anne of Bohemia's book of hours (first phase *c.*1340),[72] a manuscript that has already been discussed (Chapter 2, fig. 2.5). The same motif appears in a manuscript (*c.*1350) of the *Voeux du Paon*, now in the Pierpont Morgan Library in New York,[73] which can be connected with the Tournai atelier of Pierart dou Tielt and Jehan de Grise, where the *Roman d'Alexandre* manuscript, MS. Bodl. 264, was produced.[74]

Not much later we encounter the same motif in an English manuscript, the Bohun Psalter in the British Library (fig. 6.6).[75] What makes the migration of this artistic motif explicable is the likelihood that one of the Bohun illuminators was in fact a Fleming.[76] The fox and the stork are certainly depicted in strikingly similar poses. The only things that are missing in the equivalent scene from Anne of Bohemia's book of hours are the colours and the expressive posture of the stork, which is curiously reminiscent of a stained-glass window from the Dominican abbey in Ghent (fig. 6.7),[77] which the Flemish expat might well have seen in his youth. The window is now only partially preserved but we have enough of it to recognize the scene: the posture and appearance of the stork's feet,

6.6 *above left* The Fox and the Stork, from the Bohun Psalter, made in England in the second half of the fourteenth century for a member of the Bohun family and possibly illuminated by a Flemish artist. London, British Library, MS. Egerton 3277, fol. 47v. © British Library Board. All Rights Reserved / Bridgeman Images

6.7 *above* The stork sticking its head in a tall vessel, inspired by the fable of the Fox and the Stork. From a stained glass window from the Dominican abbey of Ghent. Ghent, University of Ghent, Het Pand. © KIK-IRPA, Brussels.

one stationary, the other raised, are remarkably similar.

Although the fable of the Fox and the Stork has a different and more ancient literary pedigree than the Reynard saga, the two were often mixed up, and English illuminators who painted Reynard scenes were always keen to add a stork for special effect. A vivid example can be found in the Smithfield Decretals.[78] The manuscript, containing a copy of Gregory IX's decretals, was copied in southern France but enriched in England, around 1340, with marginal illustrations, including some inspired by the Reynard story (fig. 6.8): at bottom left Reynard, accoutred as a bishop, preaches to an audience of birds, with the stork bringing up the rear; and on the right he is seen running off with one of the members of his congregation, the goose, while a housewife armed with her distaff is in hot pursuit.

The image at bottom right is perhaps the most iconic Reynard representation in medieval art. From illuminated manuscripts of the *Roman de Renart*, images of Reynard making off with a farmyard bird, either a cock or goose, invaded the empty spaces of all kinds of other manuscripts. Earlier than the Smithfield Decretals is the Ormesby Psalter (Oxford, Bodleian Library, MS. Douce 366), one of the greatest masterpieces of East Anglian art. The book was begun late in the thirteenth century and completed in the 1330s for Robert of Ormesby, the subprior of Norwich Cathedral. Much of the illumination, however, was undertaken in the 1310s, in a style apparently influenced by northern French artists, some of whom may have been working in England at the time. The patron was probably John de Warenne, earl of Surrey and Sussex, whose ancestor Gundrada had come from Flanders in the 1060s.[79] The Reynard story was evidently well known to one of the border artists: the fox's prey appears to be none other than Chauntecler. Again the fox is pursued by a woman with her distaff (fig. 6.9).

The longevity of this pictorial Reynard tradition is shown by the remarkable Tudor Pattern Book that is now Oxford, Bodleian Library, MS. Ashmole 1504. Produced in the third decade of the sixteenth century, the manuscript was probably copied from the same exemplar (now lost) as the so-called Helmingham Bestiary and Herbal, now at the Yale Center for British Art, Paul Mellon Collection.[80] These twin manuscripts were probably once the proud possessions of the Tollemache family of Helmingham Hall in Suffolk. Both contain illustrations of trees, animals and herbs that could be used as models for paintings, embroidery and

6.8 At bottom left Reynard, as bishop, preaches to the birds, including a stork; on the right he runs off with the goose, chased by a housewife. From the Smithfield Decretals, copied in southern France but decorated in England c.1340. London, British Library, Royal MS. 10 E IV, f. 49v. © British Library Board. All Rights Reserved / Bridgeman Images.

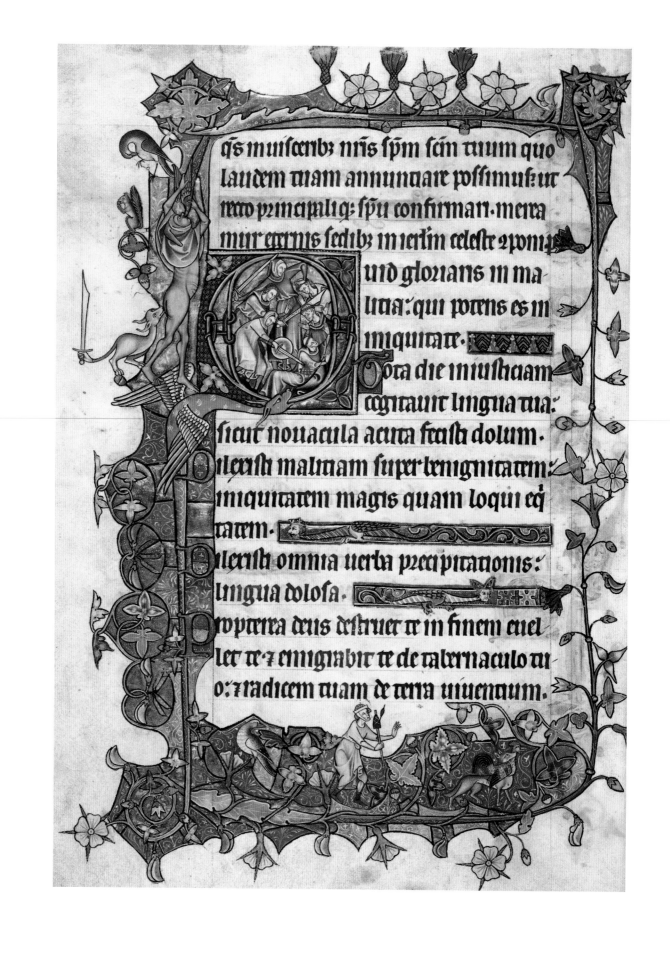

qs in uiscentib; nris spm scm truim quo
laudem truam annunciare possimus: ut
tecto principali q; spu confirman. mena
mur eternis sedib; in uerim celeste 2 pom̄ꝑ
uid glonans in ma
licia: qui potens es in
iniquitate·
Tota die iniusticiam
cogitauit lingua tua:
sicut nouacula acuta fecisti dolum·
Dilexisti maliciam super benignitatem:
iniquitatem magis quam loqui eq̄
tatem·
Dilexisti omnia uerba precipitationis:
lingua dolosa·
Propterea deus destruet te in finem euel
let te 7 emigrabit te de tabernaculo tu
o: 7 radicem tuam de terra uiuentium.

6.9 *facing page* Reynard running off with Chauntecler, chased by a woman. From the 'Ormesby Psalter', by a border artist who was probably working in the 1310s for John de Warenne, whose pedigree included Flemish ancestry. The psalter was completed in the 1330s for Robert of Ormesby, sub-prior of Norwich Cathedral. Oxford, Bodleian Library, MS. Douce 366, fol. 71v.

6.10 *above, left* Model laurel and mulberry trees, with Reynard as bishop, preaching to a rooster, a hen and a stork. From the Tudor Pattern Book, a sixteenth-century manuscript with botanical illustrations. Oxford, Bodleian Library, MS. Ashmole 1504, fol. 22v.

6.11 *above, right* A crane removing a bone from a wolf's throat, illustrating Aesop's fable of the Wolf and the Crane. From the sixteenth-century Tudor Pattern Book. Oxford, Bodleian Library, MS. Ashmole 1504, fol. 33v (detail).

sculptures. As such they provide valuable insight into the iconographic conventions and motifs that would have circulated within East Anglia.[81] Of the two manuscripts, the Bodleian Library's MS. Ashmole 1504 is later but also more interesting, since it contains, alongside the models of plants, trees and animals (each category organized alphabetically), smaller drolleries that link the manuscript to pictorial traditions that are centuries older. Almost all the Reynard motifs that we have seen in earlier medieval art are present in MS. Ashmole 1504. On the page that has model paintings of a laurel and a mulberry tree, we encounter Reynard with crosier, preaching to a rooster and hen, Chauntecler and his beloved wife Pinte, and a stork who seems to have arrived late (fig. 6.10).[82]

The scene is reminiscent of the border illustration of the British Library's Smithfield Decretals (fig. 6.8), where Reynard, again holding a bishop's staff, preaches to various birds, including the habitual latecomer, the stork.[83] In MS. Ashmole 1504 he is dressed in a blue robe – an outrageous choice, since the colour blue symbolized fidelity, which is the last thing on Reynard's mind! Was the illuminator familiar with the old Dutch proverb 'zich onder een blauwe huik verbergen' ('to hide oneself under a blue cloak'),[84] meaning to deceive others while feigning loyalty? Other foxy scenes in MS. Ashmole 1504 bear comparison with iconography found in earlier medieval manuscripts: on folio 30v a stork struggles to eat from a shallow dish while the fox is tucking in; and on folio 34r Reynard makes off with Chauntecler, chased by a woman armed with a distaff. In the Bodleian Library Tudor Pattern Book, the world of the Reynard cycle is again brought into contact with that of Aesop's fables. The image of a canine with the head of a bird down its throat (fig. 6.11) is described in the digital facsimile of Ashmole 1504 as 'a sitting fox [which] has swallowed the head of a large bird'.[85] The animals in question are actually those of Aesop's fable of the Wolf and the Crane. The crane volunteers to remove a bone that has got stuck in the wolf's throat by using its long beak, but instead of the promised reward it is told by the wolf that it has been sufficiently rewarded by not having had its head bitten off.

WILLIAM CAXTON'S *HISTORY OF REYNARD THE FOX*

From an art historical perspective it may look as if the border images in the Tudor Pattern Book are a throwback to 'the heyday of medieval grotesques',[86] but it should be remembered that Aesop and Reynard had only a few decades earlier been given a new lease of life in the new medium of print, and may actually have been regarded as topical and fashionable. In 1484 William Caxton produced an English Aesop edition with woodcut illustrations, including one of the Fox and the Stork (fol. 44r), and one of the Wolf and the Crane (fol. 35r) that looks remarkably like the one in MS. Ashmole 1504.[87] And in England the year of Reynard's greatest triumph was 1481, when Caxton published his *History of Reynard the Fox*.[88] It proved a bestseller. Before 1481 Caxton had published a number of Burgundian chivalric romances, but most of these were not commercial successes compared to *Reynard*. Caxton himself reprinted it and then redacted it for a second edition in 1489. Moreover, after Caxton generations of English printers ensured that the text remained available in new editions: Richard Pynson printed it *c.*1494, Wynkyn de Worde *c.*1515 and Thomas Gaultier in 1550. Caxton's *Reynard* was special for other reasons, too: it was not a translation from French, like most of Caxton's books, but from a Middle Dutch version of the Reynard saga. Caxton's source was a prose version of *Reynaerts historie*. The closest counterpart to Caxton's translation is the printed version that was published by Gerard Leeu in Gouda in 1479, though there is reason to suspect that Caxton may have known an earlier version.[89]

Caxton's fluency in Dutch seems remarkable today, but it was not uncommon for someone in his profession and situation. Caxton was first and foremost a mercer (a trader in fine cloth) and in that capacity he had spent decades working in the Low Countries, where the best cloth was made. In his preface to his earliest English publication, *The Recuyell of the Historyes of Troye*, translated from French, he apologized for the

> symplenes and vnperfightnes that I had in bothe langages, that
> is to wete in frenshe and in englissh. For in france was I never
> and was born and lerned myn englissh in kent in the weeld
> where I doubt not is spoken as brode and rude englissh as in
> ony place of englond, & have contynued by the space of .XXX.
> yere for the most part in the contres of Braband, flandres,
> holand, and zeland.[90]

> *the simplicity and imperfection of both of my languages, namely*
> *French and English. For I was never in France and I was born*
> *and learned my English in the Weald in Kent, where undoubtedly*
> *people speak as broad and as coarse a form of English as anywhere*

in England. And I have continued to live, for the duration of thirty years, mostly in the lands of Brabant, Flanders, Holland and Zeeland.

The suggestion here is that after thirty years in Dutch-speaking lands, Caxton had become more at home in Dutch than his mother tongue. Apologies of this kind were conventional, of course, but the rhetoric is not implausible. The Weald in Kent, where Caxton was born, is an area of England that had attracted many Dutch-speaking migrants from the middle of the fourteenth century.[91] Edward III had been so impressed with the flourishing cloth-making towns of Brabant and Flanders that he actively encouraged weavers and cloth traders to come to England,[92] and many of them settled in this region. It is likely that Caxton encountered Dutch even before he moved to the Low Countries.

Caxton published *Reynard* after he had returned to England. Despite its success with early English readers, literary critics have not been complimentary about the quality of his translation.[93] If we examine a sentence from *Reynard*, we can understand this point of view:

> Yf the fox will telle how it byfel, I wyl gyve hym the *fordele* thereof, for I can not telle it so wel but he shal *beryspe* me.[94]

> *If the fox will tell me what happened, I will give him the privilege of doing so, for I cannot tell it so well that he would not reproach me.*

Dutch speakers will have fewer problems with the two words we have italicized here than anglophone readers: they are borrowings from Dutch, as are many words in Caxton's *Reynard*. Caxton's 'double Dutch' has encouraged the view that he was translating slavishly from Dutch, but on closer inspection the situation is more complex and more interesting. For example, while 'beryspe' was probably taken over verbatim by Caxton from his Dutch source (which reads 'berispen'), 'fordele' does not occur in the corresponding passage from the Dutch source, which instead reads 'vorwaerde'.[95] Where 'vordele' does occur in *Reynaerts historie*, it only ever has the usual sense of the word, 'advantage', in which sense it was borrowed into English in the fifteenth century. The context in which Caxton here uses 'fordele' shows, however, that he was sufficiently fluent in Dutch to know that the word

6.12 *opposite* First page of William Caxton's *History of Reynard the Fox*, in the revised edition by Richard Pynson (1494). Pynson closely followed Caxton's original text, retaining many Dutch loan-words while avoiding some of Caxton's Dutch spellings. Oxford, Bodleian Library, Douce V 245, sig. Air.

¶ Here begynneth the Hyſtorye of rei
nard the foxe.

I N this hyſtorye ben wꝛy
ton the parables. goo
de lernynge and diuerſe
poyntes to be marked.
By whiche poyntes men maye lerne
to come to the ſubtyll knowleche off
ſuche thinges as now dayly ben v̓
ſed and hadde in the counceillys off
loꝛdes and prelates goſtly ⁊ woꝛldly
and alſo emonge marchauntes and
other comone people. ⁊ this boke is
maade foꝛ nede and pꝛouffyth of al
le good folke. As ferre as they in re
dyng oꝛ heryng of it ſhal mowe vn
derſtande and fele the foꝛſeyde ſutyl
deceptes that now dayly byn vſed
in the woꝛld. not to thente that men
ſholde vſe them But that euery man
ſhold eſchewe ⁊ kepe hym fꝛom the
ſubtyl falſe ſhꝛewes that they be not
decepued Then who that wylle haue
the very vndꝛſtandyng of this ma
ter. he muſte ofte and many tymes
rede in this booke and ernſtely and
dylygently marke wel ꝑ he redeth.

Foꝛ it is ſette ſubtylly lyke as ye
ſhal ſee in redynge of hyt and not o
nes to rede it. foꝛ a man ſhalle not
wyth ones ouer redyng fynde the ry
ght vnderſtandynge ne compryſe it
wel. But ofterymes to rede it ſhalle
cauſe it well to be vnderſtáde. ⁊ foꝛ
them that vnderſtandeth it. yt ſhalle
be right ioyous̔ playſaunt and pꝛof
fitable.

¶ How the lyon Kyng of alle Beſtys
ſente oute his maundementis that
alle Beeſtys ſhold come to his feſte ⁊
court.   Capitulo pꝛimo

I T was aboute the tyme of pen
thecoſte oꝛ wythſontyde that
the wodes comynly be luſty ⁊ glad
ſom And alſo the trees clad wyth le
ups and bloſſoms and the ground
wyth herbes and flourys ſwete ſmel
lynge and alſo the fowles and byꝛ
des ſyngen melodyouſly in thyer ar
monye. That the lyon the noble kyn
ge of alle beeſtes wolde in the hooly
dayes of this feeſt holde an open Co
urt at ſtade. whiche he dyde to kno
we ouer al in his ſande. And com
maunded by ſtrayte commyſſyons
and maundementis that euery beſte
ſhold come thyder. in ſuche wyſe that
alle the beſtes grete and ſmalle came
to the court ſaufe Reynard the foꝛe
¶ foꝛ he knewe hym ſelf fauty and
gylty in many thyngys ayenſt ma
ny beſtys that thider ſhold come that
he durſte not auentꝛe to goo thider
whan the kynge of al beſtes had aſ
ſembled alle his court. there was no
ne of them alle But that he had com
played ſoꝛe an reynard the foꝛe.

The firſt complaynt made Iſe
grym the wulf on reynard. Caᵒ.ii.

Segrym the wulf wyth his
lynguage and frendes came ⁊
ſtode to foꝛe the kyng and ſayde.
Hye and myghty pꝛynce my loꝛd the

A i.

had another sense in Middle Dutch, namely 'privilege, precedence'.

Instead of thinking of Caxton as a slavish translator, it would therefore be better to understand him as a bilingual speaker, whose English shows influence from the language he must have spoken and written during his decades-long stay in the Low Countries. The latest Caxton discovery is relevant here: it is a copy of a letter by Caxton, written in impeccable Dutch, in the archives of Hoorn, where Caxton was on business in 1475.[96] In linguistics, the often unconscious influence exerted by one language on another in bilingual speakers is known as interference, and this linguistic perspective provides a better and more sympathetic way of approaching Caxton's English. It explains why he was also influenced by Dutch when he was translating from French.[97] Examples of Dutch words that infiltrated his French-based books are 'butter' ('cheat', from Middle Dutch 'botter') in *The Game and Play of the Chesse* (1474); 'spynroke' ('distaff') in *The Book of the Knight of the Tower* (1484); and 'spyncop', from the Flemish dialect word 'spinnekop' ('spider'), which Caxton used in no fewer than three of his books.[98] It also explains why Dutch not only shaped Caxton's vocabulary but also other aspects of his language. For instance, in *The History of Jason* (1477), Caxton on a few occasions spells 'fleece' in Dutch fashion as 'vliese'.[99] In *The Recuyell of the Historyes of Troye*, he writes 'styfemoder' (corresponding with Dutch 'stiefmoeder') instead of his normal 'stepmoder', and 'behoeffyd' (corresponding with Dutch 'behoeft') in place of 'behoved'.[100] None of these Dutch-style spellings of words had much of an afterlife in the English language beyond Caxton, the exception being his innovative spelling of Middle English 'gost' with 'gh' (reflecting Flemish 'gheest'), which we still use today. In short, the real issue with Caxton's style is not that he translated Dutch literally, but that he could not help thinking in Dutch, even when he was translating texts from French into English.[101]

THE *REYNARD* WOODCUTS AND ENGRAVINGS

The success of Caxton's *Reynard* is shown by the many later editions, including those by the first printers to set up shop in Fleet Street in London: Richard Pynson (*c.*1449–1529/30) from Normandy and Wynkyn de Worde, probably a Dutchman, as discussed in Chapter 3. Caxton's own second edition had come out in 1489, and when he died a couple of years later, Richard Pynson prepared a slightly revised edition, published in 1494 (fig. 6.12).

Some of Caxton's 'Dutchisms' were edited out by Pynson. So instead of the spelling 'Hyer' (reflecting Middle Dutch 'hyer'/'hier'), Pynson spells the opening word 'Here'. And instead of Caxton's 'lerynge' (based on Middle Dutch 'leringe') Pynson prints 'lernynge'. What is more surprising, however, is the number of 'Dutchisms' that Pynson was content to reprint without any change, presumably because they had some currency in his own English and that of his contemporaries. 'Mowen' ('may') was not unusual in Middle English, but its use following another modal verb ('they … shal mowe understande') is peculiar and reflects Dutch usage (Caxton's source read 'si … sellen mogen verstaen'). 'Over redynge' ('perusal') is modelled on Middle Dutch 'overlesinghe'. The word is unlikely to have been of English origin; it is not even recorded in the *Oxford English Dictionary*, but Pynson must have assumed his readers would understand it.

Wynkyn de Worde in his *Reynard* edition reasserted the text's Dutch connections. Caxton's *Reynard* had been based on an unillustrated *Reynaerts historie*, such as printed by Gerard Leeu in Gouda in 1479. In 1487, however, Leeu, by that time based in Antwerp, brought out an edition of a rhymed version of *Reynaerts historie* illustrated with an impressive cycle of woodcuts by the 'Haarlem Master', so called because the same artist had earlier produced illustrations for the Haarlem-based printer Jacob Bellaert. The Haarlem Master can hardly have expected that his original woodcut cycle would dictate the future of Reynard illustrations in England and the Continent for a century and a half to come, but that is what happened. In Germany, the Dutch *Reynaerts historie* was translated into Low German as *Reynke de vos*. The first known edition was published in Lübeck in 1498, and the German artist responsible for the woodcuts simply copied the Haarlem Master's work. Wynkyn de Worde must have got hold of Leeu's illustrated *Reynaerts historie* even earlier, for it inspired him to embellish his own reprint of Caxton's *Reynard* with a series of woodcut illustrations closely modelled on those by the Haarlem Master.[102] Wynkyn's first edition (*c.*1495) is now lost, but he was undoubtedly in possession of a cycle of Reynard woodcuts by then, since he recycled some images from it to illustrate other books, the earliest of these being his edition of Lydgate's *The Horse, the Sheep, and the Goose* (*c.*1495).[103] Wynkyn's subsequent 1515 Reynard edition is preserved only in fragmentary form, but fortunately for us his cycle of woodcuts can be admired in the many sixteenth- and seventeenth-century Reynard editions that continued to use Wynkyn's Dutch-inspired woodcuts to illustrate the text. So when we look at the pictures of the 'modern' 1620 edition by the London printer Edward Allde, we are really looking back in time at the work of a late fifteenth-century book artist commissioned by Wynkyn de Worde, who in turn went back to the Haarlem Master. Edward Allde's edition, and the 1629 edition by his widow Elizabeth (fig. 6.13), who continued the printing business after her husband died, both advertised the latest Reynard book as one 'purged from all the grossenesse both in phrase and matter. As also augmented and inlarged with sundry excellent moralls and expositions upon every severall chapter.'[104] Wynkyn's woodcuts are accompanied in the margin by pieces of homely wisdom, like the one on the page shown here: 'the trappes which men now and then set for others, bring hurt to themselves'. The language has been updated, purged of much swearing, and sometimes revised to bring text and image into closer alignment.[105] Prospective buyers of *Reynard* will have been reassured by the picture opposite that there was still much 'grossenesse' to enjoy. The woodcut shows Tibert the Cat biting off one of the village priest's testicles in desperate self-defence. The priest's concubine, of course with distaff in hand, is much dismayed, but Reynard offers her the fine consolation that 'There is many a Chappell in which but one Bell rings.'

It seems apt that the next cycle of Reynard illustrations to inspire authors, readers and artists on both sides of the North Sea was also by an artist from the Low Countries: Allart van Everdingen (1621–1675). Van Everdingen is best known for his landscape paintings. His patrons were the Trip family (owners of the grand 'Trippenhuis' in Amsterdam), and it was probably for them that in the early 1650s he produced fifty-seven etchings based on the Reynard story. They were in all likelihood not originally intended as book illustrations at all but rather as a self-sufficient cycle of artworks.[106] But their potential as book illustrations did not go unnoticed. In 1752 Johann Christoph Gottsched published a modernized version of the Low German Lübeck translation of *Reynaerts historie*, along with van Everdingen's etchings. To appreciate their dramatic effect we need only look at his illustration of Bruin the Bear, with his snout trapped in a tree trunk (fig. 6.14).

Van Everdingen's background as a painter of wild and rugged landscapes shines through in this illustration, and the representations of Reynard and Bruin are of a piece: they have been imagined as animals

the t appe
which men
now and then
set for others,
bring hurt to
themselues.

uolence: there is many a Chappell in which but one Bell rings. Now whilest the Foxe thus scoffed the Priest wise, the poore Priest fell downe in a sound, so that euery man left the Cat, to reuiue the Priest: Which whilest they were doing, the Foxe returned home to Mallepardus, for he imagined the Cat was past all hope of escape: but the poore Cat seeing

all her foes busie about the Priest, shee presently began to gnaw and byte the corde till she had sheared it quite asunder in the midst: Which done, she leapt out of the hole and went roling and tumbling (like the Beare) to the Kings Court But before he got thither it was faire day, and the Sunne being risen, he entred the Court, like the pittifullest beast that euer was beheld; For by the Foxes craft his body was beaten and bruised, his bones shiuered and broken; one of his eyes lost, and his skinne rent and mangled. This when the King beheld, and saw Tybert so pittifully mangled, he grew infinitely angry, and toke counsaile once more, how to reuenge the iniuries vpon the Foxe. After some consultation Grimbart the Brocke Reynards Sisters sonne, said to the rest of the Kings Counsaile, My good Lords, though my Vncle were twice soeuil as these complaints make him; yet there is remedy enough against his mischiefes: therefore it is fit you doe him Iustice as to a man of his rancke which is, he must be the third time summoned, and if then he appeare not, make him guilty of all that is laid against him. Then the King demaunded of the Brocke, whom he thought fittest to summon him, or who would be so desperate to hazard his hands, his eares, nay his life with one so tyrannous and irreligious? Truly (answered the Brocke) if it please your Maiesty, I am that desperate person who dare aduenture to carry the message to my most subtill kinsman, if your highnesse but command me.

CHAP. 8.

How *Grimbart* the Brocke was sent to bring the Fox to the Court.

THEN said the King: Goe Grimbart for I commaund you; yet take heede of Reynard for he is subtill and malicious: The Brocke thanked his Maiesty, & so taking humble leaue, went to Mallepardus where he found Reynard and Ermelin his wife, sporting with their young whelps; then hauing saluted his Vncle and his Aunt, he said: Take heede faire Vncle that

C   your

6.14   Bruin the Bear, trapped in a cleft tree trunk.
Mezzotint etching by Allart van Everdingen, made in
the 1650s, as part of an independent cycle, probably for
the Trip family of Amsterdam. Used as a book illustration
in *Heinrichs von Alkmar Reineke der Fuchs* (1752). Oxford,
Bodleian Library, Douce A subt. 17, p. 32.

6.15 Bruin the Bear, trapped in a cleft tree trunk. Etching by Allart van Everdingen, reprinted with added colour in an edition of Sir Henry Cole's *Pleasant History of Reynard the Fox* of 1846. Oxford, Bodleian Library, Johnson e.3479, plate between pp. 16 and 17.

in the wild rather than as half-animals, half-humans. In *Reynaerts historie* Bruin's mishap takes place at night. When Bruin summons Reynard to appear before King Noble's court, he excuses his absence by claiming that he had to do the reading at evening prayers ('ic most vesper lesen').[107] To capture the gloom of night-time, in some of his illustrations van Everdingen made use of the latest technique: mezzotint. Before the invention of this technique in the 1640s, printed engravings or etchings were made by cutting lines into metal plates; when the surface of the plates was inked and then wiped dry, the ink left in the incisions produced the illustrations. In mezzotint printmaking, by contrast, the entire surface of the plate was roughened so that it would catch the ink, and the whole plate would show black if printed. By polishing selective areas of the plate lighter, tones between black and white (i.e. mezzotints) could be achieved.[108] The technique was pioneered in the printmaking centre of Amsterdam by the German amateur artist Ludwig von Siegen in the 1640s, and Allart was quick to see its potential for evoking scenes of darkness. After being exported by various Dutch artists such as Peter Lely, Jan van Somer and Abraham Blooteling, who all came to work in England, the technique flourished there, so much so that it eventually became known as *la manière anglaise*.

What the Haarlem Master did for printed Reynard editions from the late fifteenth to the mid-seventeenth century, Allart van Everdingen did in the two centuries that followed. Goethe was so impressed with Gottsched's *Reineke der Fuchs* that he sought out some of the original etchings for his private art collection. Gottshed's *Reineke* inspired Goethe to write his own Reynard verse epic, *Reineke Fuchs* (1794), later illustrated by Wilhelm von Kaulbach (1804–1874), who was clearly influenced by Allart van Everdingen's Reynard cycle.[109] In England van Everdingen's cycle lived on in the children's versions of Reynard that started appearing from the late eighteenth century onwards, and the illustrations were given a new lease of life in Sir Henry Cole's *Pleasant History of Reynard the Fox* (1843). In his preface, Henry Cole (who wrote his children's book under his pseudonym Felix Summerly) wrote that, 'For two hundred years, the Etchings in this volume, illustrative of one of the oldest and most popular fictions of the Middle Ages, have made their author, Aldert [*sic*] van Everdingen, celebrated throughout Europe, though in late times, they have become almost curiosities for the portfolio …. Their characteristic spirit, fidelity, and humour, will, I feel confident, make their revival popular with children of all ages.'[110] That Cole's confidence was justified is shown by various later editions of his children's version, including one that adds colour to van Everdingen's illustrations to make them less 'dark' (fig. 6.15).[111]

The history of Reynard the Fox is interesting from various perspectives: literary, artistic and historical. From the early twelfth century to the present, writers, printers and artists have felt drawn to it. A comprehensive history of Reynard remains to be written. If it ever is, one aspect that should receive attention is the way in which historical and cultural relations between England and the Low Countries acted as a stimulus not only for creative developments of the story in literature and art, but also for the dissemination of that literature and art beyond linguistic and political borders. In the age of manuscripts we have seen this in *Ysengrimus* and the spread of Reynard motifs from the Low Countries to England. In the age of printing, we have seen it in Caxton's *Reynard* and in the transnational influence of the Haarlem Master and Allart van Everdingen. From the very start, in the Latin *Ysengrimus* and the Old French *Roman de Renart*, the English found a place in the Reynard story, and its subsequent travels back and forth across the North Sea allowed it to evolve and so to continue its journey across borders and between peoples.

Stranguyllyon, p. 108, E., old form of strangury.

Strope, p. 41 (Du: strop) halter.

Stryke, stryked, pp. 40, 48, 85, 93, 97, 138 (Du: streken, streec, strijct). Streken, go one's way; strijcken, strike.

Valdore, p. 44 (Du: valdoer). See faldore.

Vnberisped, p. 45. See Berisp.

Vyseuase, p. 6 (Du: vyseuase) vice versa.

Wapper, wappred. p. 17 (Du: wappere, wapperen) a loaded club, beaten.

Warande, p. 53 (Du: warande in die woestine) a warren.

Wentled, wentlyng, pp. 20 27 (Du: wentelende, wentelen) tumble, wallow.

Win, (kyn, ne wyn, ne frende) p. 97. cf Icelandic, vinr.

Wrawen, p. 25 (Du: wrauwen) to thraw, writhe.

Wryued, p. 154 (Du: wreuen) rubbed.

Wyked, p. 87 (Du: ontweecken) avoided.

Yamerde, p. 59 (Du: iammerde) lamented.

Yonned, p. 85 (Du: gonden) to favour, or affect.

Yonste, p. 14 (Du: gunsten) favour.

HERE ends the History of Reynard the foxe, done into English out of Dutch by William Caxton, and now reprinted by me William Morris, at the Kelmscott Press, Upper Mall, Hammersmith in the County of Middlesex. This book was corrected for the press by Henry Halliday Sparling, and finished on the 15th day of December, 1892.

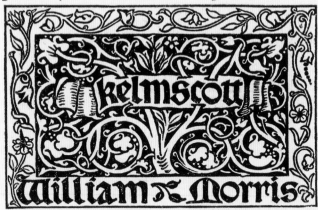

Sold by Bernard Quaritch, 15, Piccadilly, London.

The cultural, political and economic exchanges between England and the principalities of the Dutch Low Countries were always intense. The events that marked the beginning and the end of our period reveal the historic significance of traffic between England and the Low Countries. The Norman Conquest (1066) brought to the English throne a Flemish-born queen, Matilda, and accelerated a process of colonization that included people not only from present-day France but also from Flanders. Some six centuries later, the so-called Glorious Revolution (1688) and the coronation of William and Mary (1689) brought another ruler from the Low Countries to power: William of Orange, king of England, Scotland, France and Ireland and stadtholder of Holland, Zeeland, Utrecht, Guelders and Overijssel.

It is not surprising, then, that medieval and early modern historians in England and the Low Countries often looked to the other side of the North Sea to make sense of the present and the past. Their histories, real and imagined, are an important chapter in the cultural history of Anglo-Dutch relations. As we have seen, these relations had a lasting impact on book production. In the eleventh century, where we began our cultural history, the 'Winchester style' of manuscript design and illumination was exported across to the Continent. At the end of the medieval period, however, the 'Flemish style' was imported into England, and some of the best scribes and illuminators collaborated with English craftsmen to produce the finest manuscripts. The collaborations forged in the age of manuscript production were strengthened in the age of print. William Caxton, Wynkyn de Worde, Gerard Leeu and Jan van Doesborch were all cultural amphibians, capable of working in Dutch as well as English, and well aware of the book market on different sides of the North Sea.

The development of a transnational printing industry went hand in hand with developments in map-making and the emergence of an audience for ever more ambitious publications combining historical, anthropological and geographical information. Publishers both in

7.1 Glossary of 'Strange Words', mostly of Dutch origin, noted by William Morris in his hand press edition of William Caxton's *History of Reynard the Fox* (1892), which he printed using movable type and woodcuts. Oxford, Bodleian Library, Kelmscott Press d.6, final page.

England and in the Low Countries strove to meet the demand for such works, making use of the knowledge, skills and labour of authors, surveyors, cartographers, engravers and printers from both sides of the North Sea. Such Anglo-Dutch networks of merchants, craftsmen and scholars, as well as authors, artists and politicians, were fundamental to many of the cultural institutions that are still with us today, including the Bodleian Library itself.

And last but not least there is Reynard. First found in the Latin *Ysengrimus* from Ghent, Reynard conquered the West by crossing into different regions, languages (Latin, French, Dutch, English and more) and media (from manuscript to print and from text to pictures and carvings). In these evolutions, Reynard's North Sea crossings were hugely productive. Thanks to the work of writers, translators, printers, illuminators, engravers and woodcut makers, English and Dutch, the story of Reynard became part of a shared literary heritage.

We ended our final chapter with the seventeenth-century printmaker Allart van Everdingen, but the story itself does not end there. For example, William Morris (1834–1896), designer, writer and leader of the Arts and Crafts movement, travelled along some of the same roads of discovery that we have now traversed. He loved medieval manuscripts and early printed books, and learned the art of printing with handmade paper. In the final years of his life he set up a printing press, the Kelmscott Press. As he returned to 'first principles', he could think of no better books to print and redesign than those of the first English

7.2 Reynard the Fox, Bruin the Bear and the cleft tree. Magic lantern slide produced in England by Theobald & Co., *c*.1900, based on the illustrations of Wilhelm von Kaulbach for Goethe's *Reineke Fuchs* (first published 1794). Oxford, Bodleian Library, recent acquisition.

printer, William Caxton.[1] And so five of Caxton's books were reprinted, including his *History of Reynard*, which Morris produced four years before his death.

The book's colophon and the printer's mark, designed by Morris himself (fig. 7.1), are modelled on Caxton's practices. But as the glossary above the colophon shows, this is not just a reprint of Caxton. Morris thought it wise to include a 'Table of Strange Words', most of them Caxton's borrowings from Dutch. That they seem strange to us now and not to Caxton says a lot about the relevance of Dutch to a fifteenth-century merchant and its marginalization in England four centuries later.

Unlike Caxton's 'strange words', however, the story of Reynard the Fox remains current and relevant, ever finding new forms and new media. For the *North Sea Crossings* exhibition the Bodleian Library acquired a set of twelve magic lantern slides, produced in England around 1900 (fig. 7.2). They are based on the illustrations of Wilhelm von Kaulbach, the illustrator of Goethe's *Reineke Fuchs* (first published 1794), who in turn took inspiration from Allart van Everdingen (Chapter 6, fig. 6.14). Magic lanterns, first developed by the Dutch scientist Christiaan Huygens in the middle of the seventeenth century, were the most important form of visual entertainment in the nineteenth century. The introduction of moving pictures in the 1890s set in motion the decline of the old technology, and a famous landmark in the *Reynard* tradition is the stop-motion animation by pioneer Ladislas Starevich (first released 1937). Walt Disney studios also tried their hands at the story in the early 1960s. This attempt was ultimately aborted, but the character designs were later reused for Disney's 1973 vulpine version of Robin Hood.

Inspired by this long tradition of projection and animation of the Reynard stories, a current Reynard the Fox animation project shows the continuing relevance of the Reynard saga to new and contemporary audiences. As part of the outreach project *North Sea Crossings*, university students and students with SEND (special educational needs and disabilities) adapted an original Reynard story for a new medium: an animated puppet film (fig. 7.3). Another fresh take on the Reynard epic is the modern retelling of Caxton's *Reynard the Fox* by Anne Louise Avery,[2] which moves the beast epic closer to the modern novel, even as it retains various elements (place names, historical background, old words) of the medieval original. The cultural heritage of Anglo-Dutch relations has a future as well as a history.

7.3 Reynard the Fox puppet, created for *North Sea Crossings* by Katie Elspeth Williams (Instagram: @katiewilliamspuppetry), for the Flash of Splendour Reynard the Fox animation.

NOTES

Introduction: The Literary Heritage of Anglo-Dutch Relations

1 Chaucer, *Canterbury Tales*, 7.3390–97.

2 Blom and Lamberts (eds), *History of the Low Countries*, especially Milis, 'Counts, Cities and Clerics', and Blockmans, 'The Formation of a Political Union'.

3 Blockmans and Prevenier, *The Promised Lands*.

4 Willemyns, *Dutch*, pp. 4–6.

5 Ormrod, Lambert and Mackman, *Immigrant England*, pp. 102–9; Putter, 'Multilingualism', pp. 92, 105.

6 Hemptinne and Prevenier, 'La Flandre'.

7 Putter, 'The Linguistic Repertoire'.

8 Filppula, Klemola and Pavlasto, *English and Celtic*, pp. 21–2.

9 Willemyns, *Dutch*, pp. 17–21; Wal, *Geschiedenis van het Nederlands*, p. 59.

10 Willemyns, *Dutch*, p. 11.

11 Rose, *Calais*; Wallace, 'Calais'.

12 Bense, *Anglo-Dutch Relations*, p. 90.

13 E.g., the love letter (in French) addressed to George Cely in Calais, with delivery instructions in Dutch (*The Cely Letters*, no. 54).

14 Plomer, *Wynkyn de Worde*, pp. 216–19.

15 Salter and Lobel (eds), *A History of the County of Oxford*, vol. 3, pp. 1–38.

16 Emo and Menko, *Kroniek van het klooster Bloemhof*, pp. 10–11 (*Cronica Emonis*, ch. 5), 290–91 (*Cronika Menkonis*, ch. 5); pp. ix–x.

17 Translations are by the authors unless otherwise noted.

18 Wallace, *Premodern Places*, pp. 91–138.

19 Chaucer, *Canterbury Tales*, 1.272.

20 Ibid., 7.199, 239, 258, 299–301; Wallace, *Premodern Places*, p. 103.

21 Discussion in Beidler, 'The Miller's Tale'.

22 Chaucer, *Canterbury Tales*, 6.463.

23 Ibid., 7.718–20.

24 Ibid., 1.4357.

25 The variant reading is found in two fifteenth-century manuscripts from East Anglia: London, British Library, MS. Egerton 2864 and MS. Add. 5140. See Manly and Rickert,

The Text of the Canterbury Tales, vol. V, p. 430.

26 Chaucer, *Canterbury Tales*, 7.1894; Wallace, *Premodern Places*, p. 96.

27 Robbins, *Secular Lyrics*, p. 45, ll. 19–20.

28 Chaucer, *Canterbury Tales*, 7.3396.

Chapter 1 Histories

1 Van Houts, 'The Norman Conquest', pp. 843–5.

2 Van Houts, 'The Ship List', pp. 174–5.

3 Oksanen, *Flanders*, p. 11.

4 Herman de Tournai, *Les miracles de Sainte Marie de Laon*, pp. 165–8.

5 Goscelin of Saint-Bertin, *The Book of Encouragement and Consolation*, p. 26.

6 Liebermann, 'Raginald von Canterbury', p. 543 (15.55).

7 William of Malmesbury, *Gesta regum Anglorum*, vol. I, pp. 592–3 (4.342.1).

8 Van Houts, 'The Flemish Contribution', pp. 121–2.

9 Bugyis, 'Recovering the Histories of Women Religious', p. 293, n. 38.

10 Barrau, 'Did Medieval Monks Actually Speak Latin?', especially p. 297.

11 Putter, 'Multilingualism', p. 96.

12 Oksanen, *Flanders*, p. 5.

13 Hexter and Townsend, *The Oxford Handbook of Medieval Latin Literature*, pp. 50–53.

14 Keats-Rohan, *Domesday People*, vol. I, pp. 32, 38–40.

15 Ibid., pp. 60–61.

16 William of Malmesbury, *Gesta regum Anglorum*, vol. I, pp. 726–7 (5.401.1–2); John of Worcester, *The Chronicle*, vol. III, pp. 124–7 (covering the year 1111); see also Orderic Vitalis, *The Ecclesiastical History*, vol. VI, pp. 442–3; Verbrugghe et al., 'Flemish Settlements'.

17 John of Worcester, *The Chronicle*, vol. III, pp. 124–7.

18 Ibid., pp. 228–9 (covering the year 1137).

19 Gerald of Wales, *Itinerarium Kambriae*, p. 83.

20 Gerald of Wales, *The Journey*, pp. 141–2.

21 Gerald of Wales, *Itinerarium Kambriae*, p. 88.

22 Gerald of Wales, *The Journey*, p. 147.

23 Gerald of Wales, *Speculum duorum*, pp. 36–9; Putter, 'Multilingualism', pp. 103–4.

24 Jordan Fantosme, *Chronicle*, ll. 997–8; see also ll. 1796–8; Toorians, 'Flemish Settlements'.

25 Bede, *Ecclesiastical History*, book 1, ch. 1, pp. 16–17.

26 Henry of Huntingdon, *Historia Anglorum*, pp. lxvi–lxxvii.

27 Ibid., pp. 14–15.

28 Oksanen, *Flanders*, p. 178.

29 Ibid., p. 184.

30 Barrow, *The Anglo-Norman Era*, pp. 22–3, 38, 44–5.

31 Derolez, 'A Literary Tour de Force', p. 96.

32 Wallace, *Premodern Places*, p. 93.

33 De Bruijn-van der Helm et al., *Een koopman in Venetië*, pp. 34–5, 55, 329.

34 Other manuscripts read 'wilde zas' ('wild Saxon').

35 Maerlant, *Wapene Martijn*, stanza 9; Oxford, Bodleian Library, MS. Canon. Misc. 278, fol. 23r.

36 Verbij-Schillings, *Beeldvorming*.

37 Van Oostrom, *Maerlants wereld*.

38 Everett Green, *Lives of the Princesses of England*, vol. 3, pp. 6–10.

39 Loomis, 'Edward I'; Vale, 'Arthur in English Society', pp. 186–9.

40 Tahkokallio, *The Anglo-Norman Historical Canon*, p. 49.

41 Crick, *The Historia*, p. 69.

42 Gerritsen, 'Jacob van Maerlant'.

43 Maerlant, *Spiegel historiael*, 3.5.49.

44 Ibid., 3.7.11 (ll. 87–8).

45 Cordfunke, *Floris V*.

46 Lucas, 'Diplomatic Relations'; Sleiderink, *De stem van de meester*, pp. 88–97, 102–3; Spencer, *Nobility*, p. 44.

47 Heelu, *Yeeste*, I, ll. 1–7.

48 Sturler, *Les relations politiques*, pp. 142–64; Panton, *Historical Dictionary of the British Monarchy*, pp. 315–16.

49 Stein, 'The Antwerp Clerk'.

50 Lucas, 'Edward III and the Poet Chronicler John Boendale'.

51 Boendale, *Boec vander wraken*, 3.14
    (ll. 1757–822).

52 Van der Eerden, 'Eschatology in the *Boec van
    der Wraken*'.

53 Kerling, *Commercial Relations*, p. 97.

54 Dumolyn and Haemers, 'Patterns of Urban
    Rebellion', pp. 375–6.

55 Verbruggen, *The Battle of the Golden Spurs*,
    p. 375.

56 London, British Library, MS. Harley 2253,
    fols 73v–74v, www.bl.uk/manuscripts/Viewer.
    aspx?ref=harley_ms_2253_f073v [accessed
    10 March 2020].

57 Robbins (ed.), *Historical Poems*, pp. 9–13,
    ll. 65–9.

58 Ibid., ll. 17, 19–20.

59 Adam Usk, *Chronicon*, pp. xi–xxxi.

60 De Smet (ed.), 'Passio Francorum secundum
    Flemyngos', p. 314.

61 Adam Usk, *Chronicon*, p. 288.

62 Hall, 'The Courtrai Chest'.

63 Verbruggen, *The Battle of the Golden Spurs*,
    pp. 195–210.

64 Beke, *Chronographia*, cap. 6.

65 Ibid., cap. 7.

66 Verbij-Schillings, *Beeldvorming*.

67 Geoffrey of Monmouth, *The History of the
    Kings of Britain*; Levelt, 'New Evidence'.

68 *Chronicle of Gouda*, sig. a.iii.v–a.iv.r.

69 Levelt, *Jan van Naaldwijk's Chronicles of
    Holland*, pp. 228, 231, 235.

70 Westgard, 'Dissemination and Reception',
    p. 117.

71 Paris, Bibliothèque nationale de France,
    MS. Latin 5237; Westgard, 'Dissemination and
    Reception', p. 114.

72 Bede, *Ecclesiastical History*, p. lix; *Medieval
    Manuscripts in Oxford Libraries*, MS. Holkham
    misc. 7, https://medieval.bodleian.ox.ac.uk/
    catalog/manuscript_6280 [accessed 10 March
    2020].

73 London, British Library, Cotton MS. Titus D
    xxv.

74 *Brut*, cap. 249, p. 503.

75 Ibid., cap. 197, p. 220.

76 Spindler, 'Flemings in the Peasants' Revolt'.

77 London, British Library, Cotton MS. Julius B
    ii, fol. 16v.

78 Caxton, *Recuyell*.

79 Caxton, *The Cronycles of Englond*.

80 Higden, *Polychronicon*.

81 Ibid., fol. 343v.

82 Ibid., fol. 69r–v.

83 Hellinga, *William Caxton and Early Printing*.

84 Corsten, 'Caxton in Cologne'; Needham,
    'William Caxton'; Hellinga and Hellinga,
    'Caxton in the Low Countries'.

85 Veldener, *Fasciculus temporum*; see Levelt, *The
    Middle Dutch Brut*.

86 Veldener, *Fasciculus temporum*, fol. 219v.

87 Ibid., fol. 225v.

88 Ibid., fol. 222r.

89 Ibid., fol. 231v.

90 *Divisiekroniek*, fols 17r, 29r.

91 Levelt, 'New Evidence'.

92 Stocker, *A Tragicall Historie*, fol. 4r.

93 Van der Heyden, 'Emanuel van Meteren's
    History'.

94 Grimeston, *A Generall Historie of the
    Netherlands*, p. 904.

95 Ibid., p. 889.

96 *A Declaration*, pp. 2–3.

97 Ibid., p. 8.

98 Verstegan, *A Restitution*.

99 Haitsma Mulier, 'The History of Great
    Britain'.

100 Baker, *Chronicle*; Baker, *Cronyke*.

101 Helmers, *The Royalist Republic*, pp. 31–2.

102 Haitsma Mulier, 'The History of Great
    Britain', p. 137.

103 Ibid., p. 142.

104 Fleck, 'Deep Designs of Empire', pp. 190–243;
    Fleck, *The Dutch Device*, ch. 4.

105 'To the Reader', by T.M. (Thomas Manley),
    in Grotius, *De rebus Belgicis*.

106 E.g., *Engelands rouwen*; Sweerts, *Rouwe
    over het sterven*; Schoneveld, *Sea-Changes*,
    pp. 48–67.

107 Rabus, *Opkomst*, p. 107.

108 Helmers, *The Royalist Republic*.

Chapter 2 Manuscripts

1 Smeyers, *Flemish Miniatures*, p. 23.

2 Sisam, 'MSS. Bodley 340 and 342', p. 11.

3 Dronke, 'Latin and Vernacular Love-Lyrics',
   p. 401; see Sisam, 'MSS. Bodley 340 and 342',
   pp. 10–12; Kwakkel, 'Hidden in Plain Sight',
   p. 240; De Grauwe, 'Zijn olla vogala Vlaams',
   p. 44.

4 See Pulsiano, 'Jaunts, Jottings, and Jetsam',
   pp. 192–4.

5 Kwakkel, 'Book Script', p. 39.

6 Kwakkel, 'Hidden in Plain Sight'.

7 Ibid., pp. 254–5.

8 Cf. De Grauwe, 'Zijn olla vogala Vlaams'.

9 Kwakkel, 'Hebban olla vogala', pp. 6–8.

10 Kwakkel, 'Hidden in Plain Sight', p. 251.

11 Gameson, 'L'Angleterre et la Flandre',
    pp. 176–7.

12 *Catalogue général des manuscrits*, pp. 662–3; see
    also Smeyers, *Flemish Miniatures*, p. 58.

13 Drogo of Saint-Winnoc, *Historia translationis
    sanctae Lewinnae*; Meijns, 'England and
    Flanders around 1066'.

14 Newman, 'Contemplating the Trinity',
    pp. 152–6.

15 Lampen, 'De vereering van St Oswald',
    p. 150.

16 Van Houts, 'Judith of Flanders'; McGurk and
    Rosenthal, 'The Anglo-Saxon Gospelbooks
    of Judith'; Dockray-Miller, *The Books and the
    Life of Judith of Flanders*, pp. 29–48.

17 Smeyers, *Flemish Miniatures*, pp. 23–4, 34.

18 Gameson, 'L'Angleterre et la Flandre',
    pp. 172–3.

19 Smeyers, *Flemish Miniatures*, p. 34.

20 Ibid.; Ugé, *Creating the Monastic Past*,
    pp. 47–8.

21 Gameson, 'The Earliest Books of Arras
    Cathedral', pp. 251–2.

22 Smeyers, *Flemish Miniatures*, p. 60.

23 Los Angeles, J. Paul Getty Museum,
    MS. Ludwig XI 6, fols 2v, 44v; Kren,
    Illuminated Manuscripts, p. 9.

24 *Warenne (Hyde) Chronicle*, pp. 89–102.

25 Brussels, Royal Institute for Cultural
    Heritage Belgium, KIK-IRPA, object no.
    144772, and cliché no. Z011814; Crick and van
    Houts (eds), *A Social History of England*, plate
    12, p. 229; Freeman, *The Norman Conquest*,
    appendix M, pp. 754–5.

26 Blockmans and Prevenier, *The Promised
    Lands*, p. 7; Thrupp, *The Merchant Class*, p. 1.

27 Chaucer, *Canterbury Tales*, 1.447–8.

28 Good, 'The Alien Clothworkers of London'.

29 Ormrod, Lambert and Mackman, *Immigrant
    England*, p. 227.

30 Gessler (ed.), *Het Brugsche Livre des mestiers*.

31 Ibid., vol. I, pp. 33, 34.

32 Caxton, *Dialogues*, in Gessler (ed.), *Het
    Brugsche Livre des mestiers*, vol. III, p. 40.

33 Ibid., p. 42.

34 Wieck, *Time Sanctified*.

35 Smeyers, *Flemish Miniatures*, p. 138.

36 Pächt and Alexander, *Illuminated
    Manuscripts*, vol. I, pp. 21–2.

37 The Hague, Museum Meermanno – House
    of the Book, MS. 10 A 13, fol. 27v; Dennison,
    'The Dating and Localisation of The Hague
    Missal', fig. 9A, p. 530.

38 Sandler, *Gothic Manuscripts*, vol. I,
    p. 54. Sandler's conclusion, based on the
    approximate nature of the heraldry, that the
    manuscript had nothing to do with Anne of
    Bohemia (until the nineteenth-century forger

created the connection) begs the question of why a medieval illuminator would also have wished to create this impression.

39 Good, 'Richard II'.

40 Dennison, 'The Dating and Localisation of The Hague Missal', p. 519.

41 Ibid.

42 Revealing diagnostics are 'e' for 'i' in 'onser vrouwen liicht messe' (Candlemass), a spelling we have otherwise found only in a charter from Bruges from 1269 (see quotation in *Vroegmiddelnederlands woordenboek*, s.v. *ghiselhuus*), and the hitherto unrecorded form 'scoens dagh' (Wednesday). The only comparable form ('scoensdaechs') occurs in charters from Geraardsbergen, south-east of Ghent. See van Reenen, *Atlas van Vormen*.

43 Edinburgh, National Library of Scotland, MS. 10270, fol. 17v; Fleming and Mason, *Scotland and the Flemish People*, pp. 102–4.

44 Our paragraphs on Flemish Books of Hours made for English readers are much indebted to Rogers, 'Books of Hours'.

45 Ibid., p. 13.

46 *Medieval Manuscripts in Oxford Libraries*, https://medieval.bodleian.ox.ac.uk/catalog/manuscript_4464 [accessed 24 March 2020].

47 Hirsh (ed.), *Medieval Lyric*, p. 194, ll. 6–7 (emphasis added).

48 Raines (ed.), *Testamenta Eboracensia*, vol. II, p. 117.

49 Arnould and Massing, *Splendours of Flanders*, pp. 66, 116.

50 Oxford, Bodleian Library, MS. Auct. D. inf. 2. 13, fol. 98v.

51 Ibid., fol. 52r.

52 Digitized at https://libwww.freelibrary.org/digital/item/1432 [accessed 11 March 2020].

53 E.g., London, British Library, MS. Harley 3000; New Haven, Beinecke Library, MS. 310; Chicago, Newberry Library, MS. 35; The Hague, Koninklijke Bibliotheek, MS. 131 G 41.

54 Finke, 'Utrecht'; Arnould and Massing, *Splendours of Flanders*, p. 113.

55 Spufford, 'The Burgundian Netherlands'; Blockmans and Prevenier, *The Promised Lands*.

56 Smeyers, *Flemish Miniatures*, pp. 289–352.

57 Fleming and Mason, *Scotland and the Flemish People*, p. 36.

58 Vienna, Österreichische Nationalbibliothek, Codex Vindobonensis 1897, fol. 188r.

59 Ibid., fols 243v and 24v, respectively; Kren and McKendrick (eds), *Illuminating the Renaissance*, pp. 371–3.

60 Kren and McKendrick (eds), *Illuminating the Renaissance*, pp. 374–91.

61 Armstrong, 'The Language Question'.

62 Straub, *David Aubert*; Gay, 'Selected Scribe Bibliographies'.

63 Cf. Vienna, Österreichische Nationalbibliothek, Cod. 1857, fol. 114r; Kren and McKendrick (eds), *Illuminating the Renaissance*, fig. 65, p. 229.

64 See Hellinga, 'Reading an Engraving'.

65 Visser-Fuchs, *History as Pastime*, pp. 16–17.

66 Ibid., p. 65.

67 Kren and McKendrick (eds), *Illuminating the Renaissance*, pp. 277–80.

68 British Library, MS. Royal 15 E IV, fol. 14r.

69 Baltimore, Walters Art Museum, MS. W 201; The Hague, Koninklijke Bibliotheek, MS. 133 A7, I, II, II.

70 Kren and McKendrick (eds), *Illuminating the Renaissance*, pp. 255–6; Gil, 'Jean du Chesne'.

71 Amiens, Bibliothèque Municipale, MS. 200.

72 Vosters, 'De bibliotheek van Engelbrecht II'.

73 Visser-Fuchs, *History as Pastime*, pp. 290–91.

74 Van Houtte, 'The Rise and Decline of the Market of Bruges'.

75 Quoted in Syme, 'The Regulation of the English Book Trade', p. 33.

76 Scott, *The Caxton Master*; Scott, 'Introduction', in *The Mirroure of the Worlde*, pp. 1–68.

77 See *Oxford English Dictionary*, s.v. 'spincop', n., and 'bedwynge', v. The latter word, certainly authentic, has unfortunately been edited out of existence by emendation to *bend* in the latest edition of the text (Caxton, *The Booke of Ovyde*), because of a misunderstanding of the French source, 'Bien en doy mon cuer fleschir' (where *fleschir* means 'subdue, humble', not 'bend').

78 See The Hague, Koninklijke Bibliotheek, MS. 78 D 39, fol. 78v.

79 Brussels, Koninklijke Bibliotheek / Bibliothèque Royale, MS. 9106; Kren and McKendrick (eds), *Illuminating the Renaissance*, p. 158.

80 See Rundle, *The Renaissance Reform of the Book*, pp. 121–73.

81 Digital Scriptorium, http://ds.lib.berkeley.edu/HM00142_43 [accessed 11 March 2020]. Werken also worked on a second copy of this anthology: Warminster, Longleat House, MS. 30 (see Mosser, 'Longleat House, MS. 30').

82 See *Middle English Dictionary*, s.v. 'thousand'.

83 Rundle, *The Renaissance Reform of the Book*, p. 135.

84 Dumitresco, *The Early Tudor Court*, pp. 13–30. For map-making, see also Chapter 4.

85 Campbell and Foister, 'Gerard, Lucas and Susanna Horenbout'.

86 Smeyers, *Flemish Miniatures*, pp. 419–24.

87 See the Wolsey Manuscripts, www.wolseymanuscripts.ac.uk/research [accessed 11 March 2020].

88 Reeve, 'Manuscripts Copied from Printed Books'.

89 On Meghen and his handwriting see Rundle, *The Renaissance Reform of the Book*, pp. 121–73.

90 Mooney, Horobin and Stubbs, 'The Morganus Scribe', in *Late Medieval English Scribes*.

91 Meale, '"Prenes: engre"'; Kren and McKendrick (eds), *Illuminating the Renaissance*, fig. 131, p. 433.

92 Perkins, 'Introduction', and Scott, '*Prenes en gre*' – to which should be added the use of the phrase in a song by Guillaume Dufay, 'Estrinés moy'.

Chapter 3 Printed books

1 Potten and Dourish (eds), *Emprynted in Thys Manere*, pp. x–xi.

2 Werner, *Studying Early Printed Books*.

3 Putter, 'Introduction' to *Incunabula*, units 68 and 69.

4 The Bible can be seen at https://digital.bodleian.ox.ac.uk/inquire/p/cd693ffc-dbd3-4a84-a604-15634e09ef9b [accessed 11 March 2020].

5 Hellinga and Wolf, *Laurens Janszoon Coster*.

6 Cited in Dickson and Edmond, *Annals of Scottish Printing*, p. 2.

7 Wilson and Wilson, *A Medieval Mirror*, p. 23.

8 Glasgow, University Library, Sp Coll Hunterian Ds.2.3, on which see Gardham, 'Blockbook Apocalypse', and Wilson and Wilson, *A Medieval Mirror*, p. 91.

9 Blazekovic, 'Variations'.

10 Oxford, Bodleian Library, MS. Rawl. D. 1220.

11 Copenhagen, Statens Museum for Kunst, no. KKS 10458.

12 Hellinga and Hellinga, 'Caxton in the Low Countries'; Hellinga, *William Caxton and Early Printing*; Driver, 'Caxton, William'.

13 Cited from Moran, *Wynkyn de Worde*, p. 18.

14 Hellinga, *William Caxton and Early Printing*, pp. 26–32, 44–5.

15 Hellinga, 'William Caxton, Colard Mansion'; Hellinga, 'Printing', p. 74.

16 Hellinga, 'Reading an Engraving'.

17 Colin, Hellinga et al., *De vijfhonderdste verjaring*, p. 171.

18 Hellinga, 'William Caxton, Colard Mansion'.

19 Moran, *Wynkyn de Worde*.

20 Hellinga, 'Wynkyn de Worde's Native Land'.

21 Ibid.

22 Rozenski, '*The Chastising of God's Children*'.

23 Ampe, 'De vroegste Ruusbroec-verspreiding'.

24 Bazire and College (eds), *The Chastising of God's Children*, pp. 207/25–209/6 and pp. 202/25–204/17.

25 See Bod-Inc Online: C-171(1), http://incunables.bodleian.ox.ac.uk/record/C-171 [accessed 11 March 2020].

26 Goudriaan, Abels and Habermehl (eds), *Een drukker zoekt publiek*.

27 Bakker and Gerritsen, 'Collecting Ships'.

28 Duff, *The Dialogue*, p. xxiii; Bradbury and Bradbury (eds), *The Dialogue*.

29 Franssen and Simoni, 'Jan van Doesborch'; Franssen, *The World of Jan van Doesborch*.

30 Franssen, *Tussen tekst en publiek*, pp. 39–41.

31 Maslen, 'The Early English Novel'.

32 Freeman, 'Everyman'.

33 Pettegree and Walsby, *Netherlandish Books*, pp. vii–xiv; Pettegree, 'Centre and Periphery', p. 127.

34 Pettegree and Walsby, *Netherlandish Books*, pp. vii–xiv.

35 Ibid., pp. xx–xxi.

36 Ibid., pp. xiii–xx; Verbraak, 'William Tyndale'.

37 Pettegree and Walsby, *Netherlandish Books*, nos 4003, 10747, 10932, 10933, 10979, 15710, 15711, 15712, 15714, 16139.

38 Ibid., no. 3702, e.g., Ghent, Universiteitsbibliotheek, Res. 1422: *Die bibel int duitsche*, vol. 3, sig. [x.viii]v.

39 Kronenberg, 'Notes on English Printing', pp. 143–4.

40 Kronenberg, *Verboden boeken*, pp. 99–102.

41 Pettegree and Walsby, *Netherlandish Books*, no. 11141: *Ordinancie vander oorloghen*.

42 Pettegree and Walsby, *Netherlandish Books*, no. 28832: *Tafelmanieren*.

43 Pettegree and Walsby, *Netherlandish Books*, nos 2348, 9738, 17005, 17006, 29093.

44 *Aesopus moralisatus*, London, British Library, C.1.A.4, sig. A2b.

45 E.g., Pettegree and Walsby, *Netherlandish Books*, nos 15709, 15713, 15717, 15720, 15722.

46 King and Rankin, 'Print, Patronage'.

47 Neville-Singleton, 'Press, Politics and Religion'; Clegg, 'Tudor Literary Censorship'.

48 Daniell, 'Coverdale, Miles'.

49 Coverdale (ed. and trans.), *Biblia the Bible*, sig. ✠iiiir.

50 Verduyn, *Emanuel van Meteren*, p. 33.

51 Ruytinck, 'Het leven ende sterven', fol. [672]r.

52 Latré, 'The Place of Printing of the Coverdale Bible'; but see Blayney, *The Stationers' Company*, pp. 342–88.

53 Coverdale (ed. and trans.), *Biblia the Bible*, sig. ✠iiiiv.

54 Verduyn, *Emanuel van Meteren*, p. 34; King

55 Loudon, 'Rogers, Daniel'.

56 *The Byble in Englyshe*.

57 King and Rankin, 'Print, Patronage', p. 55.

58 Kronenberg, 'Notes on English Printing', p. 150; Christman, 'The Coverture of Widowhood', pp. 85–6.

59 Pettegree and Walsby, *Netherlandish Books*, nos 3080, 6185, 9065, 17287, 17288, 17289, 17290, 17291, 21001, 26376, 28127, 28128, 32147 (English religious prose); nos 4395, 4513, 4523, 6475 (English biblical translation and paraphrase).

60 Ibid., no. 27919.

61 Ibid., nos 2913, 5522, 6163, 11141, 11838, 13114, 13259, 16300, 17300, 17713, 19566, 23170, 23171, 27195, 27964, 30868 (Dutch current events); 16850, 16851, 227284 (Dutch prognostications); 5649 (Dutch ballad).

62 Ibid., nos 7680, 7681, 7695, 7699, 7702, 7717, 7718, 7750, 7751 (Dutch proclamations of Charles V); 7713, 7744, 7745 (French proclamations by Charles V); 14623, 14625 (Dutch proclamations by Henry VIII); 20688 (French proclamation by Mary of Hungary), 20689 (Dutch proclamation by Mary of Hungary).

63 Ibid., nos 10748, 10937, 10939, 10940, 10976, 10977; Driver, 'Printing', pp. 1553–4.

64 Hoftijzer, 'Henry Hexham', pp. 211–12; Sprunger, *Dutch Puritanism*, pp. 70–76, 306–18.

65 Pettegree and Walsby, *Netherlandish Books*, nos 462, 20670, 24091 (Douai); 20048 (Bruges).

66 Ibid., nos 1178, 1179, 19450.

67 Ibid., nos 7983, 16686 (Dutch sermons); 7990, 13076, 23325, 32045 (Dutch religious instruction); 27331 (Dutch polemics); 7002 (catechism); 4068, 4360, 4596–7 (biblical texts in Dutch); 4582–3 (biblical texts in Spanish); 3083–5, 3130–31, 5910, 9066, 11637, 12694, 29769 (English polemical works); 21004 (English translation of a tract of Philipp Melanchthon); 18350 (English catechism).

68 Ibid., nos 17993 (Utenhove, *De catechismus, oft kinder leere*); 17994 (*Een cort begrijp der leeringhen*).

69 Ibid., nos 17995–6; 21338 (Marten Micronius, catechism); 21340 (religious instruction); 4087 (Utenhove, *Psalmen*).

70 Thus Pettegree and Walsby, *Netherlandish Books*, no. 5072.

71 Ruytinck, *Gheschiedenissen ende handelingen*, pp. 21–3.

72 Pettegree, *Emden*, pp. 35–9.

73 Pettegree and Walsby, *Netherlandish Books*, nos 17997–8, 17999–8007.

74 Utenhove, *25 psalmen end andere ghesangen*.

75 Pettegree and Walsby, *Netherlandish Books*, nos 4186, 21341–2.

76 Verduyn, *Emanuel van Meteren*, p. 26.

77 Pettegree and Walsby, *Netherlandish Books*, nos 4148–9, 4174–6 (Psalms); 21357–8, 21366–7 (Micronius, catechism); 21359 (religious instruction).

78 Ibid., nos 21365, 21368.

79 Ibid., nos 22126, 27129, 30832.

80 Ibid., nos 22979–81; Joby, *The Dutch Language in Britain*, pp. 19, 285–8.

81 Oastler, *John Day*, pp. 4–5.

82 Ibid., p. 7.

83 King, 'John Day', p. 184.

84 King, 'John Day'; Oastler, *John Day*; King, *English Reformation Literature*, pp. 105–6.

85 Pettegree and Walsby, *Netherlandish Books*, no. 11146 (*Die warachtige beschrijvinghe vant verraedt in Enghelandt*).

86 Ruytinck, *Gheschiedenissen ende handelingen*; Joby, *The Dutch Language in Britain*, pp. 56–81.

87 Luu, *Immigrants*, pp. 70–73.

88 Joby, 'Early Modern Records in Dutch', p. 138.

89 Pettegree and Walsby, *Netherlandish Books*, nos 4211 (Datheen's Psalms); 6195 (confession); 6367 (*Eenen calender historiael*).

90 Ibid., nos 783, 13504, 22230, 22232.

91 Ibid., no. 31994 (*Send-brief*).

92 Ibid., no. 15471 (Hollyband, *Instruksie om draa en goedt Frans te leeren*).

93 Meeres, 'Records Relating to the Strangers', pp. 134–5.

94 *A Prayer to be Sayd*.

95 Willem I, *A Declaration and Publication* and *A Justification or Cleering*.

96 *Libellus supplex imperatoriae maiestati*; *A Defence and True Declaration*.

97 Dunthorne, *Britain and the Dutch Revolt*, pp. 7–8.

98 Ibid., p. 9.

99 Ibid., p. 9, n. 27.

100 Pettegree and Walsby, *Netherlandish Books*, nos 11152–6.

101 *Cort verhael*, translated from *A Short and True Discourse*.

102 Simoni, '1598: An Exchange of Dutch Pamphlets'.

103 Dunthorne, *Britain and the Dutch Revolt*, p. 24; Duke, 'William of Orange's *Apology*', p. 4.

104 Dunthorne, *Britain and the Dutch Revolt*, pp. 10–12; Gascoigne, *The Spoyle of Antwerpe*; Churchyard, *A Lamentable and Pitifull Description*; Hexham, *A True and Briefe Relation*.

105   Dunthorne, *Britain and the Dutch Revolt*, pp. 11–12.

106   Ibid., pp. 13–14; Dahl, 'Amsterdam', p. 173.

107   Stilma, *A King Translated*, pp. 54–7; Pettegree, 'Centre and Periphery', p. 125; Dover Wilson, 'Richard Schilders'.

108   Stilma, *A King Translated*, pp. 51–4.

109   Ibid., pp. 31–6.

110   Ibid., pp. 36–44.

111   Ibid., pp. 79–80.

112   Hanham, 'Who Made William Caxton's Phrase-Book?'

113   Gallagher, *Learning Languages*.

114   Bostoen, *Kaars en bril*.

115   Meurier, *The Conjugations in English and Netherdutche*.

116   Whetstone and Walraven (trans.), *The Honourable Reputation of a Souldier*, p. 11.

117   Van Dorsten, *Thomas Basson*.

118   Pettegree and Walsby, *Netherlandish Books*, nos 263, 18416, 18420, 18435, 20694, 22748 (English); 5409, 5861, 18356, 18406, 21664, 21743, 22478, 22793, 23135 (Dutch); 5786 (bilingual Dutch–French); 5591, 5785, 14516, 14519, 14522, 21682 (French).

119   Whetstone and Walraven (trans.), *The Honourable Reputation of a Souldier*, p. 13.

120   Ibid., pp. 73–103.

121   Ibid., p. 75.

122   Ibid., p. 15.

123   *Colloques ou dialogues*.

124   Whetstone and Walraven (trans.), *The Honourable Reputation of a Souldier*, p. 103.

125   Kiliaan, *Etymologicum Teutonicae linguae*; Oxford, Lincoln College Library, D.1.31.

126   Hoftijzer, 'Henry Hexham'; Osseltong, *The Dumb Linguists*; Loonen, *For to Learne to Buye and Sell*.

127   Hexham, *A Copious English and Netherduytsch Dictionarie*, sigs I11r–[Mm4]r.

128   Ibid., sigs Vu1r–Bbb2v.

129   Ibid., sig. *3r.

130   Ibid., sig. *2r–v.

131   Ibid., sig. Aaa1v.

132   Werner, *Studying Early Printed Books*.

133   Lucas, 'Printing Anglo-Saxon in Holland', p. 122; Oastler, *John Day*, pp. 19–21, 33–8; Joscelyn and Parker (eds), *Testimonie of Antiquity*.

134   Lucas, 'William Camden', p. 223.

135   Oxford, Bodleian Library, MS. Selden Supra 108, fol. 76r.

136   Lucas, 'Printing Anglo-Saxon in Holland', pp. 126, 136.

137   Lucas, 'William Camden'.

138   Hart and Carter, *Notes on a Century of Typography*.

139   Romburgh, 'Junius [Du Jon], Franciscus [Francis]'; Bremmer, 'Franciscus Junius Reads Chaucer', p. 38.

140   Seccombe and Blok, 'Vossius, Isaac'.

141   Heesakkers, 'Franciscus Junius as a Tutor'.

142   Lucas, 'Junius, his Printers and his Types', p. 177.

143   Heesakkers, 'Franciscus Junius as a Tutor'.

144   Romburgh, 'Junius [Du Jon], Franciscus [Francis]'.

145   Breuker, 'On the Course of Franciscus Junius' Germanic Studies', p. 147.

146   Lucas, 'Junius, his Printers and his Types', p. 178.

147   Breuker, 'On the Course of Franciscus Junius' Germanic Studies'.

148   Muir (ed.), *A Digital Facsimile*; Junius, *Cædmonis monachi Paraphrasis*.

149   Kiernan, 'Reading Cædmon's "Hymn"', pp. 103–4.

150   Bremmer, 'Franciscus Junius Reads Chaucer', p. 37.

151   Breuker, 'On the Course of Franciscus Junius' Germanic Studies', pp. 148–50.

152   Morison, *John Fell*, pp. 9–11.

153   Ibid., pp. 14–30.

154   Ibid., p. 59.

155   Junius, *Caedmonis monachi Paraphrasis poetica*, ed. Lucas, pp. v, xviii.

156   Morison, *John Fell*, p. 31.

157   Hart and Carter, *Notes on a Century of Typography*, pp. 162–3.

158   Morison, *John Fell*, pp. 59–64, 70–72; Hart and Carter, *Notes on a Century of Typography*, pp. 161–72.

159   Morison, *John Fell*, p. 63.

160   Lucas, 'Junius, his Printers and his Types', pp. 187–92.

161   Morison, *John Fell*, pp. 244–5.

162   Echard, *Printing the Middle Ages*, p. 42; Junius, *Etymologicum Anglicanum*.

Chapter 4 Maps

1   Morse, 'The Role of Maps'; Gautier Dalché, *La Terre*, pp. 108–16.

2   Woodward, 'Cartography and the Renaissance', pp. 7–8; Gautier Dalché, 'The Reception of Ptolemy's *Geography*'.

3   Woodward, 'Medieval *Mappaemundi*'.

4   Thrower, *Maps*, pp. 39–45.

5   London, British Library, Cotton MS. Claudius D.vi, fol. 12v, www.bl.uk/manuscripts/Viewer.aspx?ref=cotton_ms_claudius_d_vi!1_f012v [accessed 12 March 2020].

6   Harvey, 'Local and Regional Cartography'.

7   Campbell, 'Portolan Charts'.

8   Dalché, 'Maps, Travel and Exploration', pp. 153–8.

9   Thrower, *Maps*, pp. 51–6; Woodward, 'Medieval *Mappaemundi*', p. 292; Morse, 'The Role of Maps', p. 44.

10   Smallwood, 'The Date of the Gough Map'.

11   Bruges, Openbare Bibliotheek, MS. 685, fols 211v–212r, reproduced in Dewilde et al., '"So One Would Notice the Good Navigability"', p. 12, fig. 1.

12   London, British Library, Cotton MS. Augustus I.i.35, 36, 38, 39; Barber, 'Mapmaking', p. 1605.

13   *Oxford English Dictionary*, s.v. 'kenning', n.2, †4.b.

14   London, British Library, Add. MS. 22047, in part available at www.bl.uk/manuscripts/FullDisplay.aspx?ref=Add_MS_22047 [accessed 12 March 2020].

15   London, British Library, Cotton MS. Augustus I.ii.64; Barber, 'Mapmaking', p. 1605; Knighton, 'Anthony, Anthony'.

16   Jones, 'Gemini'; Barber, 'Mapmaking', p. 1620.

17   Worms, 'The London Map Trade', p. 1700; Baigent, 'Ryther, Augustine'.

18   Davies, *Renaissance Ethnography*, pp. 1–17.

19   Barber, 'Mapmaking', p. 1596.

20   Martens, 'Cities under Siege', p. 157.

21   Gregg, 'Further Insights into Anton van den Wyngaerde's Working Methods'.

22   Colvin and Foister, *The Panorama of London*, pp. 1–5.

23   Kagan, 'Philip II and the Art of the Cityscape'.

24   Colvin and Foister, *The Panorama of London*, p. 7.

25   Ibid., p. 2.

26   Ricci, 'Maps, Power and National Identity'.

27   Hessels (ed.), *Abrahami Ortelii …epistulae*, ep. 96, pp. 230–32; ep. 155, pp. 356–7; Verduyn, *Emanuel van Meteren*, p. 157.

28   Baigent, 'Hogenberg, Frans'; Karrow, *Mapmakers of the Sixteenth Century*, p. 5.

29   Verduyn, *Emanuel van Meteren*, p. 157.

30   Van der Heijden, *Leo Belgicus*.

31   Hessels (ed.), *Abrahami Ortelii … epistulae*, p. lvi.

32   Karrow, *Mapmakers of the Sixteenth Century*, pp. 1–31; van den Broecke, 'Introduction to the Life and Works of Abraham Ortelius'.

33   Hessels (ed.), *Abrahami Ortelii … epistulae*, ep. 30, pp. 772–9, at p. 774.

34 Ibid., pp. xxiii–xxv; van den Broecke 'Abraham Ortelius's Library', pp. 40–41; Karrow, *Mapmakers of the Sixteenth Century*, pp. 1–4; Voet, 'Abraham Ortelius and his World', pp. 15–18.

35 Meganck, 'Abraham Ortelius', pp. 227–8.

36 Ibid., p. 228.

37 Van den Broecke, 'Abraham Ortelius's Library', p. 30, table 1.

38 Karrow, *Mapmakers of the Sixteenth Century*.

39 Ortelius, *Theatrum orbis terrarum*, 'To the courteous Reader'.

40 Gautier Dalché, 'The Reception of Ptolemy's *Geography*'; Gautier Dalché, *La Géographie de Ptolémée*.

41 Meganck, *Erudite Eyes*.

42 Chotzen, 'Some Sidelights', p. 119.

43 Roberts and Roberts, 'De Mona Druidum Insula'.

44 Chotzen, 'Some Sidelights', p. 140.

45 Depuydt, 'Ortelius, Abraham'.

46 Chotzen, 'Some Sidelights', p. 141.

47 De Heere, *Corte Beschryvinghe*, fol. 6r.

48 Marlowe, *Tamburlaine*, part II, V.iii.151–2.

49 Ibid., part I, III.iii.50.

50 Ibid., part II, I.ii.21.

51 Ibid., part II, I.i.42–4; Keck, 'Marlowe and Ortelius's Map'.

52 This section is by Anne Louise Avery.

53 Cary, *The Tragedy of Mariam*, p. 3.

54 Cary, *The Mirror of the Worlde*.

55 Cary, *The Tragedy of Mariam*, p. 189, nn. 20 and 21.

56 Ibid., p. 6; Hodgson-Wright, 'Cary [née Tanfield], Elizabeth'.

57 Hearn, 'Somer, Paul [Pauwels] van'.

58 Camden, *Britannia*, 'Lectori'.

59 Camden, *Britain*, sig. ❧4r.

60 Oxford, Bodleian Library, MS. Smith 74, fols 1–4 (1586–96).

61 Griffiths, 'Hole [Holle], William'; Worms, 'Kip, William'; Lucas, 'William Camden', p. 224.

62 Wallis, 'Intercourse', pp. 46–7; Barber, 'Mapmaking', p. 1619.

63 Lucas, 'William Camden', pp. 225–8.

64 Van Eeghen, 'De familie van de plaatsnijder Claes Jansz Visscher'.

65 Lusardi, 'The Pictured Playhouse', p. 220; Scouloudi, *Panoramic Views of London*, pp. 24–9.

66 Wallis, 'Intercourse', pp. 31–8.

67 Van der Krogt, 'The Place of the "Atlas of Scotland"'.

68 Ibid., pp. 264–7; Worms, 'The London Map Trade'.

69 *Afbeelding, en kort-bondige beschrijving.*

70 Dryden, *Annus mirabilis*, p. 58 (stanza 230).

71 Greenlee, 'Seeing All the Anguilles', chs 7–8.

72 Ibid.

Chapter 5 People

1 Rundle, 'Good Duke Humfrey'.

2 Wakelin, *Humanism, Reading, and English Literature*, pp. 43–56.

3 Lydgate, 'On Gloucester's Approaching Marriage', stanza 8, vv. 54–6.

4 Janse, *Een pion voor een dame*; Stevenson, *Letters and Papers*, vol. 2, pp. 440–41.

5 Wakelin, *Humanism, Reading, and English Literature*, p. 43.

6 De la Mare, 'Duke Humfrey's English Palladius'.

7 Bejczy, 'Erasmus Becomes a Netherlander'.

8 Erasmus, *Opus epistolarum*, ep. 1404, vol. V, p. 366.

9 Erasmus, *The Correspondence*, letter 1404, vol. 10, p. 134.

10 Erasmus, *Opus epistolarum*, ep. 1404, vol. V, p. 367.

11 Erasmus, *The Correspondence*, letter 1404, vol. 10, p. 135, where 'Britannia' is translated 'England'.

12 Erasmus, *A Devoute Treatise*, trans. Roper.

13 Gee, 'Margaret Roper's English Version of Erasmus' *Precatio Dominica*', p. 259.

14 Goodrich, 'Thomas More and Margaret More Roper'.

15 Kaufman, 'Absolute Margaret'.

16 Mann, 'The Origins of Humanism'; Bot, *Humanisme en onderwijs*.

17 Erasmus, *De immensa dei misericordia*.

18 Savage, 'The First Visit of Erasmus to England'.

19 Erasmus, *Adagia*, II v 1 (*Adagiorum chilias secvnda*, p. 404; *Adages II*, p. 242).

20 Erasmus, *Opus epistolarum*, ep. 2283, vol. VIII, p. 373.

21 Erasmus, *The Correspondence*, letter 2283, vol. 15, p. 211.

22 Erasmus, *Moriae encomium, or, The Praise of Folly*, sig. A2v.

23 Erasmus, *Opus epistolarum*, ep. 635, vol. III, p. 57.

24 Erasmus, *The Correspondence*, letter 635, vol. 5, p. 83.

25 More, *Utopia*, ed. Surtz and Hexter, 'Thomas More to Peter Giles', pp. 250–51.

26 Erasmus, *Opus epistolarum*, ep. 3049, vol. XI, p. 221.

27 Starnes, 'A Heroic Poem', p. 74.

28 Pettegree and Walsby, *Netherlandish Books*, no. 11273; Kronenberg, 'Over verboden boeken', p. 967.

29 Kronenberg, *Verboden boeken*, p. 56.

30 Ibid., p. 63.

31 Pettegree and Walsby, *Netherlandish Books*, no. 17883.

32 Dodds, 'An Accidental Historian'.

33 Erasmus, *The Praise of Folie*.

34 *London Lickpenny*, ll. 51–4, in Dean (ed.), *Medieval English Political Writings*, pp. 222–5.

35 *Oxford English Dictionary*, s.v. 'cope', v.3; *Dictionary of the Scots Language*, s.v. 'cope', v.

36 Janssen, 'De hervormde vlugtelingen', p. 226.

37 Ibid., p. 263.

38 Yungblut, *Strangers Settled Here*, pp. 37–60.

39 Holmes, 'The "Libel of English Policy"'.

40 *Brut*, pp. 582–4.

41 Ibid., pp. 600–601.

42 *Libelle of Englyshe Polycye*, ll. 78–9.

43 Ibid., ll. 94–5.

44 Ibid., ll. 1084–5.

45 Sobecki, 'Bureaucratic Verse'.

46 *Libelle of Englyshe Polycye*, pp. vii–viii.

47 Ibid., ll. 282–99, 314–15.

48 *Brut*, p. 584, ll. 7–8.

49 Ormrod, Lambert and Mackman, *Immigrant England*, p. 243.

50 Griffiths, *The Reign of King Henry VI*, pp. 171, 177 n. 103.

51 Oxford, Bodleian Library, MS. Don. d. 152, fol. 4v.

52 Moens, *The Marriage, Baptismal, and Burial Registers*, pp. xviii–xx.

53 Pettegree, 'The Foreign Population', pp. 144–5.

54 Oxford, Bodleian Library, MS. Don. d. 152, fol. 4v.

55 *The Life and Death of Iacke Straw*.

56 Oxford, Bodleian Library, MS. Don. d. 152, fol. 4v.

57 Freeman, 'Marlowe, Kyd, and the Dutch Church Libel'.

58 Neumann, 'Imagining European Community'.

59 See Chapter 4.

60 Ruytinck, 'Het leven ende sterven', fol. [672]r.

61 Ibid., fol. [673]v.

62 Ibid.

63 Rogge, 'Het Album van Emanuel van Meteren'.

64 Hessels (ed.), *Abrahami Ortelii …epistulae*, ep. 329, pp. 770–71.

65 Levelt, 'The Manuscripts of Jan van Naaldwijk's Chronicles of Holland'.

66 Dorsten, *Poets, Patrons, and Professors*.

67 De Heere, *Corte Beschryvinghe*, fol. 39r; de Heere, *Beschrijving der Britische Eilanden*, p. 48.

68 Forster, 'Iets over Nederlandse renaissancelyriek', p. 276–7; Joby, *The Dutch Language in Britain*, pp. 285–9; de Heere, *Den hof en boomgaerd der poësien*.

69 Forster, 'Iets over Nederlandse renaissancelyriek', pp. 284–6.

70 Waterschoot, 'An Author's Strategy', p. 35.

71 Noot, *Het theatre oft toon-neel*, sig. [*Avi]r.

72 Noot, *A Theatre*.

73 Hadfield, 'Edmund Spenser's Translations'.

74 Pienaar, 'Edmund Spenser and Jonker Jan van der Noot'.

75 Noot, *A Theatre*, fol. 13r–v.

76 Ibid., fol. 14v.

77 Dorsten, *Poets, Patrons, and Professors*, pp. 76–130; Dop, *Eliza's Knights*.

78 Dorsten, *Poets, Patrons, and Professors*, pp. 131–51.

79 This section is by Robyn Adams.

80 Wooden, 'Sir Thomas Bodley's "Life of Himself"', p. 63.

81 Berkvens-Stevelinck, *Magna Commoditas*, p. 33.

82 Ibid., p. 30.

83 Bachrach, 'The Foundation of the Bodleian Library', p. 113.

84 Adams, *The Diplomatic Correspondence*.

85 The National Archives, Currency Converter, www.nationalarchives.gov.uk/currency-converter [accessed 13 March 2020].

86 *Registrum Donationum* (*Benefactors' Register*), Oxford, Bodleian Library, Library Records b. 903.

87 See www.cabinet.ox.ac.uk/armillary-sphere [accessed 13 March 2020].

88 London, British Library, MS. Cotton Galba D X, fols 204r–208r; Rotterdam, Atlas Van Stolk Museum, inv. 50442-357.

89 Adams, 'Sixteenth Century Intelligencers'.

90 Price, 'Holland's Leaguer'.

91 Karras, 'Regulation of Brothels', pp. 415–16.

92 Higgins, *Britain's Bourse*, pp. 113–14; Karras, *Common Women*, pp. 56–7.

93 Goodman, *Hollands Leaguer*, ed. Barnard, pp. 9–17.

94 Goodman, *Hollands Leaguer*, sig. [A4]v.

95 Price, *Newes from Hollands Leager*.

96 This section is by Jack Avery and Edward Holberton.

97 Pincus, *Protestantism and Patriotism*; Helmers, *The Royalist Republic*, p. 7.

98 Marvell, *The Prose Works*, vol. II, p. 242;

99 Pincus, *Protestantism and Patriotism*, pp. 21–35; Helmers, *The Royalist Republic*, pp. 160–61.

100 Ibid., *passim*.

101 MacDonald, *George Lauder*, pp. 231–9.

102 Ibid., pp. 288–9.

103 Kerrigan, *Archipelagic English*, p. 222.

104 Ibid., p. 238.

105 Marvell, *The Poems*, pp. 247–52, vv. 1–2.

106 Ibid., vv. 79–80.

107 Kerrigan, *Archipelagic English*, p. 238.

108 Van Raamsdonk, *Milton, Marvell, and the Dutch Republic*, ch. 1.

109 Helmers, *The Royalist Republic*.

110 *Den afgrysselikken start-man; Voorspookkend zinne-beeld*.

111 Oxford, Bodleian Library, MS. Rawl. poet. 6. The authors are grateful to Victoria Moul for her help in interpreting this manuscript, and for bringing it to our attention.

112 Cats, 'Aensprake van Hollandt'.

113 Jardine, *Going Dutch*, p. 134.

114 Ibid., p. 139.

115 Millar, *Sir Peter Lely*, p. 86.

116 Schurman, *The Learned Maid*.

117 Beek, *The First Female University Student*, pp. 161–3, 178–81.

118 Jardine, *Going Dutch*, pp. 263–90.

119 Evelyn, *The Diary*, vol. 3, p. 486.

120 Marvell, *The Poems*, p. 385, vv. 583–4.

121 Oxford, Bodleian Library, MS. Don. b. 8, p. 275.

122 Marvell, *The Prose Works*, vol. II, p. 225.

123 *The Declaration of His Highnes*, p. 3.

124 Jardine, *Going Dutch*, pp. 26–31.

Chapter 6 Reynard the Fox

1 Mann, *From Aesop to Reynard*, pp. 28–52.

2 Blake, 'English Versions of *Reynard the Fox*'; Varty, *Reynard, Renart, Reinaert*, pp. 221–64.

3 Varty, *Reynard the Fox*, p. 140.

4 Varty, *Reynard, Renart, Reinaert*.

5 Henryson, *Fables*, ll. 1095–6.

6 Burke, *Popular Culture*, p. 305.

7 See, e.g., Mann, *From Aesop to Reynard*, and the work published in the journals devoted to Reynardiana: *Reinardus* and *Tiecelijn*.

8 Yates, 'The Cock-and-Fox Episodes', p. 1, n. 1.

9 *Ysengrimus*, ed. and trans. Mann; Nigel de Longchamps, *Speculum stultorum*; Nigel de Longchamps, *A Mirror for Fools*; Ziolkowski, *Talking Animals*, pp. 220–34.

10 *Ysengrimus*, ed. and trans. Mann, pp. xviii–xix.

11 Ibid., p. vi.

12 *Ysengrimus*, ed. and trans. Mann, pp. 1–2 and p. 1, n. 4; pp. 483–7.

13 Strecker (ed.), *Ecbasis cuiusdam captivi*.

14 *Ysengrimus*, ed. and trans. Mann, pp. 1–2; Mann, *Ysengrimus*, p. viii.

15 Guibert de Nogent, *Autobiographie*, book III, ch. 8, pp. 342–3 (Latin with French translation); Guibert of Nogent, *The Memoirs*, p. 176 (English translation); *Ysengrimus*, ed. and trans. Mann, p. 2, n. 5.

16 Barlow, *The English Church, 1066–1154*, pp. 248–9.

17 Putter et al., '*Ysengrimus* en *Reynard the Fox*'.

18 Oksanen, *Flanders*.

19 Ibid., p. xvi.

20 Crouch, *The Reign of King Stephen*; King, *King Stephen*.

21 Chibnall, *Empress Matilda*.

22 Nieus, 'The Early Career of William of Ypres in England'.

23 Oksanen, *Flanders*, pp. 180–218.

24 *Ysengrimus*, VII, 121.

25 *Ysengrimus*, ed. and trans. Mann, p. 525, n. to VII 121; Voigt (ed.), *Ysengrimus*, p. 438.

26 E.g., Gundrada van Oosterzeele Westerscheldeke and William earl of Warenne: see *Warenne (Hyde) Chronicle*, pp. 89–102; Nieus, 'Stratégies seigneuriales anglo-flamandes', p. 170 n. 31 for Judith, daughter of Lambert of Lens (d.1054), married to earl Waltheof (d.1074).

27 Lambert of Ardres, *Historia comitum Ghisnensium*, ch. 113, p. 615; Lambert of Ardres, *The History of the Counts of Guines and Lords of Ardres*, ch. 113, p. 144.

28 *Ysengrimus*, VII, 111.

29 *Ysengrimus*, ed. and trans. Mann, pp. 522–3.

30 *Ysengrimus*, V, 1041–2.

31 Ibid., III, 659.

32 *Ysengrimus*, ed. and trans. Mann, p. 334 n.; Neilson, *Caudatus Anglicus*, pp. 35–8.

33 Bartlett, 'Symbolic Meanings of Hair', pp. 50–52.

34 William of Poitiers, *Gesta Guillelmi*, book II, 44, pp. 178–81.

35 William of Malmesbury, *Gesta regum Anglorum*, vol. I, pp. 558–61 (4.314).

36 Orderic Vitalis, *The Ecclesiastical History*, vol. IV, pp. 186–91.

37 Thomas, *The English and the Normans*, pp. 56–69.

38 *Ysengrimus*, I, 48–50.

39 *Ysengrimus*, ed. and trans. Mann, pp. 208–9, 209 n.

40 Ibid., pp. 86–7.

41 Voigt (ed.), *Ysengrimus*, p. 7.

42 *Ysengrimus*, ed. and trans. Mann, pp. xix–xx.

43 Morrison and Grollemond (eds), *Book of Beasts*, p. 158.

44 Oxford, Merton College, MS. 249; Dean and Boulton, *Anglo-Norman Literature*, pp. 191–2.

45 Morrison and Grollemond (eds), *Book of Beasts*, pp. 144–5.

46 Varty, *Reynard, Renart, Reinaert*, pp. 31–54.

47 Morrison and Grollemond (eds), *Book of Beasts*, p. 209.

48 Rigg, 'Nigel of Canterbury'; Rigg, *A History of Anglo-Latin Literature*, p. 102 and p. 349, n. 123; Mann, *From Aesop to Reynard*, pp. 99–100.

49 Rigg, *A History of Anglo-Latin Literature*, p. 350, n. 125.

50 Mann, *From Aesop to Reynard*, p. 101.

51 Ibid., p. 122.

52 Nigel de Longchamps, *Speculum stultorum*, p. 65.

53 Regenos, *The Book of Daun Burnel the Ass*, p. 85.

54 Nigel de Longchamps, *Speculum stultorum*, p. 159.

55 Mann, *From Aesop to Reynard*, p. 104.

56 *Le Roman de Renart*; Owen (trans.), *The Romance of Reynard the Fox*.

57 Mossé, 'Le *Roman de Renart*'; Chaucer, *The Legend of Good Women*, l. 2448.

58 Rickard, *Britain in Medieval French Literature*, p. 171.

59 Wackers, 'Reynaert de Vos'; van Daele, 'Alleen maar in het Land van Reynaert?'

60 Wackers, 'Nawoord'.

61 Cruse, *Illuminating the Roman d'Alexandre*; Wiechers, 'Pierart dou Tielt' and 'Jehan de Grise'.

62 Van Bruaene, 'Rhetorical Encounters'.

63 See www.bl.uk/manuscripts/FullDisplay. aspx?ref=Royal_MS_19_d_ii [accessed 14 March 2020].

64 Griffith and Putter, 'Linguistic Boundaries'.

65 Smeyers, *Flemish Miniatures*, p. 114.

66 Schouwink, 'The Fox's Funeral'.

67 Varty, *Reynard, Renart, Reinaert*, p. 140; Paris, Bibliothèque nationale de France, Département des Manuscrits, français 12583, fol. 1r, https:// gallica.bnf.fr/ark:/12148/btv1b8447178n/f5.image [accessed 14 March 2020].

68 Bennett and Smithers, *Early Middle English Verse and Prose*, pp. 65–76, 297–303.

69 Wood, 'The Romanesque Tomb-Slab'.

70 Fleming and Mason, *Scotland and the Flemish People*, p. 95.

71 Varty, *Reynard the Fox*, pp. 99–100.

72 Oxford, Bodleian Library, MS. Lat. liturg. f. 3, fol. 138v.

73 New York, Pierpont Morgan Library, Glazier

74 Dennison, 'The Artistic Context', p. 21 and plate XII (A), http://ica.themorgan.org/ manuscript/page/122/76974 [accessed 14 March 2020].

75 London, British Library, MS. Egerton 3277, fol. 47v.

76 Dennison, 'The Artistic Context'.

77 Hunt, '"Van den grave te makene"'.

78 London, British Library, Royal MS. 10 E IV, www.bl.uk/collection-items/the-smithfield-decretals [accessed 14 March 2020].

79 Law-Turner, *The Ormesby Psalter*, pp. 46–8. On Gundrada, see Chapter 2.

80 https://collections.britishart.yale.edu/vufind/ Record/2038220 [accessed 14 March 2020].

81 Barker, *Two East Anglian Picture Books*.

82 Oxford, Bodleian Library, MS. Ashmole 1504, fol. 22v.

83 Varty, *Reynard the Fox*, p. 55; London, British Library, Royal MS. 10 E IV, fol. 49v.

84 The proverb can be found written and illustrated in Pieter Bruegel's painting *Twaalf spreuken* (*Twelve Proverbs*), *c*.1558, reproduced and explicated at www.pieterbruegel.org/ twelve-proverbs [accessed 14 March 2020].

85 https://medieval.bodleian.ox.ac.uk/catalog/ manuscript_287 [accessed 14 March 2020].

86 Barker, *Two East Anglian Picture Books*, p. 37.

87 Caxton, *Fables of Esope*; London, British Library, C.11.c.17, fol. 44r (Fox and Stork) and fol. 35r (Wolf and Crane).

88 Caxton, *The History of Reynard the Fox*; Simpson (trans.), *Reynard the Fox*.

89 Schlusemann, *Die hystorie van Reynaert die vos*.

90 Hittmair (ed.), *Aus Caxtons Vorreden und Nachworthen*, p. 5.

91 Furley, *A History of the Weald of Kent*, vol. I, pp. 2, 417; vol. II, pp. 568–9.

92 Lambert and Pajic, 'Drapery in Exile'; Ormrod, 'John Kempe and Friends'.

93 See, e.g., Blake, 'William Caxton's *Reynard the Fox*'.

94 Caxton, *The History of Reynard the Fox*, p. 92.

95 Muller and Logeman, *Die Hystorie van Reynaert die Vos*, p. 128.

96 Bakker and Gerritsen, 'Collecting Ships'.

97 Ibid.

98 Hsy, *Trading Tongues*, p. 123.

99 Caxton, *The History of Jason*, pp. 86, 89, 108.

100 Caxton, *The Recuyell of the Historyes of Troye*, ed. Sommer, vol. I, p. 83 (*styfemoder*); vol. II, p. 659 (*behoeffyd*).

101 Putter et al., '*Ysengrimus* en *Reynard the Fox*'.

102 Varty, *Reynard, Renart, Reinaert*, pp. 97–9.

103 Ibid., p. 279.

104 *The Most Delectable History of Reynard the Fox* (1629), Oxford, Bodleian Library, 4° R 21(3) Art.Seld.

105 Mish, 'Reynard the Fox'; Tsuji, 'Textual Transition and Reception', pp. 48–64.

106 Verzandvoort, 'Allart van Everdingen'.

107 Hellinga (ed.), *Van den vos Reynaerde*, p. 37.

108 Barker, 'The Printed Image in the West'.

109 Verzandvoort, 'Allart van Everdingen', pp. 161–2.

110 Summerly, *The Pleasant History of Reynard the Fox*, pp. 3, 5.

111 *The Most Delectable History of Reynard the Fox* (1846).

Epilogue: North Sea Crossings – Past and Present

1 Peterson, *The Kelmscott Press*, p. 37.

2 Avery, *Reynard the Fox*.

BIBLIOGRAPHY

The alphabetical ordering of the bibliography ignores 'van', 'van de(r)' and 'de' in Dutch names, 'de la' in French names and articles at the beginning of titles of anonymous works. Pre-modern authors are alphabetized by first name (e.g. Gerald of Wales), excepting those with established surnames (e.g. Chaucer).

Adam Usk, *Chronicon*, ed. E.M. Thompson, 2nd edition, Henry Frowde, London, 1904.

Adams, R. (ed.), *The Diplomatic Correspondence of Thomas Bodley, 1585–1597*, Centre for Editing Lives and Letters, 2011, www.livesandletters.ac.uk/bodley/bodley.html [accessed 5 March 2020].

Adams, R., 'Sixteenth-Century Intelligencers and their Maps', *Imago Mundi*, vol. 63, 2011, pp. 201–16.

Afbeelding, en kort-bondige beschrijving, dan den verschrickelijcken brandt der stadt London, Marcus Willemsz Doornick, Amsterdam, 1666.

Den afgrysselikken start-man, gepast op den teegen woordijgen staat van Engelandt, n.p., [1652].

Ampe, A., 'De vroegste Ruusbroec-verspreiding in Engeland', *Ons Geestelijk Erf*, vol. 31, 1957, pp. 395–415.

Armstrong, C.A.J., 'The Language Question in the Low Countries: The Use of French and Dutch by the Dukes of Burgundy and their Administration', in *England, France, and Burgundy in the Fifteenth Century*, Hambledon, London, 1983, pp. 189–212.

Arnould, A., and J.M. Massing, *Splendours of Flanders*, Cambridge University Press, Cambridge, 1993.

Avery, A.L., *Reynard the Fox*, Bodleian Library, Oxford, 2020.

Bachrach, A.G.H., 'The Foundation of the Bodleian Library and Seventeenth Century Holland', *Neophilologus*, vol. 36, 1952, pp. 101–14.

Baigent, E., 'Hogenberg, Frans [Franz] (*c.*1540–*c.*1590), engraver', in *Oxford Dictionary of National Biography*, Oxford University Press, Oxford, 2008.

Baigent, E., 'Ryther, Augustine (d. 1593), map engraver and maker of scientific instruments', in *Oxford Dictionary of National Biography*, Oxford University Press, Oxford, 2014.

Baker, R., *A Chronicle of the Kings of England from the Time of the Romans' Government unto the Raigne of our Soueraigne Lord King Charles*, printed for Daniel Frere, London, 1643.

Baker, R., *Cronyke van het Leven en Bedryff van alle de Coningen van Engeland. Beginnende vande Regeringe der Romeijnen totte regeringe van Carolus I*, C. Dankertz, Amsterdam, 1649.

Bakker, F.J., and J. Gerritsen, 'Collecting Ships from Holland and Zeeland: A Caxton Letter Discovered', *The Library*, vol. 5, 2004, pp. 3–11.

Barber, P., 'Mapmaking in England, *ca.*1470 –1650', in *The History of Cartography*, vol. 3, part 2, ed. D. Woodward, University of Chicago Press, Chicago, 2007, pp. 1589–669.

Barker, E.E., 'The Printed Image in the West: Mezzotint', in *Heilbrunn Timeline of Art History*, Metropolitan Museum of Art, New York, 2000–, www.metmuseum.org/toah/hd/mztn/hd_mztn.htm [accessed 5 March 2020].

Barker, N., *Two East Anglian Picture Books: A Facsimile of the Helmingham Herbal and Bestiary and Bodleian MS. Ashmole 1504*, Roxburghe Club, London, 1988.

Barlow, F., *The English Church, 1066–1154: A History of the Anglo-Norman Church*, Longman, London, 1979.

Barrau, J., 'Did Medieval Monks Actually Speak Latin?', in *Understanding Monastic Practices of Oral Communication (Western Europe, Tenth–Thirteenth Centuries)*, ed. S. Vanderputten, Brepols, Turnhout, 2011, pp. 293–317.

Barrow, G.W.S., *The Anglo-Norman Era in Scottish History*, Clarendon Press, Oxford, 1980.

Bartlett, R., 'Symbolic Meanings of Hair in the Middle Ages', *Transactions of the Royal Historical Society*, 6th series, vol. 4, 1994, pp. 43–60.

Bazire, J., and E. College (eds), *The Chastising of God's Children*, Blackwell, Oxford, 1957.

Bede, *Ecclesiastical History of the English People*, ed. and trans. B. Colgrave and R.A.B. Mynors, Oxford University Press, Oxford, 1992.

Beek, P. van, *The First Female University Student: Anna Maria van Schurman (1636)*, Igitur, Utrecht, 2010.

Hier beghint die bibel int duitsche neerstelick ouergheset: ende gecorrigeert, tot profite van allen kersten menschen, Hans van Roemundt for Peter Kaetz, Antwerpen, 1525.

Beidler, P.G., 'The Miller's Tale', in *Sources and Analogues of the Canterbury Tales*, ed. R.M. Correale and M. Hamel, 2 vols, D.S. Brewer, Cambridge, 2005, vol. 2, pp. 249–76.

Bejczy, I., 'Erasmus Becomes a Netherlander', *The Sixteenth Century Journal*, vol. 28, 1997, pp. 387–99.

Beke, J. de, *Chronographia*, ed. H. Bruch, Martinus Nijhoff, The Hague, 1973.

Bennett, J.A.W., and G.V. Smithers (eds), *Early Middle English Verse and Prose*, Oxford University Press, Oxford, 1968.

Bense, J.F., *Anglo-Dutch Relations from the Earliest Times to the Death of William the Third: Being an Historical Introduction to a Dictionary of the Low-Dutch Element in the English Vocabulary*, Nijhoff, The Hague, 1925.

Berkvens-Stevelinck, C., *Magna Commoditas: History of the Leiden University Library 1575–2000*, Leiden University Press, Leiden, 2001.

Blake, N., 'English Versions of *Reynard the Fox* in the Fifteenth and Sixteenth Centuries', *Studies in Philology*, vol. 62, 1965, pp. 63–77.

Blake, N., 'William Caxton's *Reynard the Fox* and his Dutch Original', *Bulletin of the John Rylands Library*, vol. 46, 1963–4, pp. 298–325.

Blayney, P.W.M., *The Stationers' Company and the Printers of London, 1501–1557*, Cambridge University Press, Cambridge, 2013.

Blazekovic, Z., 'Variations on the Theme of the Planets' Children', in *Art and Music in the Early Modern Period: Essays in Honor of Franca Trinchieri Camiz*, ed. K.A. McIver, Ashgate, Aldershot, 2003, pp. 241–86.

Blockmans, W.P., 'The Formation of a Political Union, 1300–1588', in *History of the Low Countries*, ed. J.C.H. Blom and E. Lamberts, trans. J.C. Kennedy, new edition, Berghahn, New York and Oxford, 2006, pp. 55–140.

Blockmans, W., and W. Prevenier, *The Promised Lands: The Low Countries under Burgundian Rule, 1369–1530*, University of Pennsylvania Press, Philadelphia, 1999.

Blom, J.C.H., and E. Lamberts (eds), *History of the Low Countries*, trans. J.C. Kennedy, Berghahn, New York and Oxford, 2006.

Boendale, J. van, *Boec vander wraken*, in *Nederlandsche gedichten uit de veertiende eeuw van Jan van Boendale, Hein van Aken en anderen: naar het Oxfordsche handschrift*, ed. G.H.M. Claassens, M. Hayez, Brussels, 1869, pp. 287–488.

Bostoen, K., *Kaars en bril: de oudste Nederlandse grammatica*, repr. of *Archief van het Koninklijk Zeeuwsch Genootschap der Wetenschappen*, Koninklijk Zeeuwsch Genootschap der Wetenschappen, [Middelburg], 1984.

Bot, P.N.M., *Humanisme en onderwijs in Nederland*, Het Spectrum, Utrecht, 1955.

Bradbury, N.M., and S. Bradbury (eds), *The Dialogue of Solomon and Marcolf: A Dual-Language Edition from Latin and Middle English Printed Editions*, Medieval Institute Publications, Kalamazoo, MI, 2012.

Bremmer, R.H., Jr, 'Franciscus Junius Reads Chaucer: But Why? and How?', in *Appropriating the Middle Ages: Scholarship, Politics, Fraud*, ed. T. Shippey and M. Arnold, D.S. Brewer, Cambridge, 2001, pp. 37–72.

Breuker, P.H., 'On the Course of Franciscus Junius' Germanic Studies, with Special Reference to Frisian', in *Franciscus Junius F.F. and his Circle*, ed. R.H. Bremmer, Rodopi, Amsterdam, 1998, pp. 129–58.

Broecke, M.P.R. van den, 'Abraham Ortelius's Library Reconstructed', *Imago Mundi*, vol. 66, 2014, pp. 25–50.

Broecke, M.P.R. van den, 'Introduction to the Life and Works of Abraham Ortelius (1527–1598)', in *Abraham Ortelius and the First Atlas: Essays Commemorating the Quadricentennial of his Death, 1598–1998*, ed. M. van den Broecke, P. van der Krogt and P. Meurer, HES Publishers, Houten, 1998, pp. 29–54.

Bruaene, A. van, 'Rhetorical Encounters: *Puys*, Chambers of Rhetoric, and the Urban Literary Culture of the Burgundian Low Countries and Northern France', in *The Multilingual Muse: Transcultural Poetics in the Burgundian Netherlands*, ed. A. Armstrong and E. Strietman, MHRA and Maney Publishing, Cambridge, 2017, pp. 71–83.

Bruijn-van der Helm, J. de, F. van Buuren, M. van Donkelaar, G. Gerritsen-Geywitz and O.S.H. Lie (eds), *Een koopman in Venetië*, Verloren, Hilversum, 2001.

The Brut, or, The Chronicles of England, edited from MS. Rawl. B 171, ed. F.W.D. Brie, Kegan Paul, London, 1908

Bugyis, K.A.-M., 'Recovering the Histories of Women Religious in England in the Central Middle Ages: Wilton Abbey and Goscelin of Saint-Bertin', *Journal of Medieval History*, vol. 42, 2016, pp. 285–303.

Burke, P., *Popular Culture in Early Modern Europe*, Ashgate, London, 2009.

The Byble in Englyshe, that is to saye the Content of all the Holy Scrypture, bothe of the Olde and Newe Testament, Truly Translated after the Veryte of the Hebrue and Greke Textes, by the Dylygent Studye of Dyuerse Excellent Learned Men, expert in the Forsayde Tonges, Richard Grafton and Edward Whitchurch, Paris and London, 1539.

Eenen calendier historiael, eewelick gheduerende: waerin ghy vinden sult den opganck ende onderganck der sonnen, in alle maenden, met den jaermercten van diverseye landen, steden ende vrijheden, Anthonius de Solempne, Norwich, 1570.

Camden, W., *Britain, or, A Chorographicall Description of the Most Flourishing Kingdomes, England, Scotland, and Ireland, and the Ilands Adioyning, out of the Depth of Antiquitie Beautified VVith Mappes of the Severall Shires of England*, George Bishop and John Norton, London, 1610.

Camden, W., *Britannia, siue Florentissimorum regnorum Angliae, Scotiae, Hiberniae, et insularum adiacentium ex intima antiquitate chorographica descriptio: nunc postremò recognita, plurimis locis magna accessione adaucta, & chartis chorographicis illustrata*, George Bishop and John Norton, London, 1607.

Campbell, L., and S. Foister, 'Gerard, Lucas and Susanna Horenbout', *Burlington Magazine*, vol. 128, 1986, pp. 719–27.

Campbell, T., 'Portolan Charts from the Late Thirteenth Century to 1500', in *The History of Cartography*, vol. 1, ed. J.B. Harley and D. Woodward, University of Chicago Press, Chicago, 1987, pp. 371–463.

Cary, E., *The Mirror of the Worlde*, ed. Lesley Peterson, McGill-Queen's University Press, Montreal and Kingston, 2012.

Cary, E., *The Tragedy of Mariam, the Fair Queen of Jewry: with the Lady Falkland: Her Life, by One of her Daughters*, ed. B. Weller and M.W. Ferguson, University of California Press, Berkeley, 1994.

Catalogue général des manuscrits des bibliothèques publiques de France, vol. 26, *Départements; Lille, Dunkerque, Bergues, Roye, Péronne Ham, La Chatre*, Ministère de l'Instruction Publique, Paris, 1897.

Cats, J., 'Aensprake van Hollandt aen Carel den Tweeden' in *Alle de Werken van Jakob Cats*, ed. R. Feith, Johannes Allart, Amsterdam, 1790–99, vol. V, pp. 230–31.

Caxton, W., *The Booke of Ovyde Named Methamorphose*, ed. R. Moll, Pontifical Institute of Mediaeval Studies, Toronto, 2013.

Caxton, W., *The Cronycles of Englond*, William Caxton, Westminster, 1482.

Caxton, W., *Dialogues*, William Caxton, Westminster, 1480.

Caxton, W., *Fables of Esope*, William Caxton, Westminster, 1484.

Caxton, W., *The History of Jason*, ed. J. Munro, Early English Text Society, extra series 111, Trübner, London, 1913.

Caxton, W., *The History of Reynard the Fox*, ed. N. Blake, Early English Text Society, ordinary series 263, Oxford University Press, London, 1970.

Caxton, W., *The Recuyell of the Historyes of Troye*, William Caxton, Bruges, 1473.

Caxton, W., *The Recuyell of the Historyes of Troye*, ed. H.O. Sommer, 2 vols, Nutt, London, 1894.

The Cely Letters, 1472–1488, ed. A. Hanham, Early English Text Society, original series, vol. 273, Oxford University Press, London, 1975.

Chaucer, G., *The Canterbury Tales*, in *The Riverside Chaucer*, ed. L.D. Benson, Oxford University Press, Oxford, 1987, pp. 3–328, 795–965.

Chaucer, G., *The Legend of Good Women*, in *The Riverside Chaucer*, ed. L.D. Benson, Oxford University Press, Oxford, 1987, pp. 587–630, 1178–84.

Chibnall, M., *Empress Matilda: Queen Consort, Queen Mother and Lady of the English*, Blackwell, Oxford, 1991.

Chotzen, T.M., 'Some Sidelights on Cambro-Dutch Relations', *Transactions of the Honourable Society of Cymmrodorion*, 1937, pp. 101–44.

Christman, V., 'The Coverture of Widowhood: Heterodox Female Publishers in Antwerp, 1530–1580', *The Sixteenth Century Journal*, vol. 42, 2011, pp. 77–97.

Chronicle of Gouda: *Die cronike of die hystorie van Hollant van Zeelant ende Vrieslant ende van den sticht van Utrecht*, Gerard Leeu, Gouda, 1478.

Churchyard, T., *A Lamentable and Pitifull Description of the Wofull Warres in Flaunders*, Henry Bynneman for Ralph Nevvberie, London, 1578.

Clegg, C.S., 'Tudor Literary Censorship', Oxford Handbooks Online, 2015, www.oxfordhandbooks.com/view/10.1093/oxfordhb/9780199935338.001.0001/oxfordhb-9780199935338-e-9 [accessed 5 March 2020].

Colin, G., W. Hellinga et al., *De vijfhonderdste verjaring van de boekdrukkunst in de Nederlanden*, Koninklijke Bibliotheek, Brussels, 1973.

Colloques ou dialogues avec un dictionnaire en quatre langues, flamen, anglois, francois, & latin. Colloquien oft tsamensprekinghen, met eenen vocabulaer in vier spraken: Nederduytsch, Engelsch, Fransoys, ende Latijn, Jan Paedts Jacobszoon and Jan Bouwensz, Leiden, 1585.

Colvin, H., and S. Foister, *The Panorama of London circa 1544*, London Topographical Society, London, 1996.

Cordfunke, E.H.P., *Floris V, een politieke moord in 1296*, Walburg Pers, Zutphen, 2011.

Corsten, S., 'Caxton in Cologne', *Journal of the Printing Historical Society*, vol. 11, 1975/6, pp. 1–18.

Cort verhael om te vreden te stellen ende vernoegen alle de gene, die de waerheit niet wetende, ondiscretelick spreken vande coninginne van Engeland, van den Baenderheer van Wyllughby, ende vande Engelsche natie, [Richard Field, London], 1589.

Coverdale, M. (ed. and trans.), *Biblia the Bible, that is, The Holy Scripture of the Olde and New Testament, Faithfully and Truly Translated out of Douche and Latyn in to Englishe*, [Merten de Keyser, Antwerp], 1535.

Crick, J.C., *The Historia regum Britannie of Geoffrey of Monmouth, IV: Dissemination and Reception in the Later Middle Ages*, D.S. Brewer, Cambridge, 1991.

Crick, J., and E. van Houts (eds), *A Social History of England, 900–1200*, Cambridge University Press, Cambridge, 2011.

Crouch, D., *The Reign of King Stephen, 1135–1154*, Longman, Harlow, 2000.

Cruse, M., *Illuminating the Roman d'Alexandre: Oxford, Bodleian Library, MS Bodley 264*, D.S. Brewer, Cambridge, 2011.

Daele, Rik van, 'Alleen maar in het Land van Reynaert?', *Tiecelijn*, vol. 11, 1998, pp. 114–30.

Dahl, F., 'Amsterdam–Cradle of English Newspapers', *The Library*, vol. s5-IV, 1949, pp. 166–78.

Dalché, P., 'Maps, Travel and Exploration in the Middle Ages: Some Reflections about Anachronism', *The Historical Review/La Revue Historique*, vol. 12, 2015, pp. 143–62.

Daniell, D., 'Coverdale, Miles (1488–1569), Bible translator and bishop of Exeter', in *Oxford Dictionary of National Biography*, Oxford University Press, Oxford, 2009.

Davies, S., *Renaissance Ethnography and the Invention of the Human*, Cambridge University Press, Cambridge, 2016.

Dean, J.M. (ed.), *Medieval English Political Writings*, Medieval Institute Publications, Kalamazoo, MI, 1996.

Dean, R.J., and M.B.M. Boulton, *Anglo-Norman Literature: A Guide to Texts and Manuscripts*, Anglo-Norman Text Society, London, 1999.

The Declaration of His Highnes William Henry, by the Grace of God Prince of Orange, &c. of the Reasons Inducing Him, to Appear in Armes in the Kingdome of England, for Preserving of the Protestant Religion, and for Restoring the Lawes and Liberties of England, Scotland and Ireland, Arnout Leers, The Hague, 1688.

A Declaration of the Causes Moouing the Queene of England to Giue Aide to the Defence of the People Afflicted and Oppressed in the Lowe Countries, Christopher Barker, London, 1585.

A Defence and True Declaration of the Things Lately Done in the Lowe Countrey, whereby may Easily be Seen to Whom all the Beginning and Cause of the Late Troubles and Calamities is to be Imputed. And therewith also the Sclaunders wherewith the Aduersaries do Burden the Churches of the Lowe Countrey are Plainly Confuted, John Day, London, [1571].

Dennison, L., 'The Artistic Context of Fourteenth Century Flemish Brasses', *Transactions of the Monumental Brass Society*, vol. 14, 1986, pp. 1–38.

Dennison, L., 'The Dating and Localisation of The Hague Missal (Meermanno-Westreenanium MS 10 A 14) and the Connection between English and Flemish Miniature Painting in the Mid-Fourteenth Century', in *'Als Ich Can': Liber Amicorum in Memory of Professor Dr. Maurits Smeyers*, ed. B. Cardon, Peeters, Leuven, 2002, pp. 505–36.

Depuydt, J., 'Ortelius, Abraham (1527–1598), map maker', in *Oxford Dictionary of National Biography*, Oxford University Press, Oxford, 2004.

Derolez, A., 'A Literary Tour de Force: The Latin Translation of Maerlant's *Martijns* and the Translator's Prologues', in *Syntagmatia: Essays on Neo-Latin Literature in Honour of Monique Mund-Dopchie and Gilbert Tournoy*, ed. J. Papy and D. Sacré, Leuven University Press, Leuven, 2009, pp. 93–103.

Dewilde, B., J. Dumolyn, B. Lambert and B. Vannieuwenhuyze, '"So One Would Notice the Good Navigability": Economic Decline and the Cartographic Conception of Urban Space in Late Fifteenth- and Sixteenth-Century Bruges', *Urban History*, vol. 45, 2018, pp. 2–25.

Dickson, R., and J.P. Edmond, *Annals of Scottish Printing*, Macmillan & Bowes, Cambridge, 1890.

Dictionary of the Scots Language / Dictionar o the Scots Leid, Scottish Language Dictionaries, Edinburgh, 2004, https://dsl.ac.uk [accessed 5 March 2020].

Digital Scriptorium, www.digital-scriptorium.org [accessed 5 March 2020].

[*Divisiekroniek*]: *Die cronycke van Hollandt, Zeelandt ende Vrieslant, beghinnende van Adams tiden …*, Jan Seversz, Leiden, 1517.

Dockray-Miller, M., *The Books and the Life of Judith of Flanders*, Ashgate, Farnham, 2015.

Dodds, G.D., 'An Accidental Historian: Erasmus and the English History of the Reformation', *Church History*, vol. 82, 2013, pp. 273–92.

Dop, J.A., *Eliza's Knights: Soldiers, Poets and Puritans in the Netherlands 1572–1586*, Remak, Alblasserdam, [1981].

Dorsten, J.A. van, *Poets, Patrons, and Professors: Sir Philip Sidney, Daniel Rogers, and the Leiden Humanists*, Leiden University Press, Leiden, and Oxford University Press, London, 1962.

Dorsten, J.A. van, *Thomas Basson, 1555–1613, English Printer at Leiden*, Sir Thomas Browne Institute, Leiden, 1961.

Dover Wilson, J., 'Richard Schilders and the English Puritans', *The Library*, vol. 11, 1909, pp. 65–134.

Driver, M.W., 'Caxton, William', in *The Encyclopedia of Medieval Literature in Britain*, ed. S. Echard, R.A. Rouse, J.A. Fay, H. Fulton and G. Rector, 4 vols, Blackwell, Oxford, 2017, vol. 1, pp. 390–99.

Driver, M.W., 'Printing', in *The Encyclopedia of Medieval Literature in Britain*, ed. S. Echard, R.A. Rouse, J.A. Fay, H. Fulton and G. Rector, 4 vols, Blackwell, Oxford, 2017, vol. 4, pp. 1546–54.

Drogo of Saint-Winnoc, *Historia translationis sanctae Lewinnae*, in *Acta Sanctorum July V*, ed. Société des Bollandistes, Antwerp, 1727, pp. 613–27.

Dronke, P., 'Latin and Vernacular Love-Lyrics: Rochester and St Augustine's, Canterbury', *Revue Bénédictine*, vol. 115, 2005, pp. 400–410.

Dryden, J., *Annus mirabilis: The Year of Wonders, 1666. An Historical Poem*, Henry Herringman, London, 1667.

Duff, G. (ed.), *The Dialogue, or, Communing between the Wise King Salomon and Marcolphus*, Laurence and Bullen, London, 1902.

Duke, A., 'William of Orange's *Apology* (1580)', *Dutch Crossing*, vol. 22, 1998, pp. 3–96.

Dumitresco, T., *The Early Tudor Court and International Musical Relations*, Ashgate, Farnham, 2007.

Dumolyn, J., and J. Haemers, 'Patterns of Urban Rebellion in Medieval Flanders', *Journal of Medieval History*, vol. 31, 2005, pp. 369–93.

Dunthorne, H., *Britain and the Dutch Revolt, 1560–1700*, Cambridge University Press, Cambridge, 2013.

Echard, S., *Printing the Middle Ages*, University of Pennsylvania Press, Philadelphia, 2008.

Eeghen, I.H. van, 'De familie van de plaatsnijder Claes Jansz Visscher', *Amstelodamum: Maandblad voor de kennis van Amsterdam*, vol. 77, 1990, pp. 73–82.

Eerden, P.C. van der, 'Eschatology in the Boec van der Wraken', in *The Use and Abuse of Eschatology in the Middle Ages*, ed. W. Verbeke, D. Verhelst and A. Welkenhuysen, Leuven University Press, Leuven, 1988, pp. 425–40.

Emo and Menko, *Kroniek van het klooster Bloemhof te Wittewierum*, ed. and trans. H.P.H. Jansen and A. Janse, Verloren, Hilversum, 1991.

Engelands rouwen, en rouw-klachten over de doodt van die groote en deugt-begaefde gaedeloose koninginne van Groot Brittanje Marya Stuart, Pieter Jooste, Amsterdam, 1695.

Erasmus, D., *Adages II i 1 to II vi 100*, trans. R.A.B. Mynors, *Collected Works of Erasmus*, vol. 33, University of Toronto Press, Toronto, 1991.

Erasmus, D., *Adagiorum chilias secvnda, pars prior*, ed. M. Szymański, *Desiderii Erasmi Roterodami Opera Omnia*, vol. 2.3, Elsevier, Amsterdam, 2005.

Erasmus, D., *The Correspondence of Erasmus*, trans. R.A.B. Mynors, A. Dalzell et al., *The Collected Works of Erasmus*, vols 1–, University of Toronto Press, Toronto, 1974–.

Erasmus, D., *A Devoute Treatise upon the Pater noster*, trans. M. Roper, [Thomas Berthelet, London, 1526].

Erasmus, D., *De immensa dei misericordia: A Sermon of the Excedynge Great Mercy of God*, Thomas Berthelet, London, [1526].

Erasmus, D., *Moriae encomium, or, The Praise of Folly Written Originally in Latine*, trans. J. Wilson, William Leak, London, 1668.

Erasmus, D., *Opus epistolarum*, ed. P.S. Allen and H.M. Allen, 12 vols, Clarendon Press, Oxford, 1906–58.

Erasmus, D., *The Praise of Folie = Moriæ encomium a Booke Made in Latine*, trans. T. Chaloner, Thomas Berthelet, London, 1549.

Evelyn, J., *The Diary*, ed. E.S. de Beer, 6 vols, Clarendon Press, Oxford, 1955.

Everett Green, M.A., *Lives of the Princesses of England from the Norman Conquest*, 6 vols, Longman, Brown, Green, Longman & Roberts, London, 1857.

Filppula, M., J. Klemola and H. Pavlasto, *English and Celtic in Contact*, Routledge, London, 2008.

Finke, U., 'Utrecht – Zentrum Nordniederländischer Buchmalerei', *Oud Holland*, vol. 78, 1963, pp. 27–66.

Fleck, A., 'Deep Designs of Empire: English Representations of the Dutch from the Armada to the Glorious Revolution', Ph.D. thesis, Claremont Graduate University, 2000.

Fleck, A., *The Dutch Device: English Representations of the Dutch from the Armada to the Glorious Revolution*, forthcoming.

Fleming, A., and R.A. Mason, *Scotland and the Flemish People*, John Donald, Edinburgh, 2019.

Forster, L., 'Iets over Nederlandse renaissancelyriek vóór Heinsius en Hooft', *Tijdschrift voor Nederlandse Taal- en Letterkunde*, vol. 83, 1967, pp. 274–302.

Franssen, P.J.A., *Tussen tekst en publiek: Jan van Doesborch, drukker-uitgever en literator te Antwerpen en Utrecht in de eerste helft van de zestiende eeuw*, Rodopi, Amsterdam, 1990.

Franssen, P.J.A., *The World of Jan van Doesborch*, http://janvandoesborch.com/book [accessed 5 March 2020].

Franssen, P.J.A., and A.E.C. Simoni, 'Jan van Doesborch (?–1536), Printer of English Texts', *Quaerendo*, vol. 16, 1986, pp. 259–80.

Freeman, A., 'Everyman and Others, Part II: The Bandinel Fragments', *The Library*, vol. 9, 2008, pp. 397–427.

Freeman, A., 'Marlowe, Kyd, and the Dutch Church Libel', *English Literary Renaissance*, vol. 3, 1973, pp. 44–52.

Freeman, E.A., *The Norman Conquest of England*, vol. IV, Clarendon Press, Oxford, 1876.

Furley, R., *A History of the Weald of Kent*, 2 vols, Russell Smith, London, 1974.

Gallagher, J., *Learning Languages in Early Modern England*, Oxford University Press, Oxford, 2019.

Gameson, R., 'L'Angleterre et la Flandre aux Xe et XIe Siècles: Le témoignage des manuscrits', in *Les échanges culturels au Moyen Âge: XXXIIe Congrès de la SHMES (Université du Littoral Côte d'Opale, juin 2001)*, Éditions de la Sorbonne, Paris, 2002, pp. 165–206.

Gameson, R., 'The Earliest Books of Arras Cathedral', *Scriptorium*, vol. 61, 2007, pp. 233–85.

Gardham, J., 'Blockbook Apocalypse. Netherlands: 1430s–1440s; Sp Coll Hunterian Ds.2.3', Glasgow University Library Special Collections Department Book of the Month, April 2005, http://special.lib.gla.ac.uk/exhibns/month/apr2005.html [accessed 5 March 2020].

Gascoigne, G., *The Spoyle of Antwerpe* (1576), in *The Complete Works of George Gascoigne*, ed. J.W. Cunliffe, 2 vols, Cambridge University Press, Cambridge, 1907–10, vol. II, pp. 586–99.

Gautier Dalché, P., *La Géographie de Ptolémée en Occident (IVᵉ–XVIᵉ siècle)*, Brepols, Turnhout, 2009.

Gautier Dalché, P., 'The Reception of Ptolemy's *Geography* (End of the Fourteenth to Beginning of the Sixteenth Century)', in *The History of Cartography*, vol. 3, part 1, ed. D. Woodward, University of Chicago Press, Chicago, 2007, pp. 285–364.

Gautier Dalché, P., *La Terre: Connaissance, représentations, mesure au moyen âge*, Brepols, Turnhout, 2013.

Gay, R., 'Selected Scribe Bibliographies', in *Illuminating the Renaissance: The Triumph of Flemish Manuscript Painting in Europe*, ed. T. Kren and S. McKendrick, J. Paul Getty Museum, Los Angeles, 2003, pp. 518–21.

Gee, J.A., 'Margaret Roper's English Version of Erasmus' *Precatio Dominica* and the Apprenticeship behind Early Tudor Translation', *Review of English Studies*, original series, vol. XIII, 1937, pp. 257–71.

Gemmula vocabulorum, cum addito, Gerard Leeu, Antwerp, 1488.

Geoffrey of Monmouth, *The History of the Kings of Britain*, ed. M.D. Reeve, trans. N. Wright, Boydell Press, Woodbridge, 2007.

Gerald of Wales, *Itinerarium Kambriae*, in *Giraldi Cambrensis opera*, vol. VI, ed. J.F. Dimock, Longmans, Green, Reader, and Dyer, London, 1868.

Gerald of Wales, *The Journey through Wales*, trans. L. Thorpe, Penguin, Harmondsworth, 1978.

Gerald of Wales, *Speculum duorum, or, A Mirror of Two Men*, ed. Y. Lefèvre and R.B.C. Huygens, trans. B. Dawson, University of Wales Press, Cardiff, 1974.

Gerritsen, W.P., 'Jacob van Maerlant and Geoffrey of Monmouth', in *An Arthurian Tapestry: Essays in Memory of Lewis Thorpe*, ed. K. Varty, University of Glasgow, Glasgow, 1981, pp. 368–88.

Gessler, J. (ed.), *Het Brugsche Livre des mestiers en zijn navolgelingen*, 6 vols, Consortium der Brugsche Meesters Boekdrukkers, Bruges, 1931.

Gil, M., 'Jean du Chesne, écrivain lillois à la fin de l'époque bourguignonne', in *Manuscript Studies in the Low Countries: Proceedings of the 'Groninger Codicologendagen in Friesland'*, ed. A.M.W. As-Vijvers, J.M.M. Hermans and G.C. Huisman, Egbert Forsten, Groningen, 2008, pp. 159–84.

Good, J., 'The Alien Clothworkers of London, 1337–1381', in *The Ties that Bind: Essays in Medieval British History in Honor of Barbara Hanawalt*, ed. L.E. Mitchell, K.L. French and D.L. Biggs, Ashgate, Farnham, 2011, pp. 7–19.

Good, J., 'Richard II and the Cults of Saints George and Edward the Confessor', in *Translatio, or, The Transmission of Culture in the Middle Ages and Renaissance: Modes and Messages*, ed. L. Hollengreen, Brepols, Turnhout, 2008, pp. 161–79.

Goodman, N., *Hollands Leaguer*, ed. D.S. Barnard, Mouton, The Hague, 1970.

Goodman, N., *Hollands Leaguer, or, An Historical Discourse of the Life and Actions of Dona Britanica Hollandia the Arch-mistris of the Wicked Women of Eutopia*, Richard Barnes, London, 1632.

Goodrich, J., 'Thomas More and Margaret More Roper: A Case for Rethinking Women's Participation in the Early Modern Public Sphere', *The Sixteenth Century Journal*, vol. 39, 2008, pp. 1021–40.

Goscelin of Saint-Bertin, *The Book of Encouragement and Consolation* (*Liber confortatorius*), trans. M. Otter, Boydell & Brewer, Cambridge, 2004.

Goudriaan, K., P. Abels and N. Habermehl (eds), *Een drukker zoekt publiek: Gheraert Leeu te Gouda, 1477–1484*, Eburon, Delft, 1993.

Grauwe, L. De, 'Zijn olla vogala Vlaams, of zit de Nederlandse filologie met een koekoeksei in (haar) nest(en)?', *Tijdschrift voor Nederlandsche Taal- en Letterkunde*, vol. 120, 2004, pp. 44–56.

Greenlee, J.W., 'Seeing All the Anguilles: Eels in the Cultural Landscape of Medieval and Early Modern England', Ph.D. dissertation, Cornell University, 2020.

Gregg, R.E., 'Further Insights into Anton van den Wyngaerde's Working Methods', *Master Drawings*, vol. 51, 2013, pp. 323–42.

Griffith, G., and A. Putter, 'Linguistic Boundaries in Multilingual Miscellanies', in *Middle English Texts in Transition: A Festschrift Dedicated to Toshiyuki Takamiya*, ed. S. Horobin and L. Mooney, D.S. Brewer, Cambridge, 2014, pp. 116–24.

Griffiths, A., 'Hole [Holle], William (d. 1624), engraver', in *Oxford Dictionary of National Biography*, Oxford University Press, Oxford, 2004.

Griffiths, R.A., *The Reign of King Henry VI: The Exercise of Royal Authority, 1422–1461*, University of California Press, Berkeley, 1981.

Grimeston, E., *A Generall Historie of the Netherlands vvith the Genealogie and Memorable Acts of the Earls of Holland, Zeeland, and West-Friseland, from Thierry of Aquitaine the First Earle, Successiuely vnto Philip the Third King of Spaine: Continued vnto this Present Yeare of Our Lord 1608*, Adam Islip and George Eld, London, 1608.

Grotius, H., *De rebus Belgicis, or, The Annals and History of the Low-Country-Warrs*, trans. T. Manley, Henry Twyford and Robert Paulet, London, 1665.

Guibert de Nogent, *Autobiographie*, ed. and trans. E.-R. Labande, Belles Lettres, Paris, 1981.

Guibert of Nogent, *The Memoirs: Self and Society in Medieval France: The Memoirs of Abbot Guibert of Nogent, 1064?–c.1125*, trans. C.C.S. Bland, rev. J.F. Benton, Harper & Row, New York, 1970.

Hadfield, A., 'Edmund Spenser's Translations of Du Bellay in Jan van der Noot's A Theatre for Voluptuous Worldlings', in *Tudor Translation: Early Modern Literature in History*, ed. F. Schurink, Palgrave Macmillan, London, 2011, pp. 143–60.

Haitsma Mulier, E.O.G., 'The History of Great Britain as Seen by the Dutch of the Seventeenth Century: A Chapter from the History of Historiography', in *The Exchange of Ideas: Religion, Scholarship and Art in Anglo-Dutch Relations in the Seventeenth Century*, ed. S. Groenveld and M. Wintle, Walburg Pers, Zutphen, 1991, pp. 133–49.

Hall, E.T., 'The Courtrai Chest from New College, Oxford, Re-examined', *Antiquity*, vol. 61, issue 231, 1987, pp. 104–7.

Hanham, A., 'Who Made William Caxton's Phrase-Book?', *Review of English Studies*, vol. 56, 2005, pp. 712–29.

Hart, H., and H. Carter, *Notes on a Century of Typography at the University Press, Oxford, 1693–1794*, Clarendon Press, Oxford, 1970.

Harvey, P.D.A., 'Local and Regional Cartography in Medieval Europe', in *The History of Cartography*, vol. 1, ed. J.B. Harley and D. Woodward, University of Chicago Press, Chicago, 1987, pp. 464–501.

Hearn, K., 'Somer, Paul [Pauwels] van [Paul Vansommer] (1577/8–1621/2), portrait painter', in *Oxford Dictionary of National Biography*, Oxford University Press, Oxford, 2004.

Heelu, J. van, *Yeeste van den slag van Woeringen*, ed. J.F. Willems, *Rymkronyk van Jan van Heelu betreffende den slag van Woeringen van het jaer 1288*, M. Hayez, Brussels, 1836.

Heere, L. de, *Beschrijving der Britische Eilanden*, ed. T.M. Chotzen and A.M.E. Draak, Sinjoren, Antwerp, 1937.

Heere, L. de, *Corte Beschryvinghe van England, Scotland, ende Irland*, London, British Library, Additional MS 28330, www.bl.uk/manuscripts/Viewer.aspx?ref=add_ms_28330 [accessed 5 March 2020].

Heere, L. de, *Den hof en boomgaerd der poësien, inhoudende menigherley soorten van poëtijckelicke blommen*, Ghileyn Manilius, Ghent, 1565.

Heesakkers, C.L., 'Franciscus Junius as a Tutor: His *Paraenesis missa Alberico de Vere*', in *Franciscus Junius F.F. and his Circle*, ed. R.H. Bremmer, Rodopi, Amsterdam, 1998, pp. 93–115.

Heijden, H.A.M. van der, *Leo Belgicus: An Illustrated and Annotated Carto-Bibliography*, Canaletto, Alphen aan den Rijn, 1990.

Hellinga, L., 'Printing', in *The Cambridge History of the Book in Britain*, vol. III, *1400–1557*, ed. L. Hellinga and J.B. Trapp, Cambridge University Press, Cambridge, 1999, pp. 65–108.

Hellinga, L., 'Reading an Engraving: William's Caxton's Dedication to Margaret of York, Duchess of Burgundy', in *Across the Narrow Seas: Studies in the History and Bibliography of Great Britain and the Low Countries Presented to Anna C. Simoni*, ed. S. Roach, British Library, London, 1991, pp. 1–15.

Hellinga, L., *William Caxton and Early Printing in England*, British Library, London, 2010.

Hellinga, L., 'William Caxton, Colard Mansion and the Printer in Type 1', in *Incunabula in Transit: People and Trade*, Brill, Leiden, 2018, pp. 286–322.

Hellinga, L., 'Wynkyn de Worde's Native Land', in *Incunabula in Transit: People and Trade*, Brill, Leiden, 2018, pp. 323–39.

Hellinga, L., and W. Hellinga, 'Caxton in the Low Countries', *Journal of the Printing Historical Society*, vol. 11, 1975/6, pp. 19–32.

Hellinga, L., and C. de Wolf, *Laurens Janszoon Coster was zijn naam*, Enschede, Haarlem, 1988.

Hellinga, W. (ed.), *Van den vos Reynaerde: Teksten*, Tjeenk Willink, Zwolle, 1952.

Helmers, H., *The Royalist Republic: Literature, Politics, and Religion in the Anglo-Dutch Public Sphere, 1639–1660*, Cambridge University Press, Cambridge, 2015.

Hemptinne, T. de, and W. Prevenier, 'La Flandre au moyen âge: un pays de trilinguisme administratif', in *La langue des actes: Actes du XIe congrès international de diplomatique*, 2003, http://elec.enc.sorbonne.fr/CID2003/de-hemptinne_prevenier [accessed 5 March 2020].

Henry of Huntingdon, *Historia Anglorum (History of the English People)*, ed. and trans. D. Greenway, Oxford University Press, Oxford, 1996.

Henryson, R., *Fables*, in *Robert Henryson: The Complete Works*, ed. D.J. Parkinson, Medieval Institute, Kalamazoo, MI, 2010, https://d.lib.rochester.edu/teams/publication/parkinson-henryson-the-complete-works [accessed 23 March 2020].

Herman de Tournai, *Les miracles de Sainte Marie de Laon*, ed. and trans. A. Saint-Denis, CNRS, Paris, 2008.

Hessels, J.H. (ed.), *Abrahami Ortelii et virorum eruditorum ad eundem et ad Jacobum Colium Ortelianum epistulae*, vol. I of *Ecclesiae Londino-Batavae Archivum*, Cambridge University Press, Cambridge, 1887.

Hexham, H. *A Copious English and Netherduytsch Dictionarie / Het groot woorden-boeck*, Arnout Leers, Rotterdam, 1648.

Hexham, H., *A True and Briefe Relation of the Famous Seige of Breda: Beseiged, and Taken in vnder the Able and Victorious Conduct of his Highnesse the Prince of Orange, Captaine Generall of the States Armie, and Admirall of the Seas, &c.*, James Moxon, Delft, 1637.

Hexter, R.J., and D. Townsend, *The Oxford Handbook of Medieval Latin Literature*, Oxford University Press, Oxford, 2012.

Heyden, H.A.M. van der, 'Emanuel van Meteren's History as Source for the Cartography of the Netherlands', *Quaerendo*, vol. 16, 1986, pp. 3–29.

Higden, R., *Polychronicon*, William Caxton, Westminster, 1482.

Higgins, S., 'Britain's Bourse: Cultural and Literary Exchanges between England and the Low Countries in the Early Modern Era (*c.*1580–1620)', Ph.D. thesis, University College Cork, 2017.

Hirsh, J.C. (ed.), *Medieval Lyric: Middle English Lyrics, Ballads, and Carols*, Blackwell, Oxford, 2005.

The History of the Most Illustrious William, Prince of Orange Deduc'd from the First Founders of the Antient House of Nassau: Together with the Most Considerable Actions of the Present Prince, London, 1688.

Hittmair, R. (ed.), *Aus Caxtons Vorreden und Nachworthen*, Noske, Leipzig, 1934.

Hodgson-Wright, S., 'Cary [née Tanfield], Elizabeth, Viscountess Falkland (1585–1639), writer and translator', in *Oxford Dictionary of National Biography*, Oxford University Press, Oxford, 2014.

Hoftijzer, P., 'Henry Hexham (*c.*1585–1650), English Soldier, Author, Translator, Lexicographer, and Cultural Mediator in the Low Countries', in *Renaissance Cultural Crossroads: Translation, Print and Culture in Britain, 1473–1640*, ed. S. Barker and B. Hosington, Brill, Leiden, 2013, pp. 209–25.

Hollyband, C., *Instruksie om draa en goedt Frans te leeren, en Engels*, Thomas Vautrollier, London, 1581.

Holmes, G.A., 'The "Libel of English Policy"', *The English Historical Review*, vol. 76, 1961, pp. 193–216.

Houts, E. van, 'The Flemish Contribution to Biographical Writing in England in the Eleventh Century', in *Writing Medieval Biography, 750–1250: Essays in Honour of Frank Barlow*, ed. D. Bates, J. Crick and S. Hamilton, Boydell & Brewer, Woodbridge, 2006, pp. 111–28.

Houts, E. van, 'Judith of Flanders, Duchess of Bavaria (1030×35–1095), Noblewoman', in *Oxford Dictionary of National Biography*, Oxford University Press, Oxford, 2004.

Houts, E. van, 'The Norman Conquest through European Eyes', *English Historical Review*, vol. 110, 1995, pp. 832–53.

Houts, E. van, 'The Ship List of William the Conqueror', *Anglo-Norman Studies*, vol. 10, 1988, pp. 159–83.

Houtte, J.A. van, 'The Rise and Decline of the Market of Bruges', *Economic History Review*, vol. 19, 1966, pp. 29–47.

Hsy, J., *Trading Tongues: Merchants, Multilingualism, and Medieval Literature*, The Ohio State University Press, Columbus, 2013.

Hunt, E.M., '"Van den grave te makene": The Matter of Heraldry in a Psalter for the Count of Flanders (Royal Library of Belgium MS 10607) and in the Urban Media of Ghent', *Peregrinations*, vol. 4, 2014, pp. 87–127.

Janse, A., *Een pion voor een dame: Jacoba van Beieren (1401–1436)*, Uitgeverij Balans, Amsterdam, 2009.

Janssen, H.Q., 'De hervormde vlugtelingen van Yperen in Engeland: geschetst naar hunne brieven. Een bijdrage tot de hervormingsgeschiedenis van Yperen en Norwich', in *Bijdragen tot de oudheidkunde en geschiedenis inzonderheid van Zeeuwsch Vlaanderen 2*, Middelburg, 1857, pp. 211–304.

Jardine, L., *Going Dutch: How England Plundered Holland's Glory*, HarperCollins, London, 2008.

Joby, C., *The Dutch Language in Britain (1550–1702): A Social History of the Use of Dutch in Early Modern Britain*, Brill, Leiden, 2015.

Joby, C., 'Early Modern Records in Dutch at the Norfolk Record Office', *Dutch Crossing*, vol. 36, 2012, pp. 132–40.

John of Worcester, *The Chronicle of John of Worcester*, ed. and trans. R.R. Darlington, P. McGurk and J. Bray, 3 vols, Oxford University Press, Oxford, 1995–98.

Jones, P.M., 'Gemini [Geminus, Lambrit], Thomas (*fl.* 1540–1562)', in *Oxford Dictionary of National Biography*, Oxford University Press, Oxford, 2008.

Jordan Fantosme, *Chronicle*, ed. and trans. R.C. Johnston, Clarendon Press, Oxford, 1981.

Joscelyn, J., and M. Parker (eds), *A Testimonie of Antiquitie Shewing the Auncient Fayth in the Church of England Touching the Sacrament of the Body and Bloude of the Lord here Publikely Preached, and also Receaued in the Saxons Tyme, aboue 600. Yeares Agoe*, John Day, London, [1566].

Junius, F., *Cædmonis monachi Paraphrasis poetica Genesios ac praecipuarum sacrae paginae historiarum*, Christophorus Cunradus, Amsterdam, 1655.

Junius, F., *Caedmonis monachi Paraphrasis poetica: genesios ac praecipuarum sacrae paginae historiarum*, ed. P.J. Lucas, Rodopi, Amsterdam, 2000.

Junius, F., *Etymologicum Anglicanum*, Sheldonian Theatre, Oxford, 1743.

Kagan, R.L., 'Philip II and the Art of the Cityscape', *Journal of Interdisciplinary History*, vol. 17, 1986, pp. 115–35.

Karras, R.M., *Common Women: Prostitution and Sexuality in Medieval England*, Oxford University Press, New York, 1996.

Karras, R.M., 'The Regulation of Brothels in Later Medieval England', *Signs*, vol. 14, 1989, pp. 399–433.

Karrow, R.W., Jr, *Mapmakers of the Sixteenth Century and their Maps: Bio-Bibliographies of the Cartographers of Abraham Ortelius, 1570*, Speculum Orbis Press for The Newberry Library, Winnetka, IL, 1993.

Kaufman, P.I., 'Absolute Margaret: Margaret More Roper and "Well Learned" Men', *The Sixteenth Century Journal*, vol. 20, 1989, pp. 443–56.

Keats-Rohan, K., *Domesday People: A Prosopography of Persons Occurring in English Documents, 1066–1166*, vol. I, *Domesday Book*, Boydell Press, Woodbridge, 1999.

Keck, D., 'Marlowe and Ortelius's Map', *Notes and Queries*, vol. 52, 2005, pp. 189–90.

Kerling, N.J.M., *Commercial Relations of Holland and Zeeland with England from the Late 13th Century to the Close of the Middle Ages*, E.J. Brill, Leiden, 1954.

Kerrigan, J., *Archipelagic English: Literature, History, and Politics, 1603–1707*, Oxford University Press, Oxford, 2008.

Kiernan, K.S., 'Reading Cædmon's "Hymn"', in *Old English Literature: Critical Essays*, ed. R.M. Liuzza, Yale University Press, New Haven, CT, 2002, pp. 103–24.

Kiliaan, C., *Etymologicum Teutonicae linguae: siue, Dictionarium Teutonico-Latinum*, 3rd edition, Ex Officina Plantiniana, Antwerp, 1599.

King, E., *King Stephen*, Yale University Press, New Haven, CT, 2012.

King, J.N., *English Reformation Literature: The Tudor Origins of the Protestant Tradition*, Princeton University Press, Princeton, 1982.

King, J.N., 'John Day: Master Printer of the English Reformation', in *The Beginnings of English Protestantism*, ed. P. Marshall and A. Ryrie, Cambridge University Press, Cambridge, 2002, pp. 180–208.

King, J.N., and M. Rankin, 'Print, Patronage, and the Reception of Continental Reform: 1521–1603', *The Yearbook of English Studies*, vol. 38, 2008, pp. 49–67.

Knighton, C., 'Anthony, Anthony (d. 1563), military administrator', in *Oxford Dictionary of National Biography*, Oxford University Press, Oxford, 2008.

Kren, T., *Illuminated Manuscripts from Belgium and the Netherlands in the J. Paul Getty Museum*, J. Paul Getty Museum, Los Angeles, 2010.

Kren, T., and S. McKendrick (eds), *Illuminating the Renaissance: The Triumph of Flemish Manuscript Painting in Europe*, J. Paul Getty Museum, Los Angeles, 2003.

Krogt, P. van der, 'The Place of the "Atlas of Scotland" in the Atlas Production of Willem Jansz. and Joan Blaeu', *Scottish Geographical Journal*, vol. 121, 2005, pp. 261–8.

Kronenberg, M.E., 'Notes on English Printing in the Low Countries', *The Library*, vol. s4-IX, 1928, pp. 139–63.

Kronenberg, M.E., 'Over verboden boeken en opstandige drukkers', *Verslagen en mededelingen van de Koninklijke Vlaamse Academie voor Taal- en Letterkunde*, 1935, pp. 963–78.

Kronenberg, M.E., *Verboden boeken en opstandige drukkers in de Hervormingstijd*, P.N. van Kampen & Zoon, Amsterdam, 1948.

Kwakkel, E., 'Book Script', in E. Kwakkel and R. Thomson (eds), *The European Book in the Twelfth Century*, Cambridge University Press, Cambridge, 2018, pp. 25–42.

Kwakkel, E., 'Hebban olla vogala in historisch perspectief', *Tijdschrift voor Nederlandse Taal- en Letterkunde*, vol. 121, 2005, pp. 1–24.

Kwakkel, E., 'Hidden in Plain Sight: Continental Scribes in Rochester Cathedral Priory, 1075–1150', in *Writing in Context: Insular Manuscript Culture, 500–1200*, ed. E. Kwakkel, Leiden University Press, Leiden, 2013, pp. 231–61.

Lambert of Ardres, *Historia comitum Ghisnensium*, ed. J. Heller, Monumenta Germaniae Historiae SS 24, Hahn, Hanover, 1874.

Lambert of Ardres, *The History of the Counts of Guines and Lords of Ardres*, trans. L. Shopkow, University of Pennsylvania Press, Philadelphia, 2001.

Lambert, B., and M. Pajic, 'Drapery in Exile: Edward III, Colchester and the Flemings, 1351–1367', *History*, vol. 99, 2014, pp. 733–53.

Lampen, W., 'De vereering van St Oswald, bijzonder in de Nederlanden', *Ons Geestelijk Erf*, vol. 1, 1927, pp. 142–57.

Latré, G., 'The Place of Printing of the Coverdale Bible', *The Tyndale Society Journal*, vol. 8, 1997, pp. 5–18.

Law-Turner, F.C.E., *The Ormesby Psalter: Patrons and Artists in East Anglia*, Bodleian Library Publishing, Oxford, 2017.

Levelt, S., *Jan van Naaldwijk's Chronicles of Holland: Continuity and Transformation in the Historical Tradition of Hollland during the Early Sixteenth Century*, Verloren, Hilversum, 2011.

Levelt, S., 'The Manuscripts of Jan van Naaldwijk's Chronicles of

Holland, Cotton MSS. Vitellius F. XV and Tiberius C. IV', *Electronic British Library Journal*, 2012, article 4, www.bl.uk/eblj/2012articles/article4.html [accessed 5 March 2020].

Levelt, S., *The Middle Dutch Brut: An Edition and Translation*, Liverpool University Press, Liverpool, 2021.

Levelt, S., 'New Evidence for an Interest in Arthurian Literature in the Dutch Low Countries in the Fifteenth and Early Sixteenth Centuries', *Arthurian Literature*, vol. XXIX, 2012, pp. 101–10.

Levillain, C.-É., 'England's "Natural Frontier": Andrew Marvell and the Low Countries', in *The Oxford Handbook of Andrew Marvell*, ed. M. Dzelzainis and E. Holberton, Oxford University Press, Oxford, 2019, pp. 114–27.

The Libelle of Englyshe Polycye: A Poem on the Use of Sea-Power, 1436, ed. G. Warner, Clarendon Press, Oxford, 1926.

Libellus supplex imperatoriae maiestati caeterisq[ue] sacri imperij electoribus, principibus, atq[ue] ordinibus, nomine Belgarus ex inferiori Germania, euangelicae religionis causa per Albani Ducis tyrannidem eiectorum in comitijs Spirensibus, exhibitus, John Day, London, 1571.

Liebermann, F., 'Raginald von Canterbury', *Neues Archiv für ältere deutsche Geschichtskunde*, vol. 13, 1888, pp. 517–56.

The Life and Death of Iacke Straw, a Notable Rebell in England vvho was Kild in Smithfield by the Lord Maior of London, Iohn Danter, London, [1594].

Loomis, R.S., 'Edward I, Arthurian Enthusiast', *Speculum*, vol. 28, 1953, pp. 114–27.

Loonen, P., *For to Learne to Buye and Sell: Learning English in the Low Countries Area, 1500–1800*, APA–Holland University Press, Amsterdam, 1991.

Loudon, M., 'Rogers, Daniel (*c.*1538–1591), diplomat and author', in *Oxford Dictionary of National Biography*, Oxford University Press, Oxford, 2008.

Lucas, H.S., 'Diplomatic Relations of Edward I and Albert of Austria', *Speculum*, vol. 9, 1934, pp. 125–34.

Lucas, H.S., 'Edward III and the Poet Chronicler John Boendale', *Speculum*, vol. 12, 1937, pp. 367–9.

Lucas, P.J., 'Junius, his Printers and his Types', in *Franciscus Junius F.F. and His Circle*, ed. R.H. Bremmer, Rodopi, Amsterdam, 1998, pp. 177–98.

Lucas, P.J., 'Printing Anglo-Saxon in Holland and John Selden's *Mare Clausum seu de Dominio Maris*', *Quaerendo*, vol. 31, 2001, pp. 120–36.

Lucas, P.J., 'William Camden, Seventeenth-Century Atlases of the British Isles and the Printing of Anglo-Saxon', *The Antiquaries Journal*, vol. 98, 2018, pp. 219–44.

Lusardi, J.P., 'The Pictured Playhouse: Reading the Utrecht Engraving of Shakespeare's London', *Shakespeare Quarterly*, vol. 44, 1993, pp. 202–27.

Luu, L.B., *Immigrants and the Industries of London, 1500–1700*, Ashgate, Aldershot, 2005.

Lydgate, J., 'On Gloucester's Approaching Marriage', in *The Minor Poems of John Lydgate*, part II, *Secular Poems*, ed. H.N. MacCracken, Oxford University Press, London, 1934, poem 26, pp. 601–8.

MacDonald, A.A. (ed.), *George Lauder: Life and Writings*, D. S. Brewer, Cambridge, 2018.

McGurk, P., and J. Rosenthal, 'The Anglo-Saxon Gospelbooks of Judith, Countess of Flanders: Their Text, Make-up and Function', *Anglo-Saxon England*, vol. 24, 1995, pp. 251–308.

Maerlant, J. van, *Spiegel historiael*, ed. M. de Vries and E. Verwijs, 4 vols, Brill, Leiden, 1863–79; repr. HES Publishers, Utrecht, 1982.

Manly, J.M., and E. Rickert, *The Text of the Canterbury Tales*, 8 vols, University of Chicago Press, Chicago, 1940.

Mann, J., *From Aesop to Reynard: Beast Literature in Medieval Britain*, Oxford University Press, Oxford, 2009.

Mann, J., *Ysengrimus*, Harvard University Press, Cambridge, MA, 2013.

Mann, N., 'The Origins of Humanism', in *The Cambridge Companion to Renaissance Humanism*, ed. J. Kraye, Cambridge University Press, Cambridge, 1996, pp. 1–19.

Mare, A.C. de la, 'Duke Humfrey's English Palladius (MS. Duke Humfrey d. 2)', *Bodleian Library Record*, vol. 12, 1985, pp. 39–51.

Marlowe, C., *Tamburlaine Parts One and Two*, ed. A.B. Dawson, Oxford University Press, Oxford, 2003.

Martens, P., 'Cities under Siege: Portrayal *ad vivum* in Early Netherlandish Prints (1520–1565)', in *Ad Vivum? Visual Materials and the Vocabulary of Life-Likeness in Europe before 1800*, ed. T. Balfe, J. Woodall, C. Zittel, Brill, Leiden, 2019, pp. 151–99.

Marvell, A., *The Poems of Andrew Marvell*, ed. N. Smith, Longman, London, 2007.

Marvell, A., *The Prose Works of Andrew Marvell*, ed. A. Patterson, M. Dzelzainis, N. von Maltzahn, and N.H. Keeble, 2 vols, Yale University Press, New Haven, CT, 2003.

Maslen, R., 'The Early English Novel in Antwerp: The Impact of Jan van Doesborch', in *Narrative Developments from Chaucer to Defoe*, ed. G. Bayer and E. Klitgård, Routledge, New York, 2011, pp. 136–57.

Meale, C., '"Prenes: engre": An Early Sixteenth-Century Presentation Copy of *The Erle of Tolous*', in *Romance Reading on the Book: Essays on Medieval Narrative Presented to Maldwyn Mills*, ed. J. Fellows, R. Field, G. Rogers and J. Weiss, University of Wales Press, Cardiff, 1996, pp. 212–36.

Medieval Manuscripts in Oxford Libraries: A Catalogue of Western Manuscripts at the Bodleian Libraries and Selected Oxford Colleges, https://medieval.bodleian.ox.ac.uk [accessed 5 March 2020].

Meeres, F., 'Records Relating to the Strangers at the Norfolk Record Office', *Dutch Crossing*, vol. 38, 2014, pp. 132–53.

Meganck, T.L., 'Abraham Ortelius, Hubertus Golzius en Guido Laurinus en de studie van de Arx Britannica', *Bulletin KNOB*, vol. 98, 1999, pp. 226–36.

Meganck, T.L., *Erudite Eyes: Friendship, Art and Erudition in the Network of Abraham Ortelius (1527–1598)*, Brill, Leiden, 2017.

Meijns, B., 'England and Flanders around 1066: The Cult of the English Saints Oswald and Lewinna in the Comital Abbey of Bergues', *Anglo-Norman Studies*, vol. XXXIX, 2017, pp. 128–49.

Meurier, G., *The Conjugations in English and Netherdutche, according as Gabriel Meurier hath ordayned the same, in Netherdutche, and Frenche / De conjugatien in Engelsch ende Nederduytsche, also de selve door Gabriel Meurier in Nederduytsche ende Franchoyse zijn gemaeckt ende gheordonneert*, Thomas Basson, Leiden, 1586.

Middle English Dictionary, ed. R.E. Lewis et al., in *Middle English Compendium*, ed. F. McSparran et al., University of Michigan Library, Ann Arbor, MI, 2000–2018, https://quod.lib.umich.edu/m/middle-english-dictionary/dictionary.

Milis, L.J.R., 'Counts, Cities and Clerics: The Eleventh, Twelfth and Thirteenth Centuries', in *History of the Low Countries*, ed. J.C.H. Blom and E. Lamberts, trans. J.C. Kennedy, new edition, Berghahn, New York and Oxford, 2006, pp. 23–53.

Millar, O., *Sir Peter Lely, 1618–80*, National Portrait Gallery, London, 1978.

Mish, C.C., 'Reynard the Fox in the Seventeenth Century', *Huntington Library Quarterly*, vol. 17, 1953–4, pp. 327–44.

Moens, W.J.C., *The Marriage, Baptismal, and Burial Registers, 1571 to 1874, and Monumental Inscriptions, of the Dutch Reformed Church, Austin Friars, London*, King and Sons, Lymington, 1884.

Mooney, L., S. Horobin and E. Stubbs, *Late Medieval English Scribes*, www.medievalscribes.com [accessed 5 March 2020].

Moran, J., *Wynkyn de Worde: Father of Fleet Street*, British Library, London, 2003.

More, T., *Utopia*, ed. E. Surtz, SJ, and J.H. Hexter, trans. G.C. Richards, vol. IV of *The Complete Works of St. Thomas More*, Yale University Press, New Haven, CT, 1965.

Morison, S., *John Fell, the University Press and the 'Fell' Types*, Clarendon Press, Oxford, 1967.

Morrison, E., and L. Grollemond (eds), *Book of Beasts: The Bestiary in the Medieval World*, J. Paul Getty Museum, Los Angeles, 2019.

Morse, V., 'The Role of Maps in Later Medieval Society: Twelfth to Fourteenth Century', in *The History of Cartography*, vol. 3, part 1, ed. D. Woodward, University of Chicago Press, Chicago, 2007, pp. 25–52.

Mossé, F., 'Le *Roman de Renart* dans l'Angleterre du moyen âge', *Les Langues Modernes*, vol. 25, 1951, pp. 22–35.

Mosser, D.W., 'Longleat House, MS. 30, T. Werken and Thomas Betson', *Journal of the Early Book Society*, vol. 15, 2012, pp. 319–31.

The Most Delectable History of Reynard the Fox, Elizabeth Allde, London, 1629.

The Most Delectable History of Reynard the Fox, Cundall, London, 1846.

Muir, B.J. (ed.), *A Digital Facsimile of Oxford, Bodleian Library MS. Junius 11*, Bodleian Library, Oxford, 2004.

Muller, J.W., and H. Logeman, *Die Hystorie van Reynaert die Vos, naar den druk van 1479, vergeleken met Caxton's Engelsche vertaling*, Tjeenk Willink, Zwolle, 1892.

Needham, P., 'William Caxton and his Cologne Partners', in *Ars impressoria: Entstehung und Entwicklung des Buchdrucks – Eine internationale Festgabe für Severin Corsten zum 65 Geburtstag*, ed. H. Limburg, H. Lohse and W. Schmitz, K.G. Saur, Munich, 1986, pp. 103–31.

Neilson, G., *Caudatus Anglicus: A Mediæval Slander*, G.P. Johnston, Edinburgh, 1896.

Neumann, E., 'Imagining European Community on the Title Page of Ortelius' *Theatrum Orbis Terrarum* (1570)', *Word & Image*, vol. 25, 2009, pp. 427–42.

Neville-Singleton, P., 'Press, Politics and Religion', in *The Cambridge History of the Book in Britain*, vol. III, *1400–1557*, ed. L. Hellinga and J.B. Trapp, Cambridge University Press, Cambridge, 1999, pp. 576–607.

Newman, B., 'Contemplating the Trinity: Text, Image, and the Origins of the Rothschild Canticles', *Gesta*, vol. 52, 2013, pp. 133–59.

Nieus, J.-F., 'The Early Career of William of Ypres in England: A New Charter of King Stephen', *English Historical Review*, vol. 130, 2015, pp. 527–45.

Nieus, J.-F., 'Stratégies seigneuriales anglo-flamandes après 1066: l'honor de Choques et de la famille de Béthune', *Revue Belge de Philologie et d'Histoire*, vol. 95, 2017, pp. 163–92.

Nigel de Longchamps, *A Mirror for Fools, or, The Book of Burnel the Ass*, trans. J.H. Mozley, Blackwell, Oxford, 1961.

Nigel de Longchamps, *Speculum stultorum*, ed. J.H. Mozley and R.R. Raymo, University of California Press, Berkeley, 1960.

Noot, J. van der, *Het theatre oft toon-neel, waer in ter eender de ongelucken ende elenden die den werelts gesinden ende boosen menschen toecomen: ende op dander syde tgheluck, goet ende ruste die de gheloouighe ghenieten, vertoont worden*, John Day, London, [1568].

Noot, J. van der, *A Theatre wherein be Represented as wel the Miseries & Calamities that Follow the Voluptuous Worldlings as also the Great Ioyes and Plesures which the Faithfull do Enioy*, Henry Bynneman, London, 1569.

Oastler, C.L., *John Day, the Elizabethan Printer*, Oxford Bibliographical Society, Oxford, 1975.

Oksanen, E., *Flanders and the Anglo-Norman World, 1066–1216*, Cambridge University Press, Cambridge, 2012.

Oostrom, F. van, *Maerlants wereld*, Prometheus, Amsterdam, 1996.

Orderic Vitalis, *The Ecclesiastical History*, ed. and trans. M. Chibnall, 6 vols, Clarendon Press, Oxford, 1969–80.

Die ordinancie vander oorloghen tusschen den coninck van Enghelant ende den coninck van Schotlant, vid. Christoffel van Ruremund, Antwerp, [1542].

Ormrod, M., 'John Kempe and Friends: Flemish Weavers in Edward III's England', www.englandsimmigrants.com/page/individual-studies/john-kempe-and-friends [accessed 5 March 2020].

Ormrod, W.M., B. Lambert and J. Mackman, *Immigrant England, 1300–1550*, Manchester University Press, Manchester, 2005.

Ortelius, A., *Theatrum orbis terrarum Abrahami Orteli Antuerp. geographi regii. = The Theatre of the Whole World: Set forth by that Excellent Geographer Abraham Ortelius*, John Norton, London, 1608.

Osseltong, N.E., *The Dumb Linguists: A Study of the Earliest English and Dutch Dictionaries*, Leiden University Press, Leiden, and Oxford University Press, Oxford, 1973.

Owen, D.D.R. (trans.), *The Romance of Reynard the Fox: A New Translation*, Oxford University Press, Oxford, 1994.

Oxford English Dictionary, Oxford University Press, Oxford, https://www.oed.com.

Pächt, O., and J.J.G. Alexander, *Illuminated Manuscripts in the Bodleian Library, Oxford*, 2 vols, Clarendon Press, Oxford, 1966.

Panton, J., *Historical Dictionary of the English Monarchy*, Scarecrow Press, Plymouth, 2011.

Perkins, N., 'Introduction: The Materiality of Romance', in *Medieval Romance and Material Culture*, ed. N. Perkins, Boydell & Brewer, Woodbridge, 2015, pp. 1–22.

Peterson, W.S., *The Kelmscott Press: A History of William Morris's Typographical Adventure*, University of California Press, Berkeley, 1991.

Pettegree, A., 'Centre and Periphery in the European Book World', *Transactions of the Royal Historical Society*, 6th series, vol. 18, 2008, pp. 101–28.

Pettegree, A., *Emden and the Dutch Revolt: Exile and the Development of Reformed Protestantism*, Clarendon Press, Oxford, 1992.

Pettegree, A., 'The Foreign Population of London in 1549', *Proceedings of the Huguenot Society*, vol. 24, 1984, pp. 141–6.

Pettegree, A., and M. Walsby, *Netherlandish Books: Books Published in the Low Countries and Dutch Books Published Abroad before 1601*, Brill, Leiden, 2011.

Pienaar, W.J. Bennie, 'Edmund Spenser and Jonker Jan van der Noot', *English Studies*, vol. 8, 1926, pp. 33–76.

Pincus, S., *Protestantism and Patriotism: Ideologies and the Making of English Foreign Policy, 1650–1688*, Cambridge University Press, Cambridge, 1996.

Plomer, H., *Wynkyn de Worde and his Contemporaries*, Grafton, London, 1925.

Potten, E., and E. Dourish (eds), *Emprynted in Thys Manere: Early Printed Treasures from Cambridge University Library*, Cambridge University Library, Cambridge, 2014.

A Prayer to be Sayd in the End of the Mornyng Prayer Daily (through the Dioeces of Norwich) during the Tyme of this Hard and Sharp Wether of Frost and Snow, [Anthony de Solempne, Norwich, 1572].

Price, L., *Newes from Hollands Leager, or, Hollands Leager is Lately up Broken, This for a Certaine is Spoken*, I.W., London, [1632], http://ebba.english.ucsb.edu/ballad/20283 [accessed 5 March 2020].

Price, V.E., 'Holland's Leaguer', in *Encyclopedia of Prostitution and Sex Work*, ed. M.H. Ditmore, Greenwood, Westport, CT, 2006, pp. 211–12.

Pulsiano, 'Jaunts, Jottings, and Jetsam in Anglo-Saxon Manuscripts', *Florilegium*, vol. 19, 2002, pp. 189–97.

Putter, A. (ed.), *Incunabula: The Printing Revolution in Europe, 1455–1500*, Units 68–9, *Printing in Dutch*, Gale/British Library, London, 2010.

Putter, A., 'The Linguistic Repertoire of Medieval England, 1100–1500', in *Imagining Medieval English*, ed. T.W. Machan, Cambridge University Press, Cambridge, 2016, pp. 126–44.

Putter, A., 'Multilingualism in England and Wales, *c*.1200: The Testimony of Gerald of Wales', in *Medieval Multilingualism: The Francophone World and its Neighbours*, ed. C. Kleinhenz and K. Busby, Brepols, Turnhout, 2010, pp. 83–105.

Putter, A., E. van Houts, S. Levelt and M. Arbabzadah, 'Ysengrimus en Reynard the Fox: Engels–Nederlandse contacten als context voor de Reynaerttraditie', Tiecelijn, vol. 11, 2018, pp. 65–81.

Raamsdonk, E. van, Milton, Marvell, and the Dutch Republic, Routledge, Abingdon, 2020.

Rabus, P., Opkomst, geboorte, leven en dood van Maria Stuart, koningin van Groot Brittanje, Vrankryk en Yerland ondermengd met de voornaamste gevallen zo van staat als oorlog, welke zich hebben toegedragen beneffens een verhandeling van 't Huys van Stuart, Jan ten Hoorn, Amsterdam, 1695.

Raines, J. (ed.), Testamenta Eboracensia: A Selection of Wills from the Registry at York, 2 vols, Surtees Society, Durham, 1855.

R.B., The History of the House of Orange, or, A Brief Relation of the Glorious and Magnanimous Atchievements of His Majesties Renowned Predecessors and Likewise of his own Heroick Actions till the late Wonderful Revolution: together with the History of William and Mary King and Queen of England, Scotland, France, and Ireland &c., Nathaniel Crouch, London, 1693.

Reenen, P. van, Atlas van vormen en constructies in Middelnederlandse oorkonden van de 14de en 13de eeuw, https://vormencatalogus.middelnederlands.nl/list [accessed 27 March 2021].

Reeve, M.D., 'Manuscripts Copied from Printed Books', in Manuscripts and Methods: Essays on Editing and Transmission, ed. M.D. Reeve, Edizioni di Storia e Letteratura, Rome, 2011, pp. 175–83.

Regenos, G.W., The Book of Daun Burnel the Ass: Nigellus Wireker's Speculum Stultorum, University of Texas Press, Austin, 1959.

Ricci, A., 'Maps, Power and National Identity: The Leo Belgicus as a Symbol of the Independence of the United Provinces', Bollettino della Associazione Italiana di Cartografia, vol. 154, 2015, pp. 102–20.

Rickard, P., Britain in Medieval French Literature, 1100–1500, Cambridge University Press, Cambridge, 1956.

Rigg, A.G., A History of Anglo-Latin Literature, 1066–1422, Cambridge University Press, Cambridge, 1992.

Rigg, A.G., 'Nigel of Canterbury: What was his Name?', Medium Ævum, vol. 56, 1987, pp. 304–7.

Robbins, R.H. (ed.), Historical Poems of the XIV and XV Centuries, Columbia University Press, New York, 1959.

Robbins, R.H. (ed.), Secular Lyrics of the Fifteenth Century, Clarendon Press, Oxford, 1952.

Roberts, I., and M. Roberts, 'De Mona Druidum Insula', in Abraham Ortelius and the First Atlas: Essays Commemorating the Quadricentennial of his Death, 1598–1998, ed. M. van den Broeck, P. van der Krocht and P. Meurer, HES Publishers, Houten, 1998, pp. 347–63.

Rogers, N., 'Books of Hours Produced in the Low Countries for the English Market in the Fifteenth Century', 2 vols, M.Litt. thesis, University of Cambridge, 1982.

Rogge, H.C., 'Het Album van Emanuel van Meteren', Oud Holland, vol. 15, 1897, pp. 199–210.

Romburgh, S., 'Junius [Du Jon], Franciscus [Francis] (1591–1677), philologist and writer on art', in Oxford Dictionary of National Biography, Oxford University Press, Oxford, 2011.

Rose, S., Calais: An English Town in France, 1347–1558, Boydell & Brewer, Woodbridge, 2008.

Rozenski, S., 'The Chastising of God's Children from Manuscript to Print', Études Anglaises, vol. 66, 2013, pp. 369–78.

Rundle, D., 'Good Duke Humfrey: Bounder, Cad and Bibliophile', Bodleian Library Record, vol. 27, 2014, pp. 36–53.

Rundle, D., The Renaissance Reform of the Book and Britain: The English Quattrocento, Cambridge University Press, Cambridge, 2019.

Ruytinck, S., Gheschiedenissen ende handelingen die voornemelick aengaen de Nederduytsche natie ende gemeynten wonende in Engeland ende in 't byzonder tot Londen, ed. J.J. van Toorenenbergen, Kemink en Zoon, Utrecht, 1873.

Ruytinck, S., 'Het leven ende sterven vanden eerwerden, vromen, ende vermaerden Emanuel van Meteren', in Emanuel van Meteren, Historie der Neder-landscher ende haerder na-buren oorlogen ende geschiedenissen, Hillebrandt Iacobssz, The Hague, 1614, fols [672]r–[673]v.

Salter, H.E., and M.D. Lobel (eds), A History of the County of Oxford, vol. 3, The University of Oxford, Victoria County History, London, 1954.

Sandler, L.F., Gothic Manuscripts, 1285–1385, 2 vols, Harvey Miller, London, 1986.

Savage, H.J., 'The First Visit of Erasmus to England', PMLA, vol. 37, 1922, pp. 94–112.

Schlusemann, R., Die hystorie van Reynaert die vos und The History of Reynard the Fox: Die spätmittelalterlichen Prosabearbeitungen des Reynaert-Stoffes, Peter Lang, Frankfurt, 1991.

Schoneveld, C.W., Sea-Changes: Studies in Three Centuries of Anglo-Dutch Cultural Transmission, Rodopi, Amsterdam, 1996.

Schouwink, W., 'The Fox's Funeral in European Art: Transformations of a Literary Motif', Reinardus, vol. 6, 1993, pp. 169–79.

Schurman, A.M. van, The Learned Maid, or, Whether a Maid May be a Scholar? A Logick Exercise, Written in Latine by that Incomparable Virgin Anna Maria à Schurman of Vtrecht, John Redmayne, London, 1659.

Scott, K.L., The Caxton Master and his Patrons, Cambridge Bibliographical Society, Cambridge, 1976.

Scott, K.L. (ed.), *The Mirroure of the Worlde: MS Bodley 283*, Roxburghe Club, London, 1980.

Scott, K.L., '*Prenes en gre* All Over Again', *Journal of the Early Book Society*, vol. 19, 2016, pp. 249–66.

Scouloudi, I., *Panoramic Views of London 1600–1666*, Corporation of London, London, 1953.

Seccombe, T., and F.F. Blok, 'Vossius, Isaac (1618–1689), philologist and author', in *Oxford Dictionary of National Biography*, Oxford University Press, Oxford, 2006.

Send-brief: waer in de voorneempste stucken der pauwscher leere verhandelt, met Godes woort ende ghetuyghenissen der vaderen wederleet werden: gheschreven aen alle inwooners onfer goet-jonstighe vader- stadt S. Truyden. Mit noch eenen register, Thomas Vautrollier, London, 1581.

A Short and True Discourse for Satisfying all those vvho not Knovving the Truth, Speake Indiscreetly of hir most Excellent Maiestie, of the Lord Willughby Gouernour of hir Maiesties Succours in the Vnited Prouinces of the Low Countries, and of all the English Nation, [printed by Richard Field, London], 1589.

Shute, W., *The Triumphs of Nassau, or, A Description and Representation of all the Victories both by Land and Sea, Granted by God to the Noble, High, and Mightie Lords, the Estates Generall of the Vnited Netherland Prouinces vnder the Conduct and Command of his Excellencie, Prince Maurice of Nassau*, Adam Islip, London, 1613.

Simoni, A.E.C., '1598: An Exchange of Dutch Pamphlets and their Repercussions in England', in *From Revolt to Riches: Culture and History of the Low Countries, 1500–1700*, ed. T. Hermans and R. Salverda, University College London Press, London, 2017, pp. 100–125.

Simpson, J. (trans.), *Reynard the Fox: A New Translation*, Norton, New York, 2015.

Sisam, K., 'MSS. Bodley 340 and 342: Ælfric's *Catholic Homilies*', *The Review of English Studies*, vol. 9, no. 33, 1933, pp. 1–12.

Sleiderink, R., *De stem van de meester: De hertogen van Brabant en hun rol in het literaire leven*, Prometheus, Amsterdam, 2003.

Smallwood, T.M., 'The Date of the Gough Map', *Imago Mundi*, vol. 62, 2010, pp. 3–29.

Smet, J.M. De (ed.), '*Passio Francorum secundum Flemyngos*: Het Brugse spotevangelie op de nederlaag van de Fransen te Kortrijk (11 juli 1302)', *De Leiegouw*, vol. 19, 1977, pp. 289–319.

Smeyers, M., *Flemish Miniatures from the 8th to the Mid-16th Century: The Medieval World of Parchment*, Brepols, Turnhout, 1999.

Sobecki, S., 'Bureaucratic Verse: William Lyndwood, the Privy Seal, and the Form of the *Libelle of Englyshe Polycye*', *New Medieval Literatures*, vol. 12, 2010, p. 251–88.

Spencer, A.M., *Nobility and Kingship in Medieval England: The Earls and Edward I, 1272–1307*, Cambridge University Press, Cambridge, 2014.

Spindler, E., 'Flemings in the Peasants' Revolt, 1381', in *Contact and Exchange in Later Medieval Europe: Essays in Honour of Malcolm Vale*, ed. H. Skoda, P. Lantschner and R.L.J. Shaw, Boydell Press, Woodbridge, 2012, pp. 59–78.

Sprunger, K.L., *Dutch Puritanism: A History of English and Scottish Churches of the Netherlands in the Sixteenth and Seventeenth Centuries*, Brill, Leiden, 1982.

Spufford, P., 'The Burgundian Netherlands', in A. Arnould and J.M. Massing, *Splendours of Flanders*, Cambridge University Press, Cambridge, 1993, pp. 1–11.

Starnes, D.T., 'A Heroic Poem on the Death of Sir Thomas More – by D. Erasmus of Rotterdam', *Studies in English*, vol. 9, 1929, pp. 69–81.

Stein, R., 'The Antwerp Clerk Jan van Boendale and the Creation of a Brabantine Ideology', in *Political Representation: Communities, Ideas and Institutions in Europe (c.1200–c.1690)*, ed. M. Damen, J. Haemers and A.J. Mann, Brill, Leiden, 2018.

Stevenson, J., *Letters and Papers Illustrative of the Wars of the English in France: During the Reign of Henry the Sixth, King of England*, 2 vols, Longman, Green, Roberts, and Green, London, 1861–4.

Stilma, A., *A King Translated: The Writings of King James VI & I and their Interpretation in the Low Countries, 1593–1603*, Ashgate, Farnham, 2012.

Stocker, T. (trans.), *A Tragicall Historie of the Troubles and Ciuile Warres of the Lowe Countries, Otherwise Called Flanders*, Jhon Kyngston [and Thomas Dawson] for Tobie Smith, London, 1583.

Straub, R.E.F., *David Aubert, escripvain et clerc*, Rodopi, Amsterdam, 1995.

Strecker, K. (ed.), *Ecbasis cuiusdam captivi per Tropologiam*, Hahnsche Buchhandlung, Hanover, 1935.

Strubel, A., R. Bellon, D. Boutet and S. Lefèvre (eds), *Le Roman de Renart*, Gallimard, Paris, 1998.

Sturler, J. de, *Les relations politiques et les échanges commerciaux entre le duché de Brabant et l'Angleterre au moyen âge*, E. Droz, Paris, 1936.

Summerly, F. (Sir Henry Cole), *The Pleasant History of Reynard the Fox*, Home Treasury, London, 1854.

Sweerts, C., *Rouwe over het sterven van haare majesteit Maria Stuart*, Pieter van den Berge, Amsterdam, 1695.

Syme, S.A., 'The Regulation of the English Book Trade 1484 to 1547', *Journal of Library History*, vol. 3, 1968, pp. 32–8.

[*Tafelmanieren.*] *Englysshe. Frenche. Dutche*, Christoffel van Ruremund, Antwerp, [1530].

Tahkokallio, J., *The Anglo-Norman Historical Canon: Publishing and Manuscript Culture*, Cambridge University Press, Cambridge, 2019.

Thomas, H.M., *The English and the Normans: Ethnic Hostility, Assimilation and Identity, 1066–c.1220*, Oxford University Press, Oxford, 2003.

Thrower, N.J.W., *Maps and Civilization: Cartography in Culture and Society*, 3rd edition, University of Chicago Press, Chicago, 2008.

Thrupp, S., *The Merchant Class of Medieval London*, University of Michigan Press, Ann Arbor, 1989.

Toorians, L., 'Flemish Settlements in Twelfth-Century Scotland', *Revue Belge de Philologie et d'Histoire*, vol. 74, 1996, pp. 659–93.

Tsuji, S., 'Textual Transition and Reception of the English *Reynard the Fox*', Ph.D. thesis, Fukuoka Women's University, 2016.

Ugé, K., *Creating the Monastic Past in Medieval Flanders*, York Medieval Press, Woodbridge, 2005.

Utenhove, J. (trans.), [*Psalmen 23, 101, 115 & 128*], Nicolaes van den Berghe, London, 1552.

Utenhove, J. (trans.), *25 psalmen end andere ghesangen, diemen in de Duydtsche ghemeynte te Londen was ghebruyckende*, Gellius Ctematius, Emden, 1557.

Utenhove, J. (trans.), *Jan Łaski: De catechismus, oft kinder leere, diemen te Londen, in de Duytsche ghemeynte, is ghebruyckende*, Steven Mierdman, London, 1551.

Utenhove, J. (trans.), *Jan Łaski: Een cort begrijp der leeringhen, van die waerachtighe ende eender ghemeynten te Londen*, Steven Mierdman, London, 1551.

Vale, J., 'Arthur in English Society', in *The Arthur of the English: The Arthurian Legend in Medieval English Life and Literature*, ed. W.R.J. Barron, University of Wales Press, Cardiff, 2001, pp. 185–96.

Varty, K., *Reynard the Fox: A Study of the Fox in Medieval Art*, Leicester University Press, Leicester, 1967.

Varty, K., *Reynard, Renart, Reinaert and Other Foxes in Medieval England: The Iconographic Evidence*, Amsterdam University Press, Amsterdam, 1999.

Veldener, J., *Fasciculus temporum: dat boec dat men hiet Fasciculus temporum*, Johan Veldener, Utrecht, 1480.

Verbij-Schillings, J., *Beeldvorming in Holland: Heraut Beyeren en de historiografie omstreeks 1400*, Prometheus, Amsterdam, 1995.

Verbraak, G., 'William Tyndale and the Clandestine Book Trade: A Bibliographical Quest for the Printers of Tyndale's New Testaments', in *Infant Milk or Hardy Nourishment? The Bible for Lay People and Theologians in the Early Modern Period*, ed. W. François and A. den Hollander, Peeters, Leuven, 2009, pp. 167–89.

Verbruggen, J.F., *The Battle of the Golden Spurs (Courtrai, 11 July 1302): A Contribution to the History of Flanders' War of Liberation, 1297–1305*, ed. K. DeVries, trans. D.R. Ferguson, Boydell Press, Woodbridge, 2002.

Verbrugghe, G., S. Vanderputten, V. Van Eetvelde and W. De Clercq, 'Flemish Settlements beyond Flanders: A Review and New Perspectives on Transregional Medieval Settlement Landscapes in Britain', *The Haskins Society Journal: Studies in Medieval History*, vol. 31, 2019 (2020), pp. 21–47.

Verduyn, W.D., *Emanuel van Meteren*, Martinus Nijhoff, The Hague, 1926.

Verstegan, R., *Nederlantsche antiquiteyten met de bekeeringhe van eenighe der selve landen tot het kersten ghelooue*, Gaspar Bellerus, Antwerp, 1613.

Verstegan, R., *A Restitution of Decayed Intelligence in Antiquities concerning the most Noble and Renovvmed English Nation*, Robert Bruney, Antwerp, 1605.

Verzandvoort, E., 'Allart van Everdingen (1621–1675) and his Illustrations for J.Chr. Gottsched's *Reineke der Fuchs* (Leipzig, 1752)', *Reinardus*, vol. 8, 1995, pp. 151–63.

Visser-Fuchs, L., *History as Pastime: Jean de Wavrin and his Collection of Chronicles of England*, Shaun Tyas, Donington, 2018.

Voet, L., 'Abraham Ortelius and his World', in *Abraham Ortelius and the First Atlas: Essays Commemorating the Quadricentennial of his Death, 1598–1998*, ed. M. van den Broeck, P. van der Krocht and P. Meurer, HES Publishers, Houten, 1998, pp. 11–28.

Voigt, E. (ed.), *Ysengrimus*, Verlag der Buchhandlung des Waisenhauses, Halle, 1884.

Voorspookkend zinne-beeld, op den staat der Engelsche en Nederlandsche regeering, n.p., [1652].

Vosters, S.A., 'De bibliotheek van Engelbrecht II van Nassau', *De Oranjeboom*, vol. 46, 1993, pp. 25–63.

Vroegmiddelnederlands woordenboek, vmnw.inl.nl [accessed 23 March 2020].

Wackers, P., 'Nawoord', in *Reynaert in Tweevoud*, part 2, *Reynaerts historie*, Bert Bakker, Amsterdam, 2002, pp. 327–58.

Wackers, P., 'Reynaert de Vos', in *Van Aiol tot Zwaanridder: Personages uit middeleeuwse verhaalkunst en hun voortleven in literatuur, theater en beeldende kunst*, ed. W.P. Gerritsen and A.G. van Melle, SUN, Nijmegen, 1993, pp. 269–79.

Wakelin, D., *Humanism, Reading, and English Literature, 1430–1530*, Oxford University Press, Oxford, 2007.

Wal, M. van der, *Geschiedenis van het Nederlands*, Spectrum, Utrecht, 1992.

Wallace, D., 'Calais', in *Europe: A Literary History, 1348–1418*, ed. D. Wallace, Oxford University Press, Oxford, 2016, 2 vols, vol. I, pp. 180–90.

Wallace, D., *Premodern Places: Calais to Surinam, Chaucer to Aphra Behn*, Blackwell, Oxford, 2004.

Wallis, H., 'Intercourse with the Peaceful Muses', in *Across the Narrow Seas: Studies in the History and Bibliography of Great Britain and the Low Countries Presented to Anna C. Simoni*, ed. S. Roach, British Library, London, 1991, pp. 31–53.

Die warachtige beschrijvinghe vant verraedt in Enghelandt, John Daye [= and Nicolaes Gevaertsz], London [= Wesel], 1571.

The Warenne (Hyde) Chronicle, ed. and trans. E.M.C. van Houts and R.C. Love, Clarendon Press, Oxford, 2013.

Waterschoot, W., 'An Author's Strategy: Jan van der Noot's *Het Theatre*', in B. Westerweel (ed.), *Anglo-Dutch Relations in the Field of the Emblem*, Brill, Leiden, 1997, pp. 35–47.

Wavrin, J. de, *Recueil des croniques et anchiennes istories de la Grant Bretaigne*, ed. W. Hardy, 5 vols, Longman, Green, Longman, Roberts, and Green, London, 1864–91.

Werner, S., *Studying Early Printed Books, 1450–1800: A Practical Guide*, Wiley Blackwell, Chichester, 2019.

Westgard, J.A., 'Dissemination and Reception of Bede's *Historia Ecclesiastica Gentis Anglorum* in Germany, *c*.731–1500: The Manuscript Evidence', Ph.D. thesis, University of North Carolina, Chapel Hill, 2005.

Whetstone, G., and J. Walraven (trans.), *The Honourable Reputation of a Souldier VVith a Morall Report of the Vertues, Offices and (by Abuse) the Disgrace of his Profession. Drawen out of the Lives, Documents, and Disciplines of the Most Renowned Romaine, Grecian, and other Famous Martialistes / De eervveerdighe achtbaerheyt van een soldener. Met een stichtich verhael der deuchden, ampten, ende (by misbruyc) d'ontucht van zijn professie*, Jan Paedts Jacobszoon & Jan Bouwensz for Thomas Basson, Leiden, 1586.

Wiechers, R., 'Jehan de Grise', in *Lexicon van Boekverluchters*, www.bookilluminators.nl/met-naam-gekende-boekverluchters/boekverluchters-j-naam/jehan-de-grise [accessed 5 March 2020].

Wiechers, R., 'Pierart dou Tielt', in *Lexicon van Boekverluchters*, www.bookilluminators.nl/met-naam-gekende-boekverluchters/boekverluchters-p-naam/pierart-dou-thielt [accessed 5 March 2020].

Wieck, R.S., *Time Sanctified: The Book of Hours in Medieval Art and Life*, George Braziller, New York 2001.

Willem I, *A Declaration and Publication of the Most Worthy Prince of Orange, Contaynyng the Cause of his Necessary Defence against the Duke of Alba*, John Day, London, [1568].

Willem I, *A Justification or Cleering of the Prince of Orendge agaynst the False Sclaunders, wherewith his Ilwillers goe about to Charge him Wrongfully*, trans. A. Golding, John Day, London, [1575].

Willemyns, R., *Dutch: Biography of a Language*, Oxford University Press, Oxford, 2013.

William of Malmesbury, *Gesta regum Anglorum (The History of the English Kings)*, ed. and trans. R.A.B. Mynors, R.M. Thomson and M. Winterbottom, 2 vols, Oxford University Press, Oxford, 1998–9.

William of Poitiers, *Gesta Guillelmi*, ed. and trans. R.H.C. Davis and M. Chibnall, Clarendon Press, Oxford, 1998.

Wilson, A., and J.L. Wilson, *A Medieval Mirror: Speculum humanae salvationis*, University of California Press, Berkeley, 1998.

The Wolsey Manuscripts, www.wolseymanuscripts.ac.uk [accessed 23 March 2020].

Wood, R., 'The Romanesque Tomb-Slab at Bridlington Priory', *Yorkshire Archaeological Journal*, vol. 73, 2003, pp. 63–70.

Wooden, W.W., 'Sir Thomas Bodley's "Life of Himself" (1609) and the Epideictic Strategies of Encomia', *Studies in Philology*, vol. 83, 1986, pp. 62–75.

Woodward, D., 'Cartography and the Renaissance: Continuity and Change', in *The History of Cartography*, vol. 3, part 1, ed. D. Woodward, University of Chicago Press, Chicago, 2007, pp. 3–24.

Woodward, D., 'Medieval *Mappaemundi*', in *The History of Cartography*, vol. 1, ed. J.B. Harley and D. Woodward, University of Chicago Press, Chicago, 1987, pp. 286–370.

Worms, L., 'Kip, William (*fl. c*.1585–1618), engraver', in *Oxford Dictionary of National Biography*, Oxford University Press, Oxford, 2004.

Worms, L., 'The London Map Trade to 1640', in *The History of Cartography*, vol. 3, part 2, ed. D. Woodward, University of Chicago Press, Chicago, 2007, pp. 1693–721.

Yates, D.N., 'The Cock-and-Fox Episodes of *Isengrimus*, attributed to Simon of Ghent: A Literary and Historical Study', Ph.D. dissertation, University of North Carolina, Chapel Hill, 1979.

Ysengrimus: Text with Translation, Commentary and Introduction, ed. and trans. J. Mann, Brill, Leiden, 1987.

Yungblut, L.H., *Strangers Settled Here amongst Us: Policies, Perceptions and the Presence of Aliens in Elizabethan England*, Routledge, London, 1996.

Ziolkowski, J., *Talking Animals: Medieval Latin Beast Poetry, 750–1150*, University of Pennsylvania Press, Philadelphia, 1993.

AUTHORS

Robyn Adams is Senior Research Fellow at the Centre for Editing Lives and Letters, University College London. Her research spans book history, manuscript culture and the material processes by which collections formed and were used, both in their own time and now.

Moreed Arbabzadah studied classics (BA, MPhil, PhD) at Jesus College, University of Cambridge. He is a Fellow of Pembroke College, a Research Associate in the Faculty of History and an Affiliated Lecturer in the Faculty of Classics at the University of Cambridge.

Anne Louise Avery is a writer and art historian. She is the Director of Flash of Splendour and European Editor of the literary travel journal *Panorama*. Her retelling of the story of Reynard the Fox was published by Bodleian Library Publishing in 2020.

Jack Avery has recently completed his PhD at the University of Bristol, the National Archives and the National Maritime Museum. His work explores the relationship between news writing and literature, which is also the subject of his recently published article in *The Seventeenth Century*.

Edward Holberton is a Lecturer at the Department of English, University of Bristol. He is the author of *Poetry and the Cromwellian Protectorate: Culture, Politics, and Institutions* (Oxford University Press, 2008) and has recently co-edited (with Martin Dzelzainis) *The Oxford Handbook of Andrew Marvell* (Oxford University Press, 2019).

Elisabeth van Houts is Emeritus Honorary Professor in European Medieval History and a Fellow of Emmanuel College, University of Cambridge. She has published on Anglo-European medieval history. Her most recent book is *Married Life in the Middle Ages, 900–1300* (Oxford University Press, 2019).

Kathleen E. Kennedy is British Academy Global Professor at the University of Bristol. She has published on medieval manuscript art in edited collections and journals, and in her monograph *The Courtly and Commercial Art of the Wycliffite Bible* (Brepols, 2014).

Sjoerd Levelt is Senior Research Associate at the University of Bristol. He studies English and Dutch medieval and early modern literature and history. His first monograph, *Jan van Naaldwijk's Chronicles of Holland*, was awarded the Society for Renaissance Studies Book Prize 2012.

Ad Putter is Professor of Medieval English at the University of Bristol and Fellow of the British Academy. He has published widely on medieval literatures in a range of languages, and is the editor, with Myra Stokes, of *The Works of the Gawain Poet* (Penguin, 2014)

Pre-modern people are indexed under their first name (e.g. Alfred of Beverley is found under 'A') unless known by a surname (e.g. Aubert, Chaucer, Wolsey). All manuscripts are listed under the headword 'Manuscripts'. Saints are indexed under their name, not under 'saint'. The alphabetical ordering ignores 'von', 'van', 'van de(n/r)', 'de' and 'du'. For illustrations, which are listed by page number in italics, the information indexed includes shelfmarks of manuscripts, authors and/or titles of works, names of artists and persons depicted, and significant publishers/ printers and owners.

**BODLEIAN
LIBRARY
PUBLISHING**

First published in 2021 by the Bodleian Library
Broad Street, Oxford OX1 3BG
www.bodleianshop.co.uk

ISBN: 978 1 85124 554 3

Front cover and frontispiece: Detail of a map of Britain and Ireland showing the North Sea, from Joan Blaeu's *Atlas*, c.1645–54. © Bodleian Library, Oxford, Gough Maps 91.
Back cover: Detail of King William III's entry into The Hague from a 1692 engraving by Govard Bidloo.
© Bodleian Library, Oxford, Douce L subt. 12.

Publisher: Samuel Fanous
Managing Editor: Deborah Susman
Editor: Janet Phillips
Picture Editor: Leanda Shrimpton
Production Editor: Susie Foster
Designed and typeset by Dot Little in 10.5/15 Adobe Caslon
Printed and bound by Printer Trento S.r.l. on 150gsm Gardamatt Art paper

Adobe Caslon is a revival font created in 1990 by American type designer Carol Twombly, based on eighteenth-century specimen sheets from the Caslon foundry. When William Caslon (1692–1766) established his type foundry in London, English printing was dominated by type produced in the Netherlands. Cutting his types based on Dutch examples, especially those of the Voskens family (see p. 137), Caslon captured first the English, and subsequently the international market.

British Library Cataloguing-in-Publication Data
A CIP record of this publication is available from the British Library